Lecture Notes in Computer S

Commenced Publication in 1973
Founding and Former Series Editors:
Gerhard Goos, Juris Hartmanis, and Jan van Le

T0230550

Leopoldo Bertossi   Anthony Hunter
Torsten Schaub (Eds.)

Inconsistency Tolerance

 Springer

Volume Editors

Leopoldo Bertossi
Carleton University, School of Computer Science
Herzberg Building, 1125 Colonel By Drive, Ottawa, Canada K1S 5B6
E-mail: bertossi@scs.carleton.ca

Anthony Hunter
University College London, Department of Computer Science
Gower Street, London WC1E 6BT, UK
E-mail: a.hunter@cs.ucl.ac.uk

Torsten Schaub
Universität Potsdam, Institut für Informatik
August-Bebel-Str. 89, 14482 Potsdam, Germany
E-mail: torsten@cs.uni-potsdam.de

Library of Congress Control Number: 2004117075

CR Subject Classification (1998): H.2, D.2, F.3, F.4

ISSN 0302-9743
ISBN 3-540-24260-0 Springer Berlin Heidelberg New York

Springer is a part of Springer Science+Business Media

springeronline.com

© Springer-Verlag Berlin Heidelberg 2004
Printed in Germany

Typesetting: Camera-ready by author, data conversion by Scientific Publishing Services, Chennai, India
Printed on acid-free paper   SPIN: 11373957   06/3142   5 4 3 2 1 0

Preface

The idea for this book arose after we had organized a meeting on inconsistency tolerance at Dagstuhl in Germany in the summer of 2003. We approached a number of eminent researchers in the field to contribute to the first book devoted to the subject. The net result is a collection of papers that provide an exciting coverage of some of the key aspects of the field.

All the chapters in the collection were anonymously reviewed, chapters by editors of the book being submitted for anonymous review by the other editors. Reviewing was undertaken by other authors involved in the project and by external reviewers. We are particularly grateful to the external reviewers as we believe they made a very significant contribution to all the chapters. The external reviewers included Ofer Arieli, Pablo Barcelo, Diego Calvanese, Sergio Greco, Jerome Lang, Domenico Lembo, Peter McBrien, Nic Wilson, and Peter Wood.

October 2004

Leo Bertossi
Anthony Hunter
Torsten Schaub

Table of Contents

Introduction to Inconsistency Tolerance

Leopoldo Bertossi[1], Anthony Hunter[2], and Torsten Schaub[3],[*]

[1] School of Computer Science,
Carleton University,
1125 Colonel By Drive,
Ottawa, K1S 5B6, Canada
bertossi@scs.carleton.ca

[2] Department of Computer Science,
University College London
Gower Street, London WC1E 6BT, UK
a.hunter@cs.ucl.ac.uk

[3] Institut fur Informatik,
August-Bebel-Strasse 89,
D-14482 Potsdam, Germany
torsten@cs.uni-potsdam.de

Abstract. Inconsistency arises in many areas in advanced computing. Examples include: Merging information from heterogeneous sources; Negotiation in multi-agent systems; Understanding natural language dialogues; and Commonsense reasoning in robotics. Often inconsistency is unwanted, for example, in the specification for a plan, or in sensor fusion in robotics. But sometimes inconsistency is useful, e.g. when lawyers look for inconsistencies in an opposition case, or in a brainstorming session in research collaboration. Whether inconsistency is unwanted or useful, there is a need to develop tolerance to inconsistency in application technologies such as databases, knowledgebases, and software systems. To address this, inconsistency tolerance is being built on foundational technologies for identifying and analysing inconsistency in information, for representing and reasoning with inconsistent information, for resolving inconsistent information, and for merging inconsistent information. In this introductory chapter, we consider the need and role for inconsistency tolerance, and briefly review some of the foundational technologies for inconsistency tolerance.

1 The Need for Inconsistency Tolerance

Traditionally the consensus of opinion in the computer science community is that inconsistency is undesirable. Many believe that databases, knowledgebases, and software specifications, should be completely free of inconsistency, and try to eradicate inconsistency from them immediately by any means possible. Others

---

[*] Affiliated with the School of Computing Science at Simon Fraser University, Burnaby, Canada.

L. Bertossi et al. (Eds.): Inconsistency Tolerance, LNCS 3300, pp. 1–14, 2004.

address inconsistency by isolating it, and perhaps resolving it locally. All seem to agree, however, that data of the form q and $\neg q$, for any proposition q cannot exist together, and that the conflict must be resolved somehow.

This view is too simplistic for developing robust software or intelligent systems, and furthermore, fails to use the benefits of inconsistent information in intelligent activities, or to acknowledge the fact that living with inconsistency seems to be unavoidable. Inconsistency in information is the norm in the real-world, and so should be formalized and used, rather than always rejected.

There are cases where q and $\neg q$ can be perfectly acceptable together and hence need not be resolved. Consider for example an income tax database where contradictory information on a taxpayer can be useful evidence in a fraud investigation. Maybe the taxpayer has completed one form that states the taxpayer has 6 children (hence the tax benefits for that) and completed another that states the taxpayer has 0 children. Here, this contradictory information needs to be kept and reasoned with. A similar example is in law courts where lawyers on opposing sides (for prosecution and defence) will seek contradictions in the opposition. Moreover, they will try to direct questions and to use evidence to engineer the construction of contradictions.

In other cases, q and $\neg q$ serve as a useful trigger for various logical actions. Inconsistency is useful in directing reasoning, and instigating the natural processes of argumentation, information seeking, multi-agent interaction, knowledge acquisition and refinement, adaptation, and learning.

In a sense, inconsistency can be seen as perfectly acceptable in a system, or even desirable in a system, as long as the system has appropriate mechanisms for acting on the inconsistencies arising [27]. Of course, there are inconsistencies that do need to be resolved. But, the decision to resolve, and the approach to resolution, need to be context-sensitive. There is also the question of when to resolve inconsistencies. Immediate resolution of inconsistencies can result in the loss of valuable information if an arbitrary choice is made on what to reject. Consider for example the requirements capture stage in software engineering. Here premature resolution can force an arbitary decision to be made without the choice being properly considered. This can therefore overly constrain the requirements capture process.

The call for robust, and intelligent, systems, has led to an increased interest in inconsistency tolerance in computer science. However, introducing inconsistency tolerance is a difficult and challenging aim. In the next section, we consider some of the problems, at the level of formal logic, arising from inconsistency. Then, in the subsequent section, we review a range of foundational technologies for use in developing inconsistency tolerance.

2   Problems Arising from Inconsistency

Classical mathematical logic is very appealing for knowledge representation and reasoning: The representation is rich and the reasoning powerful. Furthermore, classical reasoning is intuitive and natural. The appeal of classical logic however, extends beyond the naturalness of representation and reasoning. It has some very important and useful properties which mean that it is well-understood and well-behaved, and that it is amenable to automated reasoning.

Much of computer science is based on classical logic. Consider for example hardware logic, software specifications, SQL databases, and knowledgebase systems. Classical logic is therefore a natural starting point for considering inconsistency tolerance. Inconsistency is very much a logical concept, and so we should consider the effect of inconsistency on classical logic.

Unfortunately, inconsistency causes problems in reasoning with classical logic. In classical logic, anything can follow from an inconsistent set of assumptions. Let Δ be a set of assumptions, let $\vdash$ be the classical consequence relation, and let α be a formula, then $\Delta \vdash \alpha$ denotes that α is an inference from Δ using classical logic. A useful definition of inconsistency for a set of assumptions Δ is that if $\Delta \vdash \alpha$ and $\Delta \vdash \neg\alpha$ then Δ is inconsistent. A property of classical logic is that if Δ is inconsistent, then for any β in the language, $\Delta \vdash \beta$. This property results from the following proof rule, called *ex falso quodlibet*, being a valid proof rule of classical logic.

$$\frac{\alpha \qquad\qquad \neg\alpha}{\beta}$$

So inconsistency causes classical logic to collapse. No useful inferences follow from an inconsistent set of assumptions. It can be described as exploding, or trivialised, in the sense that all formulae of the language are consequences of inconsistent set of assumptions.

Since much of computer science is based on classical logic, the collapse of it in the face of inconsistency is a profound problem. We need to define the mechanisms for handling information in terms of a logic. So if classical logic is not appropriate for inconsistent information, we need to look elsewhere for a logic for inconsistency tolerance, or we need to consider mechanisms on top of classical logic to manage the information.

Even if we adopt a logic that does not collapse, i.e. ex falso quodlibet does not hold, we still need ways to handle the conflicting information. If we have a database that contains both α and $\neg\alpha$, we may need to answer the query "is α true?". An obvious strategy is that we only answer queries after we have cleaned the data by removing information to restore consistency. Another strategy is to take credulous approach to answering queries and so answer positively if the fact is in the database irrespective of the existence of its complement: In this case the answer would be "yes". A third strategy is to take a skeptical approach to answering queries and so answer positively if the fact is in the database and its complement is not: In this case the answer would be "no". A fourth strategy is a qualified credulous approach which refines the credulous inference with information about the existence of its complement.

The strategy of restoring consistency is not necessarily simple. For a set of formulae Δ, one option is to remove the union of the minimally inconsistent subsets to fix the inconsistency. Consider the set of beliefs.

$$\Delta = \{\alpha, \alpha \rightarrow \beta, \beta \rightarrow \gamma, \delta \rightarrow \neg\beta, \delta\}$$

There is only one minimally inconsistent subset of Δ:

$$\{\alpha, \alpha \rightarrow \beta, \delta \rightarrow \neg\beta, \delta\}.$$

To revise Δ, we can subtract the minimally inconsistent subset, and use the remainder as the revised knowledgebase. This is the same as taking the intersection of the maximally consistent subsets as the revised knowledgebase. So the revised knowledgebase is $\{\beta \rightarrow \gamma\}$. From this example, we see that the subtraction of the minimally inconsistent subset from the knowledgebase is quite drastic. An alternative is just to remove the smallest number of assumptions in order to restore consistency. Given Δ, we only need to remove one formula to restore consistency. There are four possible clauses we could choose for this:

$$\alpha$$
$$\alpha \rightarrow \beta$$
$$\delta \rightarrow \neg\beta$$
$$\delta$$

So this gives us four choices for a revised set of assumptions. Each of these choices is a maximally consistent subset.

$$\Delta_1 = \{\alpha, \beta \rightarrow \gamma, \delta \rightarrow \neg\beta, \delta\}$$
$$\Delta_2 = \{\alpha, \alpha \rightarrow \beta, \beta \rightarrow \gamma, \delta\}$$
$$\Delta_3 = \{\alpha, \alpha \rightarrow \beta, \beta \rightarrow \gamma, \delta \rightarrow \neg\beta\}$$
$$\Delta_4 = \{\alpha \rightarrow \beta, \beta \rightarrow \gamma, \delta \rightarrow \neg\beta, \delta\}$$

Clearly, such a revision is much more modest. But then we see we have a choice to make which may call for further knowledge and/or further strategies.

The conclusion we can draw from the discussions and examples in this section is that whilst classical logic is very useful in computer science, it needs to be adapted for use with inconsistent information, and that adapting it can involve some difficult issues. This has been the subject of much research, some of which we touch upon in the next section.

3   Foundational Technologies for Inconsistency Tolerance

Inconsistency tolerance is being built on foundational technologies for identifying and analysing inconsistency in information, for representing and reasoning with inconsistent information, for resolving inconsistent information, and for merging inconsistent information.

The central position is that the collapse of classical logic in cases of inconsistency should be circumvented. In other words, we need to suspend the principle of absurdity (*ex falso quodlibet*) for many kinds of reasoning. A number of useful proposals have been made in the field of paraconsistent logics.

In addition, we need strategies for analysing inconsistent information. This need has in part driven the approach of argumentation systems which compare pros and cons for potential conclusions from conflicting information. Also important are strategies for isolating inconsistency and for taking appropriate actions, including resolution actions. This calls for uncertainty reasoning and meta-level reasoning. Furthermore, the cognitive activities involved in reasoning with inconsistent information need to be directly related to the kind of inconsistency. So, in general, we see the need for inconsistency tolerance giving rise to a range of technologies for inconsistency management.

3.1   Consistency Checking

In order to manage inconsistency in knowledge, we need to undertake consistency checking. However, consistency checking is inherently intractable in the propositional case. To address this problem of the intractability, we can consider using (A) tractable subsets of classical logic (for example binary disjunctions of literals [30]), (B) heuristics to direct the search for a model (for example in semantic tableau [56], GSAT [67], and constraint satisfaction [22]), (C) some form of knowledge compilation (for example [53, 19]), and (D) formalization of approximate consistency checking based on notions described below, such as approximate entailment [49, 66], and partial and probable consistency.

Heuristic approaches, which have received a lot of attention in automated reasoning technologies and in addressing constraint satisfaction problems, can be either complete such as semantic tableau or Davis-Puttnam procedure [20] or incomplete such as in the GSAT system [68]. Whilst in general, using heuristics to direct search has the same worst-case computational properties as undirected search, it can offer better performance in practice for some classes of theories. Note, heuristic approaches do not tend to be oriented to offering any analysis of theories beyond a decision on consistency.

In approximate entailment, classical entailment is approximated by two sequences of entailment relations. The first is sound but not complete, and the second is complete but not sound. Both sequences converge to classical entailment. For a set of propositional formulae Δ, a formula α, and an approximate entailment relation $\models_i$, the decision of whether $\Delta \models_i \alpha$ holds or $\Delta \not\models_i \alpha$ holds can be computed in polynomial time.

Partial consistency takes a different approach to approximation. Furthermore, consistency checking for a set of formulae Δ can be prematurely terminated when the search space exceeds some threshold. When the checking of Δ is prematurely terminated, partial consistency is the degree to which Δ is consistent. This can be measured in a number of ways including the proportion of formulae from Δ that can be shown to form a consistent subset of Δ. Maximum generalized satisfiability [57] may be viewed as an example of this.

Yet another approach is probable consistency checking [40]. Determining the probability that a set of formulae is consistent on the basis of polynomial time classifications of those formulae. Classifications for the propositional case can be based on tests including counting the number of different propositional letters, counting the multiple occurrences of each propositional letter, and determining the degree of nesting for each logical symbol. The more a set of formulae is tested, the greater the confidence in the probability value for consistency, but this is at the cost of undertaking the tests.

Identifying approximate consistency for a set of formulae Δ is obviously not a guarantee that Δ is consistent. However, approximate consistency checking is useful because it helps to focus where problems possibly lie in Δ, and to prioritize resolution tasks. For example, if Δ and Γ are two parts of a larger knowledgebase that is thought to be inconsistent, and the probability of consistency is much greater for Δ than Γ, then Γ is more likely to be problematical and so should be examined more closely. Similarly, if Δ and Γ are two parts of a larger knowledgebase that is thought to be inconsistent, and a partial consistency identified for Δ is greater than for Γ, then Γ seems to contain more problematical data and so should be examined more closely by the user.

In databases, inconsistency is a notion relative to the satisfaction of a given set of integrity constraints (ICs), which are properties of the admissible database states. They impose semantic restrictions on the data in order to capture the correspondence of the data with the outside world that is being modelled by the database. We say that the database is inconsistent when the ICs, expressed as logical formulas, are not satisfied by the database, which can be seen as a first-order structure [64].

From this point of view, checking satisfaction of integrity constraints amounts to determining is a sentence is true in the given database. This can be easily done by posing and answering a query to/from the database. Taking into account that databases evolve as updates on it are executed, it becomes necessary to check every database state generated in this way. This process can be simplified using an inductive approach [54]: If the database was consistent before executing a certain update, then according to the kind of update and the kind of IC, it may be necessary to check only a formula that is much simpler that the original IC; or nothing at all if the update is irrelevant to the IC at hand [13]. Most approaches to consistency handling in database are directed to either detect potential inconsistencies, so that a problematic update is rejected before execution, or to accept the update even if an inconsistency is produced, but then detect or make a diagnosis of the data participating in the inconsistency, followed by an additional, remedial or compensating update that restores or enforces consistency [32, 16].

Clearly each approach to making consistency checking viable involves some form of compromise, and none is perfect for all applications. We therefore need a variety of approaches with clearly understood foundations and inter-relationships with other approaches. Furthermore, different techniques may give us different perspectives on inconsistencies in a given knowledgebase.

3.2 Paraconsistent Logics

Reasoning with inconsistency involves some compromise on the inferential machinery of classical logic. There is a range of proposals for logics (called paraconsistent logics) for reasoning with inconsistency. Each of the proposals has advantages and disadvantages. Selecting an appropriate paraconsistent logic for an application depends on the requirements of the application.

Types of paraconsistent logic that are proving to be of use for knowledge representation and reasoning in intelligent computing systems include: (1) Weakly-negative logics which use the full classical language, but a subset of the classical proof theory [21, 5]; (2) Four-valued logics which use a subset of the classical language and a subset of the classical proof theory, together with an intuitive four-valued semantics [6, 63, 4]; (3) Signed systems which involve renaming all literals in a theory and then restoring some of the original theory by progressively adding formal equivalences between the original literals and their renamings [10]; and (4) Quasi-classical logic which uses classical proof theory but restricts the notion of a natural deduction proof by prohibiting the application of elimination proof rules after the application of introduction proof rules [11, 35, 36].

These options behave in quite different ways with sets of assumptions. None can be regarded as perfect for handling inconsistent information in general. Rather, they provide a spectrum of approaches. However, in all the approaches the aim is to stay close to classical reasoning, since, as we have acknowledged, classical logic has many appealing features for knowledge representation and reasoning.

Paraconsistent logics are central to developing tolerance to inconsistency. Key research frontiers on this subject include: (1) developing a deeper understanding of the relationship of paraconsistency and substructural logics (for more information see Chapter 9 by John Slaney entitled "Relevant Logic and Paraconsistency"); (2) developing a deeper understanding of the computational complexity of paraconsistent logics (for more information see Chapter 6 by Sylvie Coste-Marquis and Pierre Marquis entitled "On the Complexity of Paraconsistent Inference Relations"); (3) developing automated reasoning technology for paraconsistent logics such via quantified Boolean formulae (for more information see Chapter 4 by Philippe Besnard, Torsten Schaub, Hans Tompits, and Stefan Woltran entitled "Representing Paraconsistent Reasoning via Quantified Boolean Formulae").

3.3   Argumentation Systems

Argumentation is an important cognitive activity that draws on conflicting knowledge for decision-making and problem solving. It normally involves identifying relevant assumptions and conclusions for a given problem being analysed. Furthermore, this often involves identifying conflicts, resulting in the need to look for pros and cons for particular conclusions. This may also involve chains of reasoning, where conclusions are used in the assumptions for deriving further conclusions. In other words, the problem may be decomposed recursively.

Coalition Systems. These are based on identifying sets of arguments that defend each other against counter-arguments by banding together for self-defence. The seminal proposal that can be described as using coalitions is by Dung [24]. This approach assumes a set of arguments, and a binary "attacks" relation between pairs of arguments. A hierarchy of arguments is then defined in terms of the relative attacks "for" and "against" each argument in each subset of the arguments. In this way, for example, the plausibility of an argument could be defended by another argument in its coalition (i.e. its subset).

Coherence Systems. One of the most obvious strategies for handling inconsistency in a knowledgebase is to reason with consistent subsets of the knowledgebase. This is closely related to the approach of removing information from the knowledgebase that is causing an inconsistency. In coherence systems, an argument is based on a consistent subset of a inconsistent set of formulae — the inconsistency arises from the conflicting views being represented. Further constraints, such as minimality or skeptical reasoning, can be imposed on the consistent subset for it to be an allowed argument. This range of further constraints gives us a variety of approaches to argumentation including [52, 14, 7, 8, 25, 2, 34, 12].

Defeasible Logics. There are a number of proposals for defeasible logics. The common feature for these logics is the incorporation of a defeasible implication into the language. Defeasible logics have their origins in philosophy and were originally developed for reasoning problems similar to those addressed by nonmonotonic logics in artificial intelligence. In [59, 60], Pollock conceptualises the notions of reasons, prima facie reasons, defeaters, rebutting defeaters, and undercutting defeaters, in terms of formal logic. Arguments can then be defined as chains of reasons leading to a conclusion with consideration of potential defeaters at each step. Different types of argument occur depending on the nature of the reasons and defeaters. This has provided a starting point for a number of proposals for logic-based argumentation including abstract argument systems [71], conditional logic [55], and ordered logic [47].

There are many proposals for formalisms for logic-based argumentation. For general reviews of formalisms for argumentation see [31, 70, 61, 17]. Furthermore, some of these formalisms are being developed for applications in legal reasoning [62], in medical reasoning and risk assessment [26], and in agent-based systems [58]. A review of argumentation systems that relate proposals to potential application areas in knowledge engineering, decision-support, multi-agent negotiation, and software engineering, is given in [15].

3.4   Inconsistency Analysis

Given an inconsistent set of formulae Δ, we may need to know more about the nature of the inconsistency and the nature of information being offered by Δ. In some sense, we may desire inconsistency analysis based on notions that can be measured in Δ.

The seminal work on measuring inconsistency is by Shannon [69]. This work, based on probability theory, can be used in a logical setting when the worlds are the possible events. This work is also the basis of Lozinskii's work [51] for defining the quantity of information of a formula (or knowledgebase) in propositional logic. But this definition is not suitable when the knowledgebase is inconsistent. In this case, it has no classical model, so we have no "event" to count. To address this, models of maximal consistent subsets of the knowledgebase are considered.

Another related measure is the measure of contradiction. It is usual in classical logic to use a binary measure of contradiction: a knowledgebase is either consistent or inconsistent. This dichotomy is obvious when the only deductive tool is classical inference, since inconsistent knowledgebases are of no use. But, as we have identified earlier, there are now a number of paraconsistent logics developed to draw non-trivial conclusions from an inconsistent knowledgebase. So this dichotomy is not sufficient to describe the measure of contradiction of a knowledgebase, one needs more fine-grained measures.

Some interesting proposals have been made for this including: Consistency-based analyses that focus on the consistent and inconsistent subsets of a knowledgebase [39]; Information theoretic analyses that adapt Shannon's information measure [51, 72]; Probabilistic semantic analyses that consider maximal consistent probability distributions over a set of formulae [42, 43]; Epistemic actions analyses that measure the degree of information in a knowledgebase in terms of the number of actions required to identify the truth value of each atomic proposition and the degree of contradiction in a knowledgebase in terms of the number of actions needed to render the knowledgebase consistent [44]; and Model-theoretic analyses that are based on evaluating a knowledgebase in terms of three or four valued models that permit an "inconsistent" truth value [33, 37, 38].

This topic is the basis of Chapter 7 by Anthony Hunter and Sebastien Konieczny entitled "Approaches to Measuring Inconsistent Information".

3.5   Belief Revision

Given a knowledgebase Δ, and a revision α, belief revision theory is concerned with the properties that should hold for a rational notion of updating Δ with α. If $\Delta \cup \alpha$ is inconsistent, then belief revision theory assumes the requirement that the knowledge should be revised so that the result is consistent.

The AGM axioms, by Alchurron, Gardenfors and Makinson [1, 29], are postulates to delineate the behaviour of revision functions for belief sets (consider this as the set of all inferences obtained from a set of formulae). In the revision operation, as little of the belief set is changed as possible in order to include some new information. This requirement to change as little as possible precludes the change from a consistent set to an inconsistent set. In other words, some beliefs will be removed in order to maintain consistency.

The postulates appear as rational and intuitive properties that would be highly desirable. However, delivering efficient and effective systems that meet the postulates has proved to be challenging. There have been many developments of belief revision theory including iterated belief revision [18, 48], and relating belief revision to database updating [41]. These also offer intuitive abstract constraints for revision/updating. For a review of belief revision theory see [23].

There are some more concrete proposals for knowledgebase merging that adhere to belief revision postulates. In Konieczny and Pino Perez [45], there is a proposal for merging beliefs based on semantically characterizing interpretations which are "closest" to some sets of interpretations. But the approach does not exploit any meta-level information such as preferences. The approach has been generalized by considering merging with respect to integrity constraints [46].

Another approach that extends belief revision theory, called arbitration operators, is by Liberatore and Schaerf [50]. This is a form of merging restricted to merging only two knowledgebases and it forces the result to be the disjunction of the two original knowledgebases.

Proposals for belief revision that incorporate priorities include ordered theory presentations [65] and prioritized revision [28]. In ordered theory presentations, if a formula is less preferred than another which contradicts it, those aspects of it which are not contradicted are preserved. This is done by adopting an inferentially weaker formula to avoid the contradiction with the more preferred formula. This merging can be undertaken in an arbitrarily large partially ordering of formulae. In prioritized revision, a belief revision operator is defined in terms of selecting the model that satisfies the new belief and is nearest to the existing beliefs. The measure of nearness can be used in iterated belief revision where the more preferred items are used in later revisions.

Similar in spirit to belief revision is the recent work on consistent query answering in databases [3, 9]. The idea, as opposed to traditional approaches to inconsistency handling, is to live with an inconsistent database, but obtaining only consistent information (with respect to given integrity constraints) when queries are answered. That consistent information is the one that is invariant or persists under all possible minimal ways of restoring consistency of the database. There may be several alternative minimal *repairs* for a database, in consequence what is consistently true in a database instance is what is true in a collection of other instances that are the minimally repaired version of the original one. This approach shares many similarities with the problem of updating a database seen as a logical theory (or a model) by means of a set of sentences (the integrity constraints). In this case, the data is flexible, subject to repair, but the integrity constraints are hard, not to be given up. So, what is consistently true is what is true wrt to the revised database. A more precise comparison can be found in [3, 9].

4   Towards Viable Technologies

We are now at an exciting stage in the development of inconsistency tolerance. Rich foundations are being established, and a number of interesting and complementary application areas are being explored in decision-support, multi-agent systems, database systems, and software engineering.

Key frontiers in developing viable applications technologies include: Integrating data from heterogeneous databases (for more information see Chapter 3 by Leo Bertossi and Loreto Bravo entitled "Consistent Query Answers in Virtual Data Integration Systems"); Computational complexity issues in integrity maintenance (for more information see Chapter 5 by Jan Chomicki and Jerzy Marcinkowski entitled "On the Computational Complexity of Minimal-Change Integrity Maintenance in Relational Databases"); Representing and reasoning with spatial data (for more information see Chapter 8 by Andrea Rodriguez entitled "Inconsistency Issues in Spatial Databases"; and Computational complexity issues in handling XML specifications (for more information see Chapter 2 by Marcelo Arenas, Leonid Libkin and Wenfei Fan entitled "Consistency of XML specifications").

5 Conclusions

In this introduction, we have highlighted the need for inconsistency tolerance in order to create more robust and more intelligent computing systems. Inconsistency tolerance is being built on foundational technologies of identifying and analysing inconsistency in information, for representing and reasoning with inconsistent information, for resolving inconsistent information, and for merging inconsistent information. Inconsistency tolerance is now being developed for a range of applications in database, knowledgebase and software systems.

References

1. C Alchourron, P Gardenfors, and D Makinson. On the logic of theory change: partial meet contraction and revision functions. *Journal of Symbolic Logic*, 50:510–530, 1985.
2. L Amgoud and C Cayrol. On the acceptability of arguments in preference-based argumentation. In G Cooper and S Moral, editors, *Proceedings of the 14th Conference on Uncertainty in Artificial Intelligence*. Morgan Kaufmann, 1998.
3. M Arenas, L Bertossi, and J Chomicki. Consistent query answers in inconsistent databases. In *Proc. ACM Symposium on Principles of Database Systems (PODS 99)*, pages 68–79, 1999.
4. O Arieli and A. Avron. The value of the four values. *Artificial Intelligence*, 102:97–141, 1998.
5. D Batens. Paraconsistent extensional propositional logics. *Logique et Analyse*, 90–91:195–234, 1980.
6. N Belnap. A useful four-valued logic. In G Epstein, editor, *Modern Uses of Multiple-valued Logic*, pages 8–37. Reidel, 1977.
7. S Benferhat, D Dubois, and H Prade. Argumentative inference in uncertain and inconsistent knowledge bases. In *Proceedings of Uncertainty in Artificial Intelligence*, pages 1449–1445. Morgan Kaufmann, 1993.
8. S Benferhat, D Dubois, and H Prade. A logical approach to reasoning under inconsistency in stratified knowledge bases. In *Symbolic and Quantitative Approaches to Reasoning and Uncertainty*, volume 956 of *Lecture Notes in Computer Science*, pages 36–43. Springer, 1995.
9. L Bertossi and J Chomicki. Query answering in inconsistent databases. In G Saake J Chomicki and R van der Meyden, editors, *Logics for Emerging Applications of Databases*. Springer, 2003.
10. Philippe Besnard and Torsten Schaub. Signed systems for paraconsistent reasoning. *Journal of Automated Reasoning*, 20:191–213, 1998.
11. Ph Besnard and A Hunter. Quasi-classical logic: Non-trivializable classical reasoning from inconsistent information. In C Froidevaux and J Kohlas, editors, *Symbolic and Quantitative Approaches to Uncertainty*, volume 946 of *Lecture Notes in Computer Science*, pages 44–51, 1995.

12. Ph Besnard and A Hunter. A logic-based theory of deductive arguments. *Artificial Intelligence*, 128:203–235, 2001.
13. J Blakeley, N Coburn, and P Larson. Updating derived relations: detecting irrelevant and autonomously computable updates. *ACM Transactions on Database Systems*, 14(3):369–400, 1989.
14. G Brewka. Preferred subtheories: An extended logical framework for default reasoning. In *Proceedings of the Eleventh International Conference on Artificial Intelligence*, pages 1043–1048, 1989.
15. D Carbogim, D Robertson, and J Lee. Argument-based applications to knowledge engineering. *Knowledge Engineering Review*, 15:119–149, 2000.
16. S Ceri, P Fraternali, S Paraboschi, and L Tanca. Automatic generation of production rules for integrity maintenance. *ACM Transactions on Database Systems*, 19(3):367–422, 1994.
17. C Chesnevar, A Maguitman, and R Loui. Logical models of argument. *ACM Computing Surveys*, 32:337–383, 2001.
18. A Darwiche and J Pearl. On the logic of iterated belief revision. *Artificial Intelligence*, 89:1–29, 1997.
19. A Darwiche. Compiling knowledge into decomposible negation normal form. In *Proceedings of the International Joint Conference on Artificial Intelligence (IJCAI'99)*, pages 284–289, 1999.
20. M. Davis and H. Putnam. A computing procedure for quantification theory. *Journal of the ACM*, 7:201–215, 1960.
21. N C da Costa. On the theory of inconsistent formal systems. *Notre Dame Journal of Formal Logic*, 15:497–510, 1974.
22. R Dechter and J Pearl. Network-based heuristics for constraint-satisfaction problems. *Artificial Intelligence*, 34:1–38, 1987.
23. D Dubois and H Prade, editors. *Handbook of Defeasible Resoning and Uncertainty Management Systems*, volume 3. Kluwer, 1998.
24. P. Dung. On the acceptability of arguments and its fundamental role in nonmonotonic reasoning, logic programming and n-person games. *Artificial Intelligence*, 77:321–357, 1995.
25. M Elvang-Goransson and A Hunter. Argumentative logics: Reasoning from classically inconsistent information. *Data and Knowledge Engineering*, 16:125–145, 1995.
26. J Fox and S Das. *Safe and Sound: Artificial Intelligence in Hazardous Applications*. MIT Press, 2000.
27. D Gabbay and A Hunter. Making inconsistency respectable 1: A logical framework for inconsistency in reasoning. In *Fundamentals of Artificial Intelligence*, volume 535 of *Lecture Notes in Computer Science*, pages 19–32. Springer, 1991.
28. D Gabbay and O Rodrigues. A methodology for iterated theory change. In *Practical Reasoning*, volume 1085 of *Lecture Notes in Computer Science*. Springer, 1996.
29. P Gardenfors. *Knowledge in Flux*. MIT Press, 1988.
30. M Garey and D Johnson. *Computers and Intractability: A Guide to the Theory of NP-Completeness*. Freeman, 1979.
31. J Gebhardt and R Kruse. Background and perspectives of possibilistic graphical models. In A Hunter and S Parsons, editors, *Applications of Uncertainty Formalisms*, Lecture Notes in Computer Science. Springer, 1998.

32. M Gertz and W Lipeck. An extensible framework for repairing constraint violations. In S Jajodia et al., editor, *Integrity and Internal Control in Information Systems, IFIP TC11 Working Group 11.5, First Working Conference on Integrity and Internal Control in Information Systems: Increasing the confidence in Information Systems, Zurich, Switzerland, December 4-5, 1997*, pages 89–111. Chapman Hall, 1997.

33. J Grant. Classifications for inconsistent theories. *Notre Dame Journal of Formal Logic*, 19:435–444, 1978.

34. R Haenni, J Kohlas, and N Lehmann. Probabilistic argumentation systems. In D Gabbay and Ph Smets, editors, *Handbook of Defeasible Reasoning and Uncertainty Management Systems, Volume 5*, pages 221–288. Kluwer, 2000.

35. A Hunter. Reasoning with contradictory information using quasi-classical logic. *Journal of Logic and Computation*, 10:677–703, 2000.

36. A Hunter. A semantic tableau version of first-order quasi-classical logic. In *Quantitative and Qualitative Approaches to Reasoning with Uncertainty*, LNCS. Springer, 2001. 544–556.

37. A Hunter. Measuring inconsistency in knowledge via quasi-classical models. In *Proceedings of the 18th National Conference on Artificial Intelligence (AAAI'2002)*, pages 68–73. MIT Press, 2002. ISBN 0-262-51129-0.

38. A Hunter. Evaluating the significance of inconsistency. In *Proceedings of the International Joint Conference on AI (IJCAI'03)*, pages 468–473, 2003.

39. A Hunter. Logical comparison of inconsistent perspectives using scoring functions. *Knowledge and Information Systems Journal*, 2004. (in press).

40. A Hunter. Probable consistency checking for sets of propositional clauses. In *Symbolic and Quantitative Approaches to Reasoning with Uncertainty*, volume 2711 of Lecture Notes in Computer Science. Springer, 2003. pages 464 - 476.

41. H Katsuno and A Mendelzon. On the difference between updating a knowledgebase and revising it. *Belief Revision*, pages 183–203, 1992.

42. K Knight. Measuring inconsistency. *Journal of Philosophical Logic*, 31:77–98, 2001.

43. K Knight. Two information measures for inconsistent sets. *Journal of Logic, Language and Information*, 12:227–248, 2003.

44. S Konieczny, J Lang, and P Marquis. Quantifying information and contradiction in propositional logic through epistemic actions. In *Proceedings of the 18th International Joint Conference on Artificial Intellignce (IJCAI'03)*, 2003. in press.

45. S Konieczny and R Pino Perez. On the logic of merging. In *Proceedings of the Sixth International Conference on Principles of Knowledge Representation and Reasoning (KR98)*, pages 488–498. Morgan Kaufmann, 1998.

46. S Konieczny and R Pino Perez. Merging with integrity constraints. In Anthony Hunter and Simon Parsons, editors, *Qualitative and Quantitative Approaches to Reasoning and Uncertainty (ECSQARU'99)*, volume 1638 of *Lecture Notes in Computer Science*. Springer, 1999.

47. E Laenens and D Vermeir. A fixpoint semantics for ordered logic. *Journal of Logic and Computation*, 1:159–185, 1990.

48. D Lehmann. Belief revision, revised. In *Proceedings of the International Joint Conference on Artificial Intelligence (IJCAI'95)*, pages 1534–1540, 1995.

49. H Levesque. A logic of implicit and explicit belief. In *Proceedings of the National Conference on Artificial Intelligence (AAAI'84)*, pages 198–202, 1984.

50. P Liberatore and M Schaerf. Arbitration (or how to merge knowledgebases). *IEEE Transactions on Knowledge and Data Engineering*, 10:76–90, 1998.

51. E Lozinskii. Information and evidence in logic systems. *Journal of Experimental and Theoretical Artificial Intelligence*, 6:163–193, 1994.

52. R Manor and N Rescher. On inferences from inconsistent information. *Theory and Decision*, 1:179–219, 1970.

53. P Marquis. Knowledge compilation using prime implicates. In *Proceedings of the International Joint Conference on Artificial Intelligence (IJCAI'95)*, pages 837–843, 1995.

54. J-M. Nicolas. Logic for improving integrity checking in relational data bases. *Acta Informatica*, 18:227–253, 1982.

55. D Nute. Defeasible reasoning and decision support systems. *Decision Support Systems*, 4:97–110, 1988.

56. F Oppacher and E Suen. HARP: A tableau-based theorem prover. *Journal of Automated Reasoning*, 4:69–100, 1988.

57. C Papadimitriou. *Computational Complexity*. Addison-Wesley, 1994.

58. S Parsons, C Sierra, and N Jennings. Agents that reason and negotiate by arguing. *Journal of Logic and Computation*, 8:261–292, 1998.

59. J Pollock. Defeasible reasoning. *Cognitive Science*, 11:481–518, 1987.

60. J Pollock. How to reason defeasibly. *Artificial Intelligence*, 57:1–42, 1992.

61. H Prakken and G Vreeswijk. Logical systems for defeasible argumentation. In D Gabbay, editor, *Handbook of Philosophical Logic*. Kluwer, 2000.

62. H Prakken. *Logical Tools for Modelling Legal Argument*. Kluwer, 1997.

63. G Priest. Reasoning abuot truth. *Artificial Intelligence*, 39:231–244, 1989.

64. R Reiter. Towards a logical reconstruction of relational database theory. In M.Brodie, J.Mylopoulos, and J. Schmidt, editors, *On Conceptual Modeling*, pages 191–233. Springer-Verlag, 1984.

65. M Ryan. Representing defaults as sentences with reduced priority. In *Principles of Knowledge Representation and Reasoning: Proceedings of the Third International Conference*. Morgan Kaufmann, 1992.

66. M Schaerf and M Cadoli. Tractable reasoning via approximation. *Artificial Intelligence*, 74:249–310, 1995.

67. B Selman, H Levesque, and D Mitchell. A new method for solving hard satisfiability problems. In *Proceedings of the Tenth National Conference on Artificial Intelligence (AAAI'92)*, pages 440–446, 1992.

68. B. Selman, H. Levesque, and D. Mitchell. A new method for solving hard satisfiability problems. In P. Rosenbloom and P. Szolovits, editors, *Proceedings of AAAI'92*, pages 440–446. AAAI Press, 1992.

69. C Shannon. A mathematical theory of communication. *Bell System Technical Journal*, 27:379–423, 1948.

70. D Vermeir, E Laenens, and P Geerts. Defeasible logics. In *Handbook of Defeasible Reasoning and Uncertainty Management*, volume 2. Kluwer, 1998.

71. G Vreeswijk. Abstract argumentation systems. *Artificial Intelligence*, 90:225–279, 1997.

72. P Wong and Ph Besnard. Paraconsistent reasoning as an analytic tool. *Journal of the Interest Group in Propositional Logic*, 9:233–246, 2001.

Consistency of XML Specifications

Marcelo Arenas[1], Wenfei Fan[2], and Leonid Libkin[1]

[1] Department of Computer Science, University of Toronto
{marenas, libkin}@cs.toronto.edu
[2] University of Edinburgh & Bell Laboratories
wenfei@research.bell-labs.com

Abstract. Specifications of XML documents typically consist of typing information (for example, a DTD), and integrity constraints (for example, keys and foreign keys). We show that combining the two may lead to seemingly reasonable specifications that are nevertheless inconsistent: there is no XML document that both conforms to the DTD and satisfies the constraints. We then survey results on the complexity of consistency checking, and show that, depending on the classes of DTDs and constraints involved, it ranges from linear time to undecidable. Furthermore, we show that for some of the most common classes of specifications checking consistency is intractable.

1 Introduction

Although a number of dependency formalisms were developed for relational databases, functional and inclusion dependencies are the ones used most often. In fact, two subclasses of functional and inclusion dependencies, namely, keys and foreign keys, are most commonly found in practice. Both are fundamental to conceptual database design, and are supported by the SQL standard [34]. They provide a mechanism by which one can uniquely identify a tuple in a relation and refer to a tuple from another relation. They have proved useful in update anomaly prevention, query optimization and index design [1, 41].

XML (eXtensible Markup Language [11]) has become the prime standard for data exchange on the Web. XML data typically originates in databases. If XML is to represent data currently residing in databases, it should support keys and foreign keys, which are an essential part of the semantics of the data. A number of key and foreign key specifications have been proposed for XML, e.g., the XML standard (Document Type Definition, DTD) [11], XML Data [31] and XML Schema [40]. Keys and foreign keys for XML are important in, among other things, query optimization [37], data integration [7, 8, 22, 27], and in data transformations between XML and database formats [9, 18, 25, 26, 32, 38, 39].

XML data usually comes with a DTD[1] that specifies how a document is organized. Thus, a specification of an XML document may consist of both a DTD

---

[1] Throughout the chapter, by a DTD we mean its type specification; we ignore its ID/IDREF constraints since their limitations have been well recognized [12, 24].

L. Bertossi et al. (Eds.): Inconsistency Tolerance, LNCS 3300, pp. 15–41, 2004.
© Springer-Verlag Berlin Heidelberg 2004

and a set of integrity constraints, such as keys and foreign keys. A legitimate question then is whether such a specification is *consistent*, or meaningful: that is, whether there exists an XML document that both satisfies the constraints and conforms to the DTD.

In the relational database setting, such a question would have a trivial answer: one can write arbitrary (primary) key and foreign key specifications in SQL, without worrying about consistency. However, DTDs (and other schema specifications for XML) are more complex than relational schema: in fact, XML documents are typically modeled as node-labeled trees, e.g., in XSLT [19], XQuery [10], XML Schema [40], XPath [20] and DOM [3]. Consequently, DTDs may interact with keys and foreign keys in a rather nontrivial way, as shown in the following examples.

Example 1. As a simple example, consider the DTD given below:

```
<!ELEMENT db  (foo)>
<!ELEMENT foo (foo)>
```

Observe that there exists no finite XML tree conforming to this DTD, and hence this specification – that consists only of a DTD and no constraints – is inconsistent.   □

Example 2. To illustrate the interaction between XML DTDs and key/foreign key constraints, consider a DTD D, which specifies a (nonempty) collection of teachers:

```
<!ELEMENT teachers (teacher+)>
<!ELEMENT teacher  (teach, research)>
<!ELEMENT teach    (subject, subject)>
```

It says that a teacher teaches two subjects. Here we omit the descriptions of elements whose type is string (i.e., PCDATA in XML).

Assume that each teacher has an attribute name and each subject has an attribute taught_by. Attributes are single-valued. That is, if an attribute l is defined for an element type τ in a DTD, then in a document conforming to the DTD, each element of type τ must have a unique l attribute with a string value. Consider a set of unary key and foreign key constraints, Σ:

$$teacher.name \;\; \rightarrow \;\; teacher,$$
$$subject.taught\_by \;\; \rightarrow \;\; subject,$$
$$subject.taught\_by \subseteq_{FK} teacher.name.$$

That is, name is a key of teacher elements, taught_by is a key of subject elements and it is also a foreign key referencing name of teacher elements. More specifically, referring to an XML tree T, the first constraint asserts that two distinct teacher nodes in T cannot have the same name attribute value: the (string) value of name attribute uniquely identifies a teacher node. It should

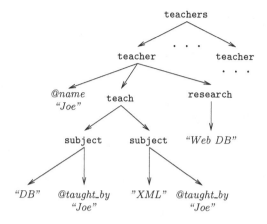

Fig. 1. An XML tree conforming to D

be mentioned that two notions of equality are used in the definition of keys: we assume string *value* equality when comparing **name** attribute values, and *node* identity when it comes to comparing **teacher** elements. The second key states that the **taught_by** attribute value uniquely identifies a **subject** node in T. The third constraint asserts that for any **subject** node x, there is a **teacher** node y in T such that the **taught_by** attribute value of x equals the **name** attribute value of y. Since **name** is a key of **teacher**, the **taught_by** attribute of any **subject** node refers to a unique **teacher** node.

Obviously, there exists an XML tree conforming to D, as shown in Figure 1. However, there is no XML tree that both conforms to D and satisfies Σ. To see this, let us first define some notation. Given an XML tree T and an element type τ, we use $ext(\tau)$ to denote the set of all the nodes labeled τ in T. Similarly, given an attribute l of τ, we use $ext(\tau.l)$ to denote the set of l attribute values of all τ elements. Then immediately from Σ follows a set of dependencies:

$$|ext(teacher.name)| = |ext(teacher)|,$$
$$|ext(subject.taught\_by)| = |ext(subject)|,$$
$$|ext(subject.taught\_by)| \leq |ext(teacher.name)|,$$

where $|\cdot|$ is the cardinality of a set. Therefore, we have

$$|ext(subject)| \leq |ext(teacher)|. \tag{1}$$

On the other hand, the DTD D requires that each teacher must teach two subjects. Since no sharing of nodes is allowed in XML trees and the collection of **teacher** elements is nonempty, from D follows:

$$1 < 2 \cdot |ext(teacher)| = |ext(subject)|. \tag{2}$$

Thus $|ext(teacher)| < |ext(subject)|$. Obviously, (1) and (2) contradict each other and as an immediate result, there exists no XML document that both satisfies Σ and conforms to D. In particular, the XML tree in Figure 1 violates the key $subject.taught\_by \to subject$.   □

This example demonstrates that a DTD may impose dependencies on the cardinalities of certain sets of objects in XML trees. These *cardinality constraints* interact with keys and foreign keys. More specifically, keys and foreign keys also enforce cardinality constraints that interact with those imposed by DTD. This makes the consistency analysis of keys and foreign keys for XML far more intriguing than its relational counterpart.

The constraints in this example are fairly simple: there is an immediate analogy between such XML constraints and relational keys and foreign keys. There have been a number of proposals for supporting more powerful keys and foreign keys for XML (e.g., [11, 12, 40, 31]). Not surprisingly, the interaction between DTDs and those complicated XML constraints is more involved.

In light of this we are interested in the following family of the *consistency* (or *satisfiability*) problems, where $\mathcal{C}$ ranges over classes of integrity constraints:

PROBLEM	:	SAT($\mathcal{C}$).
INPUT	:	A DTD D, a set Σ of $\mathcal{C}$-constraints.
QUESTION	:	Is there an XML document that conforms to D and satisfies Σ?

In other words, we want to validate XML specifications statically, at compile-time. The main reason is twofold: first, complex interactions between DTDs and constraints are likely to result in inconsistent specifications, and second, an alternative dynamic approach to validation (simply check a document to see if it conforms to the DTD and satisfies the constraints) would not tell us whether repeated failures are due to a bad specification, or problems with the documents.

This chapter presents the complexity of the consistency analysis of XML specifications. We consider DTDs and a variety of XML keys and foreign keys commonly encountered in real-life XML specifications.

The next section gives a brief introduction to XML DTDs and XML documents. It is followed by the definitions of two basic forms of XML constraints, namely, *absolute* constraints that hold in the entire document, and *relative* constraints that only hold in a part of the document. Section 4 is devoted to the consistency analyses of XML specifications with absolute constraints, and Section 5 considers relative constraints. Extensions of the basic XML constraints by means of path expressions (regular expressions and XPath [20]), such as constraints proposed by XML Schema [40], are treated in Section 6. Finally, Section 7 identifies open problems for further study, and provides references to the original papers.

2   DTDs and XML Trees

In this section, we present a formalism of XML DTDs [11] and review the XML tree model.

Document Type Definition. We formalize the notion of DTDs as follows (cf. [11, 15, 35, 23]).

Definition 1. *A* DTD *(Document Type Definition) is defined to be* $D = (E, A, P, R, r)$, *where:*

- *E is a finite set of* element types;
- *A is a finite set of* attributes, *disjoint from E;*
- *for each $\tau \in E$, $P(\tau)$ is a regular expression α, called the* element type definition *of τ:*

$$\alpha \quad ::= \quad \mathsf{S} \mid \tau' \mid \epsilon \mid \alpha|\alpha \mid \alpha, \alpha \mid \alpha*,$$

  where S denotes the string *type, $\tau' \in E$, ϵ is the empty word, and "|", "," and "*" denote union, concatenation, and the Kleene closure, respectively. In this chapter we also use the following shorthands: $\alpha+$ for $(\alpha, \alpha*)$ and $\alpha?$ for $(\epsilon|\alpha)$. We refer to the set of E types appearing in $P(\tau)$ as the alphabet of $P(\tau)$.*
- *for each $\tau \in E$, $R(\tau)$ is a set of attributes in A;*
- *$r \in E$ and is called* the element type of the root.   □

We normally denote element types by τ and attributes by l, and assume that r does not appear in $P(\tau)$ for any $\tau \in E$. We also assume that each τ in $E \setminus \{r\}$ is *connected to* r, i.e., either τ appears in $P(r)$, or it appears in $P(\tau')$ for some τ' that is connected to r.

Example 3. Let us consider the DTD D given in Example 2. In our formalism, D can be represented as (E, A, P, R, r), where $E = \{$*teachers, teacher, teach, research, subject*$\}$, $A = \{$*name, taught_by*$\}$, $r = $ *teachers* and P, R are as follows:

$P(teachers) = teacher+$	$R(teachers) = \emptyset$
$P(teacher) \;= teach,\ research$	$R(teacher) \;= \{name\}$
$P(teach) \quad= subject,\ subject$	$R(teach) \quad= \emptyset$
$P(subject) \;= \mathsf{S}$	$R(subject) \;= \{taught\_by\}$
$P(research) = \mathsf{S}$	$R(research) = \emptyset$

□

XML Trees. An XML document is typically modeled as a node-labeled tree. Below we describe valid XML documents w.r.t. a DTD, along the same lines as XQuery [10], XML Schema [40] and DOM [3].

Definition 2. *Let $D = (E, A, P, R, r)$ be a DTD. An XML tree T conforming to D, written $T \models D$, is defined to be $(V, lab, ele, att, val, root)$, where*

- V *is a finite set of* nodes;
- *lab is a function that maps each node in* V *to a label in* $E \cup A \cup \{S\}$; *a node* $v \in V$ *is called an* element of type τ *if* $lab(v) = \tau$ *and* $\tau \in E$, *an* attribute *if* $lab(v) \in A$, *and a* text node *if* $lab(v) = S$;
- *ele is a function that for any* $\tau \in E$, *maps each element* v *of type* τ *to a (possibly empty) list* $[v_1, ..., v_n]$ *of elements and text nodes in* V *such that* $lab(v_1) \ldots lab(v_n)$ *is in the regular language defined by* $P(\tau)$;
- *att is a partial function from* $V \times A$ *to* V *such that for any* $v \in V$ *and* $l \in A$, $att(v, l)$ *is defined iff* $lab(v) = \tau$, $\tau \in E$ *and* $l \in R(\tau)$;
- *val is a partial function from* V *to string values such that for any node* $v \in V$, $val(v)$ *is defined iff* $lab(v) = S$ *or* $lab(v) \in A$;
- *root is the root of* T: $root \in V$ *and* $lab(root) = r$.

For any node $v \in V$, *if* $ele(v)$ *is defined, then the nodes* v' *in* $ele(v)$ *are called the* subelements *of* v. *For any* $l \in A$, *if* $att(v, l) = v'$, *then* v' *is called an* attribute *of* v. *In either case we say that there is a* parent-child edge *from* v *to* v'. *The subelements and attributes of* v *are called its* children. *The graph defined by the parent-child relation is required to be a rooted tree.* □

Intuitively, V is the set of nodes of the tree T. The mapping *lab* labels every node of V with a symbol (tag) from $E \cup A \cup \{S\}$. Text nodes and attributes are leaves. For an element x of type τ, the functions *ele* and *att* define the children of x, which are partitioned into *subelements* and *attributes* according to $P(\tau)$ and $R(\tau)$ in the DTD D. The subelements of x are ordered and their labels satisfy the regular expression $P(\tau)$. In contrast, its attributes are unordered and are identified by their labels (names). The function *val* assigns string values to attributes and text nodes. We consider single-valued attributes. That is, if $l \in R(\tau)$ then every element of type τ has a unique l attribute with a string value. Since T has a tree structure, sharing of nodes is not allowed in T.

For example, Figure 1 depicts an XML tree valid w.r.t. the DTD given in Example 2.

Our model is simpler than the models of XQuery [10] and XML Schema [40] as DTDs support only one basic type (PCDATA or string) and do not have complex type constructs. Furthermore, we do not have nodes representing namespaces, processing instructions and references. These simplifications allow us to concentrate on the essence of the DTD/constraint interaction. It should further be noticed that they do not affect the lower bounds results in the chapter. It is also worth mentioning that we consider ordered XML trees in this paper, but removal of ordering does not affect the semantics of XML constraints and the complexity of their consistency and implication analyses.

Notation. In this chapter, we also use the following notation. Referring to an XML tree T, if x is a τ element in T and l is an attribute in $R(\tau)$, then $x.l$ denotes the l attribute value of x, i.e., $x.l = val(att(x, l))$. If X is a list $[l_1, \ldots, l_n]$ of attributes in $R(\tau)$, then $x[X] = [x.l_1, \ldots, x.l_n]$. We write $|S|$ for the cardinality of a set S.

Given a DTD $D = (E, A, P, R, r)$ and element types $\tau, \tau' \in E$, a string $\tau_1.\tau_2.\cdots.\tau_n$ over E is a *path in* D *from* τ *to* τ' if $\tau_1 = \tau$, $\tau_n = \tau'$ and for each $i \in [2, n]$, τ_i is a symbol in the alphabet of $P(\tau_{i-1})$. Moreover, we define $Paths(D) = \{p \mid$ there is $\tau \in E$ such that p is a path in D from r to $\tau\}$.

We say that a DTD is *non-recursive* if $Paths(D)$ is finite, and recursive otherwise. We also say that D is a *no-star* DTD if the Kleene star does not occur in any regular expression $P(\tau)$ (note that this is a stronger restriction than being $*$-free, which is a well-accepted concept with a standard definition [42]: a regular expression without the Kleene star yields a finite language, while the language of a $*$-free regular expression may still be infinite as it allows boolean operators including complement).

3   Integrity Constraints for XML

We consider two forms of constraints for XML: *absolute constraints* that hold on the entire document, denoted by $\mathcal{AC}$, and *relative constraints* that hold on certain sub-documents, denoted by $\mathcal{RC}$. Below we define both classes of constraints. A variation of $\mathcal{AC}$ using regular expressions will be defined in Section 6.1.

3.1   Absolute Keys and Foreign Keys

A class of absolute keys and foreign keys, denoted by $\mathcal{AC}_{K,FK}^{*,*}$ (we shall explain the notation shortly), is defined for element types as follows. An $\mathcal{AC}_{K,FK}^{*,*}$ constraint φ over a DTD $D = (E, A, P, R, r)$ has one of the following forms:

- *Key:* $\tau[X] \to \tau$, where $\tau \in E$ and X is a nonempty set of attributes in $R(\tau)$. An XML tree T satisfies this constraint, denoted by $T \models \tau[X] \to \tau$, if

$$\forall x, y \in ext(\tau) \ (x[X] = y[X] \to x = y).$$

- *Foreign key:* $\tau_1[X] \subseteq_{FK} \tau_2[Y]$, where $\tau_1, \tau_2 \in E$, X and Y are nonempty lists of attributes in $R(\tau_1)$ and $R(\tau_2)$, respectively, and $|X| = |Y|$. This constraint is satisfied by a tree T, denoted by $T \models \tau_1[X] \subseteq_{FK} \tau_2[Y]$, if $T \models \tau_2[Y] \to \tau_2$, and in addition

$$\forall x \in ext(\tau_1) \ \exists y \in ext(\tau_2) \ (x[X] = y[Y]).$$

That is, $\tau[X] \to \tau$ says that the X-attribute values of a τ element uniquely identify the element in $ext(\tau)$, and $\tau_1[X] \subseteq_{FK} \tau_2[Y]$ says that the Y-attribute values of a τ_2 element uniquely identify the element in $ext(\tau_2)$ and the list of X-attribute values of every τ_1 node in T must match the list of Y-attribute values of some τ_2 node in T. We use two notions of equality to define keys: value equality is assumed when comparing attributes, and node identity is used when comparing elements. We shall use the same symbol '$=$' for both, as it will never lead to ambiguity. It is worth remarking that keys and foreign keys are defined in terms of XML attributes, which are of the string type and can not be null values.

Constraints of $AC^{*,*}_{K,FK}$ are generally referred to as *multi-attribute* constraints as they may be defined with multiple attributes. An $AC^{*,*}_{K,FK}$ constraint is said to be *unary* if it is defined in terms of a single attribute; that is, $|X| = |Y| = 1$ in the above definition. In that case, we write $\tau.l \rightarrow \tau$ for unary keys, and $\tau_1.l_1 \subseteq_{FK} \tau_2.l_2$ for unary foreign keys. For example, the set of constraints considered in Example 2 are unary. As in relational databases, we also consider *primary keys*: for each element type, at most one key can be defined.

Example 4. To illustrate keys and foreign keys of $AC^{*,*}_{K,FK}$, let us consider a DTD $D_1 = (E_1, A_1, P_1, R_1, r_1)$, where $E_1 = \{school, course, student, subject, enroll, name\}$, $A_1 = \{student\_id, course\_no, dept\}$, $r_1 = school$ and P_1, R_1 are as follows:

$$P_1(school) = course*, \ student* \qquad R_1(school) = \emptyset$$
$$P_1(course) = subject, \ enroll* \qquad R_1(course) = \{dept, course\_no\}$$
$$P_1(student) = name \qquad\qquad\quad R_1(student) = \{student\_id\}$$
$$P_1(subject) = \mathsf{S} \qquad\qquad\qquad R_1(subject) = \emptyset$$
$$P_1(enroll) = \epsilon \qquad\qquad\qquad R_1(enroll) = \{student\_id\}$$
$$P_1(name) = \mathsf{S} \qquad\qquad\qquad R_1(name) = \emptyset$$

Typical $AC^{*,*}_{K,FK}$ constraints over D_1 include:

$$student.student\_id \ \rightarrow \ student,$$
$$course[dept, course\_no] \ \rightarrow \ course,$$
$$enroll.student\_id \subseteq_{FK} student.student\_id,$$

The first two constraints are keys in $AC^{*,*}_{K,FK}$ and the last constraint is a foreign key. The first and the last constraint are unary. □

We shall use the following notation for subclasses of $AC^{*,*}_{K,FK}$: subscripts K and FK denote keys and foreign keys, respectively. When the primary key restriction is imposed, we use subscript PK instead of K. The superscript '*' denotes multi-attribute, and '1' means unary. The first of these superscripts refers to keys, and the second to foreign keys.

In this chapter we shall be dealing with the following subclasses of $AC^{*,*}_{K,FK}$:

- $AC^{*,1}_{K,FK}$ is the class of multi-attribute keys and unary foreign keys;
- $AC^{*,1}_{PK,FK}$ is the class of primary multi-attribute keys and unary foreign keys;
- $AC^{1,1}_{K,FK}$ is the class of unary keys and unary foreign keys;
- $AC^{1,1}_{PK,FK}$ is the class of primary unary keys and unary foreign keys;
- AC^{*}_{K} is the class of multi-attribute keys.

Since every foreign key implicitly contains a key, the class $AC^{1,*}_{K,FK}$ of unary keys and multi-attributes foreign keys is equal to $AC^{*,*}_{K,FK}$. Thus, we do not consider $AC^{1,*}_{K,FK}$ in this chapter.

3.2   Relative Keys and Foreign Keys

Since XML documents are hierarchically structured, one may be interested in the entire document as well as in its sub-documents. The latter gives rise to *relative integrity constraints* [12, 13], that only hold on certain sub-documents. Below we define relative keys and foreign keys. Recall that we use $\mathcal{RC}$ to denote various classes of such constraints. We use the notation $x \prec y$ when x and y are two nodes in an XML tree and y is a descendant of x.

A class of relative keys and foreign keys, denoted by $\mathcal{RC}_{K,FK}^{*,*}$, is defined as follows. An $\mathcal{RC}_{K,FK}^{*,*}$ constraint φ over a DTD $D = (E, A, P, R, r)$ has one of the following forms:

- *Relative key*: $\tau(\tau_1[X] \rightarrow \tau_1)$, where $\tau, \tau_1 \in E$ and X is a nonempty set of attributes in $R(\tau_1)$. It says that relative to each node x of element type τ, the set of attributes X is a key for all the τ_1 nodes that are descendants of x. That is, if a tree T conforms to D, then $T \models \varphi$ if

$$\forall x \in ext(\tau) \; \forall y, z \in ext(\tau_1) \; \big((x \prec y) \land (x \prec z) \land y[X] = z[X] \rightarrow y = z\big).$$

- *Relative foreign key*: $\tau(\tau_1[X] \subseteq_{FK} \tau_2[Y])$, where $\tau, \tau_1, \tau_2 \in E$, X and Y are nonempty lists of attributes in $R(\tau_1)$ and $R(\tau_2)$, respectively, and $|X| = |Y|$. It indicates that for each x in $ext(\tau)$, X is a foreign key of descendants of x of type τ_1 that references a key Y of τ_2-descendants of x. That is, T satisfies φ, denoted by $T \models \tau(\tau_1[X] \subseteq_{FK} \tau_2[Y])$, if $T \models \tau(\tau_2[Y] \rightarrow \tau_2)$ and T satisfies

$$\forall \, x \in ext(\tau) \; \forall \, y \in ext(\tau_1) \; \big((x \prec y) \rightarrow \\ \exists \, z \in ext(\tau_2) \; ((x \prec z) \land y[X] = z[Y])\big).$$

Here τ is called the *context type* of φ. Note that absolute constraints are a special case of relative constraints when $\tau = r$: i.e., $r(\tau[X] \rightarrow \tau)$ is the usual absolute key. As in the case of absolute constraints, a relative constraint is said to be *unary* if it is defined in terms of a single attribute; that is, $|X| = |Y| = 1$ in the above definition. In that case, we write $\tau(\tau_1.l \rightarrow \tau)$ for relative unary keys, and $\tau(\tau_1.l_1 \subseteq_{FK} \tau_2.l_2)$ for relative unary foreign keys.

Example 5. Let us consider an XML document that for each country lists its administrative subdivisions (e.g., into provinces or states), as well as capitals of provinces. A DTD is given below and an XML document conforming to it is depicted in Figure 2.

```
<!ELEMENT db       (country+)>
<!ELEMENT country  (province+, capital)>
<!ELEMENT province (capital)>
```

Each country has a nonempty sequence of provinces and a capital, and for each province we specify its capital. Each country and province has an attribute *name*.

Now suppose we want to define keys for countries and provinces. One can state that country *name* is a key for *country* elements. It is also tempting to

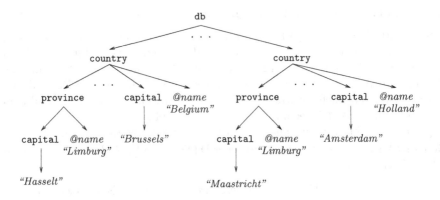

Fig. 2. An XML document storing information about countries and their administrative subdivisions

say that *name* is a key for *province*, but this may not be the case. The example in Figure 2 clearly shows that. Which *Limburg* one is interested in probably depends on whether one's interests are in database theory, or in the history of the European Union. To overcome this problem, we define *name* to be a key for province *relative* to a country; indeed, it is extremely unlikely that two provinces of the same country would have the same name. Thus, our constraints are:

$$country.name \rightarrow country,$$
$$country(province.name \rightarrow province).$$

The first constraint is like those we have encountered before: it is an *absolute* key, which applies to the entire document. The second one is a *relative constraint* which is specified for sub-documents rooted at *country* elements. It asserts that for each country, *name* is a key of *province* elements. Note that relative constraints are somewhat related to the notion of keys for weak entities in relational databases (cf. [41]). □

Following the notation for $\mathcal{AC}$, we denote subclasses of $\mathcal{RC}$ as follows:

- $\mathcal{RC}^{*,1}_{K,FK}$: the class of relative multi-attribute keys and unary foreign keys;
- $\mathcal{RC}^{*,1}_{PK,FK}$: the class of relative primary multi-attribute keys and unary foreign keys;
- $\mathcal{RC}^{1,1}_{K,FK}$: the class of relative unary keys and unary foreign keys;
- $\mathcal{RC}^{1,1}_{PK,FK}$: the class of relative primary unary keys and unary foreign keys;
- $\mathcal{RC}^{*}_{K}$: the class of relative multi-attribute keys.

As in the case of absolute constraints, every relative foreign key implicitly contains a relative key and, hence, the class $\mathcal{RC}^{1,*}_{K,FK}$ of unary keys and multi-attributes foreign keys is equal to $\mathcal{RC}^{*,*}_{K,FK}$. Thus, there is no need to consider $\mathcal{RC}^{1,*}_{K,FK}$.

4   Consistency of Absolute Keys and Foreign Keys

In this section we study the complexity of the consistency problem for absolute keys and foreign keys. We show that, in general, this problem is undecidable, and we identify several special cases of the problem that are decidable.

4.1   Undecidability of Consistency

The following result shows that in general it is not possible to verify statically whether an XML specification is consistent.

Theorem 1. $\mathsf{SAT}(\mathcal{AC}^{*,*}_{K,FK})$ *is undecidable.*   □

This theorem was proved in [23] by showing that the implication problem associated with keys and foreign keys in relational databases is undecidable, and then reducing (the complement of) the implication problem to the consistency problem for $\mathcal{AC}^{*,*}_{K,FK}$ constraints.

Given this negative result, it is desirable to find some restrictions on $\mathcal{AC}^{*,*}_{K,FK}$ that lead to decidable cases. We identify several of these classes in the next subsections.

4.2   Multi-attribute Keys

The reason for the undecidability of $\mathsf{SAT}(\mathcal{AC}^{*,*}_{K,FK})$ is that the implication problem for functional and inclusion dependencies in relational databases can be reduced to it [23]. However, this implication problem is known to be decidable – in fact, in cubic time – for single-attribute inclusion dependencies [21], thus giving us hope to get decidability for multi-attribute keys and unary foreign keys.

While the decidability of the consistency problem for $\mathcal{AC}^{*,1}_{K,FK}$ is still an open problem, a closely-related problem, the consistency problem for multi-attribute *primary* keys and unary foreign keys, $\mathsf{SAT}(\mathcal{AC}^{*,1}_{PK,FK})$, has shown to be decidable [4]. Recall that a set Σ of $\mathcal{AC}^{*,1}_{K,FK}$ constraints is said to be *primary* if for each element type τ, there is at most one key in Σ defined for τ elements. The decidability of $\mathsf{SAT}(\mathcal{AC}^{*,1}_{PK,FK})$ is shown by proving that, complexity-wise, the problem is equivalent to a certain extension of integer linear programming studied in [33]:

PROBLEM	: PDE (Prequadratic Diophantine Equations).
INPUT	: An integer $n \times m$ matrix A, a vector $\boldsymbol{b} \in \mathbb{Z}^n$, and a set $E \subseteq \{1, \ldots, m\} \times \{1, \ldots, m\} \times \{1, \ldots, m\}$.
QUESTION	: Is there a vector $\boldsymbol{x} \in \mathbb{N}^m$ such that $A\boldsymbol{x} \leq \boldsymbol{b}$ and $x_i \leq x_j \cdot x_k$ for all $(i, j, k) \in E$?

Note that for $E = \emptyset$, this is exactly the integer linear programming problem [36]. Thus, PDE can be thought of as integer linear programming extended with inequalities of the form $x \leq y \cdot z$ among variables. It is therefore NP-hard, and [33] proved an NEXPTIME upper bound for PDE. The exact complexity of the problem remains unknown.

Recall that two problems P_1 and P_2 are *polynomially equivalent* if there are PTIME reductions from P_1 to P_2 and vice versa. It is shown in [4] that $\mathsf{SAT}(\mathcal{AC}_{PK,FK}^{*,1})$ and PDE are polynomially equivalent. The following theorem is an immediate consequence of this result.

Theorem 2. $\mathsf{SAT}(\mathcal{AC}_{PK,FK}^{*,1})$ *is NP-hard, and can be solved in NEXPTIME.* $\square$

Obviously the exact complexity of $\mathsf{SAT}(\mathcal{AC}_{PK,FK}^{*,1})$ cannot be obtained without resolving the corresponding question for PDE, which appears to be quite hard [33].

The result of Theorem 2 can be generalized to *disjoint* $\mathcal{AC}_{K,FK}^{*,1}$ constraints: that is, a set Σ of $\mathcal{AC}_{K,FK}^{*,1}$ constraints in which for any two keys $\tau[X] \to \tau$ and $\tau[Y] \to \tau$ (on the same element type τ) in Σ, $X \cap Y = \emptyset$. The proof of Theorem 2 applies almost verbatim to show the following.

Corollary 1. *The restriction of* $\mathsf{SAT}(\mathcal{AC}_{K,FK}^{*,1})$ *to disjoint constraints is NP-hard, and can be solved in NEXPTIME.* $\square$

4.3   Unary Keys and Foreign Keys

One important subclass of $\mathcal{AC}_{K,FK}^{*,*}$ is $\mathcal{AC}_{K,FK}^{1,1}$, the class of unary keys and unary foreign keys. A cursory examination of existing XML specifications reveals that most keys and foreign keys are single-attribute constraints, i.e., unary. In particular, in XML DTDs, one can only specify unary constraints with ID and IDREF attributes.

The exact complexity of $\mathsf{SAT}(\mathcal{AC}_{K,FK}^{1,1})$ was established in [23] by showing that this problem is polynomially equivalent to linear integer programming [36]:

PROBLEM	: Linear Integer Programming.
INPUT	: An integer $n \times m$ matrix A and vector $\boldsymbol{b} \in \mathbb{Z}^n$.
QUESTION	: Is there a vector $\boldsymbol{x} \in \mathbb{N}^m$ such that $A\boldsymbol{x} \leq \boldsymbol{b}$?

Given that linear integer programming is known to be NP-complete, the following theorem is an immediate consequence of the polynomial equivalence of the two problems.

Theorem 3. $\mathsf{SAT}(\mathcal{AC}_{K,FK}^{1,1})$ *is NP-complete.* $\square$

Since all the flavors of the consistency problem presented so far are intractable, we next want to find suitable restrictions that admit polynomial-time algorithms. For instance, one might think that the primary key restriction would simplify the consistency analysis of $\mathcal{AC}_{K,FK}^{1,1}$ constraints. Unfortunately, as shown in [23], this is not the case.

Theorem 4. $\mathsf{SAT}(\mathcal{AC}_{PK,FK}^{1,1})$ *remains NP-complete.* $\square$

A more natural way of putting restrictions appears to be by specifying what kinds of regular expressions are allowed in the DTDs. However, the hardness result can be proved even for DTDs with neither recursion nor the Kleene star [23]. In the rest of this section, we show that the hardness result for $\mathsf{SAT}(\mathcal{AC}_{K,FK}^{1,1})$ is very robust, and withstands severe restrictions on constraints and DTDs: namely, a bound on the total number of constraints, and a bound on the depth of the DTD. However, imposing both of these bounds simultaneously makes $\mathsf{SAT}(\mathcal{AC}_{K,FK}^{1,1})$ tractable.

Recall that for a non-recursive DTD D, the set $Paths(D)$ is finite. We define the *depth* of a non-recursive DTD D as $\max_{p \in Paths(D)} length(p)$, denoted by $Depth(D)$. By a depth-d $\mathsf{SAT}(\mathcal{AC}_{K,FK}^{1,1})$ we mean the restriction of $\mathsf{SAT}(\mathcal{AC}_{K,FK}^{1,1})$ to pairs (D, Σ) with $Depth(D) \leq d$. By a k-constraint $\mathsf{SAT}(\mathcal{AC}_{K,FK}^{1,1})$ we mean the restriction of the consistency problem to pairs (D, Σ) where $|\Sigma| \leq k$. A k-constraint depth-d $\mathsf{SAT}(\mathcal{AC}_{K,FK}^{1,1})$ is a restriction to (D, Σ) with $|\Sigma| \leq k$ and $Depth(D) \leq d$. The following theorem was proved in [4].

Theorem 5. *For non-recursive no-star DTDs:*

a) *both k-constraint $\mathsf{SAT}(\mathcal{AC}_{K,FK}^{1,1})$ and depth-d $\mathsf{SAT}(\mathcal{AC}_{K,FK}^{1,1})$ are NP-hard, for $k \geq 2$ and $d \geq 2$.*

b) *for any fixed $k, d > 0$, the k-constraint depth-d $\mathsf{SAT}(\mathcal{AC}_{K,FK}^{1,1})$ is solvable in NLOGSPACE.* ☐

4.4   Linear Time Decidable Cases

While the general consistency problem is undecidable, it is possible to identify some decidable cases of low complexity. The first one is checking whether a DTD has a valid XML tree. This is a special case of the consistency problem, namely, when the given set of $\mathcal{AC}_{K,FK}^{*,*}$ constraints is empty. A more interesting special case involves keys only.

It was shown in [23] that the problem of verifying whether a given DTD has a valid XML tree can be reduced to the emptiness problem for a context free grammar. Given that this reduction can be computed in linear time and the emptiness problem for a context free grammar can be solved in linear time (cf. [30]), the problem of checking whether a DTD has a valid XML tree can be solved in linear time. It was also shown in [23] that given any DTD D and any set Σ of keys in $\mathcal{AC}_K^*$ over D, Σ can be satisfied by an XML tree valid w.r.t. D if and only if D has a valid XML tree. Thus, the following theorem is a consequence of our previous discussion.

Theorem 6. *The following problems are decidable in linear time:*

a) *Given any DTD D, whether there exists an XML tree valid w.r.t. D.*

b) *$\mathsf{SAT}(\mathcal{AC}_K^*)$.* ☐

4.5   The Implication Problem

Another classical problem, which is closely related to the consistency problem, is the *implication problem* for a class of constraints $\mathcal{C}$, denoted by $\mathsf{Impl}(\mathcal{C})$. Here, we consider it in the presence of DTDs. We write $(D, \Sigma) \vdash \phi$ if for every XML tree T, $T \models D$ and $T \models \Sigma$ imply $T \models \phi$. The implication problem $\mathsf{Impl}(\mathcal{C})$ is to determine, given any DTD D and any set $\Sigma \cup \{\phi\}$ of $\mathcal{C}$ constraints, whether or not $(D, \Sigma) \vdash \phi$.

The simple result below gives us lower bounds for the complexity of implication, if we know the complexity of the consistency problem. Recall that for a complexity class K, coK stands for $\{\bar{P} \mid P \in \mathsf{K}\}$.

Proposition 1. *For any class $\mathcal{C}$ of XML constraints that contains $\mathcal{AC}^{1,1}_{PK,FK}$, if $\mathsf{SAT}(\mathcal{C})$ is K-hard for some complexity class K that contains $DLOGSPACE$, then $\mathsf{Impl}(\mathcal{C})$ is coK-hard.* □

Along the same lines as Section 4.3 one can define k-constraint $\mathsf{Impl}(\mathcal{AC}^{1,1}_{K,FK})$ and depth-d $\mathsf{Impl}(\mathcal{AC}^{1,1}_{K,FK})$. Proposition 1 in fact remains intact under the depth-d and the k-constraint restrictions for $d \geq 2$ and $k \geq 2$. It has also been shown [23] that $\mathsf{Impl}(\mathcal{AC}^{*}_{K})$ is decidable in linear time. From these and the lower-bounds established for the consistency problem, we derive:

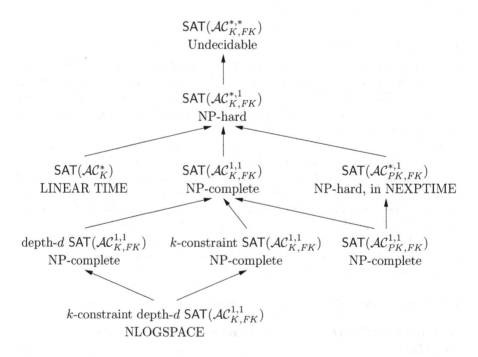

Fig. 3. A summary of the known complexity bounds for the consistency problem for absolute keys and foreign keys

Corollary 2. *For the implication problem for XML constraints,*

- $\mathsf{Impl}(\mathcal{AC}^{*,*}_{K,FK})$ *is undecidable;*
- *both k-constraint* $\mathsf{Impl}(\mathcal{AC}^{1,1}_{K,FK})$ *and depth-d* $\mathsf{Impl}(\mathcal{AC}^{1,1}_{K,FK})$ *are coNP-hard for $d \geq 2$ and $k \geq 2$, and so is* $\mathsf{Impl}(\mathcal{AC}^{*,1}_{PK,FK})$;
- $\mathsf{Impl}(\mathcal{AC}^{*,1}_{PK,FK})$ *is coNP-hard, and so are* $\mathsf{Impl}(\mathcal{AC}^{*,1}_{K,FK})$ *(and its restriction to disjoint constraints) and* $\mathsf{Impl}(\mathcal{AC}^{1,1}_{PK,FK})$;
- $\mathsf{Impl}(\mathcal{AC}^{*}_{K})$ *is in linear time.*   □

4.6   Summary

Figure 3 shows a summary of the lower and upper bounds for the consistency problem for absolute keys and foreign keys. Note that in many cases we have matching lower and upper bounds. Also notice that for k-constraint $\mathsf{SAT}(\mathcal{AC}^{1,1}_{K,FK})$, depth-$d$ $\mathsf{SAT}(\mathcal{AC}^{1,1}_{K,FK})$ and k-constraint depth-d $\mathsf{SAT}(\mathcal{AC}^{1,1}_{K,FK})$ we are only considering non-recursive no-star DTDs.

5   Consistency of Relative Keys and Foreign Keys

In this section we study the consistency problem for relative keys and foreign keys. Relative constraints appear to be quite useful for capturing information about (hierarchical) XML documents that cannot possibly be specified by absolute constraints. However, it turns out that the complexity of their consistency analysis is, in general, higher than the complexity of the consistency problem for absolute constraints. In particular, we show that even for relative unary constraints the consistency problem is undecidable. In light of this negative result, we also identify some special cases of this problem that are decidable.

5.1   Undecidability of Consistency Analysis

Given that $\mathcal{RC}^{*,*}_{K,FK}$ contains $\mathcal{AC}^{*,*}_{K,FK}$ as a proper subclass, from Theorem 1 we obtain the following corollary.

Corollary 3. $\mathsf{SAT}(\mathcal{RC}^{*,*}_{K,FK})$ *is undecidable.*   □

Since $\mathsf{SAT}(\mathcal{AC}^{*,1}_{PK,FK})$, the consistency problem associated with absolute multi-attribute keys and unary foreign keys, is decidable, one would be tempted to think that $\mathsf{SAT}(\mathcal{RC}^{*,1}_{PK,FK})$, the consistency problem for relative multi-attribute keys and unary foreign keys, is also decidable. Even more, given that $\mathsf{SAT}(\mathcal{AC}^{1,1}_{K,FK})$ is NP-complete, one would be tempted to believe that $\mathsf{SAT}(\mathcal{RC}^{1,1}_{K,FK})$, the consistency problem for relative unary keys and foreign keys, must be decidable. However, it was shown in [4] that $\mathsf{SAT}(\mathcal{RC}^{1,1}_{K,FK})$ is not decidable, even if the primary key restriction is imposed.

Theorem 7. $\mathsf{SAT}(\mathcal{RC}^{1,1}_{PK,FK})$ *is undecidable.*   □

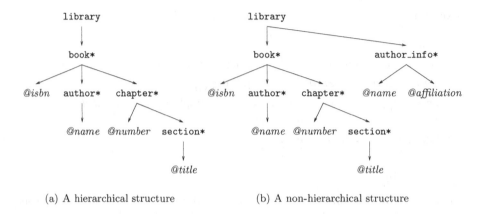

(a) A hierarchical structure   (b) A non-hierarchical structure

Fig. 4. Two schemas for storing data in a library

This undecidability was established by reduction from the Hilbert's 10th problem [29], a well known undecidable problem.

Corollary 4. $\mathsf{SAT}(\mathcal{RC}^{*,1}_{K,FK})$, $\mathsf{SAT}(\mathcal{RC}^{*,1}_{PK,FK})$ and $\mathsf{SAT}(\mathcal{RC}^{1,1}_{K,FK})$ are undecidable. $\qquad\square$

5.2 Decidable Hierarchical Constraints

Often, relative constraints for XML documents have a hierarchical structure. For example, to store information about books we can use the structure given in Figure 4 (a), with four relative constraints:

$$library(book.isbn \rightarrow book), \tag{3}$$
$$book(author.name \rightarrow author), \tag{4}$$
$$book(chapter.number \rightarrow chapter), \tag{5}$$
$$chapter(section.title \rightarrow section). \tag{6}$$

(3) says that *isbn* is a key for books, (4) says that two distinct authors of the same book cannot have the same name and (5) says that two distinct chapters of the same book cannot have the same number. Constraint (6) asserts that two distinct sections of the same chapter cannot have the same title.

This specification has a hierarchical structure: there are three context types (*library*, *book*, and *chapter*), and if a constraint restricts one of them, then it does not impose a restriction on the others. For instance, (3) imposes a restriction on the children of *library*, but it does not restrict the children of *book*. To verify if there is an XML document conforming to this schema, we can separately solve three consistency problems for absolute constraints: one for the subschema containing the element types *library*, *book* and *isbn*; another for *book*, *author*, *name*, *chapter* and *number*; and the last one for *chapter*, *section*, and *title*.

On the other hand, the example in Figure 4 (b) does not have a hierarchical structure. In this case, *author_info* stores information about the authors of books, and, therefore, the following relative foreign key is included:

$$library(author.name \subseteq_{FK} author\_info.name).$$

In this case, nodes of type *author* are restricted from context types *library* and *book*. Thus, we cannot separate the consistency problems for nodes of types *library* and *book*.

The notion of hierarchical relative constraints was introduced in [4]. Below we introduce this notion via the notion of *hierarchical* DTDs and sets of relative constraints. Then, we show that the consistency problem for these kinds of DTDs and sets of constraints is decidable and show that under some additional restrictions, it is PSPACE-complete.

Let $D = (E, A, P, R, r)$ be a non-recursive DTD and Σ be a set of $\mathcal{RC}^{1,1}_{K,FK}$-constraints over D. We say that $\tau \in E$ is a *restricted type* if $\tau = r$ or τ is the context type of some Σ-constraint. A *restricted node* in an XML tree is a node whose type is a restricted type. The *scope* of a restricted node x is the subtree rooted at x consisting of: (1) all element nodes y that are reachable from x by following some path $\tau_1.\tau_2.\cdots.\tau_n$ $(n \geq 2)$ such that for every $i \in [2, n-1]$, τ_i is not a restricted type, and (2) all the attributes of the nodes mentioned in (1). For instance, a node of type *book* in the example shown in Figure 4 (a) is a restricted node and its scope includes a node of type *book* and some nodes of types *author*, *name*, *chapter* and *number*.

Given two restricted types τ_1 and τ_2, we say that τ_1, τ_2 are a conflicting pair in (D, Σ) if the scopes of the nodes of types τ_1 and τ_2 are related by a foreign key. Formally, $\tau_1, \tau_2 \in E$ are a *conflicting pair in* (D, Σ) iff $\tau_1 \neq \tau_2$ and (1) there is a path in D from τ_1 to τ_2 and τ_2 is the context type of some constraint in Σ; and (2) there is $\tau_3 \in E$ such that $\tau_2 \neq \tau_3$ and there exists a path in D from τ_2 to τ_3 and for some $\tau_4 \in E$, either $\tau_1(\tau_3.l_3 \subseteq_{FK} \tau_4.l_4)$ or $\tau_1(\tau_4.l_4 \subseteq_{FK} \tau_3.l_3)$ is in Σ. As an example, *library* and *book* in Figure 4 (b) are a conflicting pair, whereas they are not in Figure 4 (a).

If a specification (D, Σ) does not contain conflicting pairs, then (D, Σ) is said to be *hierarchical* [4]. We define the language $\mathcal{HRC}^{1,1}_{K,FK}$ as $\{(D, \Sigma) \mid D$ is a non-recursive DTD, Σ is a set of $\mathcal{RC}^{1,1}_{K,FK}$-constraints and (D, Σ) is hierarchical$\}$. In this case, the input of $\mathsf{SAT}(\mathcal{HRC}^{1,1}_{K,FK})$ is $(D, \Sigma) \in \mathcal{HRC}^{1,1}_{K,FK}$, and the problem is to determine whether there is an XML tree conforming to D and satisfying Σ.

It was shown in [4] that if a $\mathcal{HRC}^{1,1}_{K,FK}$-specification is consistent, then a tree conforming to D and satisfying Σ can be constructed hierarchically, never looking at more than the scope of a single restricted node. More precisely, it was shown in [4] that:

Theorem 8. $\mathsf{SAT}(\mathcal{HRC}^{1,1}_{K,FK})$ *is PSPACE-hard. The problem can be solved in EXPSPACE.* □

The exponential space upper bound can be lowered by imposing some further conditions on the "geometry" of constraints involved: namely, that for any inclusion constraint $\tau(\tau_1.l_1 \subseteq_{FK} \tau_2.l_2)$, $\tau_1.l_1$ and $\tau_2.l_2$ are not too far from each other. Formally, let D be a non-recursive DTD and Σ a set of $\mathcal{RC}_{K,FK}^{1,1}$-constraints over D such that (D, Σ) is hierarchical. Given $d > 1$, (D, Σ) is d-local if, whenever τ_1, τ_2 are restricted types, τ_2 is a descendant of τ_1 and no other node on a path from τ_1 to τ_2 is a context type of a Σ-constraint, then the length of that path is at most d.

Let $d\text{-}\mathcal{HRC}_{K,FK}^{1,1}$ be the language $\{(D, \Sigma) \mid (D, \Sigma) \in \mathcal{HRC}_{K,FK}^{1,1}$ and is d-local$\}$. It was shown in [4] that:

Theorem 9. *For any $d > 1$, $\mathsf{SAT}(d\text{-}\mathcal{HRC}_{K,FK}^{1,1})$ is PSPACE-complete.*   □

5.3   A Linear Time Decidable Case

As in the case of absolute keys, it can be shown that given any DTD D and any set Σ of keys in $\mathcal{RC}_K^*$ over D, Σ can be satisfied by an XML tree valid w.r.t. D if and only if D has a valid XML tree. Thus, the following theorem is analogous to Theorem 6.

Theorem 10. $\mathsf{SAT}(\mathcal{RC}_K^*)$ *can be solved in linear time.*   □

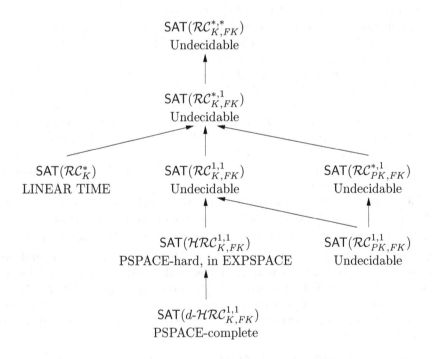

Fig. 5. A summary of the complexity bounds for the consistency problem for relative keys and foreign keys

For implication of relative constraints, note that $\mathcal{RC}_{PK,FK}^{1,1}$ and $\mathcal{HRC}_{K,FK}^{1,1}$ contain $\mathcal{AC}_{PK,FK}^{1,1}$. Thus from Proposition 1 and the lower-bounds for consistency analyses presented above. we derive:

Corollary 5. *For implication of relative constraints,*

- Impl($\mathcal{RC}_{PK,FK}^{1,1}$) *is undecidable, and so are* Impl($\mathcal{RC}_{K,FK}^{*,1}$), Impl($\mathcal{RC}_{PK,FK}^{*,1}$), Impl($\mathcal{RC}_{K,FK}^{1,1}$) *and* Impl($\mathcal{AC}_{PK,FK}^{*,1}$);
- Impl($\mathcal{HRC}_{K,FK}^{1,1}$) *is PSPACE-hard.* □

5.4   Summary

Figure 5 shows a summary of the complexity for the consistency problem for relative keys and foreign keys.

6   Consistency of Path-Expression Constraints

All the XML constraints that we have seen so far are defined for element types and in terms of attributes. As XML data is hierarchically structured, it is common to find path expressions in query languages for XML (e.g., XQuery [10], XSLT [19]). For the same reason, one is often interested in constraints specified with path expressions, either regular expressions [12, 13] or XPath [20] expressions [40]. In this section, we consider two classes of XML constraints defined with path expressions, namely, an extension of absolute constraints with regular expressions, and the class of constraints proposed by XML Schema [40] that is an extension of absolute constraints with XPath expressions.

6.1   Consistency of Regular Expression Constraints

To capture the hierarchical nature of XML data, we extend $\mathcal{AC}_{K,FK}^{*,*}$ to define absolute constraints on a collection of elements identified by a regular path expression.

We define a *regular (path) expression* over a DTD $D = (E, A, P, R, r)$ as follows:

$$\beta \quad ::= \quad \epsilon \ \mid \ \tau \ \mid \ \_ \ \mid \ \beta.\beta \ \mid \ \beta \cup \beta \ \mid \ \beta^{*},$$

where ϵ denotes the empty word, τ is an element type in E, '$\_$' stands for wildcard that matches any symbol in E and '.', '$\cup$' and '$*$' denote concatenation, union and Kleene closure, respectively. We assume that β is of the form $r.\beta'$ where β' does not include r; thus, '$\_$' is just a shorthand for $E \setminus \{r\}$. A regular expression defines a language over the alphabet E, which will be denoted by β as well.

Recall that a path in a DTD is a list of E symbols, that is, a string in E^{*}. Any pair of nodes x, y in an XML tree T with y a descendant of x uniquely determines the path, denoted by $\rho(x, y)$, from x to y. We say that y is *reachable* from x by following a regular expression β over D, denoted by $T \models \beta(x, y)$, iff $\rho(x, y) \in \beta$.

For any fixed T, let $nodes(\beta)$ stand for the set of nodes reachable from the root by following the regular expression β: $nodes(\beta) = \{y \mid T \models \beta(root, y)\}$. Note that for any element type $\tau \in E$, $nodes(r.\_^*.\tau) = ext(\tau)$.

We now define the class $\mathcal{AC}^{reg}_{K,FK}$ of XML keys and foreign keys with regular expressions. Here we only consider unary constraints. An XML $\mathcal{AC}^{reg}_{K,FK}$ constraint φ over a DTD $D = (E, A, P, R, r)$ has one of the following forms:

- *Key*: $\beta.\tau.l \rightarrow \beta.\tau$, where $\tau \in E$, $l \in R(\tau)$ and β is a regular expression over D. An XML tree T satisfies this constraint, denoted by $T \models \beta.\tau.l \rightarrow \beta.\tau$, if

$$\forall\, x, y \in nodes(\beta.\tau)\ (x.l = y.l \rightarrow x = y).$$

- *Foreign key*: $\beta_1.\tau_1.l_1 \subseteq_{FK} \beta_2.\tau_2.l_2$, where $\tau_1, \tau_2 \in E$, $l_1 \in R(\tau_1)$, $l_2 \in R(\tau_2)$ and β_1, β_2 are regular expressions over D. An XML tree T satisfies this constraint, denoted by $T \models \beta_1.\tau_1.l_1 \subseteq_{FK} \beta_2.\tau_2.l_2$, if $T \models \beta_2.\tau_2.l_2 \rightarrow \beta_2.\tau_2$ and

$$\forall\, x \in nodes(\beta_1.\tau_1)\ \exists\, y \in nodes(\beta_2.\tau_2)\ (x.l_1 = y.l_2).$$

In other words, an $\mathcal{AC}^{reg}_{K,FK}$ constraint $\beta.\tau.l \rightarrow \beta.\tau$ defines a key for the set $nodes(\beta.\tau)$ of elements, i.e., all the elements reachable via the regular path expression $\beta.\tau$; similarly, an $\mathcal{AC}^{reg}_{K,FK}$ constraint of the form $\beta_1.\tau_1.l_1 \subseteq_{FK} \beta_2.\tau_2.l_2$ defines a foreign key for the set $nodes(\beta_1.\tau_1)$ of elements that references elements in the set $nodes(\beta_2.\tau_2)$.

Example 6. Consider the XML document depicted in Figure 6, which conforms to the following DTD for schools:

```
<!ELEMENT r          (students, courses,  faculty, labs)>
<!ELEMENT students (student+)>
<!ELEMENT courses  (cs340, cs108, cs434)>
<!ELEMENT faculty  (prof+)>
<!ELEMENT labs     (dbLab, pcLab)>
<!ELEMENT student  (record)>              /* similarly for prof
<!ELEMENT cs434    (takenBy+)>            /* similarly for cs340, cs108
<!ELEMENT dbLab    (acc+)>                /* similarly for pcLab
```

Here we omit the descriptions of elements whose type is string (PCDATA). Assume that each *record* element has an attribute *id*, each *takenBy* has an attribute *sid* (for student id), and each *acc* (account) has an attribute *num*. One may impose the following constraints over the DTD of that document:

$$r.\_^*.(student \cup prof).record.id \rightarrow r.\_^*.(student \cup prof).record,$$
$$r.\_^*.cs434.takenBy.sid \subseteq_{FK} r.\_^*.student.record.id,$$
$$r.\_^*.dbLab.acc.num \subseteq_{FK} r.\_^*.cs434.takenBy.sid.$$

The first constraint says that *id* is a key for all records of *students* and *professors*. The other constraints specify foreign keys, which assert that cs434 can only be taken by students, and only students who are taking cs434 can have an account in the database lab. □

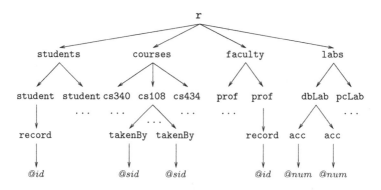

Fig. 6. An XML document

Both an upper and a lower bound for $\mathsf{SAT}(\mathcal{AC}^{reg}_{K,FK})$ were established in [4]. The lower bound already indicates that the problem is perhaps infeasible in practice, even for very simple DTDs. Finding the precise complexity of the problem remains open, and does not appear to be easy. In fact, even the current proof of the upper bound is quite involved, and relies on combining the techniques from [23] for coding DTDs and constraints as integer linear inequalities, and from [2] for reasoning about constraints given by regular expressions by using the product automaton for all the expressions involved in the constraints.

Theorem 11. $\mathsf{SAT}(\mathcal{AC}^{reg}_{K,FK})$ *is PSPACE-hard, and can be solved in NEXP-TIME.*   □

The PSPACE-hardness of $\mathsf{SAT}(\mathcal{AC}^{reg}_{K,FK})$ can be proved even for non-recursive DTDs without the Kleene star [4].

Observe that $\mathcal{AC}^{reg}_{K,FK}$ is a proper extension of the class $\mathcal{AC}^{1,1}_{K,FK}$ of unary constraints: substituting $r.\_^*.\tau$ for τ in $\mathcal{AC}^{1,1}_{K,FK}$ constraints yields equivalent $\mathcal{AC}^{reg}_{K,FK}$ constraints. Similarly, an extension of multi-attribute $\mathcal{AC}^{*,*}_{K,FK}$ constraints can be defined in terms of regular expressions, denoted by $\mathcal{AC}^{reg(*,*)}_{K,FK}$. The undecidability of the consistency problem for $\mathcal{AC}^{reg(*,*)}_{K,FK}$ is immediate from Theorem 1.

For the implication analysis of regular-expression constraints, from Proposition 1 it follows immediately:

Corollary 6. $\mathsf{Impl}(\mathcal{AC}^{reg}_{K,FK})$ *is PSPACE-hard, and* $\mathsf{Impl}(\mathcal{AC}^{reg(*,*)}_{K,FK})$ *is undecidable.*

Observe that there are practical $\mathcal{AC}^{reg}_{K,FK}$ constraints that are not expressible in $\mathcal{AC}^{1,1}_{K,FK}$, e.g., the foreign keys given in Example 6 are not definable in $\mathcal{AC}^{1,1}_{K,FK}$. In other words, $\mathcal{AC}^{reg}_{K,FK}$ is strictly more expressive than $\mathcal{AC}^{1,1}_{K,FK}$.

6.2   Consistency of XML Schema Specifications

All the results shown so far are for DTDs and keys and foreign keys. These days, the prime standard for specifying XML data is *XML Schema* [40]. It is a rather rich language that supports specifications of both types and integrity constraints. Its types subsume DTDs [11], and its constraints – even keys and foreign keys – have a slightly different semantics from what has been primarily studied in the database literature. In this section we investigate specifications that consist of a DTD and a set of constraints with the semantics proposed by XML Schema. We show that this little change of semantics complicates things considerably, as far as consistency checking is concerned.

Example 7. Recall that given any DTD D and any set Σ of keys in $\mathcal{AC}_K^*$ ($\mathcal{RC}_K^*$) over D, Σ can be satisfied by an XML tree valid w.r.t. D if and only if D has a valid XML tree. Thus, any XML specification (D, Σ) where D is non-recursive and Σ is a set of keys in $\mathcal{AC}_K^*$ ($\mathcal{RC}_K^*$) is consistent. We show here that a specification in XML Schema may not be consistent even for non-recursive DTDs in the absence of foreign keys.

Consider the following specification $S = (D, \Sigma)$ for biomedical data, where D is the following DTD:

```
<!ELEMENT seq   (clone+)>
<!ELEMENT clone (DNA, gene)>
<!ELEMENT gene  (DNA)>
```

and Σ contains only one key:

$$seq.clone.\_^*.DNA \rightarrow seq.clone.$$

The DTD describes a nonempty sequence of `clone` elements: each `clone` has a `DNA` subelement and a `gene` subelement, and `gene` in turn has a `DNA` subelement, while `DNA` carries text data (PCDATA). The key in Σ attempts to enforce the following semantic information: there exist no two `clone` elements that have the same `DNA` no matter where the `DNA` appears as their descendant. We note that the syntax of XML Schema constraints (to be formally introduced later) is different from the syntax for XML constraints presented so far in that it allows a regular expression ($\_^*.DNA$ in our example) to be the identifier of an element type.

This specification is inconsistent. XML Schema requires that for any XML document satisfying a key, the identifier (that is, $\_^*.DNA$ in our example) must *exist* and be *unique*. However, as depicted in Fig. 7, in any XML document that conforms to the DTD D, a `clone` element must have two `DNA` descendants. Thus, it violates the uniqueness requirement of the key in Σ.   □

The goal of this section is to show that the interaction of types with integrity constraints under the XML Schema semantics is more complicated than under the usual semantics for XML constraints. To focus on the nature of the interaction and to simplify the discussion, we first consider XML Schema specifications in which the type is a DTD and the constraints are absolute keys. We show that

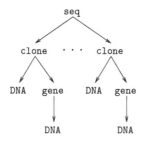

Fig. 7. An XML document conforming to the DTD D shown in Example 7

keys of XML Schema already suffice to demonstrate the complications caused by the interaction between types and constraints.

Before showing the main result of the section, we need to define the syntax and semantics of absolute keys for XML Schema specifications. Given a DTD $D = (E, A, P, R, r)$, a key *over* D is a constraint of the form

$$P[Q_1, \ldots, Q_n] \to P, \tag{7}$$

where $n \geq 1$ and $P, Q_1, \ldots, Q_n$ are regular expressions over the alphabet $E \cup A$. If $n = 1$, then the key is called unary and is denoted by $P.Q_1 \to P$. Expression P is called the *selector* of the key and is a regular expression conforming to the following BNF grammar [40] (abusing the XPath syntax):

$$\begin{aligned}
selector &::= path \mid path \cup selector \\
path &::= r.\_^*.sequence \\
sequence &::= \tau \mid \_ \mid sequence.sequence
\end{aligned}$$

Here $\tau \in E$ and $\_^*$ represents any possible finite sequence of node labels. The expressions $Q_1, \ldots, Q_n$ are called the *fields* of the key and are regular expressions conforming to the following BNF grammar [40]:

$$\begin{aligned}
field &::= path \mid path \cup field \\
path &::= \_^*.sequence.last \mid sequence.last \\
sequence &::= \epsilon \mid \tau \mid \_ \mid sequence.sequence \\
last &::= \tau \mid \_ \mid @l \mid @\_
\end{aligned}$$

Here $@\_$ is a wildcard that matches any attribute and $@l \in A$. This grammar differs from the one above in allowing the final step to match an attribute node.

Definition 3. *Given an XML tree $T = (V, lab, ele, att, val, root)$, T satisfies the constraint $P[Q_1, \ldots, Q_n] \to P$, denoted by $T \models P[Q_1, \ldots, Q_n] \to P$, if*

1) *For each $x \in nodes(P)$ and $i \in [1, n]$, there is exactly one node y_i such that $T \models Q_i(x, y_i)$. Furthermore, $lab(y_i) \in A$ or $lab(y_i) = \mathsf{S}$.*
2) *For each $x_1, x_2 \in nodes(P)$, if y_i^1, y_i^2 are the only nodes such that $T \models Q_i(x_1, y_i^1)$ and $T \models Q_i(x_2, y_i^2)$ $(i = 1, \ldots, n)$, and $val(y_i^1) = val(y_i^2)$ for every $i \in [1, n]$, then $x_1 = x_2$.* □

That is, $P[Q_1, \ldots, Q_n] \rightarrow P$ defines a key for the set $nodes(P)$ of elements, i.e., the nodes reachable from the root by following path P, by asserting that the values of $Q_1, \ldots, Q_n$ uniquely identify the elements in $nodes(P)$. It further asserts that starting from each element in $nodes(P)$ there is a unique label path conforming to the regular expression Q_i ($i \in [1, n]$).

Observe that condition 1 in the previous definition requires the uniqueness and existence of the fields involved. For example, the XML tree depicted in Fig. 7 does not satisfy the key $seq.clone.\_^*.DNA \rightarrow seq.clone$ because the uniqueness condition imposed by the key is violated. Uniqueness conditions are required by the XML Schema semantics, but they are not present in various earlier proposals for XML keys coming from the database community [12, 13, 23, 4].

Since $\mathsf{SAT}(\mathcal{AC}_K^*)$ and $\mathsf{SAT}(\mathcal{RC}_K^*)$, the consistency problems for absolute and relative keys, respectively, are decidable in linear time, one would be tempted to think that the consistency problem for keys under the XML Schema semantics can be solved efficiently. Somewhat surprisingly, it was shown in [5] that this is not the case; the uniqueness and existence condition makes the problem intractable, even for unary keys and very simple DTDs:

Theorem 12. *The consistency problem is NP-hard for unary keys of the form (7), even for non-recursive no-star DTDs.*   □

This result shows that the interaction of types and constraints under the XML Schema semantics is so intricate that the consistency check of XML Schema specifications is infeasible.

7   Selected Topics and Bibliographic Remarks

This chapter has shown that the consistency analysis of XML specifications with DTDs and constraints (keys, foreign keys) introduces new challenges and is in sharp contrast with its trivial counterpart for relational databases. Indeed, in the presence of foreign keys, compile-time verification of consistency for XML specifications is usually infeasible: the complexity ranges from NP-hard to undecidable. Worse still, the semantics of XML-Schema constraints makes the consistency analysis of specifications even more intricate.

These negative results suggest that one develops efficient approximate algorithms for static checking of XML specifications. One open question is to find performance guarantees for the approximate algorithms to prevent excessive overkill of consistent specifications. The techniques of [4, 5, 23] for establishing the complexity results of this chapter may help develop such performance guarantees; they may also help study consistency of individual XML specifications with types and constraints.

Another open problem is to close the complexity gaps. However, these are by no means trivial: for example, $\mathsf{SAT}(\mathcal{AC}_{PK,FK}^{*,1})$ was proved to be equivalent to a problem related to Diophantine equations whose exact complexity remains unknown. In the cases of $\mathsf{SAT}(\mathcal{AC}_{K,FK}^{reg})$ and $\mathsf{SAT}(\mathcal{HRC}_{K,FK}^{1,1})$, we think that it is more likely that our lower bounds correspond to the exact complexity of those problems. However, the algorithms are quite involved, and we do not yet see a way to simplify them to prove the matching upper bounds.

Bibliographic Notes. The complexity results of this chapter are taken from [4, 5, 23]: the results for the consistency analysis of absolute constraints were mostly established by [23]; relative constraints were studied in [4]; and a full treatment of XML-Schema specifications was given in [5].

Keys, foreign keys and the more general inclusion and functional dependencies have been well studied for relational databases (cf. [1]). The interaction between cardinality constraints and database schemas has been studied for object-oriented [16, 17] and extended relational data models [28]. These interactions are quite different from what we explore in this chapter because XML DTDs are defined in terms of extended context free grammars and they yield cardinality constraints more complex than those studied for traditional databases.

A number of specifications for XML keys and foreign keys have been proposed, e.g., XML Schema [40], XML-Data [31]. The notion of relative constraints was introduced by [12], which was further studied in [13]. It is worth remarking that although through the use of ID attributes in a DTD [11], one can uniquely identify an element within an XML document, it is not clear that ID attributes are intended to be used as keys rather than internal "pointers". For example, ID attributes are not scoped. In contrast to keys, they are unique within the entire document rather than among a designated set of elements. As a result, one cannot, for example, allow a student (element) and a person (element) to use the same SSN as an ID. Moreover using ID attributes as keys means that we are limiting ourselves to unary keys. Finally, one can specify at most one ID attribute for an element type, while in practice one may want more than one key.

Other constraints for semi-structured data were studied in, e.g., [2, 14]. In particular, [14] also studied the interaction between path constraints and traditional database schemas, which are quite different from XML constraints and DTDs considered here. Functional dependencies, an extension of XML keys, were recently proposed to define a normal form for XML documents [6].

Acknowledgments. M. Arenas and L. Libkin are supported in part by grants from NSERC, BUL, and PREA. W. Fan is supported in part by NSF Career Award IIS-0093168, NSFC 60228006 and EPSRC GR/S63205/01.

References

1. S. Abiteboul, R. Hull and V. Vianu. *Foundations of Databases*. Addison-Wesley, 1995.
2. S. Abiteboul and V. Vianu. Regular path queries with constraints. *J. Computer and System Sciences (JCSS)*, 58(4):428–452, 1999.

3. V. Apparao, S. Byrne, M. Champion, S. Isaacs, I. Jacobs, A. Le Hors, G. Nicol, J. Robie, R. Sutor, C. Wilson and L. Wood. Document Object Model (DOM) Level 1 Specification. W3C Recommendation, Oct. 1998. http://www.w3.org/TR/REC-DOM-Level-1/.

4. M. Arenas, W. Fan and L. Libkin. On verifying consistency of XML specifications. In *Proc. ACM Symp. on Principles of Database Systems (PODS)*, pages 259–270, 2002.

5. M. Arenas, W. Fan and L. Libkin. What's Hard about XML Schema Constraints? In *Proc. Int'l Conf. on Database and Expert Systems Applications (DEXA)*, pages 269–278, 2002.

6. M. Arenas and L. Libkin. A Normal Form for XML Documents. In *Proc. ACM Symp. on Principles of Database Systems (PODS)*, pages 85–96, 2002.

7. C. Baru, A. Gupta, B. Ludäscher, R. Marciano, Y. Papakonstantinou, P. Velikhov, and V. Chu. XML-based information mediation with MIX. In *Proc. of ACM SIGMOD Conf. on Management of Data (SIGMOD)*, pages 597–599, 1999.

8. C. Beeri and T. Milo. Schemas for integration and translation of structured and semi-structured data. In *Proc. Int'l Conf. on Database Theory (ICDT)*, pages 296–313, 1999.

9. M. Benedikt, C. Chan, W. Fan, J. Freire, and R. Rastogi. Capturing both Types and Constraints in Data Integration. In *Proc. of ACM SIGMOD Conf. on Management of Data (SIGMOD)*, pages 277–288, 2003.

10. S. Boag, D. Chamberlin, M. Fernández, D. Florescu, J. Robie and J. Siméon. XQuery 1.0: An XML Query Language. W3C Working Draft, Nov. 2003. http://www.w3.org/TR/xquery.

11. T. Bray, J. Paoli and C. M. Sperberg-McQueen. Extensible Markup Language (XML) 1.0. W3C Recommendation, Feb. 1998. http://www.w3.org/TR/REC-xml/.

12. P. Buneman, S. Davidson, W. Fan, C. Hara, and W. Tan. Keys for XML. *Computer Networks*, 39(5):473–487, 2002.

13. P. Buneman, S. Davidson, W. Fan, C. Hara, and W. Tan. Reasoning about keys for XML. *Information Systems*, 28(8):1037–1063, 2003.

14. P. Buneman, W. Fan, and S. Weinstein. Interaction between path and type constraints. *ACM Trans. on Computational Logic (TOCL)*, 4(4):530–577, 2003.

15. D. Calvanese, G. De Giacomo, and M. Lenzerini. Representing and reasoning on XML documents: A description logic approach. *J. Logic and Computation*, 9(3):295–318, 1999.

16. D. Calvanese and M. Lenzerini. Making object-oriented schemas more expressive. In *Proc. ACM Symp. on Principles of Database Systems (PODS)*, pages 243–254, 1994.

17. D. Calvanese and M. Lenzerini. On the interaction between ISA and cardinality constraints. In *Proc. IEEE Int'l Conf. on Data Engineering (ICDE)*, pages 204–213, 1994.

18. M. Carey, D. Florescu, Z. Ives, Y. Lu, J. Shanmugasundaram, E. Shekita, and S. Subramanian. XPERANTO: Publishing object-relational data as XML. In *Proc. Int'l Workshop on the Web and Databases (WebDB)*, 2000.

19. J. Clark. XSL Transformations (XSLT). W3C Recommendation, Nov. 1999. http://www.w3.org/TR/xslt.

20. J. Clark and S. DeRose. XML Path Language (XPath). W3C Recommendation, Nov. 1999. http://www.w3.org/TR/xpath.

21. S. S. Cosmadakis, P. C. Kanellakis, and M. Y. Vardi. Polynomial-time implication problems for unary inclusion dependencies. *J. ACM*, 37(1):15–46, Jan. 1990.

22. A. Eyal and T. Milo. Integrating and customizing heterogeneous e-commerce applications. *VLDB Journal*, 10(1):16–38, 2001.
23. W. Fan and L. Libkin. On XML integrity constraints in the presence of DTDs. *J. ACM*, 49(3):368–406, 2002.
24. W. Fan and J. Siméon. Integrity constraints for XML. In *PODS'00*, pages 23–34.
25. M. Fernandez, A. Morishima, D. Suciu, and W. Tan. Publishing relational data in XML: the SilkRoute approach. *IEEE Data Eng. Bull.*, 24(2):12–19, 2001.
26. D. Florescu and D. Kossmann. Storing and querying XML data using an RDMBS. *IEEE Data Eng. Bull.*, 22(3):27–34, 1999.
27. D. Florescu, L. Raschid and P. Valduriez. A methodology for query reformulation in CIS using semantic knowledge. *Int'l J. Cooperative Information Systems (IJCIS)*, 5(4):431–468, 1996.
28. P. C. Kanellakis. On the computational complexity of cardinality constraints in relational databases. *Information Processing Letters*, 11(2):98–101, Oct. 1980.
29. Y. Matiyasevich. *Hilbert's 10th Problem*. MIT Press, 1993.
30. J. E. Hopcroft, R. Motwani, and J. D. Ullman. *Introduction to Automata Theory, Languages and Computation* (2nd Edition). Addison Wesley, 2000.
31. A. Layman, E. Jung, E. Maler, H. Thompson, J. Paoli, J. Tigue, N. Mikula and S. De Rose. XML-Data. W3C Note, Jan. 1998. `http://www.w3.org/TR/1998/NOTE-XML-data`.
32. D. Lee and W. W. Chu. Constraint-preserving transformation from XML document type to relational schema. In *Proc. Int'l Conf. on Conceptual Modeling (ER)*, pages 323–338, 2000.
33. D. McAllester, R. Givan, C. Witty and D. Kozen. Tarskian set constraints. In *IEEE Symp. on Logic in Computer Science (LICS)*, pages 138–147, 1996.
34. J. Melton and A. Simon. *Understanding the New SQL: A Complete Guide*. Morgan Kaufman, 1993.
35. F. Neven. Extensions of attribute grammars for structured document queries. In *Proc. Int'l Workshop on Database Programming Languages (DBPL)*, pages 99–116, 1999.
36. C. H. Papadimitriou and K. Steiglitz. *Combinatorial Optimization: Algorithms and Complexity*. Prentice Hall, 1982.
37. L. Popa. *Object/Relational Query Optimization with Chase and Backchase*. PhD thesis, University of Pennsylvania, 2000.
38. J. Shanmugasundaram et al. E. Shekita, R. Barr, M. Carey, B. Lindsay, H. Pirahesh, and B. Reinwald. Efficiently publishing relational data as XML documents. In *Proc. of Int'l Conf. on Very Large Databases (VLDB)*, pages 65–76, 2000.
39. J. Shanmugasundaram, K. Tufte, C. Zhang, G. He, D. J. DeWitt, and J. F. Naughton. Relational databases for querying XML documents: Limitations and opportunities. In *Proc. of Int'l Conf. on Very Large Databases (VLDB)*, pages 302–314, 1999.
40. H. Thompson, D. Beech, M. Malone and N. Mendelsohn. XML Schema. W3C Recommendation, May 2001 `http://www.w3.org/XML/Schema`.
41. J. D. Ullman. *Database and Knowledge Base Systems*. Computer Science Press, 1988.
42. S. Yu. Regular Languages. In G. Rosenberg and A. Salomaa, editors, *Handbook of Formal Languages*, volume 1, pages 41–110. Springer, 1996.

Consistent Query Answers in Virtual Data Integration Systems

Leopoldo Bertossi[1] and Loreto Bravo[2]

Carleton University,
School of Computer Science,
Ottawa, Canada
{bertossi, lbravo}@scs.carleton.ca

Abstract. When data sources are virtually integrated there is no common and centralized mechanism for maintaining global consistency. In consequence, it is likely that inconsistencies with respect to certain global integrity constraints (ICs) will occur. In this chapter we consider the problem of defining and computing those answers that are consistent wrt the global ICs when global queries are posed to virtual data integration systems whose sources are specified following the local-as-view approach. The solution is based on a specification using logic programs with stable model semantics of the minimal legal instances of the integration system. Apart from being useful for computing consistent answers, the specification can be used to compute the certain answers to monotone queries, and minimal answers to non monotone queries.

1 Introduction

There is an increasing number of available information sources, many of them online, like organizational databases, library catalogues, scientific data repositories, etc., and in different formats and ranging from highly structured, like relational databases, to semi-structured, like data on the web. Many applications need to access and combine information from several databases, in consequence, a user (or application) is confronted to many different data sources.

One possibility for attacking this problem consists in bringing a possibly huge amount of data -that might be required by the application- into one single, physical, material site; and then making the application interact with this only data repository. This process is costly in term of storage, design, and refreshment, which would be necessary when the original sources are updated. That is, we have complexities that are similar to those involved in the processes associated to data warehouses, but with the difference that updating the repository could be more crucial that in data warehouses, where, most likely, decision support could be achieved without having completely up-to-date data.

An alternative solution consists in keeping the data in their sources. In this way, if the application needs answers to a query, it has to interact with the collection of available sources, first determining and selecting those that contain the relevant information. Next, queries have to be posed to those sources, on an

L. Bertossi et al. (Eds.): Inconsistency Tolerance, LNCS 3300, pp. 42–83, 2004.

individual basis; and the different results have to be combined. This can be a long, tedious, complex and error prone process if performed on an ad hoc basis. It is better to have a general, robust and uniform implementation that supports this process on a permanent and regular basis. Ideally, the application will interact with the data sources via a unique -database like - common interface.

A solution in this line consists in the *virtual integration* of the data sources via a *mediator* [75], that is, a software system that offers a common interface to a set of autonomous, independent and possibly heterogeneous data sources. Under this paradigm for data integration, the integration is virtual in the sense that the data stays in the sources, but the user -who interacts with the mediator- feels like interacting with a single database. The sources most likely do not cooperate with each other, and the mediator, except for the possibility of asking queries, has no control on the individual sources. There is no central control or maintenance mechanism either. It is also desirable that the set of participating sources is flexible and open.

It is clear that combining data from different and independent sources offers many and difficult challenges. If the integrated system is expected to keep some correspondence with the reality it is modelling, then it should keep some general, global semantic constraints satisfied. This is difficult to achieve, because most likely there will be semantic conflicts between pieces of data coming from different sources. Since there is no central, global integrity enforcement mechanism, and there is no possibility of doing any kind of *global* data cleaning, as in the datawarehouse approach to data integration, semantic problems have to be solved when the application interacts with the integration system.

More specifically, in this chapter we describe novel techniques to solve inconsistencies when queries posed to the integration system are answered. That is, only those answers to a global query that are consistent with the given global integrity constraints are returned. Apart from the problem of defining the notion of consistent answers in this scenario, there is the problem of designing query plans to consistently answering queries.

The mediator, in order to design query plans, needs to know the correspondence between the global relations offered by the mediator's interface, which determine an external query language, and the relations in the internal databases. These descriptions of the contents of the internal data sources can be expressed in different ways. In this chapter we will mostly concentrate to the *local as view* approach to data integration, according to which the sources are described as views of the global relations.

Global integrity constraints (ICs) will be expressed as first order formulas, and database instances are seen as first order structures with finite relations. We say that a database instance D is *consistent* wrt to a set IC of ICs if D satisfies IC (what is denoted by $D \models IC$, as usual). Of course, the set of global integrity constraints IC will be assumed to be logically consistent, in the sense that at least one database instance satisfies it.

This chapter is structured as follows. In Section 2 we consider virtual data integration systems, describing in general terms the main elements and issues; in particular, two alternative ways to specify the data contained in the data sources, in such a way that the mediator can make use of it. In Section 3 the semantics of virtual data integration systems with open sources under the local-as-view approach is given in detail. In Section 5 we briefly review the notion of consistent answer to a query posed to a single relational database, and some methodologies for computing them. The notion of consistent answer to a query, but now for an integration system, is defined in Section 6. With the goal of computing consistent answers in integration systems, in Section 7 logic programs with stable model semantics are used to specify the class of minimal instances of open integration systems under LAV. The results presented there are interesting in themselves, independently from consistent query answering, because they can be used to compute (ordinary) answers to both monotonic and non monotonic queries in integration systems, which extend previous results in the area. Section 8 shows how to compute consistent answers to queries posed to integration systems. The specification of minimal instances presented in Section 7 is extended in Section 9 to the case where in addition to open sources also closed and both closed and open sources are available. That specification is presented here for the first time. In Section 10, some open research issues are indicated. In Section 11 we finalize with a discussion of related work.

2   Virtual Data Integration Systems

2.1   Mediators for Data Integration

The main features of a mediator based system are: (a) The interaction with the system via queries posed to the mediator; (b) Updates via the mediator are not allowed; (c) Data sources are mutually independent and may participate in different mediated systems at the same time; (d) Sources are allowed to get in and out; (e) Data is kept in the local, individual sources, and extracted at the mediator's request.

Since the mediator offers a database like interface to the user or application, it has a *global or mediated schema*, consisting of a set of names for relations (virtual tables) and their attributes. This schema is application dependent and determines a (family of) query language(s), like in a usual relational databases from the user point of view. However, the "database" corresponding to the global schema is virtual.

A user poses queries to the mediator in terms of the relations in the global schema. However, in order to answer those global queries, the mediator needs to knows the correspondence between the global schema and the local schemas. This is achieved by means of a set of source descriptions, i.e. descriptions of what data can be found in the different sources. Having this information, when the mediator receives a query , it develops a *query plan* that determines: (a) the portions of data that are relevant to the query at hand, (b) their locations in the relevant data sources, (c) how to extract that data from the sources via queries, and (d) how to combine the answers received into a final answer for the user.

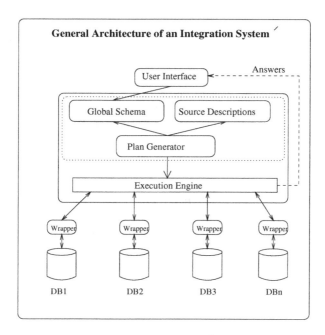

Fig. 1. Architecture of an Integration System

Figure 1 shows the main elements in the architecture of a mediator for virtual integration of data sources.

The mediator is responsible of solving problems of redundancy, complementarity, incompleteness, and consistency of data in the integration system. In this chapter we will consider this last problem, a very relevant one in this context. For example, what should the mediator do if it is asked about a person's ID card number and it gets two different numbers, each coming from a different source? The two sources, taken independently and separately, may be consistent, but taken together, possibly not. Such consistency problems are likely and natural in virtual data integration. Notice that consistency problems in virtual integration, unlike the "materialized" approaches to data integration, which offer data reconciliation solutions, cannot be solved a priori, at the physical data level.

Another element shown in Figure 1 is the *wrapper*. This is a module that is responsible for wrapping a data source in such a way that the latter can interact with the rest of integration system. It provides the mediator with data from a source as requested by the execution engine. In consequence, it presents a data source as a convenient database, with the right schema and data, the one that is understood and used by the mediator. Notice that this presentation schema may be different from the real one, the internal to the data source. Actually, it may be the case that the source is not at all internally structured as a database, but this should be transparent to the mediator. All this may require preliminary transformations, cleaning, etc., before the data can be exported to the integration system. There is a wrapper (or more) for each data source. In the following, we will assume that each data source has already a wrapper that presents it as a relational database.

Example 1. Consider a global schema for a database "containing" information about music albums: *CD(Album, Artist, Year)*, *Contract(Artist, Year, Label)*, *Songs(Album, Song)*. Now, a user wants to know the name of the label with which Norah Jones had a contract during 2002. This is asked issuing the following query to the global system Q: *Ans(L)* $\leftarrow$ *Contract(NorahJones, 2002, L)*.

Here, predicate *Ans* will contain the answers, that are to be computed using the expression on the RHS of this rule. In this case, this is the simple selection $\text{SELECT}_{X=NorahJones, Y=2002}$ Contract(X, Y, L).

It is a problem that the material data is not in the virtual global relation *Contract*, but in the data sources $DB_1(Album, Artist, Year)$, $DB_2(Album, Artist, Year, Label)$, $DB_3(Album, Song)$. In consequence, a query plan is needed in order to extract and combine the relevant data from the material sources. However, in order to design such a plan, the mediator needs to know the correspondence between the virtual global relations and the data sources. $\qquad\square$

A key element in the mediator architecture is the set of *source descriptions*, i.e. the descriptions of the available sources and their contents (as presented by the wrapper), which is achieved by establishing the relationships (mappings) between the global schema and the local schemata. These descriptions are given by means of a set of logical formulas; similar to the way in which views are defined in terms of base tables in a relational database, i.e. using queries written in a query language. Usually those query languages use logical formulas or their SQL versions.

With respect to how mappings are defined, there are two main approaches (and combinations of them): (a) *Global as View* (GAV), under which the relations in the global schema are described as views of the collection of local relations [73]; and (b) *Local as View* (LAV), under which each relation in a local source is described as a view of the global schema [61]. GLAV denotes a combination of GAV and LAV [37] where the rules can have more than one atom in the head. Another approach, called *Both as View* (BAV), consists on a specification of the transformation of the local schema into the given global schema, in such a way that each schema can be seen as defined as in terms of the other schema [65]. In Section 2.2 we describe and compare the GAV and LAV approaches.

The *plan generator* gets a user query in terms of global relations and uses the source descriptions to design a *query plan*. This is achieved by *rewriting* the original query as a set of subqueries that are expressed in terms of the local relations. The query plan includes prescriptions on how the answers from the local sources have to be combined. The query rewriting process executed by the plan generator strongly depends on whether the LAV or the GAV approach is followed. Still much theoretical and technical research is going on in relation to query plan generation. The plan is executed by the *execution engine*. Notice that it should be the plan generator who takes care of anticipating and solving potential inconsistencies. It should solve them in advance, when the plan is being generated. Later in this chapter, we will explore this issue in detail.

2.2   Description of Data Sources

The global/local schema mappings or, equivalently, the descriptions of the source contents are expressed through logical formulas that relate the global and local relations.

Global as View

In this case, the relations in the global schema are described as *views* over the tables in the union of the local schemata. This is conceptually very natural, because views are usually virtual relations defined in terms of material relations (the tables); and here we have global relations that are virtual and local sources that are materialized.

Example 2. (example 1 continued) Assume the relation *CD* is defined as the view

$$CD(Album, Artist, Year) \leftarrow DB_1(Album, Artist, Year)$$
$$CD(Album, Artist, Year) \leftarrow DB_2(Album, Artist, Year, Label).$$

Relation *CD* is defined as the union of the projections of DB_1 and DB_2 on attributes *Album, Artist, Year*, i.e. in relational terms, defined by

$$CD = \quad \Pi_{Album, Artist, Year}(DB_1) \; \cup \; \Pi_{Album, Artist, Year}(DB_2).$$

The global relation *Songs* and *Label* are defined as follows:

$$Songs(Album, Song) \leftarrow DB_1(Album, Artist, Year), DB_3(Album, Song).$$
$$Contract(Artist, Year, Label) \leftarrow DB_2(Album, Artist, Year, Label).$$

The first view is defined as, first, the join of DB_1 and DB_3 via attribute *Album*, and then, a projection on *Album, Song*. The second view is defined as the projection of DB_2 over *Artist, Year, Label*.

These views have been defined by means of *rules*. Each rule specifies that in order to compute the tuples in the relation in the LHS (the *head* of the rule), one has to go to the RHS (the *body* of the rule) and compute whatever is specified there. The attributes appearing in the head indicate that they are the attributes of interest, thus the others (in the body) can be projected out at the end. If there are more that one rule to compute a same relation, we use all of them and we take the union of the results, as for the relation *CD*.

Instead of using a rule as above, we could have used relational algebra (or relational calculus, or SQL2), in the case of the relation *Songs*,

$$Songs = \Pi_{Album, Song}(DB_1 \bowtie_{Album} DB_3).$$

The language of rules is more expressive than relational algebra, e.g. recursive views can be defined using rules, but not with relational algebra [72].   □

Once the global relations have been defined as views, we may start posing global queries, i.e. queries expressed in terms of the global relations. The problem is to answer them considering that the global relations do not contain material data. Under the GAV approach this is simple, all we need to do is *rule unfolding*.

Example 3. (example 2 continued) Consider the following global query about the music albums released in the year 2003, with their artists and songs

$Ans(Album, Artist, Song) \leftarrow \underline{CD(Album, Artist, 2003)}, \underline{Songs(Album, Song)}.$

Since it is expressed in terms of the global schema, the data has to be obtained from the sources, that is, the query has to be *rewritten* in terms of the source relations. We do this by unfolding each global relation, replacing it by its definition in terms of the local relations. We have underlined differently the goals in the body in order to keep track of the rewriting for each of them.

$Ans'(Album, Artist, Song) \leftarrow \underline{\underline{DB_1(Album, Artist, 2003)}},$
$$\underline{DB_1(Album, Artist, Year)}, \underline{DB_3(Album, Song)}.$$

$Ans'(Album, Artist, Song) \leftarrow \underline{\underline{DB_2(Album, Artist, 2003, Label)}},$
$$\underline{DB_1(Album, Artist, Year)}, \underline{DB_3(Album, Song)}.$$

These new queries do get answers directly from the sources; and the final answer is the union of two answer sets, one for each of the rules.   □

If, in addition to the view definitions, there are ICs that have to be and are satisfied by the system, unfolding is not enough for query answering [17, 19] (see Section 11 for more details).

Local as View

Under the LAV approach, each table in each local data source is described as a view (i.e. as a query expression) in terms of the global relations. This may seem somehow unnatural or unusual from the conceptual point of view, and from perspective of databases practice, because here the views contain the data, but not the "base tables". However, as we will see, this approach has some advantages.

More precisely, in the general situation we have a collection of material data sources (think of a collection of material relational tables) $S_1, \ldots, S_n$, and a global schema G for the system that integrates data from $S_1, \ldots, S_n$. Tables in $S_1, \ldots, S_n$ are seen as *views* over G, and in consequence, they can be defined by query expressions over the global schema.

Example 4. Consider the sources S_1, S_2 that are defined by the view expressions

$S_1:$ $V_1(Album, Artist, Year) \leftarrow CD(Album, Artist, Year),$
$$Contract(Artist, Year, emi), Year \geq 1990$$
$S_2:$ $V_2(Album, Song) \leftarrow Songs(Album, Song).$

Source S_1 contains a table whose entries are albums produced after 1990 by the label EMI with their artists and years. Source S_2 contains one table with songs and their albums.

Those relations that are not defined as views belong to the global schema G, in this case, we have the relations: $CD(Album, Artist, Year)$, $Songs(Album, Song)$, $Contract(Artist, Year, Label)$.   □

Notice that from the perspective of S_1, there could be other sources containing information about albums produced by EMI after 1990, and that complementary information could be exported to the global system. In this sense, the information in S_1 could be considered as "incomplete" wrt what G contains (or might contain). In other words, S_1 contains only a part of the data of the same kind in the global system. We will elaborate on this later on. Finally, also notice that in the example, and this is a general situation under LAV, the definition of each source does not depend on other sources.

Now we want to answer global queries under LAV.

Example 5. (example 4 continued) The following query posed to G asks for the songs with its album and the year they were released:

$$Ans(Album, Song, Year) \leftarrow CD(Album, Artist, Year), Songs(Album, Song).$$

This query is expressed as usual, in terms of global relations only, however, it is not possible to obtain the answers by a simple and direct computation of the RHS of the query. Now, there is no direct rule unfolding mechanism for the relations in the body, because we do not have explicit definitions for them. And the data resides in the sources, which are now defined as views.

We can see that plan generation to extract information from the sources becomes more complex under LAV than under GAV. Since a query plan is a rewriting of the query as a set of queries to the sources and a prescription on how to combine their answers (what is needed in this example), the following could be a query plan to answer the original query:

$$Ans'(Album, Song, Year) \leftarrow V_1(Album, Artist, Year), V_2(Album, Song).$$

The query has been rewritten in terms of the views; and in order to obtain the final answer, we first extract values for *Album*, *Year* from V_1; then we extract the tuples from V_2; finally, at the mediator level, we compute the join via *Album*.

Notice that due to the limited contents of the sources, we only obtain albums produced by EMI after 1990.   □

In LAV we pose a query in terms of certain relations (the global ones), but we have to answer using the contents of certain views only (the local relations). In consequence, query plan generation becomes an instance of a more general and traditional problem in databases, the one of *query rewriting using views.*

To see this connection more clearly, assume we have a collection of views $V_1, \ldots, V_n$, whose contents have already been computed, and cached or materialized. When a new query Q arrives, instead of computing its answers directly, we try to use the answers (contents) to (of) $V_1, \ldots, V_n$. A problem to consider consists in determining how much from the real answer do we get by using the pre-computed views only; and also determining what is the maximum we can get in terms of the kind of views we have available. The research carried out in query answering using views [60, 2, 49, 51, 50, 35] and query containment [2, 56, 67, 23] has become quite relevant to the area of data integration.

2.3 Comparison of Paradigms

We have seen that under GAV, rule unfolding makes plan generation simple and direct. On the other hand, GAV is not flexible to accept new sources or eliminate sources into/from the system. Actually, adding or deleting sources might imply modifying the definitions of the global relations.

LAV offers more flexibility to add new sources or delete old ones into/from the integration system, because a new source is just a new view definition. Other sources do not need to be considered at this point, because there are no other sources interfering in the process. Only the plan generator has to be aware of these changes. On the other side, plan generation is provably more difficult [2, 58, 18, 73].

2.4 Data Integration and Consistency

Notice that, so far, we have not considered any integrity constraints at the global schema level. Since the data sources are autonomous and possibly updated independently from the integration system in which they participate and from other data sources, there is not much we can do wrt to data maintenance at the global level. However, in virtual data integration, one usually assumes that certain integrity constraints hold at the global level, and they are used in the plan generation process [48, 30, 45]. Even more, in some cases the generation of a query plan is possible because certain integrity constraints (are supposed to) hold [30].

In general, we cannot be sure that such global integrity constraints hold, because they are not maintained at the global level. A more natural scenario is the one where integrity constraints are considered when queries are posed to the system. In this case, we have the problem -to be addressed in Section 6- of retrieving information from the global system that is consistent wrt certain global constraints, but the problem has to be solved at query time, as opposed to the usual approach in single databases, where all the data in the database is kept and maintained consistent, independently from potential queries.[1] This is an interesting point of view wrt integrity constraints: they constitute constraints on the answers to queries rather than on the database states.

Notice that the flexibility to add/remove sources, in particular under LAV, is likely to introduce extra sources of inconsistencies we have to take care of.

The global ICs we will consider are first order sentences written in the language of the global schema. In particular, they will be *universal integrity constraints*, i.e. sentences of the form $\forall \bar{x} \varphi(\bar{x})$, where $\varphi(\bar{x})$ is a quantifier-free formula; and also *referential integrity constraints* of the form $\forall \bar{x}(P(\bar{x}) \rightarrow \exists y(Q(\bar{x}', y)))$, where $\bar{x}' \subseteq \bar{x}$.

---

[1] Work reported in [11] departs from this practice and considers a more flexible approach to query answering in databases where databases may be inconsistent, but only answers to queries are expected to be consistent.

3   Semantics of Virtual Data Integration Systems

In the rest of this paper, unless otherwise stated, we will concentrate on the LAV approach (see Section 11 for references on the GAV approach). The semantics of virtual data integration systems is given in terms of the intended global instances. This does not mean that such instances are to be computed, but they will allow us to give a model theoretic semantics to global integrity constraint satisfaction, to query answers, etc.

A data integration system $\mathcal{G}$ under the LAV approach is specified by a set of view definitions, plus a set of material tables v_i corresponding to the views V_i defined:

$$\mathcal{G}: \qquad V_1(\bar{X}_1) \leftarrow \varphi_1(\bar{X}'_1); \quad v_1 \qquad\qquad (1)$$
$$\cdots\cdots\cdots$$
$$V_n(\bar{X}_n) \leftarrow \varphi_n(\bar{X}'_n); \quad v_n$$

Here, $\bar{X}_j \subseteq \bar{X}'_j$, and each v_i is an extension (a material relation) for view V_i, which in its turn is defined as a conjunctive view.

Until further notice we will assume that the system has all its sources open (also called sound). This means that the information stored in the sources might be incomplete. The description in (1) plus the openness assumption will determine a *a set of legal global instances*. Now we describe how.[2]

Let D be a global instance, i.e. its domain contains at least the constants appearing in the source extensions and the view definitions; and has relations (and contents) for the global schema. We denote with $\varphi_i(D)$ the set of tuples obtained by applying to D the definition of view V_i. This gives an extension for V_i in (wrt) global instance D, which can be compared with v_i. We call a global instance D *legal* if the computed extension on D of each view V_i contains the originally given extension v_i:

$$Legal(\mathcal{G}) := \{ \text{ global } D \mid v_i \subseteq \varphi_i(D); \ i = 1, \dots, n \},$$

which captures the incompleteness of the sources, because if a view is applied to a legal instance, the result will be a superset of the elements in the source. Only legal instances will determine the semantics of $\mathcal{G}$.

Example 6. Consider the system $\mathcal{G}_1$ with global relation $R(X, Y)$ and the following open sources

$$V_1(X, Y) \leftarrow R(X, Y); \qquad v_1 = \{(a, b), (c, d)\}$$
$$V_2(X, Y) \leftarrow R(X, Y); \qquad v_2 = \{(a, c), (d, e)\}.$$

The global instance D for which the relation R has the extension $R^D = \{(a, b), (c, d), (a, c), (d, e)\}$[3] is legal, because: (a) $v_1 \subseteq \varphi_1(D) = \{(a, b), (c, d), (a, c),$

---

[2] A similar semantics can be given in the case of the GAV approach [58].

[3] In the rest of this chapter we will use a simpler description for an instance of this kind. We simple write $D = \{(a, b), (c, d), (a, c), (d, e)\}$, because there is only one global relation. If there were another relation, we write $D = \{R(a, b), R(c, d), \dots\}$.

$(d, e)\}$; and (b) $v_2 \subseteq \varphi_2(D) = \{(a, b), (c, d), (a, c), (d, e)\}$. All supersets of D are also legal global instances; e.g. $\{(a, b), (c, d), (a, c), (d, e), (c, e)\} \in Legal(\mathcal{G})$, but no subset of D is legal, e.g. $\{(a, b), (c, d), (a, c)\} \notin Legal(\mathcal{G})$. □

Example 7. Let $\mathcal{D} = \{a, b, c, \dots\}$ be the underlying domain. Consider the integration system $\mathcal{G}_2$ defined by

$$V_1(X, Z) \leftarrow P(X, Y), R(Y, Z); \qquad v_1 = \{(a, b)\}$$
$$V_2(X, Y) \leftarrow P(X, Y); \qquad v_2 = \{(a, c)\}.$$

Each global instance D of the form $\{P(a, c), P(a, z), R(z, b)\}$, with $z \in \mathcal{D}$ is a legal instance, because $v_1 \subseteq \varphi_1(D) = \{(a, b)\}$ and $v_2 \subseteq \varphi_2(D) = \{(a, c), (a, z)\}$. Any superset of D is also legal, but none of its subsets is. □

Now we can define the intended answers to a global query Q. They are the *certain answers*, those that can be obtained from every legal global instance [2]:

$$Certain_{\mathcal{G}}(Q) := \{\bar{t} \mid \bar{t} \text{ is an answer to } Q \text{ in } D \text{ for all } D \in Legal(\mathcal{G})\}.$$

Example 8. (example 6 continued) Consider the following global query Q posed to system $\mathcal{G}_1$: $Ans(X, Y) \leftarrow R(X, Y)$. In this case, $Certain_{\mathcal{G}_1}(Q) = \{(a, b), (c, d), (a, c), (d, e)\}$. □

The algorithms for constructing query plans should be sound and complete wrt this semantics, more precisely they should be able to produce plans whose execution will allow us to get all and only the certain answers from a data integration system; of course, without explicitly computing all the legal instances and querying them.

4   Query Plans

There are several algorithms for generating query plans. See [62, 51] for survey of different techniques. In [45] a deductive methodology is presented. Here we will briefly describe the *inverse rules algorithm* (IRA) [29, 30]. This algorithm is conceptually simple, shows the main issues, and will be used later in this chapter in our solution to the problem of consistent query answering in integration systems.

Our framework is as follows. We are given a global query Q posed in terms of the global schema, but we need to go to the sources for the data required to evaluate Q. The problem is how to do this, or more precisely, how to rewrite Q in terms of the views available, i.e. in terms of the relations in the sources.

We will assume that we have a set of rules describing the source relations as conjunctive (Select-Project-Join) views of the global schema [1]. We also assume that the sources are open.

The input to our problem is a global query expressed, e.g. in Datalog (may be recursive, but without negation). The expected output is a new Datalog program expressed in terms of the source relations.

Example 9. Consider the local relations V_1, V_2 in sources S_1, S_2, resp., and the global relations R_1, R_2, R_3. The set of source descriptions contains

$$S_1: \quad V_1(X, Z) \leftarrow R_1(X, Y), R_2(Y, Z), \tag{2}$$
$$S_2: \quad V_2(X, Y) \leftarrow R_3(X, Y). \tag{3}$$

The idea behind IRA consists in obtaining, from these descriptions, "inverse rules" describing the global relations. Let us start from (3). Since V_2 is open, it is contained in the "extension" of the global relation R_3. That is, the only way to get tuples for V_2 is by going to pick up tuples from the RHS of (3). In other terms, we can say that V_2 "$\subseteq$" R_3, or, equivalently, V_2 "$\Rightarrow$" R_3. More precisely, we invert the rule in the description of V_2, obtaining

$$R_3(X, Y) \leftarrow V_2(X, Y),$$

now, a rule describing R_3, which we wanted. If there are (not in this case though) other rules of this kind describing R_3 (from other source description rules containing R_3 on the RHS), we just take the union.

Now, wrt inverting rule (2), a first attempt could be

$$R_1(X, Y), R_2(Y, Z) \leftarrow V_1(X, Z),$$

but this is a strange rule, with a strange head. There are several problems. If the head is seen as a conjunction, then we may split it into two rules, namely $R_1(X, Y) \leftarrow V_1(X, Z)$ and $R_2(Y, Z) \leftarrow V_1(X, Z)$, but now the two occurrences of variable Y are independent, and before it was a shared variable that allowed us to combine tables R_1, R_2 by means of a join. This connection is lost now. Another problem has to do with the unrestricted occurrence of Y in the heads; there are no conditions on Y in the bodies (this kind of rules are considered *unsafe* in databases [72]). It should not be the case that any value for Y is admissible.

A better approach is as follows: $V_1(X, Z) \leftarrow R_1(X, Y), R_2(Y, Z)$ is equivalent to $V_1(X, Z) \leftarrow \exists Y \, (R_1(X, Y) \wedge R_2(Y, Z))$ (a join followed by a projection). Inverting, we obtain $\exists Y (R_1(X, Y) \wedge R_2(Y, Z)) \leftarrow V_1(X, Z)$. This rule has an implicit universal quantification on X, Z, then each value for Y possibly depends on the values for X, Z, i.e. Y is a function of X, Z. To capture this dependence, we replace Y by a function symbol $f(X, Z)$ (a so-called "Skolem function"), obtaining

$$R_1(X, f(X, Z)) \wedge R_2(f(X, Z), Z) \leftarrow V_1(X, Z).$$

As before, we split the conjunction, obtaining the rules $R_1(X, f(X, Z)) \leftarrow V_1(X, Z)$ and $R_2(f(X, Z), Z) \leftarrow V_1(X, Z)$. In this way, we obtain the following set $\mathcal{V}^{-1}$ of inverse rules

$$R_1(X, f(X, Z)) \leftarrow V_1(X, Z)$$
$$R_2(f(X, Z), Z) \leftarrow V_1(X, Z)$$
$$R_3(X, Y) \leftarrow V_2(X, Y),$$

which can be used to compute answers to global queries.

Notice that we may need other symbolic functions, for dependencies between variables in the same or other rules. More precisely, we introduce one function symbol for each variable in the body of a view definition that is not in the head; and that function appears evaluated in the variables in the head.

Now, assume the following global query Q is posed to the integration system

$$Ans(X, Z) \leftarrow R_1(X, Y), R_2(Y, Z), R_4(X)$$
$$R_4(X) \leftarrow R_3(X, Y)$$
$$R_4(X) \leftarrow R_7(X)$$
$$R_7(X) \leftarrow R_1(X, Y), R_6(X, Y).$$

We can see that the goal R_6 cannot be computed, because there is no definition for it in $\mathcal{V}^{-1}$. Then, R_7 cannot be evaluated either; and the rule defining it can be deleted. For the same reason, the third rule in the query cannot be evaluated; and can be deleted. In this way we obtain a pruned query Q^-:

$$Ans(X, Z) \leftarrow R_1(X, Y), R_2(Y, Z), R_4(X)$$
$$R_4(X) \leftarrow R_3(X, Y).$$

In consequence, the final query produced by the plan generator, using the IRA, is $Q^- \cup \mathcal{V}^{-1}$. This is a sort of Datalog program, but with functions.

This is all and the best we have to answer the original query. With the new query program we can compute *some* answers to Q, but actually, "the most" we can. The plan can be evaluated, e.g. bottom-up, from concrete source contents [72]. The final answer may contain some tuples with the function symbol f in them; but they are eventually deleted.

We will illustrate this process with a different query. Assume that the source contents are $v_1 = \{(a, b), (a, a), (c, a), (b, a)\}$ and $v_2 = \{(a, c), (a, a), (c, d), (b, b)\}$; and the query is now Q':

$$Ans(X) \leftarrow R_1(X, Y), R_2(Y, Z), R_4(X)$$
$$Ans(X) \leftarrow R_2(X, Y)$$
$$R_4(X) \leftarrow R_3(X, Y)$$
$$R_4(X) \leftarrow R_1(X, a).$$

We have the same set $\mathcal{V}^{-1}$ of inverse rules as above, they are the same for all the queries. So, first we prune the query rules that cannot be evaluated from the inverse rules. We delete the last rule in the query, because it does not contribute to R_4 (a cannot be an f-value). We obtain the final query consisting of the rules in $\mathcal{V}^{-1}$ plus the first three rules in Q'. It can be evaluated bottom-up. The mediator will use the inverse rules applied to the sources, which requires sending one query to each source, and will obtain

$$R_1 = \{(a, f(a, b)), (a, f(a, a)), (c, f(c, a)), (b, f(b, a))\}$$
$$R_2 = \{(f(a, b), b), (f(a, a), a), (f(c, a), a), (f(b, a), a)\}$$
$$R_3 = \{(a, c), (a, a), (c, d), (b, b)\}.$$

Using the third rule of Q', we obtain $R_4 = \{a, c, b\}$. Now we can evaluate the first rule in Q', whose body becomes $\Pi_X(R_1 \bowtie R_2) \cap R_4 = \{a, c, b\} \cap \{a, c, b\} = \{a, c, b\}$. Then, $a, c, b \in Ans$. From the second rule in Q' we obtain $f(a, b), f(a, a), f(c, a), f(b, a) \in Ans$, but these tuples are not considered, because all the tuples containing function symbols are eliminated from the final answer set. So, finally $Ans = \{a, c, b\}$. $\qquad\square$

Given a Datalog query, the query plan obtained for it is a new Datalog program, but may contain function symbols (strictly speaking, for this reason, it is not a Datalog program). If the original query does not contain recursion, neither does the final query. The query plan: (a) does not contain negation, (b) can be evaluated in a bottom-up manner and always has a unique fix point, (c) can be constructed in polynomial time in the size of the original query and the source descriptions.

The plan obtained is the best we can get under the circumstances, i.e. given the query, the sources and their descriptions. More precisely, for a Datalog query Q and a set of sources defined as conjunctive views, the query plan generated with the IRA is *maximally contained* [2] in the original query Q [30]. In other words, there is no other query plan that retrieves a set of answers to Q that is a proper superset of *answers* to Q produced by IRA.

It is possible to prove [2] that for conjunctive views and Datalog queries (and open sources), a maximally contained query plan computes all the certain answers. In consequence, the inverse rules algorithm returns all the certain answers to Datalog queries [30].

We have seen in this section and also in Section 2.2 for the GAV approach, that the query plan prescribes how to rewrite the original, global, conjunctive query as a new query expressed in terms of the source relations. The new query is also a first order or Datalog query. However, for more complex queries, the "rewriting" may need to be expressed in more expressive languages, e.g. disjunctive logic programs with stable model semantics, as in Section 7, in order to capture a higher data complexity of query answering (see [22] for a discussion about what should qualify as a query rewriting).

Now, if in addition to the source descriptions, we have a set IC of global integrity constraints; it is quite likely that they are not going to be satisfied by (all) the legal instances. In consequence, instead of retrieving the certain answers to a global query, we might be interested in retrieving those answers that are *consistent wrt IC*. This notion is still to be formalized (see Section 6), but having done that, we would expect that the query plans generated by the mediator should incorporate new elements, responsible for enforcing the satisfaction of the ICs at the query answer level.

In order to formally define what is a consistent answer to a query to the integration system, we will appeal to some notions and techniques introduced, in the context of single, stand alone relational databases, to characterize and compute answers to queries that are consistent wrt to integrity constraints that the database may fail to satisfy. We review some of those relevant notions and techniques in Section 5.

5   Consistent Query Answering for Single Databases

Assume we have a single relational database instance D and a set of integrity constraints (ICs) that D may fail to satisfy. This inconsistent database can still give us "correct" answers to queries, because not all the data in it participates in the violation of the ICs. It becomes necessary to define in precise terms what is the "correct" or "consistent" information in the database; and in particular, which are the "correct answers" to a query. Having done this, it is necessary to develop mechanisms for retrieving such consistent answers; but without changing the database, restoring its consistency. See [11] for an extended discussion about why this is a natural and important problem. Here we briefly review some notions and techniques that have been given to attack these problems.

Given a relational database instance D, a query Q, and a set IC of ICs, we say that a tuple $\bar{t}$ is a *consistent answer* to Q in D wrt IC whenever $\bar{t}$ is an answer to Q in every *repair* of D, where a repair of instance D is a database instance D', over the same schema and domain, that satisfies IC, and differs from D by a minimal set of changes (insertions/deletions of whole tuples) wrt to set inclusion [3].

Intuitively speaking, consistent answers are invariant under minimal ways of restoring consistency. Repairs are just an auxiliary concept, used to characterize the consistent answers, but we *we are not interested in repairs per se*. Actually we may try to avoid to (explicitly and completely) compute them whenever possible, because this is an expensive process. In consequence, the ideal situation is the one in which we are able to compute the consistent answers to Q by posing a -hopefully- simple new query Q' to the inconsistent instance D, in such a way that the standard answers to Q' are precisely the consistent answers to Q. In some cases it is possible to generate a new first order query Q' with that property, however in other situations, the query Q' has to be written in some extension of Datalog, possibly as disjunctive normal programs [41, 27].

Example 10. Consider the database instance $D = \{P(a), P(b), R(a), R(c)\}$ and the integrity constraint $IC : \forall x(\neg P(x) \vee \neg R(x))$, stating that tables P and R do not intersect. The instance is inconsistent wrt to IC. The two repairs of D are $D_1 = \{P(a), P(b), R(c)\}$, $D_2 = \{P(b), R(a), R(c)\}$. The query $Q(x) :$ $Ans(x) \leftarrow P(x)$ has b as only consistent answer, because P becomes true only of b in both repairs. The query Q' consisting of the rules $Ans(x) \leftarrow P(x)$ and $Ans(x) \leftarrow R(x)$, has a, b, c as consistent answers, what shows that data is not cleaned from inconsistencies: the problematic tuple a is still recovered.   □

In [11], an alternative repair based semantic was used in the presence of referential integrity constraints. There, if a tuple is inconsistent (participates in a violation), the possible ways to repair are deleting the inconsistent tuple or adding a tuple with null values in the existentially quantified attributes of the constraint.

In order to compute the consistent answers to queries, two main approaches have been introduced. One of them is first order (FO) query rewriting (if the original query is first order) [3, 25, 13]; and the other consists in specification of database repairs using disjunctive logic programs with stable model semantics [4, 47, 7]. The later approach is more general, but more expensive than FO query rewriting. Despite their higher data complexity, disjunctive programs have to be applied, also to some first order queries, because in some cases, for complexity reasons, there is no FO rewriting [26, 20, 38].

5.1   Query Rewriting

Example 11. (example 10 continued) Consider again query Q. Notice that a tuple $\bar{t}$ is an answer to the query and at the same time consistent wrt to IC if it is not in R. In consequence, instead of posing the original query to the original database, we pose the new query $(P(x) \wedge \neg R(x))$, which gives us the expected answer, b, in D.

The extra condition $\neg R(x)$ imposed on the original query is the so-called *residue* of the literal $P(x)$ wrt the IC. Notice that this residue can be obtained by resolution between the query literal and the IC. We write $T^1(Q) = (P(x) \wedge \neg R(x))$. In principle, the new literal appended may have residues of its own wrt IC. We do not have any in this case, but if we had, we would append its residues, obtaining $T^2(Q)$, etc. Here, the iteration stopped and we write $T^\omega(Q) = (P(x) \wedge \neg R(x))$. See [3, 25] for details.   □

The FO query rewriting based methodology introduced in [3] via the T operator has some limitations [3, 25]. It cannot be applied to existential or disjunctive queries, like query Q' in Example 10, and only universal integrity constraints can be involved.

5.2   Logic Programming

The second approach consists in representing in a compact form the collection of all database repairs. This is like axiomatizing a class of models, namely as the intended models of a disjunctive logic program under the stable model semantics [41]. That is, the repairs correspond to certain distinguished models of the program, namely, to its stable models.

Once the specification has been given, in order to obtain consistent answers to a, say, FO query Q, the latter is transformed into a query written as logic program, which is a standard process [64, 1]; and then, this query program is "run" together with the program that specifies the repairs. This evaluation can be implemented on top of DLV, for example; a logic programming system that computes according to the stable models semantics [31, 59]. We illustrate the methodology presented in [6] by means of an example. In order to capture the repair process, the program uses annotation constants, whose intended semantics is shown in Table 1.

Example 12. (example 10 continued) The repair program $\Pi(r, IC)$ consists of:

1. Facts: $P(a, \mathbf{t_d}), P(b, \mathbf{t_d}), R(a, \mathbf{t_d}), R(c, \mathbf{t_d})$.

Whatever was true (false) or becomes true (false), gets annotated with $\mathbf{t^\star}$ ($\mathbf{f^\star}$):

Table 1. Semantic of Annotation Constants

Annotation	Atom	The tuple $P(\bar{a})$ is...
$\mathbf{t_d}$	$P(\bar{a}, \mathbf{t_d})$	a fact of the database
$\mathbf{f_d}$	$P(\bar{a}, \mathbf{f_d})$	a fact not in the database
$\mathbf{t_a}$	$P(\bar{a}, \mathbf{t_a})$	advised to be made true
$\mathbf{f_a}$	$P(\bar{a}, \mathbf{f_a})$	advised to be made false
$\mathbf{t^\star}$	$P(\bar{a}, \mathbf{t^\star})$	true or becomes true
$\mathbf{f^\star}$	$P(\bar{a}, \mathbf{f^\star})$	false or becomes false
$\mathbf{t^{\star\star}}$	$P(\bar{a}, \mathbf{t^{\star\star}})$	true in the repair
$\mathbf{f^{\star\star}}$	$P(\bar{a}, \mathbf{f^{\star\star}})$	false in the repair

2. $P(X, \mathbf{t^\star}) \leftarrow P(X, \mathbf{t_d})$
    $P(X, \mathbf{t^\star}) \leftarrow P(X, \mathbf{t_a})$
    $P(X, \mathbf{f^\star}) \leftarrow \ not\ P(X, \mathbf{t_d})$
    $P(X, \mathbf{f^\star}) \leftarrow P(X, \mathbf{f_a})$ ... the same for R ...

3. $P(X, \mathbf{f_a}) \ \vee \ R(X, \mathbf{f_a}) \ \leftarrow \ P(X, \mathbf{t^\star}), R(X, \mathbf{t^\star})$

One rule per IC; that says how to repair the IC, in this case, if x belongs both to P and R, either delete the tuple from P or from R. Passing to annotations $\mathbf{t^\star}$ and $\mathbf{f^\star}$ allows to keep repairing the DB wrt to all the ICs until the whole process stabilizes.

Repairs must be *coherent*: we use denial constraints at the program level, to prune the models that do not satisfy them

4. $\leftarrow P(X, \mathbf{t_a}), P(X, \mathbf{f_a})$
    $\leftarrow R(X, \mathbf{t_a}), R(X, \mathbf{f_a})$

Finally, annotations constants $\mathbf{t^{\star\star}}$ and $\mathbf{f^{\star\star}}$ are used to read off the literals that are inside (outside) a repair, i.e. they are used to interpret the stable models of the program as database repairs.

5. $P(X, \mathbf{t^{\star\star}}) \leftarrow P(X, \mathbf{t_a})$
    $P(X, \mathbf{t^{\star\star}}) \leftarrow P(X, \mathbf{t_d}), \ not\ P(X, \mathbf{f_a})$
    $P(X, \mathbf{f^{\star\star}}) \leftarrow P(X, \mathbf{f_a})$
    $P(X, \mathbf{f^{\star\star}}) \leftarrow \ not\ P(X, \mathbf{t_d}), \ not\ P(X, \mathbf{t_a})$.   ... etc.

The program has two stable models (and two repairs):

$\{P(a, \mathbf{t_d}), P(a, \mathbf{t^\star}), P(a, \mathbf{t^{\star\star}}), P(b, \mathbf{t_d}), P(b, \mathbf{t^\star}), P(b, \mathbf{t^{\star\star}}), R(a, \mathbf{t_d}), R(a, \mathbf{f_a}),$
$R(a, \mathbf{f^\star}), R(a, \mathbf{f^{\star\star}}), R(c, \mathbf{t_d}), R(c, \mathbf{t^\star}), R(c, \mathbf{t^{\star\star}})\} \equiv \{P(a), P(b), Q(c)\}.$

$\{P(a, \mathbf{t_d}), P(a, \mathbf{f_a}), P(a, \mathbf{f^\star}), P(a, \mathbf{f^{\star\star}}), P(b, \mathbf{t_d}), P(b, \mathbf{t^\star}), P(b, \mathbf{t^{\star\star}}),$
$R(a, \mathbf{t_d}), R(a, \mathbf{t^\star}), R(a, \mathbf{t^{\star\star}}), R(c, \mathbf{t_d}), R(c, \mathbf{t^\star}), R(c, \mathbf{t^{\star\star}})\} \equiv \{P(b), Q(a), Q(c)\}.$

If we want the consistent answers to the query $(P(\bar{x}) \wedge R(\bar{x}))$, for example, we run the repair program $\Pi(r, IC)$ together with query program $Ans(X) \leftarrow P(X, \mathbf{t^{**}}), Q(X, \mathbf{t^{**}})$, obtaining the answer $Ans = \emptyset$, as expected. With the query $Ans(X) \leftarrow P(X, \mathbf{t^{**}}), Q(X, \mathbf{f^{**}})$, we obtain the answer $Ans = \{b\}$. Finally, we can pose the disjunctive query Q' we had in Example 10 by means of the two rules $Ans(X) \leftarrow P(X, \mathbf{t^{**}})$ and $Ans(X) \leftarrow R(X, \mathbf{t^{**}})$, obtaining $Ans = \{a, b, c\}$. □

This approach can be used for Datalog$^{\vee, \neg}$ queries and universal constraints. The extension for referential constraints can be found in [11]. We have successfully experimented with consistent query answering (CQA) based on specification of database repairs using the DLV system [31].

6   Semantics of CQA in Integration Systems

In this section we will assume that we are working under the LAV approach. Actually, this scenario is more challenging than GAV and inconsistency issues are more relevant due to the flexibility to insert/delete sources into/from the system.

Let us first consider an example that will help us motivate our notions of consistency of an integration system and consistent query answering.

Example 13. (example 8 continued) We found for query Q: $R(X, Y)$, that $Certain_{\mathcal{G}_1}(Q) = \{(a, b), (c, d), (a, c), (d, e)\}$. Now assume that we have global functional dependency $FD: X \rightarrow Y$. It is not satisfied by $D = \{(a, b), (c, d), (a, c), (d, e)\}$, nor by its supersets, i.e. no legal instance satisfies it. Since the tuples $(a, b), (a, c)$ participate in the violation of FD, only $(c, d), (d, e)$ should be consistent answers to the query.

Notice that the local functional dependencies $V_1: X \rightarrow Y$, $V_2: X \rightarrow Y$ are satisfied by the sources. □

A virtual integration system does not have data at the global level. In spite of this, we would like to be able to characterize such a system as consistent or not, but we would like to do this on the basis of the data at hand, the one that is forced to be in the system, avoiding problems of consistency caused by data that is only potentially contained in the integration system. In this direction we concentrate on the *minimal* instances. We will see that this shift of semantics does not have an impact on query answering for relevant classes of queries in comparison to the semantics based on the whole class of legal instances.

Definition 1. [10] (a) A *minimal global instance* of an integration system $\mathcal{G}$ is a legal instance that does not properly contain any other legal instance. We denote by $Mininst(\mathcal{G})$ the set of minimal instances of $\mathcal{G}$.
(b) We say $\mathcal{G}$ is *consistent* wrt a set of global ICs IC if for every $D \in Mininst(\mathcal{G})$ it holds $D \models IC$. □

Example 14. (example 13 continued) System $\mathcal{G}_1$ has only $D = \{(a, b), (c, d), (a, c),$ $(d, e)\}$ as minimal instance. There FD does not hold; in consequence, $\mathcal{G}_1$ is inconsistent. □

The minimal instances will play a special role in our treatment of inconsistent integration systems. Since we have a well defined subclass of legal instances, it is natural to consider those answers to queries that hold for all the instances in the class.

Definition 2. [10] The *minimal answers* to a global query Q posed to an integration system $\mathcal{G}$ are those answers that can be obtained from every minimal instance. We denote them by $Minimal_{\mathcal{G}}(Q)$. □

Example 15. (example 14 continued) For the query $Q\colon Ans(X,Y) \leftarrow R(X,Y)$, we have $Minimal_{\mathcal{G}_1}(Q) = \{(a, b), (c, d), (a, c), (d, e)\}$, which can be obtained by querying the only minimal instance. In this case the minimal answers coincide with the certain answers.

Now consider the query $Q'\colon Ans(X,Y) \leftarrow \neg R(X,Y)$. On the basis of the underlying domain, we have $(a, e) \in Minimal_{\mathcal{G}_1}(Q')$, because the minimal instance does not contain the tuple (a, e). However, $(a, e) \notin Certain_{\mathcal{G}_1}(Q')$, because there are -non minimal- legal instances that contain the tuple (a, e). □

What was shown in the previous example holds in general, namely $Certain_{\mathcal{G}}(Q) \subseteq Minimal_{\mathcal{G}}(Q)$; and for monotone queries [1] they coincide; but for queries with negation, possibly not.

As in the case of a single database, consistent answers will be the answers that are invariant under the repairs of the system. We make these intuitions precise.

Definition 3. [10] Let $\mathcal{G}$ be an integration system and IC a set of global ICs.

(a) A *repair* of $\mathcal{G}$ wrt to IC is a global instance that satisfies IC, and minimally differs from a minimal instance (wrt to inclusion of sets of tuples). We denote by $Repairs^{IC}(\mathcal{G})$ the set of repairs of $\mathcal{G}$ wrt IC.
(b) A ground tuple $\bar{t}$ is a *consistent answer* to a global query Q wrt IC if for every $D \in Repairs^{IC}(\mathcal{G})$, it holds $D \models Q[\bar{t}]$, i.e. $\bar{t}$ is an answer to Q in D. We denote by $Consis_{\mathcal{G}}^{IC}(Q)$ set of consistent answers to Q. □

Example 16. (example 14 continued) Consider system $\mathcal{G}_1$ with the global $FD\colon X \to Y$. Since $D = \{(a, b), (c, d), (a, c), (d, e)\}$ is the only minimal instance, and it does not satisfy FD, the system has two repairs wrt FD, namely $D^1 = \{(a, b), (c, d), (d, e)\}$ and $D^2 = \{(c, d), (a, c), (d, e)\}$.

Now, for the query $Q\colon Ans(X,Y) \leftarrow R(X,Y)$, we have $Consis_{\mathcal{G}_1}^{FD}(Q) = \{(c, d), (d, e)\}$, as expected. For the existential query $Q''(X)\colon Ans(X) \leftarrow R(X,Y)$, we have $Consis_{\mathcal{G}_1}^{FD}(Q'') = \{a, c, d\}$. This shows that the value a is not lost through the repair process and is still recovered as a consistent answer. □

This example shows that repairs may not be legal instances. The two repairs in it are not. This flexibility is necessary to make the system repairable. Remember that the repairs are just an auxiliary notion that we use to define the consistent answers to queries.

Here we are considering repairs that treat deletions and insertions of tuples symmetrically. Other approaches may privilege certain kinds of changes, e.g. in [20] insertions are preferred to deletions in the presence of referential ICs, with the purpose of giving a better account of the openness (or incompleteness) of the sources (see Section 11 for a more detailed discussion of alternative approaches). However, adapting our specifications and methodologies for query answering to this kind of special repairs is rather straightforward.

Also notice that an alternative definition of consistent answer in terms of being true in all consistent legal instances does not always work, because, in the presence of functional dependencies, most likely there won't be any consistent legal instances (see Example 13). Nevertheless, this alternative direction is studied in [57].

Except for strange cases -that we will exclude- where the set of ICs is *non generic* [11], i.e. it entails by itself (independently from the data) that a ground literal belong (or does not belong) to the database, the consistent answers are real answers. More precisely, for generic ICs, we have $Consis_{\mathcal{G}}^{IC}(Q) \subsetneqq Minimal_{\mathcal{G}}(Q)$ [10]. If $\mathcal{G}$ is consistent wrt IC, then $Consis_{\mathcal{G}}^{IC}(Q) = Minimal_{\mathcal{G}}(Q)$. The problem with non generic ICs is that they force specific data items, which may have not been in the original instance, to belong (not to belong) to every (any) repair, something that can be easily achieved without appealing to ICs. This situation is illustrated in the following example.

Example 17. (example 16 continued) Assume that, in addition to the functional dependency, IC also contains the non generic constraint $\forall x \forall y (x = a \land y = e \rightarrow R(x,y))$, saying that tuple (a,e) belongs to R. In this case, there is only one repair for $\mathcal{G}_1$, namely $D^3 = \{(a,e),(c,d),(d,e)\}$. Now, $Consis_{\mathcal{G}_1}^{IC}(Q) = \{(a,e),(c,d),(d,e)\} \not\subseteq Minimal_{\mathcal{G}_1}(Q)$. □

Having defined what a consistent answer is, we need to find mechanisms for computing them.

7 Logic Programming Specification of Minimal Instances

In this section we will show how to specify the minimal instances of a virtual integration system under LAV using logic programs with stable model semantics [41, 42]. This specification is -as we will see- interesting and useful in itself, but in Section 8 it will also be used as the basis for computing consistent answers to queries.

7.1   The Simple Specification

We will start by giving a preliminary version of the specification program. This version is simpler to explain than the general, definitive one, and already contains the key ideas.

Example 18. (example 7 continued) It is easy to verify that the class of minimal instances for the system is $Mininst(\mathcal{G}) = \{\{P(a, c), P(a, z), R(z, b)\} \mid z \in \mathcal{D}\}$. Now, the set $\mathcal{V}^{-1}$ of inverse rules is

$$P(X, f(X, Z)) \leftarrow V_1(X, Z)$$
$$R(f(X, Z), Z) \leftarrow V_1(X, Z)$$
$$P(X, Y) \leftarrow V_2(X, Y).$$

Inspired by these inverse rules, we give the following specification program $\Pi(\mathcal{G}_2)$:

- Facts: $dom(a)$, $dom(b)$, $dom(c)$, $\ldots, V_1(a, b)$, $V_2(a, c)$.
- $P(X, Y) \leftarrow V_1(X, Z), F_1^Y(X, Z, Y),$
  $R(Y, Z) \leftarrow V_1(X, Z), F_1^Y(X, Z, Y),$
  $P(X, Y) \leftarrow V_2(X, Y).$
- $F_1^Y(X, Z, Y) \leftarrow V_1(X, Z), dom(Y), choice((X, Z), (Y)).$

Here, $dom(x)$ is a domain predicate with elements in $\mathcal{D}$, F_1^Y is a predicate corresponding to view V_1 and the existential variable Y in its definition; and $choice((X, Z), (Y))$ is the choice operator introduced in [39], which non-determin-istically chooses a unique value for Y for each combination of values in (X, Z). In this way, the functional dependency $X, Z \rightarrow Y$ is enforced; and inclusion of redundant tuples in the global instances is (partly) avoided.

A program with choice Π can be always transformed into a normal program, $SV(\Pi)$ [39] with stable model semantics [40]. The so-called *choice models* of the original program Π are in one-to-one correspondence with the stable models of its *stable version* $SV(\Pi)$.

In our example, the stable models of $SV(\Pi(\mathcal{G}_2))$ are

$$\mathcal{M}_a = \{dom(a), \ldots, V_1(a, b), V_2(a, c), P(a, c), R(a, b), P(a, a)\};$$
$$\mathcal{M}_b = \{dom(a), \ldots, V_1(a, b), V_2(a, c), P(a, c), R(b, b), P(a, b)\};$$
$$\mathcal{M}_c = \{dom(a), \ldots, V_1(a, b), V_2(a, c), P(a, c), R(c, b)\}; \text{ etc.}$$

Here we show only their relevant parts, skipping domain atoms, and atoms containing the F_1 predicate. In this example we find a one-to-one correspondence between the models of $\Pi(\mathcal{G}_2)$ and the minimal instances of $\mathcal{G}_2$.   □

More generally, the preliminary version of the specification contains the following elements:

1. Facts: $dom(a)$ for every constant $a \in \mathcal{D}$, and $V_i(\bar{a})$ whenever $\bar{a} \in v_i$ for a source extension v_i in $\mathcal{G}$.

2. For every view (source) predicate V_i with definition $V_i(\bar{X}) \leftarrow P_1(\bar{X}_1), \ldots,$ $P_n(\bar{X}_n)$, the rule

$$P_j(\bar{X}_j) \leftarrow V_i(\bar{X}), \bigwedge_{X_l \in (\bar{X}_j \setminus \bar{X})} F_i^{X_l}(\bar{X}, X_l).$$

3. For every predicate $F_i^{X_l}(\bar{X}, X_l)$ introduced in 2., the rule

$$F_i^{X_l}(\bar{X}, X_l) \leftarrow V_i(\bar{X}), dom(X_l), choice((\bar{X}), (X_l)).$$

It can be proved [16] that

$$Mininst(\mathcal{G}) \subseteq \text{ class of stable models of } SV(\Pi(\mathcal{G})) \subseteq Legal(\mathcal{G}). \qquad (4)$$

Queries expressed as logic programs can be answered by running them together with $\Pi(\mathcal{G})$ under the cautious stable model semantics (that sanctions as true what is true of all stable models). As a consequence of (4) we obtain that for monotone queries Q the answers obtained using $\Pi(\mathcal{G})$ coincide with $Certain_{\mathcal{G}}(Q)$ and $Minimal_{\mathcal{G}}(Q)$.

The inclusions in (4) suggest that equality may not be achieved. The following example shows that that is the case.

Example 19. Let $\mathcal{D} = \{a, b, c, \ldots\}$ be the underlying domain. The system $\mathcal{G}_3$ is defined by

$$V_1(X) \leftarrow P(X, Y); \qquad v_1 = \{a\}$$
$$V_2(X, Y) \leftarrow P(X, Y); \qquad v_2 = \{(a, c)\}.$$

Here we have $Mininst(\mathcal{G}_3) = \{\{P(a, c)\}\}$, however, the legal global instances corresponding to stable models of $\Pi(\mathcal{G}_3)$ are of the form $\{\{P(a, c), P(a, z)\} \mid z \in \mathcal{D}\}$, that is, we obtain from the program more legal instances (or stable models) than the minimal instances. The reason is that V_2, being open, forces $P(a, c)$ to be in all legal instances, what makes the same condition on V_1 being automatically satisfied, i.e. no other values for Y are needed. Nevertheless, the choice operator, as used above, may still choose, and it does, other values $z \in \mathcal{D}$.

As mentioned before, the simple version of the specification program for this system -even not being sound as a specification of the class of minimal instances- can be used to correctly compute minimal and certain answers to monotone queries. For instance, consider the following monotonic queries containing comparisons

$$Ans \leftarrow P(X, Y), Y \neq c \qquad (5)$$
$$Ans(Y) \leftarrow P(a, Y), Y \neq c. \qquad (6)$$

The boolean query (5) has answer *false* in the class $\{\{P(a, c), P(a, z)\} \mid z \in \mathcal{D}\}$, because it is not true of all the instances in it. Query (6) has empty answer in the same class. In the minimal instance $\{P(a, c)\}$, the queries have answer *false*, and $\emptyset$, respectively. We can see that these queries are correctly answered. $\square$

At this point we could compare what can be obtained using the simple spec-ification of minimal instances and what could we obtain by trying to use the inverse rules algorithm. Notice that the latter algorithm does not consider com-parisons other than equalities [30]. The inverse rules can be seen as defining a sort of generic, symbolic instance, which is obtained by propagating the source contents through the inverses rules (from the bodies to the heads in them) and the function symbols.

For example, the set $\mathcal{V}^{-1}$ of inverse rules for the system in Example 19 consists of $P(X, f(X)) \leftarrow V_1(X)$ and $P(X, Y) \leftarrow V_2(X, Y)$. If we propagate the values in the sources, we obtain a "generic instance" containing f-values, namely

$$D_f = \{P(a, c), P(a, f(a))\}, \tag{7}$$

that represents a family of legal instances, each of which can be obtained by interpreting f on the underlying domain $\mathcal{D}$. Basically, this class coincides with the class we obtained using the program above (and then it represents a superset of the minimal instances, but a subset of the legal instances). A difference is that with the specification program we obtain the instances explicitly.

If we attempt to use "instance" (7) to evaluate the queries (5) and (6) (this is the idea behind the IRA for conjunctive, built-in free queries in [30]), we obtain, assuming that $f(a)$ is different from c because they are syntactically different, that the answer to (5) is $Ans = true$, whereas query (6) gets the answer $Ans = \{f(a)\}$, which, after elimination of the f-value, becomes $Ans = \emptyset$.

The problem with this methodology for query answering based on generic instances with functional values we just attempted, is that it does not capture the minimal instances, actually the only minimal instance $\{P(a, c)\}$ is missed by the assumption that $f(a) \neq c$. In order to make this approach work, we would have to consider alternative values for function f. Our explicit approach based on the choice operator achieves this, and can be naturally extended -as we will do in Section 7.2- in such a way that not only monotonic queries, but also non monotonic queries containing negation, can be handled correctly (the latter, wrt the minimal answer semantics).

Example 20. (example 19 continued) Assume $\mathcal{G}_3$ is extended with the source definition $V_3(X, Y) \leftarrow R(X, Y)$; $v_3 = \{(a, c)\}$. Then, the minimal instance is $\{\{P(a, c), R(a, c)\}\}$, and the instances obtained from the program are $\{\{P(a, c), P(a, z), R(a, c)\} \mid z \in \mathcal{D}\}$. Now the query

$$Ans \leftarrow P(X, Y), \ not \ R(X, Y) \tag{8}$$

has answer *false* both in the minimal instance and in the class of the instances obtained from the specification program. In the later case, in the sense that the query is not true in all the models of the program. That is, also in this case the simple specification is giving us the right minimal answers.

On the other side, the same query evaluated in the new IRA-induced, generic instance $D_f = \{P(a, c), P(a, f(a)), R(a, c)\}$ has answer *true* if the functional term is assumed to be different from c.   □

This example shows that even for some non monotonic queries, the simple specification program returns the correct minimal answers. It is an interesting open problem to characterize the class of system descriptions and non monotonic queries for which the simple specification returns the correct minimal answers (however, see [16] for some results in this direction). On the other side, a naive application of the IRA to a query containing negation, as (8), does not give the correct answer.

It is a natural question as to whether the program with Skolem functions introduced by IRA (as in [30]) could be used, instead of the functional predicates, for specifying the repairs, pruning at the end the ground functional terms when queries are answered. In [16] it is shown -and this applies to both the simple and refined version of the specification program- that doing so does not necessarily capture the repairs of the system. The intuitive reason behind is that using the function symbols may prevent us from detecting violations to the ICs by the minimal instances. Actually, as Examples 19 and 20 already show, keeping the functional symbols may fail to properly capture the minimal instances, which is a problem when queries with negations or comparisons are to be answered.

In this work, when we answer non monotone queries, we are interested in the minimal answers. Actually, the consistent answers as defined here are a subset of the minimal answers (see Section 6). Wrt to the certain answers to non monotone queries, we can see that negated sub-queries can always be made false by adding extra data to the legal instances of an integration system with *open* sources. We believe that the notion of minimal answer to a non monotone query posed to an open system is the natural notion to use[4], instead of the notion of certain answer.

7.2   The Refined Specification

If we want $\Pi(\mathcal{G})$ to specify only the minimal instances, then the program has to be refined. The new version $\Pi(\mathcal{G})$ detects in which cases it is necessary to use the function predicates. This is achieved by means of a stronger condition, $add_{V_i}(\bar{X})$, in the choice rules, i.e. $F_i^{X_l}(\bar{X}, X_l) \leftarrow add_{V_i}(\bar{X}), dom(X_l), choice((\bar{X}), (X_l))$, where $add_{V_i}(\bar{X})$ is true only when the openness of V_i is not satisfied through other views; and this can be further specified by means of extra rules. The general refined version is described and analyzed in detail in [16]. For it, the class of stable models of the program provably coincides with the minimal instances. In consequence, the program can be used to compute minimal answers to arbitrary queries and certain answers to monotone queries.

The refined version of the program uses annotation constants to be placed in an extra argument added to the global relations. Their intended semantics is given in Table 2. Annotation t_d is used to read off the atoms in the minimal instances. The others are annotations that are used to compute intermediate atoms. We illustrate the refined version by means of an example.

---

[4] Assuming, as we have done in this chapter, that the sources are defined as conjunctive views or disjunctions thereof. In particular, they are defined without negation.

Table 2. Semantic of Annotation Constants for Minimal Models

annotation	atom	the tuple $P(\bar{a})$ is ...
$\mathbf{t_d}$	$P(\bar{a}, \mathbf{t_d})$	an atom of the minimal legal instances
$\mathbf{o}$	$P(\bar{a}, \mathbf{o})$	an obligatory atom in all the minimal legal instances
$\mathbf{v_i}$	$P(\bar{a}, \mathbf{v_i})$	an optional atom introduced to satisfy the openness of view V_i
$\mathbf{nv_i}$	$P(\bar{a}, \mathbf{nv_i})$	an optional atom introduced to satisfy the openness of a view other than V_i

Example 21. (example 19 continued) The refined program $\Pi(\mathcal{G}_3)$ is:

$$dom(a), dom(c), ..., V_1(a), V_2(a, c). \tag{9}$$

$$P(X, Y, \mathbf{v_1}) \leftarrow add_{V_1}(X), F_1^Y(X, Y). \tag{10}$$

$$add_{V_1}(X) \leftarrow V_1(X), \; not \; aux_{V_1}(X). \tag{11}$$

$$aux_{V_1}(X) \leftarrow var_{V_1, Z}(X, Z). \tag{12}$$

$$var_{V_1, Z}(X, Z) \leftarrow P(X, Z, \mathbf{nv_1}). \tag{13}$$

$$F_1^Y(X, Y) \leftarrow add_{V_1}(X), dom(Y), choice((X), (Y)). \tag{14}$$

$$P(X, Y, \mathbf{o}) \leftarrow V_2(X, Y). \tag{15}$$

$$P(X, Y, \mathbf{nv_1}) \leftarrow P(X, Y, \mathbf{o}). \tag{16}$$

$$P(X, Y, \mathbf{t_d}) \leftarrow P(X, Y, \mathbf{v_1}). \tag{17}$$

$$P(X, Y, \mathbf{t_d}) \leftarrow P(X, Y, \mathbf{o}). \tag{18}$$

Rules (10) to (13) ensure that if there is an atom in source V_1, e.g. $V_1(\bar{a})$, and if an atom of the form $P(\bar{a}, Y)$ was not added by view V_2, then it is added by rule (10) with a Y value given by the functional predicate $F_1^Y(\bar{a}, Y)$. This function predicate is calculated by rule (14). Rule (15) enforces the satisfaction of the openness of V_2 by adding obligatory atoms to predicate P, and rule (16) stores this atoms with the annotation $\mathbf{nv_1}$ implying that they were added by a view different from V_1. The last two rules gather with annotation $\mathbf{t_d}$ the elements that were generated by both views. Those are the atoms in the minimal instances.

The only stable model of this program is $\{dom(a), dom(c), \ldots, V_1(a), V_2(a, c), P(a, c, \mathbf{t_d}), P(a, c, \mathbf{o}), P(a, c, \mathbf{nv_1}), aux_{V_1}(a)\}$, which corresponds to the only minimal legal instance $\{P(a, c)\}$. $\qquad\square$

We have obtained an answer set programming specification of the minimal instances of an open integration system under LAV. From it, the minimal answers to complex queries, e.g. non stratified Datalog queries [1], can be computed using the cautions or skeptical answer set semantics that sanctions as true what is true of all stable models. Notice that the refined version (and also the simple version) of the specification program $\Pi(\mathcal{G})$ is a non stratified program, whose data complexity [1] is likely to be higher than polynomial [27]. As with the simple program, the refined program can be used to compute the certain answers to monotone queries.

It is interesting to observe that the specification $\Pi(\mathcal{G})$ we just gave can be seen as a considerable extension of the original IRA algorithm since it can be used to obtain the certain answers to monotone queries involving comparisons (see Example 19), and the minimal answers to non-monotone queries.

There are several issues and possible extensions that are discussed in detail in [16]. We briefly mention some of them here. First, we do not need to make any assumption about the underlying domain for the logic programming based specifications of minimal instances to work properly. All we need is that it -possibly properly- contains the active domains of the sources and the constants that may appear in the view definitions. However, if the program is to be run with a system like DLV, we need to have a finite number of elements in the domain. We can always simulate the potential infiniteness of the underlying domain by means of a sufficiently large finite domain [16]. This can be achieved by introducing fresh constants. This subject related to a finite vs. infinite underlying domain certainly deserves further investigation. Any case, computing with infinite stable models has started to receive attention from the answer set programming community [14].

A possible extension, also discussed in [16], consists in having views defined by disjunctions of conjunctive queries. Inspiration for the specification programs can be found in the extension of the IRA to the case of disjunctive sources [29].

We will use the specification of minimal instances as a basis for the computation of consistent answers (see Section 8). In Section 9, the specification is extended to the case where also closed sources participate in the integration system.

8 Computing Consistent Answers in Integration Systems

We will see two methodologies for consistently answering queries posed to virtual integration systems under LAV. The first one, in Section 8.1, is based on first-order query rewriting. The second one, to be presented in Section 8.2, is much more general, and provides a solution based on the specification of the repairs of the minimal instances of an open integration systems. Both methodologies eventually rely on the specification of minimal instanced presented in Section 7.

8.1   Query Rewriting for CQA

In this section we will describe a methodology, first presented in [10], that provides a partial solution to the problem of CQA under the LAV approach. It builds upon the query rewriting approach to CQA for single relational databases described in Section 5.1. The limitations of that approach are inherited by the solution for the case of integration of data sources. In consequence, this solution applies to queries Q that are conjunctions of literals, but without projection (or existential quantification); and global integrity constraints that are universal. In consequence, referential ICs are excluded.

The high level description of the rewriting based algorithm for CQA in integration system is as follows: Given as input a set IC of global integrity constraints, and global query Q that is a conjunction of literals, we do the following

Meta–Algorithm (19)

1. Rewrite $Q(\bar{X})$ into the first-order query $T^\omega(Q(\bar{X}))$ using IC.[5]
2. Transform $T^\omega(Q(\bar{X}))$ into a recursion-free Datalog$^\neg$ query program $\Pi(T^\omega (Q))$ (this is straightforward [64]).
3. Find a query plan, $Plan(\Pi(T^\omega(Q)))$ to answer the query $\Pi(T^\omega(Q))$ posed to the global system.
4. Evaluate the query plan on the view extensions of $\mathcal{G}$ to compute the answer set.

A problem with this algorithm is that the program $\Pi(T^\omega(Q))$ may contain negation, that is introduced at the first step. We give some examples.

Example 22. Consider the integration system

$$V_1(X,Y) \leftarrow P(X,Y); \qquad v_1 = \{(a,d)\}$$
$$V_2(X,Z) \leftarrow P(X,Y), R(Y,Z); \qquad v_2 = \{(a,b),(b,c)\}.$$

The minimal instances are of the form $D_{uv} = \{P(a,u), R(u,b), P(b,v), R(v,c), P(a,d)\}$, with $u,v \in \mathcal{D}$. Now consider the global IC $IC : \forall x \forall y (\neg P(x,y) \vee \neg R(x,y))$. The system is inconsistent, because the minimal instances obtained with $u = c, v = a$, i.e. $D_{ca} = \{P(a,c), R(c,b), P(b,a), R(a,c), P(a,d)\}$ is inconsistent. The same happens with D_{bb}. The other minimal instances are consistent. Then, the repairs are all the $D_{u,v}$ above, except for the last two combinations, which in their turn contribute with the repairs $D^1_{ca} = \{R(c,b), P(b,a), R(a,c), P(a,d)\}$, $D^2_{ca} = \{P(a,c), R(c,b), P(b,a), P(a,d)\}$, $D^1_{bb} = \{P(a,b), R(b,b), R(b,c), P(a,d)\}$ $D^2_{bb} = \{P(a,b), P(b,b), R(b,c), P(a,d)\}$. Now, consider the query $Q : P(X,Y)$?. The only answer to this query in common to all repairs is $\{P(a,d)\}$, then this is the only consistent answer.

On the rewriting side, if we want the consistent answers to the same query relative to IC, we rewrite the query as follows $T(Q) : (P(X,Y) \wedge \neg R(X,Y))$ (see Example 11), which produces the following query program that contains negation: $Ans(X,Y) \leftarrow P(X,Y), not\ R(X,Y)$. ☐

Example 23. (example 6 continued) *FD* can be written in the form

$$\forall x \forall y \forall z (\neg R(x,y) \vee \neg R(x,z) \vee y = z). \tag{20}$$

If the query $Q : R(X,Y)$? is posed to the system, we have to find the residues of $R(X,Y)$ wrt (20), and we obtain after the first step the rewritten query

$$T^\omega(Q(X,Y)) : R(X,Y) \wedge \neg \exists Z (R(X,Z) \wedge Z \neq Y). \tag{21}$$

---

[5] We are assuming here that $T^\omega(Q(\bar{X}))$ produces a finite formula. Conditions for this to happen in terms of Q and IC are studied in [3, 25]. However, those conditions are satisfied by the most common universal ICs found in database practice.

Query (21) is translated into the following Datalog⁻ program $\Pi(T^\omega(Q(X,Y)))$:

$$Ans(X,Y) \leftarrow R(X,Y), \; not \; S(X,Y) \tag{22}$$

$$S(X,Y) \leftarrow R(X,Z), dom(Y), Y \neq Z \tag{23}$$

$$dom(a), dom(b), dom(c), dom(d), dom(e), ... \tag{24}$$

The domain extends the *active domain* [1] that contains the constants in the sources and those that may appear in the view definitions. This is a form of materialization of a domain closure assumption, however we are not necessarily closing wrt the active domain, but wrt a superset of it that contains fresh constants. This allows us to correctly compute certain answers (see [16] for a detailed discussion of this issue). The introduction of the *dom* predicate in programs is a general way to make the rules *safe* [72]. Despite these considerations, in this example, the domain predicate is not necessary, because (21) is logically equivalent to

$$T^\omega(Q(X,Y)): \; R(X,Y) \; \wedge \; \neg\exists Z(R(X,Y) \; \wedge \; R(X,Z) \; \wedge \; Z \neq Y).$$

In consequence, program $\Pi(T^\omega(Q(X,Y)))$ can be written as the set of safe rules $Ans(X,Y) \leftarrow R(X,Y), \; not \; S(X,Y)$ and $S(X,Y) \leftarrow R(X,Y), R(X,Z), Y \neq Z$.

At step 3. of algorithm (19), we need a query plan to answer the query expressed by (22)-(24). As we can see, the query contains negation and comparisons. □

Algorithms like IRA are designed to deal with negation-free queries without comparisons [30]. On the other side, $\Pi(T^\omega(Q))$ does not contain recursion but contains negation. In consequence, an algorithm like IRA, if it is going to be applied in this context, has to be extended in order to handle queries that are, e.g. non recursive Datalog programs with negation and comparisons.

Some very limited extensions of the IRA algorithm have been proposed in order to include negation [10, 74, 35]. However, we can use our specification of the minimal instances (see Section 7) as a general query plan mechanism for eventually computing consistent answers to queries. In Algorithm (19) that specification can be used in the third step. All one needs to do is combine the query obtained after the second step (with its predicates expanded with a new, final argument with the annotation $\mathbf{t_d}$ in it) with the specification of the minimal instances. The combined program is run under the cautions stable model semantics.

Example 24. (example 22 continued)   The query $Ans(X,Y) \leftarrow P(X,Y),$ $not \; R(X,Y)$ has to be combined with the specification of the minimal instances of the integration system, which is essentially the same as the one given in Example 18. If we want or need[6] to use the refined version of the specification of minimal instances, then the query has to be first transformed into $Ans(X,Y) \leftarrow P(X,Y,\mathbf{t_d}), \; not \; R(X,Y,\mathbf{t_d})$. □

---

[6] In this example this is not necessary, because the simple program correctly specifies the class of minimal instances. In [16] sufficient conditions are identified for this to happen.

8.2   CQA from Specifications of Repairs

A more general methodology that the one presented in Section 8.1 is based on a logic programming specifications of the repairs of the minimal instances of an integration system. First results were presented in [15], and full details can be found in [16]. This methodology works for queries expressed in extensions of Datalog, in particular, for first-order queries; and universal ICs combined with acyclic sets of referential ICs. In the rest of this section, we will assume that sources are open, and defined as conjunctive views over the global schema. However the solution can be extended to combinations of closed and open sources (see Section 9), and views defined as disjunctions of conjunctive queries [16].

Figure 2 describes the methodology in general terms. In order to compute the consistent answer to a global query, the query is expressed as a query program, which is run in combination with other programs that specifies, in two layers, the minimal instances of the integration systems, first, and then, the repairs of the minimal instances. Of course, the same specification program can be used with different queries. The specification of minimal instances is the one presented in Section 7.

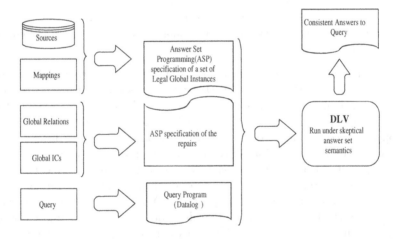

Fig. 2. Computing Consistent Answers

What we have so far is a specification of minimal instances of an open integration system, but they may not satisfy certain global ICs. In consequence, we may consider specifying their repairs wrt those ICs. For this we can apply the ideas and techniques developed to specify repairs of single databases (Section 5). Actually, we can combine into a repair program, $\Pi(\mathcal{G}, IC)$, the program that specifies the minimal instances with a program that specifies the repairs of each minimal instance. This is because a minimal instance can be seen as (or is) a single database instance. Instead of a full treatment (see [16]), we give an example.

Example 25. (example 21 continued) Consider system $\mathcal{G}_3$, but now with the global integrity constraint Sym: $\forall x \forall y (P(x,y) \rightarrow P(y,x))$. Since $Mininst(\mathcal{G}_3) = \{\{P(a,c)\}\}$, an the only instance does not satisfy Sym, the system is inconsistent.

The repair program, $\Pi(\mathcal{G}_3, Sym)$, consists of two layers. The first one is exactly program $\Pi(\mathcal{G}_3)$ in Example 21 that specifies the minimal instances; and the second layer is the following subprogram that repairs the minimal instances; it builds on the atoms annotated with $\mathbf{t_d}$ in the first layer:

$$P(X,Y,\mathbf{t^\star}) \leftarrow P(X,Y,\mathbf{t_a}), dom(X), dom(Y).$$
$$P(X,Y,\mathbf{t^\star}) \leftarrow P(X,Y,\mathbf{t_d}), dom(X), dom(Y).$$
$$P(X,Y,\mathbf{f^\star}) \leftarrow dom(X), dom(Y), \; not \; P(X,Y,\mathbf{t_d}).$$
$$P(X,Y,\mathbf{f^\star}) \leftarrow P(X,Y,\mathbf{f_a}), dom(X), dom(Y).$$
$$P(X,Y,\mathbf{f_a}) \vee P(Y,X,\mathbf{t_a}) \leftarrow P(X,Y,\mathbf{t^\star}), P(Y,X,\mathbf{f^\star}), dom(X), dom(Y).$$
$$P(X,Y,\mathbf{t^{\star\star}}) \leftarrow P(X,Y,\mathbf{t_a}), dom(X), dom(Y).$$
$$P(X,Y,\mathbf{t^{\star\star}}) \leftarrow P(X,Y,\mathbf{t_d}), dom(X), dom(Y), \; not \; P(X,Y,\mathbf{f_a}).$$
$$P(X,Y,\mathbf{f^{\star\star}}) \leftarrow P(X,Y,\mathbf{f_a}), dom(X), dom(Y).$$
$$P(X,Y,\mathbf{f^{\star\star}}) \leftarrow dom(X), dom(Y), \; not \; P(X,Y,\mathbf{t_d}),$$
$$\qquad not \; P(X,Y,\mathbf{t_a}).$$
$$\leftarrow P(X,Y,\mathbf{t_a}), P(X,Y,\mathbf{f_a}).$$

The stable models of this program are:

$$\mathcal{M}_1 = \{dom(a), \; dom(c), \ldots, \; V_1(a), \; V_2(a,c), \; P(a,c,\mathbf{nv_1}), \; P(a,c,\mathbf{v_2}),$$
$$P(a,c,\mathbf{t_d}), \; P(a,c,\mathbf{t^\star}), \; aux_{V_1}(a), \; P(a,a,\mathbf{f^\star}), \; P(c,a,\mathbf{f^\star}), \; P(c,c,\mathbf{f^\star}),$$
$$P(a,a,\mathbf{f^{\star\star}}), \qquad P(c,a,\mathbf{t_a}), \qquad P(c,c,\mathbf{f^{\star\star}}), \qquad \underline{P(a,c,\mathbf{t^{\star\star}})}, P(c,a,\mathbf{t^\star}),$$
$$\underline{P(c,a,\mathbf{t^{\star\star}})}\}.$$

$$\mathcal{M}_2 = \{dom(a), \; dom(c), \ldots, \; V_1(a), \; V_2(a,c), \; P(a,c,\mathbf{nv_1}), \; P(a,c,\mathbf{v_2}),$$
$$P(a,c,\mathbf{t_d}), \; P(a,c,\mathbf{t^\star}), \; aux_{V_1}(a), \; P(a,a,\mathbf{f^\star}), \; P(c,a,\mathbf{f^\star}), \; P(a,c,\mathbf{f^\star}),$$
$$P(c,c,\mathbf{f^\star}), \qquad P(a,a,\mathbf{f^{\star\star}}), \qquad P(c,a,\mathbf{f^{\star\star}}), \qquad P(a,c,\mathbf{f^{\star\star}}), \qquad P(c,c,\mathbf{f^{\star\star}}),$$
$$P(a,c,\mathbf{f_a})\}.$$

By reading the literals annotated with $\mathbf{t^{\star\star}}$, we see that the first model corresponds to the repair $\{P(a,c), P(c,a)\}$; the second one, to the empty repair. $\square$

Repair programs can be given for specifying the repairs of any open integration system under the LAV approach with conjunctive view definitions; and for any set of ICs containing universal and acyclic referential integrity constraints [15, 16].

The restriction to sets of ICs that do not contain cycles in its referential ICs has to do with limitations of the logic programming based approach to the specification of repairs of single relational databases as presented in Section 5. Fundamental, theoretical reasons behind these limitations, that are inherited by our repair programs for integration systems, are studied in depth in [26, 20, 38].

With the repair programs, we can now compute consistent answers to global queries. Let $Q(\bar{x})$ be a query posed to an integration system $\mathcal{G}$. The methodology is as follows. First the query gets its literals annotated with $\mathbf{t}^{\star\star}, \mathbf{f}^{\star\star}$, e.g. if the query is first order, say $Q(\cdots P(\bar{u}) \cdots \neg R(\bar{v}) \cdots)$, we pass to $Q' := Q(\cdots P(\bar{u}, \mathbf{t}^{\star\star}) \cdots R(\bar{v}, \mathbf{f}^{\star\star}) \cdots)$. Next, a query program $\Pi(Q')$ with an $Ans(\bar{X})$ predicate is produced from Q (this is standard [64]). Finally, the program $\Pi := \Pi(Q') \cup \Pi(\mathcal{G}, IC)$ is run under the stable model semantics; and the ground atoms $Ans(\bar{t}) \in \bigcap\{S \mid S$ is a stable model of $\Pi\}$ are collected in the answer set to be returned to the user.

Example 26. (example 25 continued) Consider $\mathcal{G}_3$ and the global query Q : $P(X, Y)$? From it we generate Q' : $P(X, Y, \mathbf{t}^{\star\star})$, which in its turn is transformed into the query program $\Pi(Q')$: $Ans(X, Y) \leftarrow P(X, Y, \mathbf{t}^{\star\star})$. Next, we form $\Pi = \Pi(\mathcal{G}_3, Sym) \cup \Pi(Q')$, with $\Pi(\mathcal{G}_3, Sym)$ as in Example 25.

Now, the models of program Π are those of $\Pi(\mathcal{G}_3, Sym)$ but extended with ground Ans atoms, namely they are: $\overline{\mathcal{M}}_1 = \mathcal{M}_1 \cup \{Ans(a, c), Ans(c, a)\}$; $\overline{\mathcal{M}}_2 = \mathcal{M}_2 \cup \emptyset$. Since there are no Ans atoms in common, then query has no consistent answers (as expected). □

Example 27. (example 16 continued) The program that computes the consistent answers to query $Q(X, Y)$: $R(X, Y)$? from system $\mathcal{G}_1$ wrt FD is:

Subprogram for minimal instances:

$dom(a). dom(b). dom(c). dom(d). dom(e). \ldots V_1(a, b). V_1(c, d). V_2(c, a). V_2(e, d).$

$$R(X, Y, \mathbf{t_d}) \leftarrow V_1(X, Y).$$
$$R(Y, X, \mathbf{t_d}) \leftarrow V_2(X, Y).$$

Repair subprogram:

$$R(X, Y, \mathbf{t}^\star) \leftarrow R(X, Y, \mathbf{t_a}), dom(X), dom(Y).$$
$$R(X, Y, \mathbf{t}^\star) \leftarrow R(X, Y, \mathbf{t_d}), dom(X), dom(Y).$$
$$R(X, Y, \mathbf{f}^\star) \leftarrow dom(X), dom(Y), \ not \ R(X, Y, \mathbf{t_d}).$$
$$R(X, Y, \mathbf{f}^\star) \leftarrow R(X, Y, \mathbf{f_a}), dom(X), dom(Y).$$
$$R(X, Y, \mathbf{f_a}) \vee R(X, Z, \mathbf{f_a}) \leftarrow R(X, Y, \mathbf{t}^\star), R(X, Z, \mathbf{t}^\star), Y \neq Z,$$
$$dom(X), dom(Y), dom(Z).$$
$$R(X, Y, \mathbf{t}^{\star\star}) \leftarrow R(X, Y, \mathbf{t_a}), dom(X), dom(Y).$$
$$R(X, Y, \mathbf{t}^{\star\star}) \leftarrow R(X, Y, \mathbf{t_d}), dom(X), dom(Y), \ not \ R(X, Y, \mathbf{f_a}).$$
$$\leftarrow R(X, Y, \mathbf{f_a}), R(X, Y, \mathbf{t_a}).$$

Query subprogram:

$$Ans(X, Y) \leftarrow R(X, Y, \mathbf{t}^{\star\star}).$$

The Ans atom in common to the two stable models are $Ans(c,d), Ans(d,e)$, then the set of consistent answers to the query is $\{(c,d),(d,e)\}$.

Here we have used the simple version of the program that specifies the minimal instances. In this case the specification is *sound*, i.e. it does not compute any model that does not correspond to a minimal instance. Classes of system descriptions for which the simple specification has a sound behavior wrt the class of minimal instances are studied in [16]. The example here falls into one of those classes. $\square$

The specifications we have presented are sound and complete for CQA for sets of ICs consisting of universal integrity constraints and acyclic sets of referential integrity constraints [16]. Views can be defined by disjunctions of conjunctive formulas; and queries can be arbitrary Datalog¬ queries.

9   Specification of Minimal Instances: Mixed Case

So far we have assumed that all the sources are open. Now we will consider the *mixed case*, where some of the sources may be *closed* or closed and open (*clopen*). In consequence, a virtual data integration system will have a description like the one in (1), but each source will have a label indicating if it is open, closed or clopen [43]. Intuitively speaking, a closed source contains a superset of the data of its kind in the system, and the clopen source contains exactly all the data of its kind in the system.

More precisely, if a material source relation v, defined as the view $V(\bar{X}) \leftarrow \varphi_V(\bar{X})$ of the global system, has been defined as a closed (clopen) source, then in any legal instance D, it must hold $v \supseteq \varphi_V(D)$ (resp. $v = \varphi_V(D)$).

In this section we will describe how to modify the program that specifies the minimal instances presented in Section 7 when some of the sources are declared closed or clopen.

Example 28. For the domain $\mathcal{D} = \{a,b,c,\dots\}$, consider the integration system $\mathcal{G}_4$:

$$V_1(X,Z) \leftarrow P(X,Y), R(Y,Z); \qquad v_1 = \{(a,b)\} \quad open \qquad (25)$$
$$V_2(X,Y) \leftarrow P(X,Y); \qquad v_2 = \{(a,c)\} \quad clopen \qquad (26)$$

In Example 18 we had the same sources and definitions, but then they were all declared open; and we had $Mininst(\mathcal{G}_2) = \{\{P(a,c), P(a,z), R(z,b)\} \mid z \in \mathcal{D}\}$. Now, the label on the second sources forces relation P to be $\{(a,c)\}$. In consequence, we obtain $Mininst(\mathcal{G}_4) = \{\{P(a,c), R(c,b)\}\}$. $\square$

It is clear that the closed and clopen labels will impose additional restrictions on the legal instances we had for the purely open case, when all sources are open. In particular, these labels will never force to add new tuples to the legal instances. Actually, if a source is declared closed, then that source will contribute with the empty set of tuples to the minimal instances of the integration system.

With open, closed and clopen sources, the sets of legal and minimal instances will always be subsets of the same sets for the case where the same sources are all declared open. In order to obtain the minimal instances in the mixed case, all we have to do is filter out some of the minimal instances obtained in the purely open case, namely those that violate the closedness condition for some of the sources. This can be captured at the logic program specification level by means of a program denial constraint, which has the effect of discarding some of the stable models.

In the mixed case, the program $\Pi_{mix}(\mathcal{G})$ that specifies the minimal instances consists of the program $\Pi(\mathcal{G})$ we had for the open case in Section 7 (as if all the sources were open) plus a denial constraint of the form $\leftarrow P_1(\bar{X}_1), \ldots, P_n(\bar{X}_n),\ not\ V(\bar{X})$, for each closed (or clopen) source v with view definition $V(\bar{X}) \leftarrow P_1(\bar{X}_1), \ldots, P_n(\bar{X}_n)$. That is, the open sources contribute with rules to the program, the clopen sources both with rules and program constraints, and the closed sources with program constraints only.

With these modifications, the obtain the same correspondence between the stable models of the program $\Pi_{mix}(\mathcal{G})$ and the minimal instances of the mixed integration system $\mathcal{G}$.

Example 29. (example 28 continued) The program $\Pi_{mix}(\mathcal{G}_4)$ that specifies the minimal instances of system $\mathcal{G}_4$ is:

$$dom(a).\ \ dom(b).\ \ dom(c).\ \ \ldots\ \ V_1(a,b).\ \ V_2(a,c).$$

$$P(X,Y) \leftarrow V_1(X,Z), F_1^Y(X,Z,Y)$$
$$R(Y,Z) \leftarrow V_1(X,Z), F_1^Y(X,Z,Y)$$
$$P(X,Y) \leftarrow V_2(X,Y)$$
$$F_1^Y(X,Z,Y) \leftarrow V_1(X,Z), dom(Y), choice((X,Z),(Y))$$
$$\leftarrow P(X,Y),\ not\ V_2(X,Y).$$

This program, excluding the last denial, coincides with program $\Pi(\mathcal{G}_2)$ in Example 18, where the same sources and definitions are considered, but all the sources are open only. With the denial constraint, that enforces the closeness of source V_2, the only stable model of $\Pi_{mix}(\mathcal{G}_4)$ is $\{dom(a), \ldots, V_1(a,b), V_2(a,c), P(a,c), F_1^Y(a,b,c), R(c,b)\}$, which corresponds to the only minimal instance $\overline{\{\{P(a,c), R(c,b)\}\}}$. □

Notice that the solution we have reached via logic programs is similar in spirit to the solution presented in [43], where the mixed case is treated. There tableaux with constraints are used to compactly represent the legal instances and obtain certain answers. The tableaux capture the open part, and the constraints, as in our solution, the closed part.

10   Ongoing and Future Work

There are still many relevant open issues in this line of research. Consistency issues have barely investigated in the context of virtual data integration systems. Other research results obtained by other authors in this direction are described in Section 11.

The solution to the problem of *certain and consistent query answering* in virtual data integration system under the LAV approach presented in Sections 7 and 8.2, resp. are quite general, and conceptually clear, however many implementation issues are still open. They have to be addressed in order to use those solutions in real database applications.

A first step would be to implement certain and consistent query answering for the most common queries and constraints found in database practice. Ad hoc mechanisms could be derived from the logic programming specifications. In this direction, [13] shows how to derive, for some classes of queries, first order rewritings from the logic programs that specify repairs of single databases. Of course, by complexity reasons, this is not always possible [11].

In more general terms, the research should be focused on the specialization, optimization, and evaluation of the logic programs we have presented. Specialization has to do with deriving program for particular classes of queries and constrains from the general ones, that are better behaved in terms of evaluation. Optimization has to do with producing equivalent programs that can be more easily evaluated, in particular, the interaction of the logic programming system with the underlying databases has to be optimized. Some optimizations for CQA in single databases are introduced in [7, 13].

Evaluation issues are also extremely relevant. They have to do with splitting the program, caching intermediate results, reusing previous computations, localizing computations to the relevant parts of the data sources. Answering a particular query may not require a full computation of the repairs, but only partial computation could suffice. It becomes important to detect which are the relevant portions of data [32].

Query evaluation is a crucial point. Current implementations of answer set programming are not oriented to the problem of query answering as found in databases, where open queries are usually posed and a set of answers is returned to the user. Instead, the emphasis in answer set programming has been placed on computation of (some) models, and answering ground queries. Actually, the evaluation methodology in such systems is, in general terms, based on massive grounding of the program, full computation of stable models, and recollection of atoms in the intersection of all of them. Grounding is already a problem if the program is to be grounded on the full active domain of the databases, because the ground program generated can be huge. See [31, 59] for a discussion of implementation details.

Query evaluation methodologies that are directed by the query seem to be necessary for applications in databases, in particular, the development and implementation of "magic sets" methods [1] for disjunctive logic programs under the stable model semantics is a promising area of research. Recent research has started addressing this problem [46].

Most of the research around query answering in virtual data integration systems starts from a fixed class of mappings that describe the contents of the sources. Given a class, the semantics and query answering mechanisms are provided. However, in spite of the fact that design issues of data integration systems have been studied [8, 9, 71], the analysis of the impact of particular forms of design on the syntax of the mappings and on query answering has been largely neglected. In particular, if would be interesting to investigate how the integration system is to be designed if certain restrictions on the mappings are to be satisfied. Determining what is a *good design* for a virtual data integration in terms of the query answering features of the system is something that deserves further investigation.

11   Related Work

Here we will mention only those papers that more or less explicitly consider consistency issues in virtual data integration systems. Other important papers on virtual data integration have been cited in the main body of this paper, including those that assume that certain integrity constraints hold when query plans are derived.

An early approach to virtual data integration is presented in [68]. There, operations on the relations and attributes in the sources are defined, e.g. meet, join, aggregate, add. These operators applied to a set of source databases generate a global virtual database schema. In this way, mappings are derived and express the global relations as results of a set of operations on the source relations. When a query is posed, it is translated to the sources relations by considering the operators in the inverse order in which they where applied.

In [69], a model is presented where the integration system is considered to have a real global database, and the sources are views obtained by applying projections and selections to this global database. In this framework, the possibility of having inconsistencies in the instances is considered. Inconsistency is reflected in the fact that it can be impossible for the sources to be views of this single global database instance. For example. Consider the global schema with a binary relation R with attributes A, B. Let source I have elements $\{a\}$, and source II, elements $\{b\}$, and the respective views $V_1 = \Pi_A(R)$, $V_2 = \Pi_A(R)$. In this case, there is an instance inconsistency, because even though both sources are views of the single global database and they have the same view definitions, their elements are different. In order to handle this situation, the notion of approximate answer is introduced, actually a lower bound and an upper bound are given, corresponding, respectively, to the intersection and union of all the possible answers of the rewriting of the query using the views. No complexity analysis is provided. Global integrity constraints are not considered.

In [19], the use of integrity constraints in a data integration system under the GAV approach for clopen and open sources is studied. In the clopen[7] case, the authors argue that the integration system can be seen as a single database, and therefore, the query answering process in the presence of ICs can be done appealing to the concept of repair [3] and CQA mechanisms for single databases [3, 47, 6]. If the sources are open and there are no ICs, queries can be answered by unfolding. If there are ICs, the semantic is given by the set of legal instances that satisfy both the open mappings and the integrity constraints. Their legal instances can be seen as repairs (in our sense) of the *retrieved global database* that is obtained by propagating the source elements through the mapping. Repairs admit only tuple insertions. Since [19] considers as legal those databases that satisfy the ICs, it holds that their "certain answers" correspond to our consistent answers. If there are no legal instances (in their sense), the integration system is said to be "inconsistent". In this case, tuple deletions are also needed in order to achieve consistency.

In [17] the same semantics as in [19] is consider, for GAV and open sources. There they present an algorithm for rewriting a conjunctive query [1] in order to retrieve the "certain answers" (our consistent answers). This algorithm handles foreign key constraints and assumes that the key constraints are preserved by the mapping, i.e. that the retrieved global instance will not violate the key constraints. For these integrity constraints there will always be legal instances (in their sense), and therefore the integration system is consistent. The rewritten query can be unfolded with the mapping in order to calculate their "certain answers". In [19] an implementation of this method is presented. The complexity of the rewriting is polynomial wrt data complexity.

According to the semantic considered in [17, 19], if a key constraint is not satisfied, then there is no legal instance. This is why in [57] the loosely-sound semantic (in opposition to the previous strictly-sound semantic) is introduced. Now, a database is legal if it is satisfies the integrity constraints and if there is no other database that is *better*. A database is better than another if the portion of the former that is contained in the retrieved global database is greater that the one of the latter. In this way, we have that the inconsistencies wrt foreign key constraints are solved by adding tuples to the retrieved global database, and those wrt key constraints, by deleting a minimal number of tuples from it. The global instances in this case correspond to a subclass of the repairs introduced in [10] for integration systems.

In order to compute the legal instances for the loosely-sound semantic, a Datalog¬ program under cautious stable model semantics is used. This program calculates a maximal superset of the retrieved global database that satisfies the key constraints. In order to retrieve the certain answers, the query is transformed as defined in [17] and added to that program. This approach works for global relations defined by Datalog queries (and then, GAV is followed). The complexity of retrieving the "certain answers" becomes co-NP-complete.

---

[7] In several papers, instead of open, clopen and closed, the terms *sound*, *exact* and *complete* are used, resp.

Still under the GAV approach, the results in [57] were extended in [21], considering key constraints and inclusion dependencies, and also queries that are expressed as unions of conjunctive queries. For the strictly-sound semantics two cases are analyzed. In the first case, where only inclusion dependencies (IDs) are considered, the integration system cannot be "inconsistent"; so there is at least one legal database. The rewriting of a query becomes the mapping rules plus the query that is successively unfolded by rules that represent the inclusion dependencies. The second case considers the combination of key dependencies (KDs) and non-key-conflicting IDs (NKC), i.e. IDs where the target (global) relation has no key dependencies or where the target attributes are not a strict superset of the key of the target relation. The rewriting of a query is the same as in the first case plus some rules that enforce that if a global relation violates a KD, then all the tuples are an answer to the query.

For the loosely-sound semantics, the rewriting in [21] is expressed with the same Datalog¬ program presented in [57]. In order to repair wrt the IDs, this program is coupled with the query rewriting for the case of only IDs and strictly-sound semantics. The data complexity under the strictly-sound semantics for NKC integration systems is PTIME. For loosely-sound semantics, it becomes coNP-complete.

In [32] logic programs for consistent query answering in virtual integration systems are presented. The GAV approach is followed and the global relations can be defined using stratified Datalog¬ queries. The ICs considered are universal integrity constraints and the queries are expressed in non-recursive Datalog¬. The specification program is a disjunctive Datalog¬ program consisting of three hierarchically evaluated modules. The first one uses the mapping and the data sources to compute the "retrieved global database" (as in [19]). The second one enforces the satisfaction of the integrity constraints through repair rules; and the third one corresponds to the query. The structure of each of them depends on the mappings, ICs and query, respectively.

The source of complexity for the program in [32] comes from the second module. In consequence, optimizations are introduced. The optimization process consists of three steps: pruning the rules that are not relevant for computing the answers to the query, next determining and computing the set of facts that need to be repaired, and finally, recombining the repairs in order to compute the answers. The second step decomposes the facts in two sets, those that might be repaired and those that for sure are not going to be repaired. The recombination process presents the repairs in a compact way in order to query them as a relational database. For this, an extra attribute marking each fact is added to each relation. This attribute is a string of zeros and ones. A one (zero) in position i means that the fact is (not) in the repair i. The facts for which no repairs are calculated in the second step are marked with '111...11'. The query needs to be reformulated in order to pose it directly to the marked database. Experiments show that the optimizations significantly improve the performance of the naive and direct techniques.

It seems that the optimizations presented in [32] can be adapted to the logic programs we have presented for CQA.

Finally, we will just mention that there seem to be interesting connections between the area of consistently querying virtual data integration systems and other areas, like querying incomplete databases [66, 44], merging inconsistent theories [63, 5], semantic reconciliation of data [54], schema mapping [71, 28, 70], data exchange [33, 34], and query answering in peer-to-peer systems [55, 52, 53, 36, 12, 24].

Acknowledgements: This chapter reports on research funded by DIPUC, CON-ICYT, FONDECYT, Carleton University Start-Up Grant 9364-01, NSERC Grant 250279-02, CoLogNet. L. Bertossi is Faculty Fellow of the IBM Center for Advanced Studies, Toronto Lab. We are grateful to Jan Chomicki, Alvaro Cortes, Claudio Gutierrez, Alberto Mendelzon, Pablo Barcelo, Alon Halevy, Enrico Franconi, Andrei Lopatenko, Ariel Fuxman, and Giuseppe De Giacomo for collaboration, useful conversations and remarks. Comments received from anonymous referees are highly appreciated.

References

1. Abiteboul, S.; Hull, R. and Vianu, V. *Foundations of Databases.* Addison-Wesley, 1995.

2. Abiteboul, A. and Duschka, O. Complexity of Answering Queries Using Materialized Views. In *Proc. ACM Symposium on Principles of Database Systems (PODS 98)*, 1998, pp. 254-263.

3. Arenas, M., Bertossi, L. and Chomicki, J. Consistent Query Answers in Inconsistent Databases. In *Proc. 18th ACM Symposium on Principles of Database Systems (PODS 99)*, 1999, pp. 68–79.

4. Arenas, M., Bertossi, L. and Chomicki, L. Answer Sets for Consistent Query Answering in Inconsistent Databases. *Theory and Practice of Logic Programming*, 2003, 3(4-5): 393-424.

5. Baral, C., Kraus, S., Minker, J. and Subrahmanian, V. S. Combining Knowledge Bases Consisting of First-Order Theories. *Computational Intelligence*, 1992, 8:45-71.

6. Barcelo, P. and Bertossi, L. Logic Programs for Querying Inconsistent Databases. In *Proc. International Symposium on Practical Aspects of Declarative Languages (PADL 03)*, Springer LNCS 2562, 2003, pp. 208–222.

7. Barcelo, P., Bertossi, L. and Bravo, L. Characterizing and Computing Semantically Correct Answers from Databases with Annotated Logic and Answer Sets. Chapter in book *Semantics of Databases*, Springer LNCS 2582, 2003, pp. 1–27.

8. Batini, C., Lenzerini, M. and Navathe, S.B. A Comparative Analysis of Methodologies for Database Schema Integration. *ACM Computing Surveys*, 1986, 18(4): 323-364.

9. Bergamaschi, S., Castano, S., Vincini, M., and Beneventano, D. Semantic Integration of Heterogeneous Information Sources. *Data and Knowledge Engineering*, 2001, 36(3):215-249.

10. Bertossi, L., Chomicki, J., Cortes, A. and Gutierrez, C. Consistent Answers from Integrated Data Sources. In *Flexible Query Answering Systems*, Springer LNAI 2522, 2002, pp. 71–85.

11. Bertossi, L. and Chomicki, J. Query Answering in Inconsistent Databases. Chapter in book *Logics for Emerging Applications of Databases*, J. Chomicki, G. Saake and R. van der Meyden (eds.), Springer, 2003.

12. Bertossi, L. and Bravo, L. Query Answering in Peer-to-Peer Data Exchange Systems. arXiv.org paper cs.DB/0401015. To appear in *Proc. International Workshop on Peer-to-Peer Computing & DataBases (P2P&DB 04)*, Springer LNCS.

13. Bertossi, L. and Bravo, L. In preparation.

14. Bonatti, P. Reasoning with Infinite Stable Models. *Artificial Intelligence*, 2004, 156(1):75-111.

15. Bravo, L. and Bertossi, L. Logic Programs for Consistently Querying Data Integration Systems. In *Proc. International Joint Conference on Artificial Intelligence (IJCAI 03)*, Morgan Kaufmann, 2003, pp. 10–15.

16. Bravo, L. and Bertossi, L. Disjunctive Deductive Databases for Computing Certain and Consistent Answers to Queries from Mediated Data Integration Systems. To appear in Journal of Applied Logic (extended version of [15])

17. Cali, A., Calvanese, D., De Giacomo, G. and Lenzerini, M. Data Integration Under Integrity Constraints. In *Proc. Conference on Advanced Information Systems Engineering (CAISE 02)*, Springer LNCS 2348, 2002, pp. 262–279.

18. Cali, A., Calvanese, D., De Giacomo, G. and Lenzerini, M. On the Expressive Power of Data Integration Systems. In *Proc. of the International Conference on Conceptual Modeling (ER 02)*, Springer LNCS 2503, 2002, pp. 338–350.

19. Cali, A., Calvanese, D., De Giacomo, G. and Lenzerini, M. On the Role of Integrity Constraints in Data Integration. *IEEE Data Engineering Bulletin*, 2002, 25(3): 39-45.

20. Cali, A., Lembo, D. and Rosati, R. On the Decidability and Complexity of Query Answering over Inconsistent and Incomplete Databases. In *Proc. of the ACM Symposium on Principles of Database Systems (PODS 03)*, ACM Press, 2003, pp. 260-271.

21. Cali, A., Lembo, D. and Rosati, R. Query Rewriting and Answering under Constraints in Data Integration Systems. In *Proc. of the International Joint Conference on Artificial Intellience (IJCAI 03)*, Morgan Kaufmann, 2003, pp. 16-21.

22. Calvanese, D., De Giacomo, G., Lenzerini, M., and Vardi, M. Y. What is Query Rewriting? In *Proc. of the International Workshop on Knowledge Representation meets Databases (KRDB 00)*, CEUR Electronic Workshop Proceedings, 2000, pp. 17-27.

23. Calvanese, D., De Giacomo, G., Lenzerini, M., and Vardi, M. Y. View-based Query Containment. In *Proc. of the ACM Symposium on Principles of Database Systems (PODS 03)*, ACM Press, 2003, pp. 56–67.

24. Calvanese, D., De Giacomo, G., Lenzerini, M. and Rosati, R. Logical Foundations of Peer-To-Peer Data Integration. In *Proc. of the ACM Symposium on Principles of Database Systems (PODS 04)*, ACM Press, 2004, pp. 241-251.

25. Celle, A. and Bertossi, L. Querying Inconsistent Databases: Algorithms and Implementation. In *Computational Logic - CL 2000, Stream: International Conference on Rules and Objects in Databases (DOOD 00)*, Springer LNAI 1861, 2000, pp. 942-956.

26. Chomicki, J. and Marcinkowski, J. Minimal-Change Integrity Maintenance Using Tuple Deletions. arXiv.org paper cs.DB/0212004. To appear in *Information and Computation*.

27. Dantsin, E., Eiter, T., Gottlob, G. and Voronkov, A. Complexity And Expressive Power Of Logic Programming. *ACM Computer Surveys*, 2001, 33(3):374-425.

28. Doan, A., Domingos, P. and Halevy, A. Learning to Match the Schemas of Data Sources: A Multistrategy Approach. *Machine Learning*, 2003, 50(3): 279-301.
29. Duschka, O. Query Planning and Optimization in Information Integration. PhD Thesis, Stanford University, December 1997.
30. Duschka, O., Genesereth, M. and Levy, A. Recursive Query Plans for Data Integration. *Journal of Logic Programming*, 2000, 43(1):49-73.
31. Eiter, T., Faber, W.; Leone, N. and Pfeifer, G. Declarative Problem-Solving in DLV. Chapter in book *Logic-Based Artificial Intelligence*, J. Minker (ed.), Kluwer, 2000, pp. 79-103.
32. Eiter, T., Fink, M., Greco, G. and Lembo, D. Efficient Evaluation of Logic Programs for Querying Data Integration Systems. In *Proc. International Conference on Logic Programming (ICLP 03)*, Springer LNCS 2916, 2003, pp. 163-177.
33. Fagin, R., Kolaitis, P., Miller, R. and Popa, L. Data Exchange: Semantics and Query Answering. In *Proc. Int. Conf on Database Theory (ICDT 03)*, Springer LNCS 2572, 2003, pp. 207-224.
34. Fagin, R., Kolaitis, P. and Popa, L. Data Exchange: Getting to the Core. In *Proc. of the ACM Symposium on Principles of Database Systems (PODS 03)*, ACM Press, 2003, pp. 90-101.
35. Flesca, S. and Greco, S. Rewriting Queries Using Views. *Transactions on Knowledge and Data Engineering*, 2001, 13(6): 980-995.
36. Franconi, E., Kuper, G., Lopatenko, L., Serafini, L. A Robust Logical and Computational Characterisation of Peer-to-Peer Database Systems. In *Proc. International Workshop on Databases, Information Systems and Peer-to-Peer Computing (DBISP2P 03)*, Springer LNCS 2944, 2004, pp. 64-76.
37. Friedman, M., Levy, A. and Millstein, T. Navigational Plans for Data Integration. In *Proc. National Conference on Artificial Intelligence (AAAI 99)*, AAAI Press, 1999, pp. 67-73.
38. Fuxman, A. and Miller, R.J. Towards Inconsistency Management in Data Integration Systems. In *Proceedings of the IJCAI-03 Workshop on Information Integration on the Web*.
39. Giannotti, F., Pedreschi, D., Sacca, D. and Zaniolo, C. Non-Determinism in Deductive Databases. In *Proc. International Conference on Deductive and Object-Oriented Databases (DOOD 91)*, Springer LNCS 566, 1991, pp. 129–146.
40. Gelfond, M. and Lifschitz, V. The Stable Model Semantics for Logic Programming. In *Logic Programming, Proceedings of the Fifth International Conference and Symposium (ICLP/SLP 88)*, MIT Press, 1988, pp. 1070-1080.
41. Gelfond, M. and Lifschitz, V. Classical Negation in Logic Programs and Disjunctive Databases. *New Generation Computing*, 1991, 9:365–385.
42. Gelfond, M. and Leone, N. Logic Programming and Knowledge Representation - The A-Prolog Perspective. *Artificial Intelligence*, 2002, 138(1-2):3-38.
43. Grahne, G. and Mendelzon, A. Tableau Techniques for Querying Information Sources through Global Schemas. In *Proc. of the International Conference on Database Theory (ICDT 99)*, Springer LNCS 1540, 1999, pp. 332–347.
44. Grahne, G. Information Integration and Incomplete Information. *IEEE Computer Society Bulletin on Data Engineering*, September 2002, pp. 46-52.
45. Grant, J. and Minker, M. A Logic-based Approach to Data Integration. *Theory and Practice of Logic Programming*, 2002, 2(3):323-368.
46. Greco, S. Binding Propagation Techniques for the Optimization of Bound Disjunctive Queries. *IEEE Transactions on Knowledge and Data Engineering*, 2003, 15(2):368-385.

47. Greco, G., Greco, S. and Zumpano, E. A Logical Framework for Querying and Repairing Inconsistent Databases. *IEEE Transactions on Knowledge and Data Engineering*, 2003, 15(6):1389-1408.

48. Gryz, J. Query Rewriting Using Views in the Presence of Functional and Inclusion Dependencies. *Information Systems*, 1999, 24(7):597–612.

49. Gupta, A. and Singh Mumick, I. (eds.) *Materialized Views: Techniques, Implementations, and Applications.* MIT Press, 1999.

50. Halevy, A.Y. Theory of Answering Queries Using Views. *SIGMOD Record*, 2000, 29(4) 40-47.

51. Halevy, A.Y. Answering Queries Using Views: A Survey. *VLDB Journal*, 2001, 10(4): 270-294.

52. Halevy, A., Ives, Z., Suciu, D. and Tatarinov, I. Schema Mediation in Peer Data Management Systems. In *Proc. of the International Conference on Data Engineering (ICDE 03)*, IEEE Computer Society, 2003, pp. 505-518.

53. Halevy, A.Y. Corpus-Based Knowledge Representation. In *Proc. International Joint Conference on Artificial Intelligence (IJCAI 03)*, Morgan Kaufmann, 2003, pp. 1567-1572.

54. Hull, R. Managing Semantic Heterogeneity in Databases: A Theoretical Perspective. In *Proc. of the ACM Symposium on Principles of Database Systems (PODS 97)*, ACM Press, 1997, pp. 51-61.

55. Kementsietsidis, A., Arenas, M. and Miller, R.J. Mapping Data in Peer-to-Peer Systems: Semantics and Algorithmic Issues. In *Proc. of the ACM International Conference on Management of Data (SIGMOD 03)*, ACM Press, 2003, pp. 325-336.

56. Kolaitis, Ph. and Vardi, M. Conjunctive-Query Containment and Constraint Satisfaction. *J. Computer and Systems Sciences*, 2000, 61(2): 302-332.

57. Lembo, D., Lenzerini, M. and Rosati, R. Source Inconsistency and Incompleteness in Data Integration. In *Proc. International Workshop Knowledge Representation meets Databases (KRDB 02)*, CEUR Electronic Workshop Proceedings, 2002.

58. Lenzerini, M. Data Integration: A Theoretical Perspective. In *Proc. ACM Symposium on Principles of Database Systems (PODS 02)*, ACM Press, 2002, pp. 233-246.

59. Leone, N. et al. The DLV System for Konwledge Representation and Reasoning. arXiv.org paper cs.LO/0211004. To appear in *ACM Transactions on Computational Logic*.

60. Levy, A.Y., Mendelzon, A., Sagiv, Y. and Srivastava, D. Answering Queries Using Views. In *Proceedings of the ACM Symposium on Principles of Database Systems (PODS 95)*, ACM Press, 1995, pp. 95-104.

61. Levy, A., Rajaraman, A. and Ordille, J. Querying Heterogeneous Information Sources using Source Descriptions. In *Proc. International Conference on Very Large Databases (VLDB 96)*, Morgan Kaufmann, 1996, pp. 251–262.

62. Levy, A. Logic-Based Techniques in Data Integration. Chapter in *Logic Based Artificial Intelligence*, J. Minker (ed.), Kluwer Publishers, 2000.

63. Lin, J. and Mendelzon, A. Merging Databases under Constraints. *International Journal of Cooperative Information Systems*, 1996, 7(1):55-76.

64. Lloyd, J.W. *Foundations of Logic Programming.* Second ed., Springer-Verlag, 1987.

65. McBrien, P. and Poulovassilis, A. Data Integration by Bi-Directional Schema Transformation Rules. In *Proc. International Conference on Data Engineering (ICDE 03)*, IEEE Computer Society, 2003, pp. 227–238.

66. Meyden, R.v.d. Logical Approaches to Incomplete Information: A Survey. Chapter in *Logics for Databases and Information Systems*, J.Chomicki and G. Saake (eds.), Kluwer, 1998, pp. 307-356.
67. Millstein, T., Halevy, A. and Friedman, M. Query Containment for Data Integration Systems. *Journal of Computer and Systems Sciences*, 2003, 66(1): 20-39.
68. Motro A. Superviews: Virtual Integration of Multiple Databases. *IEEE Transactions on Software Engineering*, 1987, 13(7):785–798.
69. Motro A. Multiplex: A Formal Model for Multidatabases and Its Implementation. In *Proc. International Workshop on Next Generation Information Technology and Systems*, Springer LNCS 1649, 1999, pp. 138–158.
70. Pottinger, R., and Bernstein, Ph. Creating a Mediated Schema Based on Initial Correspondences. *IEEE Data Engineering Bulletin*, 2002, 25(3): 26-31.
71. Rahm, E. and Bernstein, Ph.A. A Survey of Approaches to Automatic Schema Matching. *VLDB Journal*, 2001, 10:334-350.
72. Ullman, J.D. *Principles of Database and Knowledge-Base Systems*. Computer Science Press, 1988.
73. Ullman, J.D. Information Integration Using Logical Views. *Theoretical Computer Science*, 2000, 239(2): 189-210.
74. Wei, F. and Lausen, G. Containment of Conjunctive Queries with Safe Negation. In *Proc. International Conference of Database Theory (ICDT 03)*, Springer LNCS 2572, 2003, pp. 346-360
75. Wiederhold, G. and Genesereth, M. The Conceptual Basis for Mediation Services. *IEEE Expert*, 1997, 12(5): 38-47.

Representing Paraconsistent Reasoning via Quantified Propositional Logic*

Philippe Besnard[1], Torsten Schaub[2,**], Hans Tompits[3], and Stefan Woltran[3]

[1] IRIT-CNRS,
118, route de Narbonne, F–31062 Toulouse Cedex
besnard@irit.fr
[2] Institut für Informatik, Universität Potsdam,
Postfach 90 03 27, D–14439 Potsdam, Germany
torsten@cs.uni-potsdam.de
[3] Institut für Informationssysteme 184/3, Technische Universität Wien,
Favoritenstraße 9–11, A–1040 Vienna, Austria
{tompits, stefan}@kr.tuwien.ac.at

Abstract. Quantified propositional logic is an extension of classical propositional logic where quantifications over atomic formulas are permitted. As such, quantified propositional logic is a fragment of second-order logic, and its sentences are usually referred to as *quantified Boolean formulas* (QBFs). The motivation to study quantified propositional logic for paraconsistent reasoning is based on two fundamental observations. Firstly, in recent years, practicably efficient solvers for quantified propositional logic have been presented. Secondly, complexity results imply that there is a wide range of paraconsistent reasoning problems which can be efficiently represented in terms of QBFs. Hence, solvers for QBFs can be used as a core engine in systems prototypically implementing several of such reasoning tasks, most of them lacking concrete realisations. To this end, we show how certain paraconsistent reasoning principles can be naturally formulated or reformulated by means of quantified Boolean formulas. More precisely, we describe polynomial-time constructible encodings providing axiomatisations of the given reasoning tasks. In this way, a whole variety of a priori distinct approaches to paraconsistent reasoning become comparable in a uniform setting.

1 Introduction

Paraconsistent reasoning, that is, reasoning from inconsistent information, is a central yet rather complex task underlying the vital reasoning capacities of in-

---

* The third and fourth author were partially supported by the Austrian Science Foundation (FWF) under grant P15068, as well as by the European Commission under project IST-2001-33570 INFOMIX and the IST-2001-33123 CologNeT Network of Excellence.
** Affiliated with the School of Computing Science at Simon Fraser University, Burnaby, Canada.

L. Bertossi et al. (Eds.): Inconsistency Tolerance, LNCS 3300, pp. 84–118, 2004.
© Springer-Verlag Berlin Heidelberg 2004

telligent agents. In view of our daily information feed, it even becomes more and more important every day. As opposed to neighbouring fields like database systems or nonmonotonic reasoning, whose mainstream has or is about to converge to a canonical approach, viz. relational algebra or answer-set programming, respectively, the inherent manifoldness of reasoning from inconsistent information (still) offers a whole variety of different approaches. As a consequence, there is a lack of implemented systems for paraconsistent reasoning.

In this chapter, we address paraconsistent reasoning from the perspective of *quantified propositional logic*, which is an extension of classical propositional logic where quantifications over atomic formulas are permitted. As such, quantified propositional logic is a fragment of second-order logic, and its sentences are usually referred to as *quantified Boolean formulas* (QBFs).

The motivation to study quantified propositional logic for paraconsistent reasoning is based on two fundamental observations. Firstly, in recent years, practicably efficient solvers for quantified propositional logic have been presented. Secondly, in view of results from complexity theory, a wide range of paraconsistent reasoning problems can be efficiently represented in terms of QBFs. Hence, solvers for QBFs can be used as a core engine in systems prototypically implementing several of such reasoning tasks, most of them lacking concrete realisations.

The basic contribution of this chapter is to illustrate how paraconsistent reasoning principles can be naturally formulated or reformulated by means of quantified Boolean formulas. That is to say, we are interested in *encodings* of paraconsistency in terms of QBFs. More specifically, given a paraconsistent inference relation $\vdash_P$, we provide a mapping $\mathcal{T}_P[\cdot;\cdot]$, assigning, to each theory T and each formula φ, a QBF $\mathcal{T}_P[T;\varphi]$ such that

1. $T \vdash_P \varphi$ iff $\mathcal{T}_P[T;\varphi]$ is valid in quantified propositional logic,
2. the size of $\mathcal{T}_P[T;\varphi]$ is polynomial in the size of T and φ, and
3. determining the validity of QBFs resulting from translation $\mathcal{T}_P[\cdot;\cdot]$ is not computationally harder than checking inference under $\vdash_P$.

Hence, encodings of this kind provide *axiomatisations* of the respective inference relation which are efficiently computable. In this way, a whole variety of a priori distinct approaches to paraconsistent reasoning can be compared in a uniform setting.

Our chapter is organised as follows. We start with an introduction to quantified propositional logic in Section 2, including basic intuitions, historical remarks, formal preliminaries, and complexity issues. Notably, this section introduces half a dozen basic QBF modules that can be used as building blocks for assembling axiomatisations of numerous reasoning tasks. These modules are then used in Section 3 to conduct three case-studies, demonstrating how existing approaches to paraconsistent reasoning can be axiomatised and thus implemented by means of QBFs.

2   Quantified Propositional Logic

2.1   Overview and Motivation

As mentioned previously, the language of quantified propositional logic is an extension of classical propositional logic in which formulas may contain quantifications over propositional atoms. Sentences of this language are called *quantified Boolean formulas* (QBFs), and often in the literature one identifies this term with the language of quantified propositional formulas *simpliciter*.

As in first-order logic, the quantifiers permitted in quantified propositional logic are either *existential* or *universal*. We illustrate the underlying ideas by some simple examples.

Consider the propositional formula

$$(p \rightarrow q) \wedge (q \rightarrow p). \tag{1}$$

Clearly, setting both p and q jointly to either true or false makes (1) true, otherwise the formula evaluates to false. Hence, (1) is *satisfiable* but not *valid*.

Imagine we want to talk about satisfiability or validity *within the logical language itself*. In other words, we want to capture the *meta-linguistic* concept of truth assignments within a suitable extension of the object language. To this end, we express a proposition of form

"there exist truth assignments to p and q such that $(p \rightarrow q) \wedge (q \rightarrow p)$ evaluates to true"

in the language of QBFs, using the formula

$$\exists p \exists q \left((p \rightarrow q) \wedge (q \rightarrow p) \right). \tag{2}$$

Analogously, in order to talk about validity of a formula, say of (1), we may write

$$\forall p \forall q \left((p \rightarrow q) \wedge (q \rightarrow p) \right). \tag{3}$$

Hence, we extended the alphabet of classical propositional logic by two *quantifier symbols*, $\exists$ and $\forall$. We call $\exists$ the *existential (Boolean) quantifier symbol* and $\forall$ the *universal (Boolean) quantifier symbol*. By the intuitive meaning of quantifiers, we immediately get that QBF (2) evaluates to true, whereas QBF (3) evaluates to false.

However, using the extended language, we can construct further formulas, for instance,

$$\exists p \forall q \left((p \rightarrow q) \wedge (q \rightarrow p) \right); \text{ or} \tag{4}$$

$$\forall p \exists q \left((p \rightarrow q) \wedge (q \rightarrow p) \right). \tag{5}$$

Formula (4) can be interpreted like this:

"Does there exist a truth assignment to p such that, for all truth assignments to q, formula (1) evaluates to true?"

By inspecting the usual truth conditions for $(p \to q) \wedge (q \to p)$, it is clear that this is not the case. On the other hand, QBF (5) evaluates to true.

QBFs of form (2)–(5) are all *closed* QBFs since each variable v occurs in the scope of a quantifier $\exists v$ or $\forall v$. *Open* formulas like

$$\exists q \left((p \to q) \wedge (q \to p) \right) \tag{6}$$

can be evaluated, analogously to open formulas in predicate logic, with respect to interpretations, i.e., given truth assignments for the *free* variables (in our case, p).

All formulas (1)–(6) are *well-formed QBFs*. So, each classical propositional formula is *a fortiori* a QBF. Moreover, for every atom p, we allow the unary operators $\exists p$ and $\forall p$ to appear "anywhere" in a QBF, not just at the beginning of a formula. For instance,

$$\exists p \left(\exists q \, (p \to q) \wedge \forall q \, (q \to p) \right)$$

is also a well-formed QBF. It is left to the reader to show that this formula evaluates to true.

In general, QBFs can be seen as a *conservative extension* of classical propositional logic, i.e., to each QBF we can assign a logically equivalent propositional formula. However, the advantage of QBFs is their compactness: to express a QBF as a logically equivalent propositional formula, one has to face an exponential increase of the formula size, in general.

In summarising, one may consider QBFs as an extension of classical propositional logic in which reasoning over truth assignments within the object language can be expressed. A different way to think of QBFs is to regard them as a subclass of second-order logic, restricting predicates to be of arity 0, and therefore to consider formulas without function symbols and object variables.

2.2   Usability of QBFs

Historically, among the first logical analyses of systems dealing with quantifiers over propositional variables are the investigations due to Russell ("theory of implication" [63]) and Łukasiewicz and Tarski ("erweiterter Aussagenkalkül" [45]), not to mention the monumental *Principia Mathematica* [70]. The particular idea of quantifying propositional variables was extended in Leśniewski's system of *prototethic logic* [42, 65] where variables whose values are *truth functions* are allowed and quantification is defined over these variables.[1]

However, it took several decades until, in the beginning of the seventies of the last century, propositional quantification got into the spotlight of computer science, in particular of the new and developing field of complexity theory [34].

---

[1] A more elaborate overview on these early historical aspects of propositional quantification can be found in §28 of Church's *Introduction to Mathematical Logic* [21].

Meyer and Stockmeyer [48] were the first who showed that the evaluation problem for QBFs is complete for the complexity class PSPACE—this class comprises all problems which can be decided by deterministic Turing machines with a space requirement polynomially related to the representation size of the problem. In fact, what was considered there were Boolean expressions, and the quantifiers were part of the problem description and not of the language. Already in [47], the same authors introduced the *polynomial hierarchy* [67] as an analogue to the arithmetic hierarchy of recursion theory. Starting from $\Sigma_1^P = \text{NP}$ (NP comprises all problems which can be decided by nondeterministic Turing machines in polynomial time), they defined classes Σ_{k+1}^P, for $k \geq 1$,

> "as the family of sets of words accepted in nondeterministic polynomial time by Turing machines with oracles for sets Σ_k^P" [48].

In that paper, it was already shown that each member of the hierarchy possesses a complete decision problem, given by the evaluation problem of QBFs having a specific quantifier structure (viz., of QBFs being in prenex normal form[2] and such that both the leading quantifier and the number of quantifier alternations is fixed). Other classes, like Π_k^P and Δ_k^P, which are today identified as basic components of the polynomial hierarchy, first appeared in [67, 72].

In view of the above completeness results, the evaluation problem for QBFs plays the same role for the respective classes of the polynomial hierarchy as the satisfiability problem for classical propositional logic, SAT, does for the central complexity class NP. More precisely, hardness for a particular class in the polynomial hierarchy can be shown by reducing the evaluation problem for the respective class of QBFs into the problem under consideration (see [41, 66, 16] for prominent PSPACE-completeness results, or [36, 30] for complexity results for nonmonotonic logics which reside on the second level of the polynomial hierarchy). On the other hand, if we know membership for a problem in some class of the polynomial hierarchy, we are guaranteed that there must exist an efficient encoding in terms of QBFs having a restricted number of quantifier alternations.

Note that the latter observation allows us to find appropriate translation schemas into QBFs such that the resultant formulas can be employed to decide the original problem. Moreover, in many cases, satisfying truth assignments to the free variables in such QBFs correspond to solutions of the original reasoning task. Such encodings provide us thus with a *uniform axiomatisation* for all the considered problems, which leads to further insights as well as allowing the comparison of differing problems in a well-studied and common setting. In fact, this is one of the aims of this article, where different paraconsistent reasoning principles are represented as QBFs, summarising and extending previous work [12, 13]. Other application areas of this general methodology, such as expressing planning problems or different forms of nonmonotonic reasoning in terms of QBFs, is reported, e.g., in [60, 6, 69, 27, 31, 68, 25, 28, 53].

---

[2] The notion of a prenex normal form for QBFs is defined analogously as for formulas in first-order logic; cf. also Section 2.4 for more details.

However, the practical impact of this line of research clearly depends on the capabilites of suitable QBF-solvers which can be applied as underlying inference engines in order to solve the reduced problems. In contrast to similar methods using reductions to SAT, where impressive results have been achieved by employing sophisticated SAT-solvers (for instance in the area of planning [37, 38]), practical implementations for evaluating QBFs lagged behind for quite a long time. This changed when Kleine-Büning *et al.* [39] presented the first implemented QBF-solver, which was based on a generalisation of the resolution principle [62]. Later, an alternative—and more promising—approach was presented by Cadoli *et al.* [17] relying on an adaption of the Davis-Putnam-Logemann-Loveland (DPLL) procedure [24, 23] for propositional logic to quantified propositional logic. Starting from this seminal paper, a number of other solvers for QBFs have been developed, like, e.g., the systems described in [32, 35, 43, 61, 73], which are based on improvements of the DPLL procedure for QBFs and by adapting several methods known from propositional logic, or by introducing new methods. It is worth mentioning that one of these solvers was also designed to run on a distributed system [32, 64]. Hence, the availability of such a parallel algorithm, and the fact that we can represent a complex problem by means of QBFs faithfully, we directly obtain a distributed decision procedure for this particular problem. This convenient situation obviously avoids designing special-purposed distributed algorithms for the problem under consideration.

Recently, Ayari and Basin [6] argued that DPLL procedures need not to be the best choice in general, and an alternative approach for solving QBFs was thus put forth (a similar idea is also outlined in [54]). These new ideas promise to be very efficient, at least on some particular classes of QBFs, a situation similar to the case when *binary decision diagrams* (BDDs) [15, 49] were proposed to evaluate QBFs.

2.3   Formal Postulates of Quantified Propositional Logic

Definition 1. *The* alphabet (*or* signature) *of the language of quantified propositional logic consists of the following items:*

1. *a* countable set of *propositional variables* (*or* atoms);
2. *the* logical constants *"⊤" and "⊥";*
3. *the* logical connectives *"¬", " ∨ ", " ∧ ", " → ", and " ≡ ";*
4. *the* quantification symbols *"∃" and "∀"; and*
5. *the* auxiliary symbols *"(" and ")".*   □

Definition 2. *The set of* quantified Boolean formulas (*QBFs*), *or* (well-formed) *formulas of quantified propositional logic, is inductively defined as follows:*

1. *any propositional variable and any logical constant is a QBF;*
2. *if Φ is a QBF, then $(\neg\Phi)$ is a QBF;*
3. *if Φ and Ψ are QBFs, then $(\Phi \wedge \Psi)$, $(\Phi \vee \Psi)$, $(\Phi \rightarrow \Psi)$, and $(\Phi \equiv \Psi)$ are QBFs;*

4. *if p is a propositional variable and Φ is a QBF, then $(\exists p\,\Phi)$ and $(\forall p\,\Phi)$ are QBFs;*
5. *the only QBFs are those given by 1–4.* □

We tacitly assume the usual conventions concerning the ommission of parentheses in formulas where no ambiguities can arise. Furthermore, we use upper-case Greek letters as meta-variables for QBFs, whilst lower-case Greek letters stand for propositional formulas (i.e., quantifier-free QBFs).

By a *theory* we understand a finite set of quantifier-free formulas. Often, we identify a theory, T, with the (finite) conjunction of its elements $\bigwedge_{\phi\in T}\phi$. Furthermore, for $T = \emptyset$, we define $\bigwedge_{\phi\in T} = \top$.

Let $\mathbf{Q} \in \{\exists, \forall\}$ be a quantifier symbol. For a formula $\mathbf{Q}p\Psi$, we call Ψ the *scope* of $\mathbf{Q}p$. Moreover, given a finite set P of atoms, $\mathbf{Q}P\Psi$ stands for any QBF $\mathbf{Q}p_1\mathbf{Q}p_2\ldots\mathbf{Q}p_n\Psi$ such that the variables $p_1,\ldots,p_n$ are pairwise distinct and $P = \{p_1,\ldots,p_n\}$.

Our definition of quantified Boolean formulas is rather unrestricted in two ways: Firstly, in contrast to some formalisations of QBFs in the literature, we allow quantifiers to appear *anywhere* in a formula. Secondly, we do not stipulate any restriction on the quantification, i.e., we do not require that a quantified variable p in $\mathbf{Q}p\Phi$ ($\mathbf{Q} \in \{\exists, \forall\}$) occurs in the scope Φ of $\mathbf{Q}p$. For example, $(\exists p\,(q \wedge r))$ is a QBF, and so is $(\exists p\,(\forall p\,(p \rightarrow q)))$.

As usual, an occurrence of a variable p in a QBF Φ is *free* iff it does not appear in the scope of a quantifier $\mathbf{Q}p$, otherwise the occurrence of p is *bound*. If Φ contains no free variable occurrences, then Φ is *closed*, otherwise Φ is *open*. Furthermore, $\Phi[p_1/\Psi_1,\ldots,p_n/\Psi_n]$ denotes the result of uniformly substituting in Φ each free occurrence of a variable p_i by a formula Ψ_i, for $1 \leq i \leq n$.

The semantics of quantified propositional logic is based on the following notion. Let P be a non-empty set of atoms. A *(two-valued) interpretation, I, (over P)* is a function assigning to each atom from P an element from $\{t, f\}$. If $I(p) = t$, then p is *true under I*, otherwise p is *false under I*. We usually view interpretations as subsets of P such that p is true under I just in case $p \in I$. Interpretations induce truth values of general formulas recursively in the following way.

Definition 3. *Let P be a non-empty set of atoms and Φ a QBF such that all atoms occurring in Φ belong to P. The* truth value, $v_I(\Phi)$, *of Φ under an interpretation $I : P \rightarrow \{t, f\}$ is defined by the following conditions:*

1. *if $\Phi = \top$, then $v_I(\Phi) = t$, and if $\Phi = \bot$, then $v_I(\Phi) = f$;*
2. *if $\Phi = p$, for an atom p, then $v_I(\Phi) = I(p)$;*
3. *if $\Phi = \neg\Psi$, then $v_I(\Phi) = t$ if $v_I(\Psi) = f$, otherwise $v_I(\Phi) = f$;*
4. *if $\Phi = (\Phi_1 \wedge \Phi_2)$, then $v_I(\Phi) = t$ if $v_I(\Phi_1) = v_I(\Phi_2) = t$, otherwise $v_I(\Phi) = f$;*
5. *if $\Phi = (\Phi_1 \vee \Phi_2)$, then $v_I(\Phi) = t$ if $v_I(\Phi_1) = 1$ or $v_I(\Phi_2) = 1$, otherwise $v_I(\Phi) = f$;*
6. *if $\Phi = (\Phi_1 \rightarrow \Phi_2)$, then $v_I(\Phi) = t$ if $v_I(\Phi_1) = f$ or $v_I(\Phi_2) = t$, otherwise $v_I(\Phi) = f$;*
7. *if $\Phi = (\Phi_1 \equiv \Phi_2)$, then $v_I(\Phi) = t$ if $v_I(\Phi_1) = v_I(\Phi_2)$, otherwise $v_I(\Phi) = f$;*

8. *if* $\Phi = \forall p\Psi$, *then* $v_I(\Phi) = t$ *if* $v_I(\Psi[p/\top]) = v_I(\Psi[p/\bot]) = t$, *otherwise* $v_I(\Phi) = f$;

9. *if* $\Phi = \exists p\Psi$, *then* $v_I(\Phi) = t$ *if* $v_I(\Psi[p/\top]) = t$ *or* $v_I(\Psi[p/\bot]) = t$, *otherwise* $v_I(\Phi) = f$.

Observe that it obviously holds that

$$v_I(\forall p\Psi) = v_I(\Psi[p/\top] \wedge \Psi[p/\bot]) \quad \text{and}$$
$$v_I(\exists p\Psi) = v_I(\Psi[p/\top] \vee \Psi[p/\bot]).$$

We say that Φ is *true under* I if $v_I(\Phi) = t$, otherwise Φ is *false under* I. If $v_I(\Phi) = t$, then I is a *model* of Φ. If Φ possesses some model, then Φ is *satisfiable*, otherwise Φ is *unsatisfiable*. If Φ is true under every interpretation, then Φ is *valid*. As usual, we also write $\models \Phi$ to express that Φ is valid.

It is easily seen that the truth value of a QBF Φ under interpretation I depends only on the free variables in Φ. Hence, without loss of generality, for determining the truth value of QBFs, we may restrict our attention to interpretations which contain only atoms occurring free in the given QBF. In particular, closed QBFs are either true under every interpretation or false under every interpretation, i.e., they are either valid or unsatisfiable. So, for closed QBFs, there is no need to refer to particular interpretations. As well, if a closed QBF Φ is valid, we say that Φ *evaluates to true*, and, correspondingly, if Φ is unsatisfiable, we say that Φ *evaluates to false*. Two formulas (i.e., ordinary propositional formulas or QBFs) are *(logically) equivalent* iff they possess the same models. Thus, formulas Φ and Ψ are logically equivalent iff $\Phi \equiv \Psi$ is valid.

We also use $\models$ to refer to the semantic consequence relation between a theory (i.e., a finite set of propositional formulas) and a propositional formula, defined in the usual way. Accordingly, for a theory T, the deductive closure of T, i.e., the set of all semantic consequences of T, is given by $Cn(T) = \{\varphi \mid T \models \varphi\}$. Furthermore, $var(T)$ denotes the set of all atoms occurring in T.

Similar to classical first-order logic, there are several results concerning the shifting and renaming of quantifiers. We list some fundamental relations below and refer the interested reader to [29, 71] for a fuller discussion.

Proposition 1. *Let* p, q *be atoms and* $\mathbf{Q} \in \{\forall, \exists\}$. *Furthermore, let* Φ, Ψ *be QBFs such that* Ψ *does not contain free occurrences of* p. *Then,*

1. $\models (\neg\exists p\,\Phi) \equiv \forall p(\neg\Phi)$,
2. $\models (\neg\forall p\,\Phi) \equiv \exists p(\neg\Phi)$,
3. $\models (\Psi \circ \mathbf{Q}p\,\Phi) \equiv \mathbf{Q}p(\Psi \circ \Phi)$, *for* $\circ \in \{\wedge, \vee, \rightarrow\}$, *and*
4. $\models (\mathbf{Q}q\,\Psi) \equiv (\mathbf{Q}p\,\Psi[q/p])$.

2.4   Computational Complexity

We assume the reader familiar with the basic concepts of complexity theory (see, e.g., [52] for a comprehensive introduction). Relevant for our purposes are the elements of the *polynomial hierarchy* [67], introduced in [48] as a computational analogue to the arithmetic hierarchy of recursion theory, consisting of the following sequence of classes:

$$\Delta_0^P = \Sigma_0^P = \Pi_0^P = P,$$

and, for all $k \geq 0$,

$$\Delta_{k+1}^P = P^{\Sigma_k^P}, \quad \Sigma_{k+1}^P = NP^{\Sigma_k^P}, \quad \text{and} \quad \Pi_{k+1}^P = \text{co-}\Sigma_{k+1}^P.$$

Here, P is the class of all problems solvable on a deterministic Turing machine in polynomial time; NP is similarly defined but using a nondeterministic Turing machine as underlying computing model; and, for complexity classes C and A, the notation C^A stands for the *relativised version* of C, consisting of all problems which can be decided by Turing machines of the same sort and time bound as in C, only that the machines have access to an oracle for problems in A. As well, co-C is the class of all problems which are complementary to the problems in C. We note that NP $= \Sigma_1^P$, co-NP $= \Pi_1^P$, and P $= \Delta_1^P$.

The *cumulative polynomial hierarchy* is given by the union $\bigcup_{k=0}^{\infty} \Sigma_k^P$. We say that a problem is located *at the kth level of the polynomial hierarchy* iff it is contained in Δ_{k+1}^P and it is either Σ_k^P-hard or Π_k^P-hard.

A further relevant family of complexity classes is given by the sequence of classes D_k^P, $k \geq 1$, where each D_k^P consists of all problems expressible as the conjunction of a problem in Σ_k^P and a problem in Π_k^P. Notice that, for all $k \geq 1$, $\Sigma_k^P \subseteq D_k^P \subseteq \Sigma_{k+1}^P$ holds; in fact, both inclusions are widely conjectured to be strict. Moreover, any problem in D_k^P can be solved with two Σ_k^P oracle calls, and is thus intuitively easier than a problem complete for Δ_{k+1}^P.

The classes Σ_k^P and Π_k^P are closely related to the evaluation problem of QBFs—in particular, to QBFs which are given in *prenex normal form*: A QBF Φ is in prenex normal form iff it is of the form

$$Q_1 P_1 Q_2 P_2 \ldots Q_n P_n \phi,$$

where ϕ is a propositional formula, $Q_i \in \{\exists, \forall\}$ such that $Q_i \neq Q_{i+1}$ for $1 \leq i \leq n-1$, and P_i are disjoint sets of propositional variables for $1 \leq i \leq n$. If $Q_1 = \exists$, then Φ is called an $(n, \exists)$-*QBF*, and if $Q_1 = \forall$, then Φ is called an $(n, \forall)$-*QBF*. Without going into details, we mention that any QBF is easily transformed into an equivalent QBF in prenex normal form (by applying, among other reduction steps, the equivalences depicted in Proposition 1).

Proposition 2. *For every $k \geq 1$, we have that*

1. *deciding the truth for closed $(k, \exists)$-QBFs is Σ_k^P-complete, and*
2. *deciding the truth for closed $(k, \forall)$-QBFs is Π_k^P-complete.*

These complexity results are central for our subsequent encodings. In particular, we are interested in representing a given paraconsistent inference relation $\vdash_P$ via a QBF-encoding $T_P[\cdot; \cdot]$ such that

1. $\mathcal{T}_P[\cdot;\cdot]$ is *faithful*, i.e., for each theory T and each formula φ, $T \vdash_P \varphi$ iff $\mathcal{T}_P[T;\varphi]$ evaluates to true,
2. $\mathcal{T}_P[T;\varphi]$ is computable in polynomial time, for each theory T and each formula φ, and
3. determining the truth values of the QBFs resulting from $\mathcal{T}_P[\cdot;\cdot]$ is not computationally harder than checking inference under $\vdash_P$.

The translation $\mathcal{T}_P[\cdot;\cdot]$ is then called an *adequate translation*. For instance, if checking $T \vdash_P \varphi$, for a given theory T and a given formula φ, is known to be in complexity class Σ_2^P, our desired translation $\mathcal{T}_P[T;\varphi]$ should lead, for each T and φ, to a $(2,\exists)$-QBF, i.e., a QBF with at most one quantifier alternation, whose size is polynomial in the size of T and φ.

2.5   Basic QBF-Modules

We next discuss how QBFs can be employed to express some fundamental reasoning tasks concerning the consistency of propositional theories. Computing tasks of this kind will be required frequently throughout the paper as subtasks for other problems. Hence, the "modules" discussed in this section play the role of "building blocks" for the subsequent encodings of different paraconsistent reasoning tasks.

Expressing consistency. First of all, since existential quantification refers to satisfiability, we are easily capable to decide whether a given theory W is consistent, i.e., whether $W \not\models \bot$. Indeed, simply define

$$Cons[W] = \exists P (\bigwedge_{\psi \in W} \psi),$$

where $P = var(W)$. Hence, $Cons[W]$ is always closed, and the following relation is easily seen:

Proposition 3. *A theory W is consistent iff $Cons[W]$ evaluates to true.*

We now extend this simple module as follows. Assume we have given two propositional theories, W and R, and we want to identify all subsets $S \subseteq R$ such that $W \cup S$ is consistent, i.e., our task is to compute all subsets of R consistent with W.

The basic idea is to use new atoms such that the truth assignments to these atoms correspond to the possible subsets of R. More precisely, let $G = \{g_\phi \mid \phi \in R\}$ be a set of new variables, not occurring in W or R. Variables from G are called "guessing variables", since they are used to guess a certain subset of R.
Consider the following encoding:

$$Cons^G[W; R] = \exists P \Big(\bigwedge_{\psi \in W} \psi \wedge \bigwedge_{\phi \in R} (g_\phi \to \phi) \Big),$$

where P consists of all variables occurring in R or W. Observe that we now have an *open* QBF where the guessing variables G are free. The relation between subsets of R which are consistent with W and models of $Cons^G[W; R]$ is a one-to-one correspondence, as desired:

Proposition 4. *Let W and R be theories, and $G = \{g_\phi \mid \phi \in R\}$ a set of variables not occurring in W or R. Moreover, let $S \subseteq R$ and $I \subseteq G$ such that, for each $\phi \in R$, $\phi \in S$ iff $g_\phi \in I$.*
   Then, $W \cup S$ is consistent iff $Cons^G[W; R]$ is true under I.

Example 1. Consider $W = \{\neg p \vee \neg q\}$ and $R = \{p, q\}$. All proper subsets of R are consistent with W, but $W \cup R$ is inconsistent. For R as given, we choose

$$G = \{g_p, g_q\}$$

as corresponding set of guessing variables.
   Consider now the encoding $Cons^G[W; R]$, given by

$$\exists pq \left((\neg p \vee \neg q) \wedge (g_p \to p) \wedge (g_q \to q) \right). \tag{7}$$

It can be checked that all interpretations $I \subset G$ are models of (7), but the interpretation $I = G$ is not a model of (7). This coincides with the observation that exactly the proper subsets of R, viz. $S_1 = \emptyset$, $S_2 = \{p\}$, and $S_3 = \{q\}$, are consistent with W, while $S_4 = \{p, q\}$ is not.

Expressing maximal consistent subsets. We also require to express the *maximal* subsets of R which are consistent (with some W). For instance, in the above example, we should rule out the subset $S_1 = \emptyset$, since $S_1 \subset S_2$ (as well as $S_1 \subset S_3$) and thus S_1 is not maximal.
   Formally, a subset S of R is *maximal consistent (with W)* iff S is consistent (with W) and each S' with $S \subset S'$ is inconsistent (with W). Due to the monotonicity of classical propositional logic, the following characterisation is equivalent:

Proposition 5. *Let W and R be theories, and $S \subseteq R$.*
   Then, S is maximal consistent with W iff

1. *$W \cup S$ is consistent, and*
2. *for each $\phi \in (R \setminus S)$, $W \cup S \cup \{\phi\}$ is inconsistent.*

We express these tests as follows: For any theories W and R, let $G = \{g_\phi \mid \phi \in R\}$ be a set of variables such that $G \cap var(W \cup R) = \emptyset$. Then, define

$$Cons^G_{max}[W; R] = Cons^G[W; R] \wedge \bigwedge_{\phi \in R} \left(\neg g_\phi \to \neg Cons^{G \setminus \{g_\phi\}}[W \cup \{\phi\}; R \setminus \{\phi\}] \right).$$

Intuitively, $Cons^G_{max}[W; R]$ guesses a subset S of R (via atoms G). With the first conjunct $Cons^G[W; R]$, it is checked whether the guess is consistent with W. The second conjunct checks maximality for S as follows: For each $\phi \in R$, if ϕ is contained in the guess (i.e., if g_ϕ is true), we are immediately done. Otherwise, $\neg Cons^{G\backslash\{g_\phi\}}[W \cup \{\phi\}; R \backslash \{\phi\}]$ must evaluate to true. Observe that we use the same set G in this module (except for removing ϕ, which itself is "added" to the first argument W) as in the previous test. Hence, we check whether S is *not* consistent with $W \cup \{\phi\}$. This coincides precisely with the second condition in Proposition 5.

The formal result is as follows:

Proposition 6. *Let W and R be theories, and $G = \{g_\phi \mid \phi \in R\}$ a set of variables not occurring in W or R. Moreover, let $S \subseteq R$ and $I \subseteq G$ such that, for each $\phi \in R$, $\phi \in S$ iff $g_\phi \in I$.*

Then, S is maximal consistent with W iff $Cons^G_{max}[W; R]$ is true under I.

Expressing minimal models. Besides the selection of maximal subsets satisfying a certain criterion, it is sometimes also necessary to characterise subsets which are *minimal* with respect to a specific condition. Indeed, a widely-used method in nonmonotonic reasoning is inference based on *minimal models*. In such an approach, the inference relation is specified not in terms of all models of a given theory but only in terms of models which are minimal with respect to a certain ordering. Following the seminal work of McCarthy [46], minimal-model reasoning can be expressed in terms of a schema of second-order logic, known as *circumscription schema* (or *circumscription* for short). However, in the propositional case, instances of the circumscription schema are actually nothing else than specific QBFs. In the following, we characterise models which are minimal with respect to a specific ordering in terms of a QBF module corresponding to propositional circumscription.

Let T be a theory and (P, Q, Z) a partition of $var(T)$. Assume two models I and I' of T, and define $I \leq_{P;Z} I'$ iff the following conditions are satisfied:

1. $\{q \in Q \mid v_I(q) = t\} = \{q \in Q \mid v_{I'}(q) = t\}$;
2. $\{p \in P \mid v_I(p) = t\} \subseteq \{p \in P \mid v_{I'}(p) = t\}$.

A model I of T is called $(P; Z)$-*minimal* if no model I' of T with $I' \neq I$ satisfies $I' \leq_{P;Z} I$.

Informally, the partition (P, Q, Z) can be interpreted as follows: The set P contains the variables to be minimised, Z are those variables that can vary in minimising P, and the remaining variables Q are fixed in minimising P.

For a theory T and a partition (P, Q, Z) of $var(T)$, where $P = \{p_1, \ldots, p_n\}$ and $Z = \{z_1, \ldots, z_m\}$, we define the QBF $Circ[T; P; Z]$, called the (*parallel*) *circumscription* (*schema*) of P in T, as

$$T \wedge \forall \tilde{P} \forall \tilde{Z}\Big((T\{P/\tilde{P}, Z/\tilde{Z}\} \wedge \bigwedge_{1 \leq i \leq n} (\tilde{p}_i \rightarrow p_i)) \rightarrow \bigwedge_{1 \leq i \leq n} (p_i \rightarrow \tilde{p}_i)\Big),$$

where $\tilde{P} = \{\tilde{p}_1, \ldots, \tilde{p}_n\}$ and $\tilde{Z} = \{\tilde{z}_1, \ldots, \tilde{z}_m\}$ are sets of new variables corresponding to P and Z, respectively, and $T\{P/\tilde{P}, Z/\tilde{Z}\}$ results from T by uniform substitution of the variables in $\tilde{P} \cup \tilde{Z}$ for those in $P \cup Z$.

Now, the main property of $Circ[T; P; Z]$ is given by the following result:

Proposition 7 ([46]). *Let T be a theory, (P, Q, Z) a partition of $var(T)$, and $I \subseteq var(T)$.*

Then, I is a $(P; Z)$-minimal model of T iff I is a model of $Circ[T; P; Z]$.

Derivability testing. Finally, we define further modules for expressing derivability. Recall that, for any theory T and any propositional formula φ, it holds that $T \models \varphi$ iff $T \cup \{\neg \varphi\}$ is inconsistent. We thus define

$$\mathcal{D}eriv[W; \varphi] = \neg \mathcal{C}ons[W \cup \{\neg \varphi\}]$$

and obtain the following property:

Proposition 8. *For any theory W and any formula φ, $W \models \varphi$ iff $\mathcal{D}eriv[W; \varphi]$ is valid.*

More generally, defining

$$\mathcal{D}eriv^G[W; R; \varphi] = \neg \mathcal{C}ons^G[W \cup \{\neg \varphi\}; R]$$

yields the following characterisation:

Proposition 9. *Let W and R be theories, φ a formula, and $G = \{g_\phi \mid \phi \in R\}$ a set of variables not occurring in W, R, or φ. Moreover, let $S \subseteq R$ and $I \subseteq G$ such that, for each $\phi \in R$, $\phi \in S$ iff $g_\phi \in I$.*

Then, $W \cup S \models \varphi$ iff $\mathcal{D}eriv^G[W; R; \varphi]$ is true under I.

3   QBFs for Paraconsistent Reasoning: Case Studies

In this section, we show how QBFs can be successfully used to express different families of paraconsistent inference relations, exploiting the basic QBF modules introduced above. We first deal with formalisms based on maximal-consistent subsets. Afterwards, in Section 3.2, we discuss a class of inference relations using a consistency-driven rewriting technique based on Reiter's default logic. Finally, Section 3.3 is devoted to approaches using minimal-model reasoning in many-valued logics.

3.1   Reasoning from Maximal-Consistent Subsets

A simple but very popular approach to reasoning from an inconsistent knowledge base is reasoning from consistent subsets [59, 58, 14, 51, 7, 8]. Consider an inconsistent knowledge base in the form of a theory T:

$$\phi \wedge (\psi \rightarrow \varphi); \tag{8}$$
$$\psi \wedge \neg \phi; \tag{9}$$
$$(\psi \wedge \varphi) \rightarrow \eta; \tag{10}$$
$$(\psi \wedge \neg \eta) \vee \neg \phi; \tag{11}$$
$$\phi \vee \psi \vee \varphi \vee \eta. \tag{12}$$

Clearly, this theory is inconsistent. One way to proceed is to consider the maximal consistent subsets of T, which are:

$$S = \{(8), (10), (12)\};$$
$$S' = \{(8), (11), (12)\};$$
$$S'' = \{(9), (10), (11), (12)\}.$$

Let us see what follows from these maximal consistent subsets of T:

- S entails ϕ and $\psi \rightarrow (\varphi \wedge \eta)$.
- S' entails ϕ and $\psi \wedge \varphi \wedge \neg\eta$.
- S'' entails $\neg\phi$ and ψ, as well as $\varphi \rightarrow \eta$.

Among the most cautious conclusions are those formulas that follow from the intersection of S, S', and S'':

$$\phi \vee \psi \vee \varphi \vee \eta.$$

Definition 4. *Let T be a theory. A formula φ is a* free consequence *of T, symbolically $T \vdash_{\text{FREE}} \varphi$, iff φ is entailed by the intersection of all maximal consistent subsets of T.*

In the above example, $\phi \vee \psi \vee \varphi \vee \eta \vee \chi$ is a free consequence of T, for any formula χ. By contrast, $\phi \vee \psi$ is not a free consequence of T even though $\phi \vee \psi$ is entailed by S and similarly by S' as well as by S''. Thus, free consequences need not be very informative and other notions have been introduced in the literature.

According to [20], a systematic account of reasoning from consistent subsets arises from distinguishing between selection mechanisms (among consistent subsets) and reasoning principles (to be applied to the selected consistent subsets).

In the general case, T is a *prioritised theory*, which means that it comes in the form $T = T_1 \cup \cdots \cup T_n$ (possibly, $n = 1$), where each T_i is a stratum such that strata with lower index contain formulas of greater importance. We assume the T_i's to be disjoint whereas not all authors do so. Here, we use the partition requirement in order to keep things simple. A *subtheory* of a prioritised theory T is of the form $S = S_1 \cup \cdots \cup S_n$ such that $S_i = T_i \cap S$ for $i = 1, \ldots, n$. Moreover, the *level* of a subtheory of T is defined by $a(S) = \min\{i \in \{1, \ldots, n\} \mid S_i \neq T_i\}$.

Definition 5. *Given $T = T_1 \cup \cdots \cup T_n$, we define the orderings $\ll^{\text{T}}$ ("subtheory-based preference"), $\ll^{\text{BO}}$ ("best-out preference"), and $\ll^{\text{INCL}}$ ("inclusion-based preference") as follows, where $S = S_1 \cup \cdots \cup S_n$ and $S' = S'_1 \cup \cdots \cup S'_n$ range over the set of all consistent subtheories of T:*

- $S \ll^{\text{T}} S'$ *iff $S \subset S'$;*
- $S \ll^{\text{BO}} S'$ *iff $a(S) < a(S')$; and*
- $S \ll^{\text{INCL}} S'$ *iff there exists some $k \in \{1, \ldots, n\}$ such that $S_k \subset S'_k$ and $S_i = S'_i$, for all $i \in \{1, \ldots, k-1\}$.*

Then, a consistent subtheory of T is σ-preferred iff it is maximal with respect to $\ll^\sigma$, where σ ranges over $\{\text{T}, \text{BO}, \text{INCL}\}$. Also, $\sigma(T)$ denotes the set of all σ-preferred subtheories of T.

Considering that all formulas in the above example form the unique stratum of T, we get that $\sigma(T) = \{S, S', S''\}$ in all three cases for σ (i.e., T, BO, and INCL). A more interesting situation is T being stratified, e.g., as follows:

$$T_1 = \{(8), (9)\}; \qquad T_2 = \{(10)\}; \qquad T_3 = \{(11), (12)\}.$$

Clearly, introducing strata cannot alter $\ll^\text{T}$, and the T-preferred subtheories of T are still as above: $\{S, S', S''\}$. Although $\ll^\text{BO}$ depends in general on strata, it happens here that the BO-preferred subtheories of T are also the same. The INCL-preferred subtheories of T are just S and S''.

Definition 6. *Let $T = T_1 \cup \cdots \cup T_n$ be a prioritised theory, φ a propositional formula, and $\sigma \in \{\text{T}, \text{BO}, \text{INCL}\}$. Then,*

- *φ is an EXI-σ consequence of T, written $T \vdash_{\text{EXI-}\sigma} \varphi$, iff $\varphi \in \bigcup_{S \in \sigma(T)} Cn(S)$,*
- *φ is a UNI-σ consequence of T, written $T \vdash_{\text{UNI-}\sigma} \varphi$, iff $\varphi \in \bigcap_{S \in \sigma(T)} Cn(S)$, and*
- *φ is an ARG-σ consequence of T, written $T \vdash_{\text{ARG-}\sigma} \varphi$, iff $\varphi \in \bigcup_{S \in \sigma(T)} Cn(S)$ but $\neg\varphi \notin \bigcup_{S \in \sigma(T)} Cn(S)$.*

Considering that all formulas in our example form the unique stratum of T, we get that $\phi \vee \psi$ is a UNI-T consequence of T, whereas $\psi \wedge \neg\phi$ is an EXI-T consequence of T because $\psi \wedge \neg\phi$ is entailed by S'' even though it is neither entailed by S nor S'. However, $\psi \wedge \neg\phi$ fails to be an ARG-T consequence of T. A reason is that ϕ (from which $\neg(\psi \wedge \neg\phi)$ is classically deduced) is entailed by S, and analogously by S'. An example of an ARG-T consequence of T is ψ.

Assume now that T is equipped with the stratification given above. UNI-T consequences and UNI-BO consequences are the same as in the non-stratified case. On the other hand, $(\psi \wedge \varphi) \to \eta$ is a new UNI-INCL consequence. Moreover, $\phi \wedge \psi \wedge \neg\eta$ is no longer an EXI-INCL consequence. Accordingly, $(\psi \wedge \varphi) \to \eta$ is a new ARG-INCL consequence.

All these notions compare, by way of set-inclusion of the respective sets of consequences of a given theory, as depicted in Figure 1 (cf. also [20]).

Hence, the free consequences of a given theory T comprise the smallest set of consequences of T and the set of EXI-T consequences is the largest (apart from the classical consequences $Cn(T)$).

Other notions have been defined as well, either in the non-prioritised case or in the prioritised case, most of them technically involved.

The complexity of checking EXI-σ, UNI-σ, and ARG-σ consequences, for $\sigma \in \{\text{T}, \text{BO}, \text{INCL}\}$, was analysed in [19]. There, the following results were shown: The problem of deciding whether a formula is an EXI-σ consequence of a given theory is Σ_2^P-complete for $\sigma \in \{\text{T}, \text{BO}, \text{INCL}\}$. The corresponding problem for UNI-T and UNI-INCL consequences is Π_2^P-complete, while for UNI-BO it is known to be in Δ_2^P. As for ARG-σ, the problem is in Δ_3^P, for each $\sigma \in \{\text{T}, \text{BO}, \text{INCL}\}$.

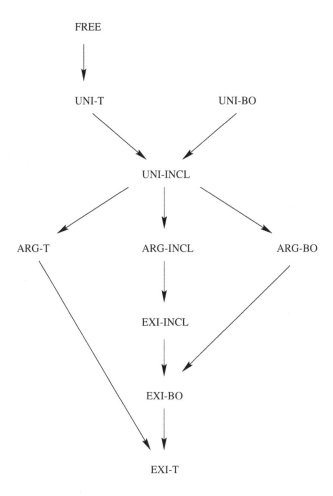

Fig. 1. Relations between different paraconsistent inference relations based on maximal subsets

Encodings. From our considerations in Section 2.5, it is quite easy to construct QBF encodings for expressing EXI-T, UNI-T, and ARG-T consequences. Indeed, it just suffices to combine the modules $\mathcal{C}ons_{max}^G[\cdot;\cdot]$ and $\mathcal{D}eriv^G[\cdot;\cdot]$ in a suitable manner, for a set G of guessing variables. More precisely, given a theory T and a formula φ, we use simultaneously the modules $\mathcal{C}ons_{max}^G[\emptyset;T]$ and $\mathcal{D}eriv^G[\emptyset;T;\varphi])$ to check whether a guess for a subset $S \subseteq T$ is maximal consistent and whether φ is entailed by S, respectively. Observe that the *same set* G of guessing variables is used for expressing both tasks. If there exists at least one interpretation $I \subseteq G$ making both $\mathcal{C}ons_{max}^G[\emptyset;T]$ and $\mathcal{D}eriv^G[\emptyset;T;\varphi])$ true, we directly get an encoding for EXI-T consequences. If under each $I \subseteq G$ which is a model of $\mathcal{C}ons_{max}^G[\emptyset;T]$, also $\mathcal{D}eriv^G[\emptyset;T;\varphi])$ is true, then we have an encoding for UNI-T consequences.

Finally, ARG-T consequences are easily encoded via two independent tests for checking EXI-T inference.

Theorem 1. *Let T be a theory, φ a formula, and $G = \{g_\phi \mid \phi \in T\}$ a set of new guessing atoms not occurring in T or φ. Then,*

1. *$T \vdash_{\text{EXI-T}} \varphi$ iff $\mathcal{T}_{\text{EXI-T}}[T; \varphi] = \exists G\big(Cons_{max}^G[\emptyset; T] \wedge Deriv^G[\emptyset; T; \varphi]\big)$ is valid,*
2. *$T \vdash_{\text{UNI-T}} \varphi$ iff $\mathcal{T}_{\text{UNI-T}}[T; \varphi] = \forall G\big(Cons_{max}^G[\emptyset; T] \rightarrow Deriv^G[\emptyset; T; \varphi]\big)$ is valid, and*
3. *$T \vdash_{\text{ARG-T}} \varphi$ iff $\mathcal{T}_{\text{ARG-T}}[T; \varphi] = \mathcal{T}_{\text{EXI-T}}[T, \varphi] \wedge \neg \mathcal{T}_{\text{EXI-T}}[T, \neg\varphi]$ is valid.*

Observe that the size of each of the above encodings is clearly polynomial in the size of T and φ. Hence, each of the encodings is computable in polynomial time. Furthermore, it is easy to check that $\mathcal{T}_{\text{EXI-T}}[T; \varphi]$ can be transformed in polynomial time into a $(2, \exists)$-QBF, whilst $\mathcal{T}_{\text{UNI-T}}[T; \varphi]$ can be transformed, likewise in polynomial time, into a $(2, \forall)$-QBF, for each T and φ. Therefore, recalling that checking EXI-T and UNI-T consequence is complete for Σ_2^P and Π_2^P, respectively, both $\mathcal{T}_{\text{EXI-T}}[\cdot; \cdot]$ and $\mathcal{T}_{\text{UNI-T}}[\cdot; \cdot]$ are adequate.

Concerning $\mathcal{T}_{\text{ARG-T}}[T; \varphi]$, since this encoding can be transformed in polynomial time into an equivalent QBF which is the conjunction of a $(2, \exists)$-QBF and a $(2, \forall)$-QBF, for each T and φ, it follows that checking ARG-T consequence is not only in Δ_3^P but actually in the easier class D_2^P.

Next, we consider the notion of free consequence. To this end, we call, for a given theory T, the set of all $\phi \in T$ which are a UNI-T consequence of T the *free base* of T.

The following property is also observed in [7].

Proposition 10. *Let T be a theory. Then, a formula φ is a free consequence of T iff φ is classically entailed by the free base of T.*

Note that, by definition, the free base of T is given by $T \cap \bigcap_{S \in T(T)} Cn(S)$. Hence, Proposition 10 expresses that $T \vdash_{\text{FREE}} \varphi$ just in case $T \cap \bigcap_{S \in T(T)} Cn(S) \models \varphi$. By the properties of $Cn(\cdot)$, this in turn entails that $T \vdash_{\text{FREE}} \varphi$ only if $\varphi \in \bigcap_{S \in T(T)} Cn(S)$, which rephrases the relation that every free consequence of T is a UNI-T consequence of T, as depicted in Figure 1.

Theorem 2. *Let T be a theory, φ a formula, and $G = \{g_\phi \mid \phi \in T\}$ a set of new guessing variables.*
Then, $T \vdash_{\text{FREE}} \varphi$ iff

$$\mathcal{T}_{\text{FREE}}[T; \varphi] = \forall G\Big(\bigwedge_{\phi \in T} \big(\mathcal{T}_{\text{UNI-T}}[T, \phi] \rightarrow g_\phi\big) \rightarrow Deriv^G[\emptyset; T; \varphi]\Big)$$

is valid.

We now turn our attention to the other approaches considered, where prioritised theories are used to realise a more fine-grained selection mechanism among consistent subsets. As it turns out, the basic reasoning principles EXI-σ, UNI-σ, and ARG-σ are encoded along the lines of Theorem 1, but we have to replace the module $Cons^G_{max}[T]$ in an appropriate way.

We start with the consequence relations based on best-out preference. The encoding relies on the following proposition.

Proposition 11. *Let $S = S_1 \cup \ldots \cup S_n$ be a consistent subset of a prioritised theory $T = T_1 \cup \ldots \cup T_n$, with $S_i = S \cap T_i$.*
Then, S is BO*-preferred iff $T_1 \cup \ldots \cup T_{a(S)}$ is inconsistent or $S = T$.*

This motivates the subsequent encoding, which works as follows. First, $Cons^G[\emptyset; T]$ yields all consistent subsets of T via the guessing variables G. By the above result, we have that T is BO-preferred whenever T is consistent. Hence, if each $g_\phi \in G$ is assigned to true, we are done. Otherwise, for a guessed subset $S \subset T$, the encoding checks, for $i = 1, \ldots, n$, that whenever i is the level, $a(S)$, of S, then $T_1 \cup \ldots \cup T_{a(S)}$ is inconsistent. Recall that the level of a subtheory S of T is defined by $a(S) = \min\{j \in \{1, \ldots, n\} \mid S_j \neq T_j\}$.

Lemma 1. *Let $T = T_1 \cup \ldots \cup T_n$ be a prioritised theory and $G = G_1 \cup \ldots \cup G_n = \{g_\phi \mid \phi \in T\}$ a set of corresponding guessing variables. Moreover, let $S \subseteq T$ and $I \subseteq G$ such that, for each $\phi \in T$, $\phi \in S$ iff $g_\phi \in I$.*
Then, S is BO*-preferred iff $\mathcal{BO}^G[T]$, given by*

$$Cons^G[\emptyset; T] \wedge \left(\neg G \rightarrow \bigwedge_{i=1,\ldots,n} ((G_1 \wedge \ldots \wedge G_{i-1} \wedge \neg G_i) \rightarrow \neg Cons[T_1 \cup \ldots \cup T_i]) \right),$$

is true under I.

In accord to Theorem 1, we obtain the following encodings for expressing the relations $\vdash_{\text{EXI-BO}}$, $\vdash_{\text{UNI-BO}}$, and $\vdash_{\text{ARG-BO}}$, respectively, by replacing the module $Cons^G_{max}[\emptyset; T]$ by $\mathcal{BO}^G[T]$ in the corresponding translations.

Theorem 3. *Let T be a prioritised theory, φ a formula, and $G = \{g_\phi \mid \phi \in T\}$ a set of new guessing atoms not occurring in T or φ. Then,*

1. *$T \vdash_{\text{EXI-BO}} \varphi$ iff $\mathcal{T}_{\text{EXI-BO}}[T; \varphi] = \exists G (\mathcal{BO}^G[T] \wedge Deriv^G[\emptyset; T; \varphi])$ is valid,*
2. *$T \vdash_{\text{UNI-BO}} \varphi$ iff $\mathcal{T}_{\text{UNI-BO}}[T; \varphi] = \forall G (\mathcal{BO}^G[T] \rightarrow Deriv^G[\emptyset; T; \varphi])$ is valid, and*
3. *$T \vdash_{\text{ARG-BO}} \varphi$ iff $\mathcal{T}_{\text{ARG-BO}}[T; \varphi] = \mathcal{T}_{\text{EXI-BO}}[T, \varphi] \wedge \neg \mathcal{T}_{\text{EXI-BO}}[T, \neg\varphi]$ is valid.*

Similar as for ARG-T consequences, the encoding $\mathcal{T}_{\text{ARG-BO}}[\cdot; \cdot]$ yields that checking ARG-BO consequences lies in the easier subclass D_2^P of Δ_3^P. Moreover, although the encoding $\mathcal{T}_{\text{EXI-BO}}[\cdot; \cdot]$ is adequate, $\mathcal{T}_{\text{UNI-BO}}[\cdot; \cdot]$ is not because checking UNI-BO consequences is in Δ_2^P but $\mathcal{T}_{\text{UNI-BO}}[T; \varphi]$ can be transformed in polynomial time into an equivalent $(2, \forall)$-QBF, for any T and φ. However, we can simplify $\mathcal{T}_{\text{UNI-BO}}[\cdot; \cdot]$ using the following observation:

Proposition 12. *For a prioritised theory $T = T_1 \cup \ldots \cup T_n$ and a formula φ, we have that $T \vdash_{\text{UNI-BO}} \varphi$ iff there exists some $i \in \{0, \ldots, n\}$ such that $T_1 \cup \ldots \cup T_i$ is consistent and $T_1 \cup \ldots \cup T_i \models \varphi$.*

Observe that the case $i = 0$ is required for dealing with the case where T_1 is already inconsistent. We thus obtain the following optimised encoding for checking UNI-BO consequences, avoiding explicit quantifier alternations:

Theorem 4. *Let $T = T_1 \cup \ldots \cup T_n$ be a prioritised theory, and φ a formula.*
Then, $T \vdash_{\text{UNI-BO}} \varphi$ iff $\bigvee_{i=0,\ldots,n} \big(\mathit{Cons}[T_1 \cup \ldots \cup T_i] \wedge \mathit{Deriv}[T_1 \cup \ldots \cup T_i; \varphi]\big)$
is valid.

Finally, we define a module for expressing the INCL-preferred subsets of a given prioritised theory. The following result is the basis for this module, albeit other characterisations are also possible.

Proposition 13. *Given a consistent subtheory $S = S_1 \cup \ldots \cup S_n$ of a prioritised theory $T = T_1 \cup \ldots \cup T_n$, it holds that S is INCL-preferred iff, for each $i \in \{1, \ldots, n\}$ and each $\phi \in T_i \setminus S$, $S_1 \cup \ldots \cup S_i \cup \{\phi\}$ is inconsistent.*

This leads to the following encoding:

Lemma 2. *Let $T = T_1 \cup \ldots \cup T_n$ be a prioritised theory and $G = G_1 \cup \ldots \cup G_n = \{g_\phi \mid \phi \in T\}$ a set of corresponding guessing atoms. Moreover, let $S \subseteq T$ and $I \subseteq G$ such that, for each $\phi \in T$, $\phi \in S$ iff $g_\phi \in I$.*
Then, S is INCL-preferred iff

$$\mathit{Incl}^G[T] = \mathit{Cons}^G[\emptyset; T] \wedge \bigwedge_{i=1,\ldots,n,\phi \in T_i} \big(\neg g_\phi \to \neg \mathit{Cons}^{G_\phi^i}[\{\phi\}, T_\phi^i]\big)$$

is true under I, where $G_\phi^i = (G_1 \cup \ldots \cup G_i) \setminus \{g_\phi\}$ and $T_\phi^i = (T_1 \cup \ldots \cup T_i) \setminus \{\phi\}$.

Again, the encodings for checking EXI-INCL, UNI-INCL, and ARG-INCL consequences, respectively, follow the same pattern as for the previous variants.

Theorem 5. *Let T be a prioritised theory, φ a formula, and $G = \{g_\phi \mid \phi \in T\}$ a set of new guessing atoms not occurring in T or φ. Then,*

1. *$T \vdash_{\text{EXI-INCL}} \varphi$ iff $\mathcal{T}_{\text{EXI-INCL}}[T; \varphi] = \exists G\big(\mathit{Incl}^G[T] \wedge \mathit{Deriv}^G[\emptyset; T; \varphi]\big)$ is valid,*
2. *$T \vdash_{\text{UNI-INCL}} \varphi$ iff $\mathcal{T}_{\text{UNI-INCL}}[T; \varphi] = \forall G\big(\mathit{Incl}^G[T] \to \mathit{Deriv}^G[\emptyset; T; \varphi]\big)$ is valid, and*
3. *$T \vdash_{\text{ARG-INCL}} \varphi$ iff $\mathcal{T}_{\text{ARG-INCL}}[T; \varphi] = \mathcal{T}_{\text{EXI-INCL}}[T; \varphi] \wedge \neg \mathcal{T}_{\text{EXI-INCL}}[T; \neg\varphi]$ is valid.*

Analogous to the previous encodings we have that $\mathcal{T}_{\text{EXI-INCL}}[\cdot; \cdot]$ and $\mathcal{T}_{\text{UNI-INCL}}[\cdot; \cdot]$ are adequate, whilst $\mathcal{T}_{\text{ARG-INCL}}[\cdot; \cdot]$ exhibits that checking ARG-INCL consequences lies actually in D_2^P.

3.2   Signed Systems

The basic idea behind the approach taken by signed systems [11] is as follows. An inconsistent theory is transformed into a consistent one by renaming all literals occurring in the theory. Then, some of the original contents of the theory is restored by introducing progressively formal equivalences linking the original literals to their renamings. This is done as long as consistency is preserved. The overall approach provides us with a family of paraconsistent consequence relations.

For illustration, consider a theory containing the four statements

$$p,\ \neg p,\ q, (\neg q \lor r). \tag{13}$$

Clearly, this theory is inconsistent. We start with transforming the theory by renaming all of its literals:

$$p^+,\ p^-,\ q^+,\ (q^- \lor r^+).$$

The renamings indicate what renamed literals were denials of each other—making explicit whether the renamed literals were "positive" or "negative". In this way, we obtain a *signed* theory. Then, we restore some of the original contents of the theory by progressively introducing formal equivalences of the form $p^+ \equiv \neg p^-$, linking the original literals to their renamings. We do this up to the point where introducing any further equivalence would reinstate inconsistency. As a result, we can apply classical logic to reason from this signed theory extended with increasingly many equivalences (actually, the equivalences we use are slightly different because we deal at once with the signed and unsigned language). Then, a later interpretation of the signed formulas gets us back to the original language, classical inferences having thus been turned into seemingly paraconsistent ones.

The primary technical means for dealing with "signed theories" is *default logic* [57], whose central concepts are *default rules* along with their induced *extensions* of an initial set of premises. A default rule (or *default* for short) $\frac{\alpha : \beta}{\gamma}$ has two types of antecedents: a *prerequisite* α which is established if α is derivable and a *justification* β which is established if β is consistent. If both conditions hold, the *consequent* γ is concluded by default. For convenience, we denote the prerequisite of a default δ by $prereq(\delta)$, its justification by $justif(\delta)$, and its consequent by $conseq(\delta)$. Accordingly, for a set D of defaults, we define $prereq(D) = \{prereq(\delta) \mid \delta \in D\}$, $justif(D) = \{justif(\delta) \mid \delta \in D\}$, and $conseq(D) = \{conseq(\delta) \mid \delta \in D\}$.

A *default theory* is a pair (D, T) where D is a set of default rules and T is a set of propositional formulas. A set E of formulas is an *extension* of (D, T) iff $E = \bigcup_{n \in \omega} E_n$, where $E_1 = T$ and, for $n \geq 1$, $E_{n+1} = Cn(E_n) \cup \{\gamma \mid \frac{\alpha : \beta}{\gamma} \in D, \alpha \in E_n, \neg\beta \notin E\}$. We refer the reader for further details on default logic to the literature [57, 9].

The formal approach behind signed systems can then be described as follows. We start with a finite set of propositional formulas (i.e., a theory) T. Then, we proceed as follows. First, we transform T into conjunctive normal form (CNF).[3] This is a conjunction of disjunctions of literals, or simply a set of clauses. In this

---

[3] Such a transformation is not strictly necessary; see [11] on how this is avoided by distinguishing among positive and negative formula occurrences.

way, T is transformed into a finite set of clauses. It is worth noticing that this transformation does not affect the logical contents of the original theory.

Next, we rename the propositions in T as follows. Let φ be a formula in CNF. Then, we define $\varphi^{\pm}$ as the formula obtained from φ by replacing each occurrence of $\neg p$ by p^- and by replacing all remaining occurrences of p by p^+. In this way, we turn the initial theory T into the *consistent* theory $T^{\pm} = \{\phi^{\pm} \mid \phi \in T\}$. This is so because each formula ϕ of T is substituted by a formula $\phi^{\pm}$ which is always a *positive* formula.

Finally, we consider the default theory comprised of $T^{\pm}$ and a set of default rules $D_P = \{\delta_p \mid p \in P\}$, where P is a suitably chosen set of propositional atoms and

$$\delta_p = \frac{: p^+ \equiv \neg p^-}{(p \equiv p^+) \wedge (\neg p \equiv p^-)}, \tag{14}$$

for each $p \in P$. Intuitively, such default rules provide means for closing the gap between $T^{\pm}$ and T. That is, by checking whether the justification $p^+ \equiv \neg p^-$ is consistent, we test whether or not we can reintroduce the "law of (non-)contradiction" for the proposition p without getting an inconsistent theory. If this is the case, we "restore" the original meaning of the propositions p^+ and p^- by adding the equivalences $p \equiv p^+$ and $\neg p \equiv p^-$. Considering in turn each propositional letter p, we are thus gradually restoring the original contents of the theory—except that we stop at the borderline of inconsistency by leaving blank all propositions involved in genuine contradictions.

Consider the theory

$$\{p, \neg p, q, (q \to r)\}. \tag{15}$$

Transforming the elements of this theory into CNF yields the theory given in (13), i.e., $\{p, \neg p, q, (\neg q \vee r)\}$. Next, we rewrite this set of clauses into the consistent theory

$$\{p^+, p^-, q^+, (q^- \vee r^+)\} \tag{16}$$

by substituting $\neg p, \neg q$ by p^-, q^- and p, q, r by p^+, q^+, r^+, respectively.

We then proceed by adding, for each propositional atom occurring in the original theory, a corresponding default rule as defined in (14). This yields three default rules δ_p, δ_q, and δ_r, since the original theory is built from the propositional atoms p, q, and r. In full detail, $\delta_p, \delta_q, \delta_r$ have the following form:

$$\frac{: p^+ \equiv \neg p^-}{(p \equiv p^+) \wedge (\neg p \equiv p^-)}, \quad \frac{: q^+ \equiv \neg q^-}{(q \equiv q^+) \wedge (\neg q \equiv q^-)}, \quad \frac{: r^+ \equiv \neg r^-}{(r \equiv r^+) \wedge (\neg r \equiv r^-)} .$$

Consider the default theory obtained from theory (16) along with the three latter default rules:

$$\left(\{\delta_p, \delta_q, \delta_r\}, \{p^+, p^-, q^+, (q^- \vee r^+)\} \right). \tag{17}$$

Clearly, the first default rule is inapplicable, since its justification $p^+ \equiv \neg p^-$ is inconsistent in the presence of p^+ and p^-. In contrast, the second and the third default rule are applicable and consequently restore the original meaning of q^+, q^-, r^+, and r^-.[4] Accordingly, we obtain a single extension containing the propositions q and r (from the alphabet of our inconsistent initial theory) along with p^+, p^-, q^+, r^+.

Using this definition, we define the first family of paraconsistent consequence relations based on signed theories:

Definition 7. *Let T be a theory, φ a propositional formula, and $\mathcal{E}$ the set of all extensions of $(D_P, T^\pm)$. Moreover, for each set S of formulas and signed formulas, let $\Pi_S = \{ conseq(\delta_p) \mid p \in P, \neg justif(\delta_p) \notin S \}$. Then,*

- *φ is a credulous unsigned[5] consequence of T, symbolically written as $T \vdash_c \varphi$, iff $\varphi \in \bigcup_{E \in \mathcal{E}} Cn(T^\pm \cup \Pi_E)$,*
- *φ is a skeptical unsigned consequence of T, symbolically written as $T \vdash_s \varphi$, iff $\varphi \in \bigcap_{E \in \mathcal{E}} Cn(T^\pm \cup \Pi_E)$, and*
- *φ is a prudent unsigned consequence of T, symbolically written as $T \vdash_p \varphi$, iff $\varphi \in Cn(T^\pm \cup \bigcap_{E \in \mathcal{E}} \Pi_E)$.*

For illustration, consider the inconsistent theory $T = \{p, q, \neg p \vee \neg q\}$. For obtaining the above paraconsistent consequence relations, T is turned into the default theory $(D_P, T^\pm) = (\{\delta_p, \delta_q\}, \{p^+, q^+, p^- \vee q^-\})$. We obtain two extensions, viz. $Cn(T^\pm \cup \{conseq(\delta_p)\})$ and $Cn(T^\pm \cup \{conseq(\delta_q)\})$. The following relations show how the different consequence relations behave: on the one hand, we have $T \vdash_c p$, $T \not\vdash_s p$, and $T \not\vdash_p p$, but, on the other hand, for instance, it holds that $T \vdash_c p \vee q$, $T \vdash_s p \vee q$, and $T \not\vdash_p p \vee q$.

For a complement, the following "signed" counterparts are defined.

Definition 8. *Given the prerequisites of Definition 7, we say that*

- *φ is a credulous signed consequence of T, symbolically written as $T \vdash_c^\pm \varphi$, iff $\varphi^\pm \in \bigcup_{E \in \mathcal{E}} Cn(T^\pm \cup \Pi_E)$,*
- *φ is a skeptical signed consequence of T, symbolically written as $T \vdash_s^\pm \varphi$, iff $\varphi^\pm \in \bigcap_{E \in \mathcal{E}} Cn(T^\pm \cup \Pi_E)$, and*
- *φ is a prudent signed consequence of T, symbolically written as $T \vdash_p^\pm \varphi$, iff $\varphi^\pm \in Cn(T^\pm \cup \bigcap_{E \in \mathcal{E}} \Pi_E)$.*

As shown in [11], these relations compare to each other in the following way:

Proposition 14. *Let $C_i(T) = \{\varphi \mid T \vdash_i \varphi\}$ and similarly $C_i^\pm(T) = \{\varphi \mid T \vdash_i^\pm \varphi\}$, for $i \in \{p, s, c\}$. Then, we have*

---

[4] Notice that the contribution of a default rule like δ_r to the theory formation process is in no way sufficient for deriving r, even though it is a necessary condition. Applying δ_r merely re-establishes the original meaning of r and $\neg r$ from r^+ and r^-, respectively. In our example, r is derived from q and $\neg q \vee r$ due to the preceding restoration of q and r.

[5] The term "unsigned" indicates that only unsigned formulas are taken into account.

1. $C_i(T) \subseteq C_i^{\pm}(T)$, and
2. $C_p(T) \subseteq C_s(T) \subseteq C_c(T)$ and $C_p^{\pm}(T) \subseteq C_s^{\pm}(T) \subseteq C_c^{\pm}(T)$.

That is, signed derivability gives more conclusions than unsigned derivability, and within each series of consequence relations the strength of the relation is increasing. For a detailed formal elaboration, along with further refined consequence relations, we refer the reader to [11].

Encodings. In [12], it was shown that, given a theory T, the outcome of the different paraconsistent consequence relations solely depends on those defaults δ_p from D_P where p occurs in T. With a slight abuse of notation, in what follows we write D_T to denote this particular set of defaults for a given T.

The next result is of importance, since it leads us to a simple appealing encoding to compute the extensions of the kind of default theories under consideration.

Proposition 15. *Let T be a theory, $(D_T, T^{\pm})$ its corresponding default theory, and $C \subseteq D_T$.*
   Then, $Cn(T^{\pm} \cup conseq(C))$ is an extension of $(D_T, T^{\pm})$ iff justif(C) is maximal consistent with $T^{\pm}$.

Reconsider our example theory $T = \{p, \neg p, q, \neg q \vee r\}$ and its corresponding default theory (17), having $justif(D_T) = \{p^+ \equiv \neg p^-, q^+ \equiv \neg q^-, r^+ \equiv \neg r^-\}$. It is quite easy to see that $T^{\pm} = \{p^+, p^-, q^+, q^- \vee r^+\}$ is not consistent with $p^+ \equiv \neg p^-$, but with $\{q^+ \equiv \neg q^-, r^+ \equiv \neg r^-\}$. Thus, $justif(\{\delta_q, \delta_r\})$ is the maximal subset of $justif(D)$ consistent with T. We thus get as single extension the deductive closure of $T^{\pm} \cup conseq(\{\delta_q, \delta_r\}) = T^{\pm} \cup \{q \equiv q^+, \neg q \equiv q^-, r \equiv r^+, \neg r \equiv r^-\}$ yielding $Cn(p^+, p^-, q^+, q, r^+, r)$.

Indeed, Proposition 15 gives us a suitable basis for the desired QBF-encodings which represent a more compact axiomatics than the encodings given in [27] for arbitrary default theories.

Theorem 6. *Let T be a theory, $(D_T, T^{\pm})$ its corresponding default theory, and $G = \{g_\delta \mid \delta \in D_T\}$ a set of new guessing variables. Moreover, let $C \subseteq D_T$ and $I \subseteq G$ such that, for each $\delta \in D_T$, $\delta \in C$ iff $g_\delta \in I$.*
   Then, the set $Cn(T^{\pm} \cup conseq(C))$ is an extension of $(D_T, T^{\pm})$ iff the QBF $Cons_{max}^G[T^{\pm}; justif(D_T)]$ is true under I.

Having a characterisation of the extensions in terms of models of QBFs, it is quite easy to decide the respective paraconsistent consequence relations. In particular, encodings for the relations $\vdash_c$, $\vdash_c^{\pm}$, $\vdash_s$, and $\vdash_s^{\pm}$ are obtained by combining, in a suitable way, the above encoding with the module for expressing derivability.

Theorem 7. *Let T be a theory, φ a formula, and $(D_T, T^{\pm})$ as before. Moreover, let $G = \{g_\delta \mid \delta \in D_T\}$ be a set of guessing variables. Then,*

1. $T \vdash_c \varphi$ iff

$$\mathcal{T}_c[T; \varphi] = \exists G \big(\mathcal{C}ons_{max}^G [T^\pm; justif(D_T)] \wedge \mathcal{D}eriv^G [T^\pm; conseq(D_T); \varphi] \big)$$

is valid,

2. $T \vdash_s \varphi$ iff

$$\mathcal{T}_s[T; \varphi] = \forall G \big(\mathcal{C}ons_{max}^G [T^\pm; justif(D_T)] \rightarrow \mathcal{D}eriv^G [T^\pm; conseq(D_T); \varphi] \big)$$

is valid,

3. $T \vdash_c^\pm \varphi$ iff $\mathcal{T}_c^\pm[T; \varphi] = \mathcal{T}_c[T; \varphi^\pm]$ is valid, and
4. $T \vdash_s^\pm \varphi$ iff $\mathcal{T}_s^\pm[T; \varphi] = \mathcal{T}_s[T; \varphi^\pm]$ is valid.

Observe that the sets D_T, $justif(D_T)$, and $conseq(D_T)$ have the same cardinality. Hence, in the above result, one set of guessing variables, G, is sufficient.

It remains to deal with the prudent consequence relations. To begin with, as pointed out in [11], the inference relation $\vdash_p$ captures the notion of free consequence. Hence, $\mathcal{T}_{FREE}[\cdot; \cdot]$ can be used as encoding for $\vdash_p$. However, for a more direct encoding of prudent consequence, we can show the following property:

Lemma 3. Let T be a theory, $(D_T, T^\pm)$ its corresponding default theory, and φ a formula.

Then, the following conditions are equivalent:

1. $T \vdash_p \varphi$;
2. for each $C \subseteq D_T$, if, for each $\delta \in D_T$, $T \vdash_s conseq(\delta)$ only if $\delta \in C$, then $T^\pm \cup conseq(C) \models \varphi$.

This leads to the following encoding:

Theorem 8. Let T be a theory, $(D_T, T^\pm)$ its corresponding default theory, φ a formula, and $G = \{g_\delta \mid \delta \in D_T\}$ a set of new guessing variables.

Then, $T \vdash_p \varphi$ iff

$$\forall G \big(\bigwedge_{\delta \in D_T} (\mathcal{T}_s^\pm[T^\pm; conseq(\delta)] \rightarrow g_\delta) \rightarrow \mathcal{D}eriv^G [T^\pm; conseq(D_T); \varphi] \big)$$

is valid.

An encoding for $T \vdash_p^\pm \varphi$ is easily obtained by replacing φ by $\varphi^\pm$ in the above encoding.

Similar to the paraconsistent inference relations based on maximal subsets, the complexity of the signed and unsigned inference relations is located at the second level of the polynomial hierarchy. This was shown in [12] on the basis of the above encodings, by inspecting the quantifier order of the resultant QBFs.[6] As well, the respective encodings are adequate.

---

[6] Incidentally, the complexity results for $\vdash_s$ and $\vdash_s^\pm$ have independently been obtained by Coste-Marquis and Marquis as well [22].

3.3   Multi-valued Approaches

The idea underlying the three-valued approaches to paraconsistent reasoning is to counterbalance the effect of contradictions by providing a third truth value, accounting for contradictory propositions. As already put forth in [55], this provides us with inconsistency-tolerating three-valued models. However, this approach turns out to be rather weak in that it invalidates certain classical inferences, even if there is no contradiction. Intuitively, this is because there are too many three-valued models, in particular those assigning the inconsistency-tolerating truth-value to propositions that are unaffected by contradictions. For instance, the three-valued logic LP [55] denies inference by disjunctive syllogism. That is, ψ is not derivable from the (consistent!) premise $(\phi \vee \psi) \wedge \neg \phi$. As pointed out in [22], this deficiency applies also to the closely related paraconsistent systems J_3 [26], L [44], and RP [33]. As a consequence, none of the aforementioned systems coincides with classical logic when reasoning from consistent premises.

The pioneering work to overcome this deficiency was done by Priest [56]. The key idea is to restrict the set of three-valued models by taking advantage of some preference criterion that aims at "minimising inconsistency". In this way, a "maximum" of a classically inconsistent knowledge base should be recovered. While minimisation is understood in Priest's seminal work [56], proposing his logic LP_m, as preferring three-valued models as close as possible to two-valued interpretations, the overall approach leaves room for different preference criteria. Another criterion is postulated in [10] by giving more importance to the given knowledge base. In this approach, one prefers three-valued models that are as similar as possible to two-valued models of the knowledge base in the sense that those models assign *true* to as many items of the knowledge base as possible. Furthermore, [40] considers cardinality-based versions of the last two preference criteria. Even more criteria are conceivable by distinguishing symbols having different importance.

Syntactically, we use propositional formulas in the standard way, but adopt the semantics as follows. A *three-valued interpretation*, M, is a function assigning to each atom a truth value from $\{t, f, o\}$. Intuitively, the truth value o takes care for contradictory propositions. In general, the assignment of truth values to arbitrary formulas, given a three-valued interpretation M, is realised by means of a function $v_M(\cdot)$, which is specified according to the following truth tables, under the usual condition that $v_M(p) = M(p)$, for any atom p:

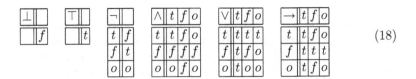

(18)

We sometimes leave an interpretation M implicit and simply write $\phi : x$ instead of $v_M(\phi) = x$, for $x \in \{t, f, o\}$. Also, with a slight abuse of notation, an interpretation may be specified as a finite set of expressions of form $p : x$, where p is an atom and x is as before, containing only the relevant elements and omitting the implicit part.

A *three-valued model* of a formula ϕ is an interpretation that assigns either t or o to ϕ. Modelhood extends to sets of formulas in the standard way. Accordingly, given a set T of formulas and a formula ϕ, we define $T \models \phi$ if each model of T is a model of ϕ. Whenever necessary, we write $\models_3$ and $\models_2$ to distinguish three-valued from two-valued entailment.

Note that the truth value of $\phi \rightarrow \psi$ differs from that of $\neg\phi \vee \psi$ only in the case of a three valued interpretation M with $v_M(\phi) = o$ and $v_M(\psi) = f$, resulting in $v_M(\phi \rightarrow \psi) = f$ and $v_M(\neg\phi \vee \psi) = o$. This difference is prompted by the fact that t and o indicate modelhood, which motivates the assignment of the same truth values to $\phi \rightarrow \psi$ no matter whether we have $\phi : t$ or $\phi : o$. This has actually to do with the difference between *modus ponens* and *disjunctive syllogism*: The latter yields ψ from $\phi \wedge \neg\phi \wedge \neg\psi$ because $\phi \vee \psi$ follows from ϕ. The overall inference seems wrong because, in the presence of $\phi \wedge \neg\phi$, $\phi \vee \psi$ is satisfied (by $\phi : o$) with no need for ψ to be t. As pointed out in [40], one may actually view the connective $\rightarrow$ as

"the 'right' generalisation of classical implication because $\rightarrow$ is the internal implication connective [5] for the defined inference relation in the sense that a deduction (meta)theorem holds for it: $T \cup \{\phi\} \models_3 \psi$ iff $T \models_3 \phi \rightarrow \psi$."

On the other hand, a formula composed of the connectives $\neg, \vee$, and $\wedge$ can never be inconsistent; that is, each such formula has at least one three-valued model [18]. Finally, we mention that the entailment problem for $\models_3$ is co-NP-complete, no matter whether $\rightarrow$ is included or not [50, 18, 22].

As mentioned previously, Priest's logic LP_m [56] was conceived to overcome the failure of disjunctive syllogism in LP [55]. LP amounts to the three-valued logic obtained by restricting the language to formulas in which only the connectives $\neg, \vee$, and $\wedge$ are permitted (and defining $\phi \rightarrow \psi$ as $\neg\phi \vee \psi$). In LP_m, modelhood is then limited to models containing a minimal number of *propositional variables* being assigned o. This allows for drawing

"all classical inferences except where inconsistency makes them doubtful anyway" [56].

Formally, the consequence relation of LP_m can be defined as follows.

Definition 9. *For three-valued interpretations M and N, define the partial ordering $M \leq_m N$ iff, for each atom p, $v_M(p) = o$ implies $v_N(p) = o$. Then, $T \models_m \varphi$ iff every three-valued model of T that is minimal with respect to $\leq_m$ is a three-valued model of φ.*

Unlike this, the approach of Besnard and Schaub [10] prefers three-valued models that assign the truth value t to as many items of the knowledge base T as possible:

Definition 10. *For three-valued interpretations M and N, define the partial ordering $M \leq_n N$ iff $\{\phi \in T \mid v_M(\phi) = o\} \subseteq \{\phi \in T \mid v_N(\phi) = o\}$. Then, $T \models_n \varphi$ iff every three-valued model of T that is minimal with respect to $\leq_n$ is a three-valued model of φ.*

The major difference between the two approaches defined above is that the restriction of modelhood in LP_m focuses on models as close as possible to two-valued *interpretations*, whilst the approach of Definition 10 aims at models next to two-valued *models* of the considered premises. According to [10], the effects of making the formula select its preferred models can be seen by looking at $T = \{p, \neg p, (\neg p \vee q)\}$: While LP_m yields two $\leq_m$-preferred models, $\{p : o, q : t\}$ and $\{p : o, q : f\}$, from which one obtains $p \wedge \neg p$, the second approach yields q as additional conclusion. In fact, $\{p : o, q : t\}$ is the only $\leq_n$-preferred model of the premises $\{p, \neg p, (\neg p \vee q)\}$; it assigns t to $(\neg p \vee q)$, while this premise is attributed o by the second $\leq_m$-preferred model $\{p : o, q : f\}$. Hence, the latter is not $\leq_n$-preferred. So, while $T \not\models_m q$ and $T \models_n q$, we note that $T \cup \{(p \vee \neg q)\} \not\models_l q$ for $l = m, n$. On the other hand, $\models_n$ is clearly more syntax-dependent than $\models_m$ since the items within the knowledge base are used for distinguishing $\leq_n$-preferred models.

In fact, both inference relations $\models_m$ and $\models_n$ amount to their classical (two-valued) counterpart, whenever the set of premises is classically consistent. Also, it is shown in [22] that deciding entailment for $\models_m$ and $\models_n$ is Π_2^P-complete, no matter whether $\rightarrow$ is included or not. A logical analysis of both relations can be found in [40] and in the original literature [56, 10].

Encodings. We start with an encoding of the underlying three-valued logic introduced above by means of classical propositional logic.

To this end, we introduce, for each atom p, a globally new atom p' and define $P' = \{p' \mid p \in P\}$ for a given set P of atoms.

Let M be a three-valued interpretation over a set P of atoms. We define the *associated two-valued interpretation*, a_2^M, over $P \cup P'$ by setting

$$\begin{aligned}
a_2^M(p) = a_2^M(p') &= t && \text{if } M(p) = t, \\
a_2^M(p) = a_2^M(p') &= f && \text{if } M(p) = f, \text{ and} \\
a_2^M(p) = f \text{ and } a_2^M(p') &= t && \text{if } M(p) = o,
\end{aligned}$$

for any atom $p \in P$. Conversely, for a given two-valued interpretation $I \subseteq P \cup P'$ satisfying $v_I(p \rightarrow p') = t$, for any $p \in P$, we define the *associated three-valued interpretation*, a_3^I, by setting

$$a_3^I(p) = \begin{cases} I(p) & \text{if } I(p) = I(p'), \\ o & \text{if } I(p) = f \text{ and } I(p') = t, \end{cases}$$

for any $p \in P$.

Moreover, we need the following parameterised translation:

Definition 11. *For any atom p and any propositional formula ϕ and ψ, we define*

1. (a) $\tau[p;t] = p$,
   (b) $\tau[p;f] = \neg p'$,
   (c) $\tau[p;o] = \neg p \wedge p'$,
2. (a) $\tau[\neg\phi;t] = \tau[\phi;f]$,
   (b) $\tau[\neg\phi;f] = \tau[\phi;t]$,
   (c) $\tau[\neg\phi;o] = \tau[\phi;o]$,
3. (a) $\tau[\phi \wedge \psi;t] = \tau[\phi;t] \wedge \tau[\psi;t]$,
   (b) $\tau[\phi \wedge \psi;f] = \tau[\phi;f] \vee \tau[\psi;f]$,
   (c) $\tau[\phi \wedge \psi;o] = \neg\tau[\phi \wedge \psi;f] \wedge \neg\tau[\phi \wedge \psi;t]$,
4. (a) $\tau[\phi \vee \psi;t] = \tau[\phi;t] \vee \tau[\psi;t]$,
   (b) $\tau[\phi \vee \psi;f] = \tau[\phi;f] \wedge \tau[\psi;f]$,
   (c) $\tau[\phi \vee \psi;o] = \neg\tau[\phi \vee \psi;t] \wedge \neg\tau[\phi \vee \psi;f]$,
5. (a) $\tau[\phi \rightarrow \psi;t] = \tau[\phi;f] \vee \tau[\psi;t]$,
   (b) $\tau[\phi \rightarrow \psi;f] = \neg\tau[\phi;f] \wedge \tau[\psi;f]$,
   (c) $\tau[\phi \rightarrow \psi;o] = \neg\tau[\phi;f] \wedge \tau[\psi;o]$.

For computing the three-valued models of a set T of formulas, we use

$$\mathcal{N}[T] = \bigwedge_{\phi \in T} \neg\tau[\phi;f].$$

For example, consider $T = \{p, \neg p, (\neg p \vee q)\}$. We get:

$$\begin{aligned}
\mathcal{N}[T] &= \neg\tau[p;f] \wedge \neg\tau[\neg p;f] \wedge \neg\tau[(\neg p \vee q);f] \\
&= \neg\neg p' \wedge \neg\tau[p;t] \wedge \neg(\tau[\neg p;f] \wedge \tau[q;f]) \\
&= \neg\neg p' \wedge \neg p \wedge \neg(\tau[p;t] \wedge \neg q') \\
&= \neg\neg p' \wedge \neg p \wedge \neg(p \wedge \neg q').
\end{aligned}$$

Now, the latter formula is equivalent to $p' \wedge \neg p \wedge (\neg p \vee q')$, which is in turn equivalent to $p' \wedge \neg p$ by absorption. Hence, $\mathcal{N}[T]$ possesses four two-valued models (over $\{p, p', q, q'\}$), viz.

$$I_1 = \{p'\}, \quad I_2 = \{p', q\}, \quad I_3 = \{p', q'\}, \quad \text{and} \quad I_4 = \{p', q, q'\}.$$

In order to establish a correspondence among the four two-models of $\mathcal{N}[T]$ and the three three-valued models of T, assigning o to p and varying on q, the relation between the underlying sets of atoms $P = \{p, q\}$ and $P' = \{p', q'\}$ must be fixed. In fact, this is accomplished by adding $r \rightarrow r'$ for every $r \in P$. Observe that in the above example, I_2 does not have a corresponding three-valued interpretation.

In this way, we obtain the following result.

Theorem 9. *Let φ be a formula with $P = var(\varphi)$, let $P' = \{p' \mid p \in P\}$, and let $x \in \{t, f, o\}$.*

Then, the following conditions hold:

1. *For any three-valued interpretation M over P, if $v_M(\varphi) = x$, then $\bigwedge_{p \in P}(p \rightarrow p') \wedge \tau[\varphi;x]$ is true under a_2^M, the associated two-valued interpretation of M.*

2. *For any two-valued interpretation I over $P \cup P'$, if $\bigwedge_{p \in P}(p \to p') \wedge \tau[\varphi; x]$ is true under I, then $v_{\mathsf{a}_3^I}(\varphi) = x$, where a_3^I is the associated three-valued interpretation of I.*

Since the formula $\tau[\varphi; t] \vee \tau[\varphi; f] \vee \tau[\varphi; o]$ is clearly a tautology of classical logic, we immediately get the following relation between the three-valued models of a theory and the two-valued models of the corresponding encoding:

Corollary 1. *Let T be a theory with $P = var(T)$, and let $P' = \{p' \mid p \in P\}$.*

Then, there is a one-to-one correspondence between the three-valued models of T and the two-valued models of the formula

$$\bigwedge_{p \in P} (p \to p') \wedge \mathcal{N}[T], \tag{19}$$

with $\mathcal{N}[T] = \bigwedge_{\phi \in T} \neg \tau[\phi; f]$.

In particular, the three-valued model of T corresponding to a two-valued model I of (19) is given by the associated three-valued interpretation a_3^I of I.

For illustration, consider $T = \{p, \neg p, (\neg p \vee q)\}$ along with

$$(p \to p') \wedge (q \to q') \wedge \mathcal{N}[T],$$

which is equivalent to

$$(p \to p') \wedge (q \to q') \wedge (p' \wedge \neg p).$$

Unlike above, we obtain now as two-valued models I_1, I_3, and I_4 being in a one-to-one correspondence with the three three-valued models, $\{p : o, q : t\}$, $\{p : o, q : o\}$, and $\{p : o, q : f\}$, of T, respectively.

Before dealing with the reductions for the inference relations $\models_m$ and $\models_n$, it is instructive to see that the results developed so far already allow for a straightforward encoding of three-valued entailment, and, in particular, inference in logic LP [55]:

Theorem 10. *Let T be a theory with $var(T) = P$, and let φ be a formula.*

Then, $T \models_3 \varphi$ iff $Deriv[\bigwedge_{p \in P}(p \to p') \wedge \mathcal{N}[T]; \neg \tau[\varphi; f]]$ is valid.

To be precise, we obtain (original) inference in LP [55] when restricting T and φ to formulas whose connectives are among $\neg$, $\wedge$, and $\vee$ only.

Let us now turn to Priest's logic LP_m [56]. For this, we must, roughly speaking, enhance the encoding of LP in order to account for the principle of "minimising inconsistency" used in LP_m. This is accomplished by means of the QBF module expressing propositional circumscription, as defined in Section 2.5.

Theorem 11. *Let T be a theory with $P = var(T)$, and let φ be a propositional formula. Furthermore, let $G = \{g_p \mid p \in var(T)\}$ be a set of new variables, and let $Q = P \cup P' \cup G \cup var(\varphi)$.*

Then, $T \models_m \varphi$ iff

$$\forall Q \Big(Circ[(\bigwedge_{p \in P}((p \to p') \wedge (g_p \equiv \tau[p; o]))) \wedge \mathcal{N}[T]; G; P \cup P'] \to \neg \tau[\varphi; f] \Big)$$

is valid.

To be precise, we obtain (original) inference in LP_m [56] when restricting T and φ to formulas whose connectives are among $\neg$, $\wedge$, and $\vee$ only.

We obtain an axiomatisation of Besnard and Schaub's approach [10] in a completely analogous fashion:

Theorem 12. *Let T, P, and φ be as in Theorem 11, let $G = \{g_\phi \mid \phi \in T\}$ be a set of new guessing variables, and let $Q = P \cup P' \cup G \cup var(\varphi)$.*

Then, $T \models_n \varphi$ iff

$$\forall Q\Big(\mathit{Circ}[(\textstyle\bigwedge_{p \in P}(p \rightarrow p') \wedge \bigwedge_{\phi \in T}(g_\phi \equiv \tau[\phi;o]) \wedge \mathcal{N}[T]; G; P \cup P'] \rightarrow \neg\tau[\varphi;f]\Big)$$

is valid.

It is a straightforward matter to check that the encodings given in the above theorems are adequate with respect to checking the corresponding inference relations. We also mention that alternative translations of the considered three-valued paraconsistent logics into QBFs are given in [13], based on different QBF modules for expressing the minimisation principles employed in the relations $\models_m$ and $\models_n$, respectively. Furthermore, although we do not detail it here, we stress that other multi-valued paraconsistent logics can analogously be treated in terms of reductions to QBFs. As a case in point, similar to the characterisations given in Theorems 11 and 12, [3] describes in effect axiomatisations of various four-valued paraconsistent logics into two-valued quantified propositional logic based on specific forms of propositional circumscription.

4   Conclusion

In this chapter, we discussed how differing approaches to paraconsistent reasoning can be expressed in a uniform framework by means of quantified propositional logic. We have started by introducing basic formulas that are used as building blocks for modeling advanced reasoning tasks. To a turn, we have demonstrated, by means of three case-studies, how specific paraconsistent inference problems can be mapped onto decision problems of QBFs.

The overall approach has several benefits. To begin with, it allows us to compare distinct approaches by looking at their axiomatisation as QBFs. Moreover, this axiomatisation provides an executable specification that can be given to existing QBF-solvers. In view of the considerable sophistication offered nowadays by these solvers, we obtain prototypical implementations with a relatively efficient performance.

The idea of encoding paraconsistent formalisms by means of QBFs is also investigated in [2]; interestingly, this approach uses signed formulas, as described in Section 3.2, for expressing inferences while preferences are expressed by QBFs. The idea of signed systems has recently been applied to database repair [4]. In this context, it is an interesting question in how far approaches to database repair and consistent query answering using annotated logics [1] (as a form of multi-valued logics) can be encoded by means of QBFs.

References

1. M. Arenas, L. Bertossi, and J. Chomicki. Consistent query answers in inconsistent databases. In *Proceedings of the Eighteenth ACM SIGACT-SIGMOD-SIGART Symposium on Principles of Database Systems (PODS '99)*, pages 68–79. ACM Press, 1999.

2. O. Arieli. Paraconsistent preferential reasoning by signed quantified Boolean formulae. In *Proceedings of the 16th European Conference on Artificial Intelligence (ECAI 2004)*, 2004. To appear.

3. O. Arieli and M. Denecker. Reducing preferential paraconsistent reasoning to classical entailment. *Journal of Logic and Computation*, 13(4):557–580, 2003.

4. O. Arieli, M. Denecker, B. V. Nuffelen, and M. Bruynooghe. Database repair by signed formulae. In *Proceedings of the Third Conference on Foundations of Information and Knowledge Systems (FoIKS '04)*, volume 2942 of *Lecture Notes in Computer Science*, pages 14–30. Springer-Verlag, 2004.

5. A. Avron. Simple consequence relations. *Information and Computation*, 92:105–139, 1991.

6. A. Ayari and D. Basin. QUBOS: Deciding quantified Boolean logic using propositional satisfiability solvers. In M. Aagaard and J. O'Leary, editors, *Proceedings of the Fourth International Conference on Formal Methods in Computer-Aided Design (FMCAD 2002)*, volume 2517 of *Lecture Notes in Computer Science*, pages 187–201. Springer-Verlag, 2002.

7. S. Benferhat, D. Dubois, and H. Prade. Argumentative inference in uncertain and inconsistent knowledge bases. In *Proceedings of the Ninth Conference on Uncertainty in Artificial Intelligence (UAI '93)*, pages 411–419, 1993.

8. S. Benferhat, D. Dubois, and H. Prade. Some syntactic approaches to the handling of inconsistent knowledge bases: A comparative study. Part 1: The flat case. *Studia Logica*, 58(1):17–45, 1997.

9. P. Besnard. *An Introduction to Default Logic*. Springer-Verlag, 1989.

10. P. Besnard and T. Schaub. Circumscribing inconsistency. In *Proceedings of the 15th International Joint Conference on Artificial Intelligence (IJCAI '97)*, pages 150–155. Morgan Kaufmann Publishers, 1997.

11. P. Besnard and T. Schaub. Signed systems for paraconsistent reasoning. *Journal of Automated Reasoning*, 20:191–213, 1998.

12. P. Besnard, T. Schaub, H. Tompits, and S. Woltran. Paraconsistent reasoning via quantified Boolean formulas, I: Axiomatising signed systems. In S. Flesca, S. Greco, N. Leone, and G. Ianni, editors, *Proceedings of the Eighth European Conference on Logics in Artificial Intelligence (JELIA '02)*, volume 2424 of *Lecture Notes in Computer Science*, pages 320–331. Springer-Verlag, 2002.

13. P. Besnard, T. Schaub, H. Tompits, and S. Woltran. Paraconsistent reasoning via quantified Boolean formulas, II: Circumscribing inconsistent theories. In *Proceedings of the Seventh European Conference on Symbolic and Quantitative Approaches to Reasoning with Uncertainty (ECSQARU '03)*, volume 2711 of *Lecture Notes in Computer Science*, pages 528–539. Springer-Verlag, 2003.

14. G. Brewka. Preferred subtheories: An extended logical framework for default reasoning. In N. S. Sridharan, editor, *Proceedings of the Eleventh International Joint Conference on Artificial Intelligence (IJCAI '89)*, pages 1043–1048. Morgan Kaufmann Publishers, 1989.

15. R. E. Bryant. Graph-based algorithms for Boolean function manipulation. *IEEE Transactions on Computers*, C-35(8):677–691, 1986.

16. T. Bylander. The computational complexity of propositional STRIPS planning. *Artificial Intelligence*, 69(1–2):165–204, 1994.

17. M. Cadoli, A. Giovanardi, and M. Schaerf. An algorithm to evaluate quantified Boolean formulae. In *Proceedings of the 15th National Conference on Artificial Intelligence (AAAI '98)*, pages 262–267. AAAI Press/MIT Press, 1998.

18. M. Cadoli and M. Schaerf. On the complexity of entailment in propositional multivalued logics. *Annals of Mathematics and Artificial Intelligence*, 18:29–50, 1996.

19. C. Cayrol, M. Lagasquie-Schiex, and T. Schiex. Nonmonotonic reasoning: From complexity to algorithms. *Annals of Mathematics and Artificial Intelligence*, 22(3–4):207–236, 1998.

20. C. Cayrol and M.-C. Lagasquie-Schiex. Non-monotonic syntax-based entailment: A classification of consequence relations. In C. Froidevaux and J. Kohlas, editors, *Proceedings of the Third European Conference on Symbolic and Quantitative Approaches to Reasoning and Uncertainty (ECSQARU '95)*, volume 946 of *Lecture Notes in Computer Science*, pages 107–114. Springer-Verlag, 1995.

21. A. Church. *Introduction to Mathematical Logic, Volume I*. Princeton University Press, 1956.

22. S. Coste-Marquis and P. Marquis. Complexity results for paraconsistent inference relations. In D. Fensel, F. Giunchiglia, D. McGuiness, and M. Williams, editors, *Proceedings of the Eighth International Conference on Principles of Knowledge Representation and Reasoning (KR '02)*, pages 61–72. Morgan Kaufmann Publishers, 2002.

23. M. Davis, G. Logemann, and D. Loveland. A machine program for theorem proving. *Communications of the ACM*, 5(7):394–397, 1962.

24. M. Davis and H. Putman. A computing procedure for quantification theory. *Journal of the ACM*, 7(3):201–215, 1960.

25. J. Delgrande, T. Schaub, H. Tompits, and S. Woltran. On computing solutions to belief change scenarios. In S. Benferhat and P. Besnard, editors, *Proceedings of the Sixth European Conference on Symbolic and Quantitative Approaches to Reasoning with Uncertainty (ECSQARU '01)*, volume 2143 of *Lecture Notes in Computer Science*, pages 510–521. Springer-Verlag, 2001.

26. I. D'Ottaviano and N. da Costa. Sur un problème de Jaśkowski. In *Comptes Rendus de l'Académie des Sciences de Paris*, volume 270, pages 1349–1353, 1970.

27. U. Egly, T. Eiter, H. Tompits, and S. Woltran. Solving advanced reasoning tasks using quantified Boolean formulas. In *Proceedings of the 17th National Conference on Artificial Intelligence (AAAI 2000)*, pages 417–422. AAAI Press/MIT Press, 2000.

28. U. Egly, R. Pichler, and S. Woltran. On deciding subsumption problems. In *Proceedings of the Fifth International Symposium on the Theory and Applications of Satisfiability Testing (SAT 2002)*, pages 89–97, 2002.

29. U. Egly, H. Tompits, and S. Woltran. On quantifier shifting for quantified Boolean formulas. In *Proceedings of the SAT 2002 Workshop on Theory and Applications of Quantified Boolean Formulas (QBF 2002)*, pages 48–61, 2002.

30. T. Eiter and G. Gottlob. On the computational cost of disjunctive logic programming: Propositional case. *Annals of Mathematics and Artificial Intelligence*, 15(3–4):289–323, 1995.

31. T. Eiter, V. Klotz, H. Tompits, and S. Woltran. Modal nonmonotonic logics revisited: Efficient encodings for the basic reasoning tasks. In U. Egly and C. Fermüller, editors, *Proceedings of the Eleventh International Conference on Automated Reasoning with Analytic Tableaux and Related Methods (TABLEAUX 2002)*, volume 2381 of *Lecture Notes in Computer Science*, pages 100–114. Springer-Verlag, 2002.

32. R. Feldmann, B. Monien, and S. Schamberger. A distributed algorithm to evaluate quantified Boolean formulas. In *Proceedings of the 17th National Conference on Artificial Intelligence (AAAI 2000)*, pages 285–290. AAAI Press/MIT Press, 2000.

33. A. Frisch. Inference without chaining. In J. McDermott, editor, *Proceedings of the Tenth International Joint Conference on Artificial Intelligence (IJCAI '87)*, pages 515–519. Morgan Kaufmann Publishers, 1987.

34. M. R. Garey and D. S. Johnson. *Computers and Intractability.* W. H. Freeman, 1979.

35. E. Giunchiglia, M. Narizzano, and A. Tacchella. QuBE: A system for deciding quantified Boolean formulas satisfiability. In R. Goré, A. Leitsch, and T. Nipkow, editors, *Proceedings of the First International Joint Conference on Automated Reasoning (IJCAR 2001)*, volume 2083 of *Lecture Notes in Computer Science*, pages 364–369. Springer-Verlag, 2001.

36. G. Gottlob. Complexity results for nonmonotonic logics. *Journal of Logic and Computation*, 2(3):397–425, 1992.

37. H. Kautz, D. McAllester, and B. Selman. Encoding plans in propositional logic. In L. Aiello, J. Doyle, and S. Shapiro, editors, *Proceedings of the Fifth International Conference on Principles of Knowledge Representation and Reasoning (KR '96)*, pages 374–384. Morgan Kaufmann Publishers, 1996.

38. H. Kautz and B. Selman. Planning as satisfiability. In B. Neumann, editor, *Proceedings of the Tenth European Conference on Artificial Intelligence (ECAI '92)*, pages 359–363. John Wiley & Sons, 1992.

39. H. Kleine Büning, M. Karpinski, and A. Flögel. Resolution for quantified Boolean formulas. *Information and Computation*, 117(1):12–18, 1995.

40. S. Konieczny and P. Marquis. Three-valued logics for inconsistency handling. In S. Flesca, S. Greco, N. Leone, and G.Ianni, editors, *Proceedings of the Eighth European Conference on Logics in Artificial Intelligence (JELIA '02)*, volume 2424 of *Lecture Notes in Computer Science*, pages 332–344. Springer-Verlag, 2002.

41. R. E. Ladner. The computational complexity of provability in systems of modal propositional logic. *SIAM Journal on Computing*, 6(3):467–480, 1977.

42. S. Leśniewski. Grundzüge eines neuen System der Grundlagen der Mathematik. *Fundamenta Mathematica*, 14:1–81, 1929.

43. R. Letz. Lemma and model caching in decision procedures for quantified Boolean formulas. In U. Egly and C. Fermüller, editors, *Proceedings of the Eleventh International Conference on Automated Reasoning with Analytic Tableaux and Related Methods (TABLEAUX 2002)*, volume 2381 of *Lecture Notes in Computer Science*, pages 160–175. Springer-Verlag, 2002.

44. H. Levesque. A knowledge-level account of abduction. In N. S. Sridharan, editor, *Proceedings of the Eleventh International Joint Conference on Artificial Intelligence (IJCAI '89)*, pages 1061–1067. Morgan Kaufmann Publishers, 1989.

45. J. Łukasiewicz and A. Tarski. Untersuchungen über den Aussagenkalkül. *Comptes Rendus Séances Société des Sciences et Lettres Varsovie*, 23(Cl. III):30–50, 1930.

46. J. McCarthy. Circumscription - A form of nonmonotonic reasoning. *Artificial Intelligence*, 13:27–39, 1980.

47. A. R. Meyer and L. J. Stockmeyer. The equivalence problem for regular expressions with squaring requires exponential space. In *13th Annual Symposium on Switching and Automata Theory*, pages 125–129, 1972.

48. A. R. Meyer and L. J. Stockmeyer. Word problems requiring exponential time. In *ACM Symposium on Theory of Computing (STOC '73)*, pages 1–9. ACM Press, 1973.

49. S. Minato. *Binary Decision Diagrams and Applications for VLSI CAD*. Kluwer, 1996.
50. D. Mundici. Satisfiability in many-valued sentential logic is NP-complete. *Theoretical Computer Science*, 52(1-2):145–153, 1987.
51. B. Nebel. Belief revision and default reasoning: Syntax-based approaches. In J. Allen, R. Fikes, and E. Sandewall, editors, *Proceedings of the Second International Conference on Principles of Knowledge Representation and Reasoning (KR '91)*, pages 417–428. Morgan Kaufmann Publishers, 1991.
52. C. Papadimitriou. *Computational Complexity*. Addison-Wesley, 1994.
53. D. Pearce, H. Tompits, and S. Woltran. Encodings for equilibrium logic and logic programs with nested expressions. In P. Brazdil and A. Jorge, editors, *Proceedings of the Tenth Portuguese Conference on Artificial Intelligence (EPIA '01)*, volume 2258 of *Lecture Notes in Computer Science*, pages 306–320. Springer-Verlag, 2001.
54. D. Plaisted, A. Biere, and Y. Zhu. A satisfiability procedure for quantified Boolean formulae. *Discrete Applied Mathematics*, 130:291–328, 2003.
55. G. Priest. Logic of paradox. *Journal of Philosophical Logic*, 8:219–241, 1979.
56. G. Priest. Reasoning about truth. *Artificial Intelligence*, 39:231–244, 1989.
57. R. Reiter. A logic for default reasoning. *Artificial Intelligence*, 13(1–2):81–132, 1980.
58. N. Rescher. *Plausible Reasoning*. Van Gorcum, Amsterdam, 1976.
59. N. Rescher and R. Manor. On inference from inconsistent premises. *Theory and Decision*, 1:179–219, 1970.
60. J. Rintanen. Constructing conditional plans by a theorem prover. *Journal of Artificial Intelligence Research*, 10:323–352, 1999.
61. J. Rintanen. Improvements to the evaluation of quantified Boolean formulae. In T. Dean, editor, *Proceedings of the 16th International Joint Conference on Artificial Intelligence (IJCAI '99)*, pages 1192–1197. Morgan Kaufmann Publishers, 1999.
62. J. A. Robinson. A machine-oriented logic based on the resolution principle. *Journal of the ACM*, 12(1):23–41, 1965.
63. B. Russell. The theory of implication. *American Journal of Mathematics*, 28(2):159–202, 1906.
64. S. Schamberger. Ein paralleler Algorithmus zum Lösen von Quantifizierten Boole'schen Formeln. Master's thesis, Universität Gesamthochschule Paderborn, 2000.
65. J. Srzednicki and Z. Stachniak, editors. *Lesniewski's Systems Protothetic*. Dordrecht, 1998.
66. R. Statman. Intuitionistic propositional logic is polynomial-space complete. *Theoretical Computer Science*, 9:67–72, 1979.
67. L. J. Stockmeyer. The polynomial-time hierarchy. *Theoretical Computer Science*, 3(1):1–22, 1976.
68. H. Tompits. Expressing default abduction problems as quantified Boolean formulas. *AI Communications*, 16:89–105, 2003.
69. H. Turner. Polynomial-length planning spans the polynomial hierarchy. In S. Flesca, S. Greco, N. Leone, and G. Ianni, editors, *Proceedings of the Eighth European Conference on Logics in Artificial Intelligence (JELIA '02)*, volume 2424 of *Lecture Notes in Computer Science*, pages 111–124. Springer-Verlag, 2002.
70. A. N. Whitehead and B. Russell. *Principia Mathematica*, volume 1–3. Cambridge University Press, 1910–13.
71. S. Woltran. *Quantified Boolean Formulas – From Theory to Practice*. PhD thesis, Technische Universität Wien, Institut für Informationssysteme, 2003.

72. C. Wrathall. Complete sets and the polynomial-time hierarchy. *Theoretical Computer Science*, 3(1):23–33, 1976.
73. L. Zhang and S. Malik. Towards a symmetric treatment of satisfaction and conflicts in quantified Boolean formula evaluation. In P. V. Hentenryck, editor, *Proceedings of the Eighth International Conference on Principles and Practice of Constraint Programming (CP 2002)*, volume 2470 of *Lecture Notes in Computer Science*, pages 200–215. Springer-Verlag, 2002.

On the Computational Complexity of Minimal-Change Integrity Maintenance in Relational Databases[*]

Jan Chomicki[1] and Jerzy Marcinkowski[2]

[1] Dept. of Computer Science and Engineering,
University at Buffalo,
Buffalo, NY 14260-2000
chomicki@cse.buffalo.edu
[2] Instytut Informatyki,
Wrocław University,
51-151 Wrocław, Poland
Jerzy.Marcinkowski@ii.uni.wroc.pl

Abstract. We address the problem of minimal-change integrity maintenance in the context of integrity constraints in relational databases. Using the framework proposed by Arenas, Bertossi, and Chomicki [5], we focus on two basic computational issues: *repair checking* (is a database instance a repair of a given database?) and *consistent query answers* (is a tuple an answer to a given query in every repair of a given database?). We study the computational complexity of both problems, delineating the boundary between the tractable and the intractable. We review relevant semantical issues and survey different computational mechanisms proposed in this context. Our analysis sheds light on the computational feasibility of minimal-change integrity maintenance. The tractable cases should lead to practical implementations. The intractability results highlight the inherent limitations of any integrity enforcement mechanism, e.g., triggers or referential constraint actions, as a way of performing minimal-change integrity maintenance.

1 Introduction

Inconsistency is a common phenomenon in the database world today. Even though integrity constraints successfully capture data semantics, the actual data in the database often fails to satisfy such constraints. This may happen because the data is drawn from a variety of independent sources as in data integration (see Lenzerini's survey [57]), or the data is involved in complex, long-running activities like workflows.

How to deal with inconsistent data? The traditional way is to not allow the database to become inconsistent by aborting updates or transactions leading to

---

[*] This material is based upon work supported by the National Science Foundation under Grant No. IIS-0119186 and UB start-up funds.

L. Bertossi et al. (Eds.): Inconsistency Tolerance, LNCS 3300, pp. 119–150, 2004.

integrity violations. We argue that in present-day applications this scenario is becoming increasingly impractical. First, if a violation occurs because of data from multiple, independent sources being merged (a scenario identified by Lin and Mendelzon [58]), there is no single update responsible for the violation. Moreover, the updates have typically already committed. For example, if we know that a person should have a single address but multiple data sources contain different addresses for the same person, it is not clear how to fix this violation through aborting some update. Second, the data may have become inconsistent through the execution of some complex activity and it is no longer possible to trace the inconsistency to a specific action.

In the context of triggers or referential integrity, more sophisticated methods for handling integrity violations have been developed. For example, instead of being aborted an update may be propagated. In general, the result is at best a consistent database state, typically with no guarantees on its distance from the original, inconsistent state (the research of Ludäscher, May, and Lausen [59] is an exception).

In our opinion, integrity restoration should be a separate process that is executed after an inconsistency is detected. Such an approach is also advocated by Embury et al. [36] under the name of *data reconciliation*. The restoration should have a minimal impact on the database by trying to preserve as many tuples as possible. This scenario is called from now on *minimal-change integrity maintenance*.

We claim that a central notion in the context of integrity restoration is that of a *repair* [5]. A repair is a database instance that satisfies integrity constraints and minimally differs from the original database (which may be inconsistent).

One can interpret the postulate of minimal change in several different ways, depending on whether the information in the database is assumed to be *correct* and *complete*. If the information is complete but not necessarily correct (it may violate integrity constraints), the only way to fix the database is by *deleting* some parts of it. This is a common approach in data warehousing. On the other hand, if the information is both incorrect and incomplete, then both insertions and deletions should be considered. Thus, in some data integration approaches, for example the work of Lenzerini, Lembo, and Rosati [56, 57], the completeness assumption is not made. For large classes of constraints, e.g., denial constraints, the restriction to deletions has no impact, since only deletions can remove integrity violations. Another dimension of change minimality is whether updates to selected attributes of tuples are considered as a way to remove integrity violations.

Regardless of what notion of minimal change is assumed, a basic computational problem in the context of integrity maintenance is *repair checking*, namely checking whether a given database instance is a repair of the original database. The complexity of this problem, under different notions of minimal change, is studied in the present paper. Repair checking algorithms can typically be converted to algorithms for nondeterministically computing repairs.

Sometimes when the data is retrieved online from multiple, autonomous sources, it is not possible to restore the consistency of the database by constructing a single repair. In that case one has to settle for computing, in response to queries, *consistent query answers* [5], namely answers that are true in every repair of the given database. Such answers constitute a conservative "lower bound" on the information present in the database. The problem of computing consistent query answers is the second computational problem studied in the present paper. The notion of consistent query answer proposed by Arenas, Bertossi and Chomicki [5] has been used and extended in many papers [6, 7, 8, 4, 9, 11, 12, 16, 20, 19, 21, 27, 28, 25, 34, 41, 45, 46, 49, 62, 64]. This research has been surveyed by Bertossi and Chomicki [14].

We describe now the setting of our results. We analyze the computational complexity of repair checking and consistent query answers along several different dimensions. We characterize the impact of the *class of queries* and the *class of integrity constraints* under consideration.

Our results shed light on the computational feasibility of minimal-change integrity maintenance. The tractable cases should lead (and to some degree already have led) to practical implementations. The intractability results highlight the inherent limitations of any integrity enforcement mechanism, e.g., triggers or referential constraint actions [59, 60], as ways of performing minimal-change integrity maintenance.

The plan of the paper is as follows. In the first three sections, we discuss first-order (or equivalently: relational algebra) queries. In Section 2, we define the basic framework. In Section 3, we consider denial constraints, for which repairs are obtained by deleting facts. In Section 4, we discuss more general universal constraints and inclusion dependencies, under different notions of repair. In Section 5, we study aggregation queries in the presence of functional dependencies. In Section 6, we summarize related research and in Section 7 we draw conclusions and discuss future work. Several key proofs are presented in detail. Other proofs can be found in the original sources.

2   Basic Notions

In the following we assume we have a fixed relational database schema R consisting of a finite set of relations (which are finite sets of tuples). We also have an infinite set of attributes (column labels) U from which relation attributes are drawn. We have a fixed, infinite database domain D, consisting of uninterpreted constants, and an infinite numeric domain N consisting of all rational numbers. Those domains are disjoint. The database instances can be seen as finite, first-order structures over the given schema, that share the domains D and N. Every attribute in U is typed, thus all the instances of R can only contain in a single attribute either uninterpreted constants or numbers. Since each instance is finite, it has a finite active domain which is a subset of $D \cup N$. (The property that attribute values are atomic is often called *First Normal Form* or *1NF*.) As usual, we allow the standard built-in predicates over N ($=, \neq, <, >, \leq, \geq$) that have infinite, fixed extensions. With all these elements we can build a first order language $\mathcal{L}$.

2.1   Integrity Constraints

Integrity constraints are closed first-order $\mathcal{L}$-formulas. In the sequel we will denote relation symbols by $P, P_1, \ldots, P_m$, tuples of variables and constants by $\bar{x}_1, \ldots, \bar{x}_m$, and quantifier-free formulas referring to built-in predicates by φ.

In this paper we consider the following basic classes of integrity constraints:

1. *Universal integrity constraints*: $\mathcal{L}$-sentences

$$\forall \bar{x}_1, \ldots, \bar{x}_n. \left(\bigvee_{i=1}^{m} P_i(\bar{x}_i) \ \vee \ \bigvee_{i=m+1}^{n} \neg P_i(\bar{x}_i) \ \vee \ \varphi(\bar{x}_1, \ldots, \bar{x}_n) \right).$$

   We assume that all variables appearing in positive literals appear also in at least one negative literal.

2. *Denial constraints*: $\mathcal{L}$-sentences

$$\forall \bar{x}_1, \ldots, \bar{x}_n. \left(\bigvee_{i=1}^{n} \neg P_i(\bar{x}_i) \ \vee \ \varphi(\bar{x}_1, \ldots, \bar{x}_n) \right).$$

   They are a special case of universal constraints.

3. *Binary constraints*: universal constraints with at most two occurrences of database relations.

4. *Functional dependencies (FDs)*: $\mathcal{L}$-sentences

$$\forall \bar{x}_1 \bar{x}_2 \bar{x}_3 \bar{x}_4 \bar{x}_5. \left(\neg P(\bar{x}_1, \bar{x}_2, \bar{x}_4) \ \vee \ \neg P(\bar{x}_1, \bar{x}_3, \bar{x}_5) \ \vee \ \bar{x}_2 = \bar{x}_3 \right).$$

   They are a special case of binary denial constraints. A more familiar formulation of the above FD is $X \to Y$ where X is the set of attributes of P corresponding to $\bar{x}_1$ and Y the set of attributes of P corresponding to $\bar{x}_2$ (and $\bar{x}_3$).

5. *Referential integrity constraints*, also known as *inclusion dependencies (INDs)*: $\mathcal{L}$-sentences

$$\forall \bar{x}_1 \ \exists \bar{x}_3. \left(\neg P_1(\bar{x}_1) \ \vee \ P_2(\bar{x}_2, \bar{x}_3) \right),$$

   where the $\bar{x}_i$'s are sequences of distinct variables, with $\bar{x}_2$ contained in $\bar{x}_1$; and database relations P_1, P_2. Again, this is often written as $P_1[Y] \subseteq P_2[X]$ where X (resp. Y) is the set of attributes of P_2 (resp. P_1) corresponding to $\bar{x}_2$. If P_1 and P_2 are clear from the context, we omit them and write the dependency simply as $Y \subseteq X$. If an IND can be written without any existential quantifiers, then it is called *full*.

Several examples of integrity constraints are presented later in Examples 1, 2, and 8.

Given a set of FDs and INDs IC and a relation P_1 with attributes U_1, a *key* of P_1 is a minimal set of attributes X of P_1 such that IC entails the FD

$X \rightarrow U_1$. In that case, we say that each FD $X \rightarrow Y \in IC$ is a *key* dependency and each IND $P_2[Y] \subseteq P_1[X] \in IC$ (where P_2 is also a relation) is a *foreign key constraint*. If, additionally, X is the primary (one designated) key of P_1, then both kinds of dependencies are termed *primary*.

The above constraint classes are the most common in database practice. They exhaust the constraints supported by present-day database management systems. The SQL:1999 standard [60] proposes general assertions that can be expressed using arbitrary SQL queries (and thus subsume arbitrary first-order constraints). However, such constraints have not found their way into practical DBMS implementations yet and are unlikely to do so in the near future. In fact, most systems allow only restricted versions of FDs and INDs in the form of key dependencies and foreign key constraints, resp.

Definition 1. *Given a database instance r of R and a set of integrity constraints IC, we say that r is* consistent *if* $r \vDash IC$ *in the standard model-theoretic sense;* inconsistent *otherwise.*

We assume that we are dealing with *satisfiable* sets of constraints.

2.2   Repairs

Given a database instance r, the *set* $\Sigma(r)$ *of facts* of r is the set of ground facts $\{P(\bar{a}) \mid r \vDash P(\bar{a})\}$, where P is a relation name and $\bar{a}$ a ground tuple. (There is clearly a straightforward correspondence between r and $\Sigma(r)$. However, we will find it more convenient to talk about the set of facts true in a first-order structure than about the structure itself.)

Definition 2. *The* distance $\Delta(r, r')$ *between database instances r and r' is defined as the symmetric difference of r and r':*

$$\Delta(r, r') = \big(\Sigma(r) - \Sigma(r')\big) \cup \big(\Sigma(r') - \Sigma(r)\big).$$

Definition 3. *For the instances* r, r', r'', $r' \leq_r r''$ *if* $\Delta(r, r') \subseteq \Delta(r, r'')$, *i.e., if the distance between r and r' is less than or equal to the distance between r and* r''.

Definition 4. *Given a set of integrity constraints IC and database instances r and r', we say that r' is a* repair *of r w.r.t. IC if* $r' \vDash IC$ *and r' is* $\leq_r$*-minimal in the class of database instances that satisfy IC.*

We denote by $Repairs_{IC}(r)$ the set of repairs of r w.r.t. IC. This set is nonempty because IC is satisfiable.

We will study in Section 4 some notions of repair that differ from that in Definition 4. Also, there is clearly a connection between the above notion of repair and the concepts of belief revision [42]. We discuss this connection in Section 6.

2.3   Queries

Queries are formulas over the same language $\mathcal{L}$ as the integrity constraints. A query is *closed* (or a *sentence*) if it has no free variables. A closed query without quantifiers is also called *ground*. *Conjunctive queries* [24, 2] are queries of the form

$$\exists \bar{x}_1, \ldots \bar{x}_m. \left(P_1(\bar{x}_1) \wedge \cdots \wedge P_m(\bar{x}_m) \wedge \varphi(\bar{x}_1, \ldots, \bar{x}_m) \right)$$

where the variables of x_i are disjoint from that of x_j if $i \neq j$, and $\varphi(\bar{x}_1, \ldots, \bar{x}_m)$ is a conjunction of built-in atomic formulas. A conjunctive query is *simple* if it has no repeated relation symbols and φ is of the form $c_1(\bar{x}_1) \wedge \cdots \wedge c_m(\bar{x}_m)$.

The following definition is standard [2]:

Definition 5. *A tuple $\bar{t}$ is an* answer *to a query $Q(\bar{x})$ in an instance r iff $r \models Q(\bar{t})$.*

2.4   Consistent Query Answers

Given a query $Q(\bar{x})$ to r, we want as *consistent* answers those tuples that are unaffected by the violations of IC, even when r violates IC.

Definition 6. [5] *A tuple $\bar{t}$ is a* consistent answer *to a query $Q(\bar{x})$ in a database instance r w.r.t. a set of integrity constraints IC iff $\bar{t}$ is an answer to query $Q(\bar{x})$ in every repair r' of r w.r.t. IC. An $\mathcal{L}$-sentence Q is* consistently true *in r w.r.t. IC if it is true in every repair of r w.r.t. IC. In symbols:*

$$r \models_{IC} Q(\bar{t}) \iff r' \models Q(\bar{t}) \quad \textit{for every repair } r' \textit{ of } r \textit{ w.r.t. } IC.$$

Note: If the set of integrity constraints IC is clear from the context, we omit it for simplicity.

2.5   Examples

Example 1. Consider the following instance of a relation *Person*

Name	City	Street
Brown	Amherst	115 Klein
Brown	Amherst	120 Maple
Green	Clarence	4000 Transit

and the functional dependency *Name* $\rightarrow$ *City Street*. Clearly, the above instance does not satisfy the dependency. There are two repairs: one is obtained by removing the first tuple, the other by removing the second. The consistent answer to the query *Person*(n, c, s) is just the tuple (Green,Clarence,4000 Transit). On the other hand, the query $\exists s.\ Person(n, c, s)$ has two consistent answers: (Brown,Amherst) and (Green,Clarence). Similarly, the query

$$Person(\text{Brown, Amherst, 115 Klein}) \vee Person(\text{Brown, Amherst, 120 Maple})$$

is consistently true in the given instance of *Person*. Notice that for the last two queries the approach based on removing all inconsistent tuples and evaluating the original query using the remaining tuples gives different, less informative results.

Example 2. We give here some examples of denial constraints. Consider the relation *Emp* with attributes *Name*, *Salary*, and *Manager*, with *Name* being the primary key. The constraint that *no employee can have a salary greater that that of her manager* is a denial constraint:

$$\forall n, s, m, s', m'. \; \bigl(\neg Emp(n, s, m) \vee \neg Emp(m, s', m') \vee s \leq s'\bigr).$$

Similarly, single-tuple constraints (CHECK constraints in SQL2) are a special case of denial constraints. For example, the constraint that *no employee can have a salary over \$200000* is expressed as:

$$\forall n, s, m. \; \bigl(\neg Emp(n, s, m) \vee s \leq 200000\bigr).$$

Note that a single-tuple constraint always leads to a single repair which consists of all the tuples of the original instance that satisfy the constraint.

2.6   Computational Problems

We consider here the following complexity classes:

- *P*: the class of decision problems solvable in polynomial time by deterministic Turing machines;
- *NP*: the class of decision problems solvable in polynomial time by nondeterministic Turing machines;
- *co-NP*: the class of decision problems whose complements are solvable in *NP*;
- Σ_2^p: the class of decision problems solvable in polynomial time by nondeterministic Turing machines with an *NP* oracle;
- Π_2^p: the class of decision problems whose complements are solvable in Σ_2^p;
- AC^0: the class of decision problems solvable by constant-depth, polynomial-size, unbounded fan-in circuits $(AC^0 \subset P)$.

Assume a class of databases $\mathcal{D}$, a class of queries $\mathcal{Q}$ and a class of integrity constraints $\mathcal{C}$ are given. We study here the complexity of the following problems:

- *repair checking*, i.e., the complexity of the set

$$B_{IC} = \{(r, r') : r, r' \in \mathcal{D} \wedge r' \in Repairs_{IC}(r)\},$$

- *consistent query answers*, i.e., the complexity of the set

$$D_{IC,\Phi} = \{r : r \in \mathcal{D} \wedge r \models_{IC} \Phi\},$$

for a fixed sentence $\Phi \in \mathcal{Q}$ and a fixed finite set $IC \in \mathcal{C}$ of integrity constraints. This formulation is called *data complexity* (introduced by Chandra and Harel [23] and Vardi [63]), because it captures the complexity of a problem as a function of the number of tuples in the database instance only. The database schema, the query and the integrity constraints are assumed to be fixed. (This is not the only relevant notion of complexity. Under *combined complexity*, also introduced by Vardi [63], the constraints and the query are also part of the input. However, in the database context the consensus is that data complexity is of paramount importance, because the size of the database is typically several orders of magnitude larger than the size of the constraints and the query. Thus, data complexity reflects the real computational cost of evaluating a query more faithfully than combined complexity. Consequently, almost all existing results about the complexity of computing consistent query answers are about data complexity, the work of Calì, Lembo, and Rosati [20] being an exception.)

It is easy to see that even under a single key FD, there may be exponentially many repairs and thus the approach to computing consistent query answers by generating and examining all repairs is not feasible.

Example 3. Consider the functional dependency $A \to B$ and the following family of relation instances r_n, $n > 0$, each of which has $2n$ tuples (represented as columns) and 2^n repairs:

r_n							
A	a_1	a_1	a_2	a_2	$\cdots$	a_n	a_n
B	b_0	b_1	b_0	b_1	$\cdots$	b_0	b_1

On the other hand, Definitions 4 and 6 immediately yield the following result.

Proposition 1. *For every set of universal constraints F and $\mathcal{L}$-sentence Φ, B_F is in co-NP and $D_{F,\Phi}$ is in Π_2^p.*

Proof. An instance r' is not a repair of r if it violates the integrity constraints or there is another instance r'' which satisfies the constraints and is closer (in the sense of $\leq_r$) to r than r'. The first condition can be checked in P; the second, in NP.

A sentence Φ is not consistently true in r if there is a repair r' of r in which Φ is false. Any repair r' of r can only contain tuples with the same constants as those occurring in the tuples of r. Thus the size of r' is polynomially bounded. Therefore, checking if there is a repair r' of r in which Φ is false can be done in NP with an NP oracle, i.e., it is in Σ_2^p.

In fact, B_F is in *co-NP* not only for universal but also for arbitrary first-order constraints. On the other hand, for non-universal constraints (e.g., INDs), the size of a repair cannot always be bounded and thus even the decidability of $D_{F,\Phi}$ is not guaranteed.

3   Denial Constraints

A distinctive property of denial constraints is that their violations can only be removed by deleting tuples from the database. Therefore, repairs (in the sense of Definition 4) are always *subsets* of the original database. This property has a positive influence on the computational complexity of integrity maintenance. Most of the notions of repair that differ for broader classes of constraints (see Section 4) coincide in the case of denial constraints.

3.1   Query Rewriting

Query rewriting is based on the following idea: *Given a query Q and a set of integrity constraints, construct a query Q′ such that for every database instance r the set of answers to Q′ in r is equal to the set of consistent answers to Q in r.*

Query rewriting was first proposed by Arenas, Bertossi, and Chomicki [5] in the context of domain relational calculus. The approach presented there was based on concepts from semantic query optimization (Chakravarthy, Grant, and Minker [22]), in particular the notion of a *residue*.

Residues are associated with literals of the form $P(\bar{x})$ or $\neg P(\bar{x})$ (where $\bar{x}$ is a vector of different variables of appropriate arity). For each literal $P(\bar{x})$ and each constraint containing $\neg P(\bar{x})$ in its clausal form (possibly after variable renaming), a local residue is obtained by removing $\neg P(\bar{x})$ and the quantifiers for $\bar{x}$ from the (renamed) constraint. For each literal $\neg P(\bar{x})$ and each constraint containing $P(\bar{x})$ in its clausal form (possibly after variable renaming), a local residue is obtained by removing $P(\bar{x})$ and the quantifiers for the variables occurring only in $\bar{x}$ from the (renamed) constraint. Finally, for each literal the global residue is computed as the conjunction of all local residues (possibly after normalizing variables).

Intuitively, the residues of a literal represent the conditions that must be true if the literal is true (and thus its negation is false).

Example 4. The constraint

$$\forall n, s, m, s', m'. \left(\neg Emp(n, s, m) \vee \neg Emp(m, s', m') \vee s \leq s' \right)$$

produces for $Emp(n, s, m)$ the following local residues:

$$\forall s', m'. \left(\neg Emp(m, s', m') \vee s \leq s' \right)$$

and

$$\forall s', m'. \left(\neg Emp(m', s', n) \vee s' \leq s \right).$$

The global residue is the conjunction of the local residues.

We consider queries that are conjunctions of positive and negative literals. The rewritten query is obtained in two steps. First, for every literal, an expanded version is constructed as the conjunction of this literal and its global residue. Second, the literals in the query are replaced by their expanded versions.

Example 5. Under the constraint

$$\forall n, s, m, s', m'.\ \bigl(\neg Emp(n, s, m) \vee \neg Emp(m, s', m') \vee s \leq s'\bigr),$$

the query $Emp(n, s, m)$ is rewritten into

$$Emp(n, s, m) \wedge \forall s', m'.\ \bigl(\neg Emp(m, s', m') \vee s \leq s'\bigr)$$
$$\wedge \forall s', m'.\ \bigl(\neg Emp(m', s', n) \vee s' \leq s\bigr).$$

A set of constraints is *generic* if it does not imply any ground literal. The results by Arenas, Bertossi, and Chomicki [5] imply the following:

Proposition 2. *For every generic set F of binary denial constraints and quantifier-free $\mathcal{L}$-sentence $\Phi(\bar{t})$ where*

$$\Phi = P_1(\bar{x}_1) \wedge \cdots P_m(\bar{x}_m) \wedge \neg P_{m+1}(\bar{x}_{m+1}) \wedge \cdots \wedge \neg P_n(\bar{x}_n) \wedge \varphi(\bar{x}_1, \ldots, \bar{x}_n)$$

and $\bar{t}$ is a vector of constants, $D_{F, \Phi(\bar{t})}$ is in P.

This is because query rewriting is done in a database-independent way and thus does not increase data complexity. In fact, since data complexity of evaluating first-order queries is in AC_0, so is $D_{F, \Phi}$.

The paper [5] shows that query rewriting is also applicable to full inclusion dependencies. But then the literal expansion step might need to be iterated until no changes occur. Also, care needs to be taken about the termination of the expansion (this is addressed by Celle and Bertossi [21]). However, query rewriting does not generalize to non-binary constraints, general INDs, or queries involving disjunction or quantifiers. The latter is particularly disappointing, since disjunctions or existential quantifiers in queries are necessary to extract *partial information* from the database. For example, in Example 1, we would like to be able to derive from the database that Brown lives in Amherst at 115 Klein or 120 Maple. Moreover, non-binary constraints and disjunctions do not necessarily lead to intractability, as shown below.

3.2   Conflict Hypergraph

Given a set of denial constraints F and an instance r, all the repairs of r with respect to F can be succinctly represented as the *conflict hypergraph*. This is a generalization of the *conflict graph* defined by Arenas, Bertossi, and Chomicki [7] for FDs only.

Definition 7. *The* conflict hypergraph *$\mathcal{G}_{F,r}$ is a hypergraph whose set of vertices is the set $\Sigma(r)$ of facts of an instance r and whose set of edges consists of all the sets*

$$\{P_1(\bar{t}_1), P_2(\bar{t}_2), \ldots P_l(\bar{t}_l)\}$$

such that $P_1(\bar{t}_1), P_2(\bar{t}_2), \ldots P_l(\bar{t}_l) \in \Sigma(r)$, and there is a constraint

$$\forall \bar{x}_1, \bar{x}_2, \ldots, \bar{x}_l.\ \bigl(\neg P_1(\bar{x}_1) \vee \neg P_2(\bar{x}_2) \vee \ldots \vee \neg P_l(\bar{x}_l) \vee \neg \varphi(\bar{x}_1, \bar{x}_2, \ldots, \bar{x}_l)\bigr)$$

in F such that $P_1(\bar{t}_1), P_2(\bar{t}_2), \ldots P_l(\bar{t}_l)$ violate together this constraint, which means that there exists a substitution ρ such that $\rho(\bar{x}_1) = \bar{t}_1, \rho(\bar{x}_2) = \bar{t}_2, \ldots \rho(\bar{x}_l) = \bar{t}_l$ and $\varphi(\bar{t}_1, \bar{t}_2, \ldots \bar{t}_l)$ is true.

Note that there may be edges in $\mathcal{G}_{F,r}$ that contain only one vertex. Also, the size of the conflict hypergraph is polynomial in the number of tuples in the database instance.

Example 6. The conflict graph of the instance of the relation *Emp* from Example 1 is represented in Figure 1.

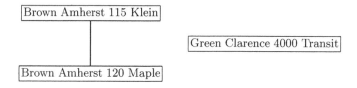

Fig. 1. Conflict hypergraph

By an *independent set* in a hypergraph we mean a subset of its set of vertices which does not contain any edge.

Proposition 3. *For each repair r' of r w.r.t. F, $\Sigma(r')$ is a maximal independent set in $\mathcal{G}_{F,r}$, and vice versa.*

Proof. Take an instance r' such that $\Sigma(r')$ is not a maximal independent set in $\mathcal{G}_{F,r}$. Then it contains an edge or is not maximal. In the first case, it means that r' violates the constraints; in the second, that r' is not minimal in $\leq_r$. On the other hand, if r' is not a repair, then it violates the constraints or is not minimal in $\leq_r$. In both cases, $\Sigma(r')$ is not a maximal independent set.

Proposition 3 yields the following result:

Proposition 4. [4] *For every set of denial constraints F and $\mathcal{L}$-sentence Φ, B_F is in P and $D_{F,\Phi}$ is in co-NP.*

Proof. Checking whether r' satisfies F is in P. The repair r' has also to be a maximal subset of r' that satisfies F. Checking that property can be done as follows: try all the tuples $\bar{t}$ in $r - r'$, one by one. If $r' \cup \{\bar{t}\}$ satisfies F, then r' is not maximal. Otherwise, if for no such tuple $\bar{t}$, $r' \cup \{\bar{t}\}$ satisfies F, no superset of r' can satisfy F (violations of denial constraints cannot be removed by adding tuples) and r' is maximal. The fact that $D_{F,\Phi}$ is in *co-NP* follows immediately from the definition of consistent query answer.

Note that the repairs of an instance r can be computed nondeterministically by picking a vertex of $\mathcal{G}_{F,r}$ which does not belong to a single-vertex edge and adding vertices that do not result in the addition of an entire edge.

3.3   Positive Results

Theorem 1. [27, 28] *For every set F of denial constraints and a ground sentence Φ, $D_{F,\Phi}$ is in P.*

Proof. We assume the sentence is in CNF [1], i.e., of the form $\Phi = \Phi_1 \wedge \Phi_2 \wedge \ldots \Phi_l$, where each Φ_i is a disjunction of ground literals. Φ is true in every repair of r if and only if each of the clauses Φ_i is true in every repair. So it is enough to provide a polynomial algorithm which will check if a given ground clause is consistently *true* in an instance r.

It is easier to think that we are checking if a ground clause is **not** consistently true in r. This means that we are checking, whether there exists a repair r' in which $\neg \Phi_i$ is true for some i. But $\neg \Phi_i$ is of the form

$$P_1(\bar{t}_1) \wedge P_2(\bar{t}_2) \wedge \ldots \wedge P_m(\bar{t}_m) \wedge \neg P_{m+1}(\bar{t}_{m+1}) \wedge \ldots \wedge \neg P_n(\bar{t}_n),$$

where the $\bar{t}_j$'s are tuples of constants. WLOG, we assume that all the facts in the set $\{P_1(\bar{t}_1), \ldots, P_n(\bar{t}_n))\}$ are mutually distinct.

The nonderministic algorithm selects for every j, $m + 1 \le j \le n$, $P_j(\bar{t}_j) \in \Sigma(r)$, an edge $E_j \in \mathcal{G}_{F,r}$ such that $P_j(\bar{t}_j) \in E_j$, and constructs a set of facts S such that

$$S = \{P_1(\bar{t}_1), \ldots, P_m(\bar{t}_m)\} \cup \bigcup_{m+1 \le j \le n, P_j(\bar{t}_j) \in \Sigma(r)} (E_j - \{P_j(\bar{t}_j)\})$$

and *there is no edge $E \in \mathcal{G}_{F,r}$ such that $E \subseteq S$*. If the construction of S succeeds, then a repair in which $\neg \Phi_i$ is true can be built by adding to S new facts from $\Sigma(r)$ until the set is maximal independent. The algorithm needs $n - m$ nondeterministic steps, a number which is independent of the size of the database (but dependent on Φ), and in each of its nondeterministic steps selects one possibility from a set whose size is polynomial in the size of the database. So there is an equivalent polynomial-time deterministic algorithm.

In the case when the set F of integrity constraints consists of only one FD per relation the conflict hypergraph has a very simple form. It is a disjoint union of full multipartite graphs. If this single dependency is a key dependency, then the conflict graph is a union of disjoint cliques. Because of this very simple structure we hoped that it would be possible, in such a situation, to compute in polynomial time the consistent answers not only to ground queries, but also to all conjunctive queries. As we are going to see now, this is only possible if the conjunctive queries are suitably restricted.

Theorem 2. [27, 28] *Let F be a set of FDs, each dependency over a different relation among $P_1, P_2, \ldots, P_k$. Then for each closed simple conjunctive query Q,*

---

[1] This assumption does not reduce the generality of our results, because every ground query can be converted to CNF independently of the database, and thus without affecting the data complexity of query evaluation. However, from a practical point of view, CNF conversion may lead to unacceptably complex queries.

there exists a closed query Q' such that for every database instance r, $r \models_F Q$ iff $r \models Q'$. Consequently, $D_{F,Q}$ is in P.

Proof. We present the construction for $k = 2$ for simplicity; the generalization to an arbitrary k is straightforward. Let P_1 and P_2 be two different relations of arity k_1 and k_2, resp. Assume we have the following FDs: $Y_1 \to Z_1$ over P_1 and $Y_2 \to Z_2$ over P_2. Let $\bar{y}_1$ be a vector of arity $|Y_1|$, $\bar{y}_2$ a vector of arity $|Y_2|$, $\bar{z}_1$ and $\bar{z}'_1$ vectors of arity $|Z_1|$, and $\bar{z}_2$ and $\bar{z}'_2$ vectors of arity $|Z_2|$. Finally, let $\bar{w}_1, \bar{w}'_1, \bar{w}''_1$ (resp. $\bar{w}_2, \bar{w}'_2, \bar{w}''_2$) be vectors of arity $k_1 - |Y_1| - |Z_1|$ (resp. $k_2 - |Y_2| - |Z_2|$). All of the above vectors consist of distinct variables. The query Q is of the following form

$$\exists \bar{y}_1, \bar{z}_1, \bar{w}_1, \bar{y}_2, \bar{z}_2, \bar{w}_2.\big(P_1(\bar{y}_1, \bar{z}_1, \bar{w}_1) \wedge P_2(\bar{y}_2, \bar{z}_2, \bar{w}_2) \wedge c_1(\bar{y}_1, \bar{z}_1, \bar{w}_1) \wedge c_2(\bar{y}_2, \bar{z}_2, \bar{w}_2)\big).$$

Then, the query Q' (which is also closed) is as follows:

$$\begin{aligned}
\exists \bar{y}_1, &\bar{z}_1, \bar{w}_1, \bar{y}_2, \bar{z}_2, \bar{w}_2 \forall \bar{z}'_1, \bar{w}'_1, \bar{z}'_2, \bar{w}'_2 \exists \bar{w}''_1, \bar{w}''_2.\Big(P_1(\bar{y}_1, \bar{z}_1, \bar{w}_1) \wedge P_2(\bar{y}_2, \bar{z}_2, \bar{w}_2) \\
&\wedge c_1(\bar{y}_1, \bar{z}_1, \bar{w}_1) \wedge c_2(\bar{y}_2, \bar{z}_2, \bar{w}_2) \wedge \big(P_1(\bar{y}_1, \bar{z}'_1, \bar{w}'_1) \wedge P_2(\bar{y}_2, \bar{z}'_2, \bar{w}'_2) \Rightarrow \\
&P_1(\bar{y}_1, \bar{z}'_1, \bar{w}''_1) \wedge P_2(\bar{y}_2, \bar{z}'_2, \bar{w}''_2) \wedge c_1(\bar{y}_1, \bar{z}'_1, \bar{w}''_1) \wedge c_2(\bar{y}_2, \bar{z}'_2, \bar{w}''_2)\big)\Big).
\end{aligned}$$

Chomicki and Marcinkowski [28] describe the generalizations of Theorems 1 and 2 to the non-ground case. The generalized version of the algorithm presented in the proof of Theorem 1 has been implemented as a part of a database middleware system Hippo [25, 26].

The above line of research is continued by Fuxman and Miller [41]. They make the observation that the query

$$Q_1 \equiv \exists e_1, e_2, s.\ \big(R(e_1, s) \wedge R(e_2, s) \wedge e_1 \neq e_2\big)$$

is consistently false if and only if there is a perfect matching in the graph of the relation R (the first argument of R is understood to be the key here). This implies that Q_1 is an example of a tractable query which cannot be answered by query rewriting (see the discussion earlier in this section), because perfect matching is not first order definable. Fuxman and Miller [41] generalize this perfect matching technique to a wider class of queries on databases over binary schemata.

3.4 Negative Results

We show now that Theorems 1 and 2 are the strongest possible (assuming the arity of relations is not restricted), because relaxing any of their conditions leads to *co-NP-completeness*. This is the case even though we limit ourselves to *key* FDs.

Theorem 3. [27, 28] *There exist a key FD f and a closed conjunctive query*

$$Q \equiv \exists x, y, y', z.\ \big(R(x, y, c) \wedge R(z, y', d) \wedge y = y'\big),$$

for which $D_{\{f\},Q}$ is co-NP-complete.

Proof. Reduction from MONOTONE 3-SAT. The FD is $A \to BC$. Let $\beta = \phi_1 \wedge \ldots \phi_m \wedge \psi_{m+1} \ldots \wedge \psi_l$ be a conjunction of clauses, such that all occurrences of variables in ϕ_i are positive and all occurrences of variables in ψ_i are negative. We build a database r_β with the facts $R(i, p, c)$ if the variable p occurs in the clause ϕ_i and $R(i, p, d)$ if the variable p occurs in the clause ψ_i. Now, there is an assignment which satisfies β if and only if there exists a repair of the database r_β in which Q is false.

As an example, consider the following monotone formula

$$\beta_0 = s \wedge (p \vee q) \wedge \neg p \wedge (\neg q \vee \neg s).$$

The corresponding database r_{β_0} contains the following facts:

$$R(1, s, c), R(2, p, c), R(2, q, c), R(3, p, d), R(4, q, d), R(4, s, d).$$

Clearly, β_0 is unsatisfiable. Also, Q is true in every repair of r_{β_0}.

To show the $\Rightarrow$ implication, select for each clause ϕ_i one variable p_i which occurs in this clause and whose value is 1 and for each clause ψ_i, one variable p_i which occurs in ψ_i and whose value is 0. The set of facts $\{R(i, p_i, c) : i \leq m\} \cup \{R(i, p_i, d) : m + 1 \leq i \leq l\}$ is a repair in which the query Q is false. The $\Leftarrow$ implication is even simpler.

Note that the query in Theorem 3 is nonsimple.

Theorem 4. [27, 28] *There is a set F of two key dependencies and a closed conjunctive query $Q \equiv \exists x, y.\ R(x, y, b)$, for which $D_{F,Q}$ is co-NP-complete.*

The above result was obtained first in a slightly weaker form – for non-key FDs – in [7, 4].

Theorem 5. [27, 28] *There exist a denial constraint f and a closed conjunctive query $Q \equiv \exists x, y.\ R(x, y, b)$, for which $D_{\{f\}, Q}$ is co-NP-complete.*

For the *co-NP-hard* cases identified above, no approach to the computation of consistent query answers based on query rewriting can work. This is because (a) such approaches produce queries that are evaluable in AC^0, and (b) the relevant *co-NP-complete* problems are not in AC^0.

4   Beyond Denial Constraints

4.1   Different Notions of Repair

The basic notion of repair (Definition 4) requires that the *symmetric* difference between a database and its repair is minimized. But as we have seen, in the context of denial constraints every repair is a subset of the database. Thus, insertions are not used in constructing repairs. The situation is different for more general constraints.

Example 7. Consider the integrity constraint $\forall x.\big(\neg P(x) \vee R(x)\big)$ and the database $\{P(1)\}$. Then there are two repairs: $\emptyset$ and $\{P(1), R(1)\}$.

Allowing repairs constructed using insertions makes sense if the information in the database may be incomplete[2]. The latter is common in data integration applications where the data is pulled from multiple sources, typically without any guarantees on its completeness. On the other hand, if we know that the data in the database is complete but possibly incorrect, as in data warehousing applications, it is natural to consider only repairs constructed using deletions. Current language standards like SQL:1999 [60] allow only deletions in their repertoire of referential integrity actions. Moreover, the restriction to deletions guarantees that the number of repairs is finite. This restriction is also beneficial from the computational point of view, as we will see later. Note that the symmetric restriction to insertions would make sense only in the context of inclusion dependencies: denial constraints cannot be fixed by insertions.

Example 8. Consider a database with two relations *Employee(SSN,Name)* and *Manager(SSN)*. There are functional dependencies $SSN \rightarrow Name$ and $Name \rightarrow SSN$, and an inclusion dependency $Manager[SSN] \subseteq Employee[SSN]$. The relations have the following instances:

Employee

SSN	Name
123456789	Smith
555555555	Jones
555555555	Smith

Manager

SSN
123456789
555555555

The instances do not violate the IND but violate both FDs. If we consider only the FDs, there are two repairs: one obtained by removing the third tuple from *Employee*, and the other by removing the first two tuples from the same relation. However, the second repair violates the IND. This can be fixed by removing the first tuple from *Manager*. So if we consider all the constraints, there are two deletion-only repairs:

Employee

SSN	Name
123456789	Smith
555555555	Jones

Manager

SSN
123456789
555555555

and

Employee

SSN	Name
555555555	Smith

Manager

SSN
555555555

---

[2] *Incompleteness* here does not mean that the database contains *indefinite information* in the form of nulls or disjunctions [61]. Rather, it means that *Open World Assumption* is adopted, i.e., the facts missing from the database are not assumed to be false.

Finally, insertions may lead to infinitely many repairs of the form

Employee

SSN	Name
123456789	c
555555555	Smith

Manager

SSN
123456789
555555555

where c is an arbitrary string different from *Smith* (this is forced by one of the FDs).

Example 9. To see the plausibility of repairing by insertion, consider Example 1 again. Suppose the only constraint is that *City* is a foreign-key, referencing the key of another relation *Cities*. Then if Clarence does not occur as a key value in the current instance of *Cities*, then one possible repair is to delete the tuple ⟨Green, Clarence, 4000 Transit⟩ (the city name may be erroneous). But it is also possible that not all the cities are in the current instance of *Cities*, thus another way of resolving the inconsistency is to insert a tuple with city name = Clarence into *Cities*. If *Cities* has more than one attribute, then infinitely many such repairs arise (all possible values for the nonkey attributes have to be considered). In practice, the nonkey attributes will receive null values in such a case.

In the next subsection, we will consider deletion-only repairs. Afterwards, we will revert to Definition 4.

4.2   Repairing by Deletion

We modify here Definition 4 to allow only repairs obtained by deletion of one or more tuples from the original instance. The definition of consistent query answers remains unchanged.

We also use B_I^- (resp. $D_{I,\Phi}^-$) to denote the problem of repair of repair checking (resp. consistent query answers), in order to indicate that due to the different notion of repair those problems are different from the corresponding problems B_I and $D_{I,\Phi}$ studied earlier.

We establish first a general relationship between the problems of repair checking and consistent query answers.

Theorem 6. *In the presence of full foreign key constraints, the problem of repair checking is logspace-reducible to the complement of the problem of consistent query answers.*

Proof. We discuss here the case of the database consisting of a single relation R_0. Assume r is the given instance of R_0 and r' is an another instance of R_0 satisfying the set of integrity constraints IC. We define a new relation S_0 having the same attributes as R_0 plus an additional attribute Z. Consider an instance s of S_0 built as follows:

- for every tuple $(x_1, \ldots, x_k) \in r'$, we add the tuple $(x_1, \ldots, x_k, c_1)$ to s;
- for every tuple $(x_1, \ldots, x_k) \in r - r'$, we add the tuple $(x_1, \ldots, x_k, c_2)$ to s.

Consider also another relation P having a single attribute W, and a foreign key constraint $i_0 : P[W] \subseteq S_0[Z]$. The instance p of P consists of a single tuple c_2. We claim that $P(c_2)$ is consistently true in the database instance consisting of s and p w.r.t. $IC \cup \{i_0\}$ iff r' is not a repair of r w.r.t. IC.

We now characterize the computational complexity of repair checking and consistent query answers for FDs and INDs.

Proposition 5. *For every set of INDs I and $\mathcal{L}$-sentence Φ, B_I^- and $D_{I,\Phi}^-$ are in P.*

Proof. For a given database instance r, a single repair is obtained by deleting all the tuples violating I (and only those).

We consider now FDs and INDs together. We want to identify the cases where both repair checking and computing consistent query answers can be done in P. The intuition is to limit the interaction between the FDs and the INDs in the given set of integrity constraints in such a way that one can use the polynomial-time results presented earlier.

Lemma 1. [28] *Let $IC = F \cup I$ be a set of constraints consisting of a set of key FDs F and a set of foreign key constraints I but with no more than one key per relation. Let r be a database instance and r' be the unique repair of r with respect to the foreign key constraints in I. Then r'' is a repair of r w.r.t. IC if and only if it is a repair of r' w.r.t. F.*

Proof. The only thing to be noticed here is that repairing r' with respect to key constraints does not lead to new inclusion violations. This is because the set of key values in each relation remains unchanged after such a repair (which is not necessarily the case if we have relations with more than one key).

Corollary 1. *Under the assumptions of Lemma 1, B_{IC}^- is in P.*

The repairs w.r.t. $IC = F \cup I$ of r are computed by (deterministically) repairing r w.r.t. I and then nondeterministically repairing the result w.r.t. F (as described in the previous section).

We can also transfer the polynomial-time results about consistent query answers obtained for FDs only.

Corollary 2. *Let Φ a quantifier-free $\mathcal{L}$-sentence or a simple conjunctive closed $\mathcal{L}$-query. Then under the assumptions of Lemma 1, $D_{IC,\Phi}^-$ is in P.*

Unfortunately, the cases identified above are the only ones we know of in which both repair checking and consistent query answers are in P.

For acyclic INDs (and arbitrary FDs), the repair checking problem is still in P. Surprisingly, consistent query answers becomes in this case a *co-NP-hard* problem, even in the case of key FDs and primary key foreign key constraints. If we relax any of the assumptions of Lemma 1, the problem of consistent query answers becomes intractable, even under acyclicity.

Definition 8. [2] *Let I be a set of INDs over a database schema R. Consider a directed graph whose vertices are relations from R and such that there is an edge $E(P, R)$ in the graph if and only if there is an IND of the form $P[X] \subseteq R[Y]$ in I. A set of inclusion dependencies is* acyclic *if the above graph does not have a cycle.*

Theorem 7. [28] *Let $IC = F \cup I$ be a set of constraints consisting of a set of FDs F and an acyclic set of INDs I. Then B_{IC}^{-} is in P.*

Proof. First compare r and r' on relations which are not on the left-hand side of any IND in I. Here, r' is a repair if and only if the functional dependencies are satisfied in r' and if adding to it any additional tuple from r would violate one of the functional dependencies. Then consider relations which are on the left-hand side of some INDs, but the inclusions only lead to already checked relations. Again, r' is a repair of those relations if and only if adding any new tuple (i.e. any tuple from r but not from r') would violate some constraints. Repeat the last step until all the relations are checked.

The above proof yields a nondeterministic polynomial-time procedure for computing the repairs w.r.t. $IC = F \cup I$.

To our surprise, Theorem 7 is the strongest possible positive result. The problem of consistent query answers is already intractable, even under additional restrictions on the FDs and INDs.

Theorem 8. [28] *There exist a database schema, a set IC of integrity constraints consisting of key FDs and of an acyclic set of primary foreign key constraints, and a ground atomic query Φ such that $D_{IC,\Phi}^{-}$ is co-NP-hard.*

We show also that relaxing the acyclicity assumption in Theorem 7 leads to the intractability of the repair checking problem (and thus also the problem of consistent query answers), even though alternative restrictions on the integrity constraints are imposed.

Theorem 9. [28] *There exist a database schema and a set IC of integrity constraints, consisting of one FD and one IND, such that B_{IC}^{-} is co-NP-hard.*

Theorem 10. [28] *There exist a database schema and a set IC of integrity constraints, consisting of key FDs and foreign key constraints, such that B_{IC}^{-} is co-NP-hard.*

We complete the picture by considering arbitrary FDs and INDs.

Theorem 11. [28] *For an arbitrary set IC of FDs and INDs, B_{IC}^{-} is co-NP-complete.*

Theorem 12. [28] *For an arbitrary set IC of FDs and INDs, and quantifier-free $\mathcal{L}$-sentence Φ, $D_{IC,\Phi}^{-}$ is Π_2^p-complete.*

Proof. The membership in Π_2^p follows from the definition of consistent query answer. We show Π_2^p-hardness below.

Consider a quantified boolean formula β of the form

$$\beta \equiv \forall p_1, p_2, \ldots p_k \exists q_1, q_2, \ldots q_l \; \psi$$

where ψ is quantifier-free and equals to $\psi_1 \wedge \psi_2 \wedge \ldots \psi_m$, where ψ_i are clauses. We will construct a database instance r_β, over a schema with a single relation $R(A, B, C, D)$, such that $R(a, a, \psi_1, a)$ is a consistent answer if and only if β is true. The integrity constraints will be $A \to B$ and $C \subseteq D$.

There are 3 kinds of tuples in r_β. For each occurence of a literal in ψ we have one tuple of the first kind (we adopt the convention that ψ_{m+1} is ψ_1):

- $R(p_i, 1, \psi_j, \psi_{j+1})$ if p_i occurs positively in ψ_j,
- $R(q_i, 1, \psi_j, \psi_{j+1})$ if q_i occurs positively in ψ_j,
- $R(p_i, 0, \psi_j, \psi_{j+1})$ if p_i occurs negatively in ψ_j,
- $R(q_i, 0, \psi_j, \psi_{j+1})$ if q_i occurs negatively in ψ_j.

For each universally quantified variable p_i we have two tuples of the second kind: $R(p_i, 1, a_i, a_i)$ and $R(p_i, 0, a_i, a_i)$. Finally, there is just one tuple of the third kind: $R(a, a, \psi_1, a)$.

Consider a repair s of r_β. Call s *white* if it does not contain any tuple of the first kind. Call s *black* if for each clause ψ_i of ψ, s contains some tuple of the form $R(\_, \_, \psi_i, \psi_{i+1})$. We claim, that each repair of r_β is either white or black. Indeed, if some $R(\_, \_, \psi_j, \psi_{j+1})$ is in s (i.e. if s is not white) then, since the $C \subseteq D$ constraint is satisfied in s, there must be some tuple of the form $R(\_, \_, \psi_{j-1}, \psi_j)$ in s. But the last implies that also some $R(\_, \_, \psi_{j-2}, \psi_{j-1})$ must be in s, and so on.

Notice, that it follows from the $C \subseteq D$ constraint that if a repair s is white, then $R(a, a, \psi_1, a)$ cannot be in s. On the other hand, it is easy to see that if s is black, then $R(a, a, \psi_1, a)$ is in s.

Now, for a repair s of r_β define σ_s^1 (respectively σ_s^2) as the substitution resulting from projecting the set of the tuples of the first (resp. second) kind in s on the first two attributes. Notice that σ_s^1 and σ_s^2 agree on the shared arguments: this is since s satisfies the functional dependency. From the construction of r_β it follows that if s is black then $\sigma_s^1(\psi)$ is true (for each ψ_j there is either a variable x occurring positively in ψ, such that $\sigma_s^1(x) = 1$ or variable x occurring negatively in ψ, such that $\sigma_s^1(x) = 0$).

To end the proof we need to show that β is false if and only if there exists some white repair of r_β.

Suppose β is false. Let σ be such a valuation of the variables $p_1, p_2, \ldots p_k$ that the formula $\sigma(\beta)$ (with free variables $q_1, q_2, \ldots q_l$) is not satisfiable. The set s_σ of all the tuples from r_β which are of the form $R(p_i, \sigma(p_i), a_i, a_i)$ is consistent. So there exists a repair s such that $s_\sigma \subseteq s$. But if s is black then σ_s^1 is a substitution which agrees with σ and satisfies ψ, which is a contradiction. So s must be white.

For the opposite direction, suppose β is true, and s is some white repair of r_β. This means that s contains only tuples of the second kind, and the projection of s on the first two attributes is some valuation σ of the variables $p_1, p_2, \ldots p_k$. Since β is true, there exists a valuation σ' of the variables $q_1, q_2, \ldots q_l$ such that $\sigma'\sigma(\psi)$ is true. Now, the union of s and the set of all the tuples of the first kind which are of the form $R(p_i, \sigma(p_i), \psi_j, \psi_{j+1})$ or of the form $R(q_i, \sigma'(q_i), \psi_j, \psi_{j+1})$ is a consistent superset of s, which contradicts the assumption that s was a repair.

4.3   Repairing by Insertion and Deletion

Calì, Lembo, and Rosati [20] study the complexity of query answering when the database is possibly not only inconsistent but also incomplete. Like in the paper of Arenas, Bertossi, and Chomicki [5] and the follow-up work, consistency is defined by means of integrity constraints, and an answer to a query is understood to be consistent if it is true in all possible repairs. Six definitions of the notion of repair are considered by Calì, Lembo, and Rosati [20], only one of which coincides with Definition 4. Each of those notions postulates that a repair satisfy the integrity constraints.

The *sound*, *exact*, and *complete* semantics do not impose any minimality conditions on repairs. The sound semantics requires that a repair is a superset of the database; the exact semantics – that it is equal to the database; and the complete semantics – that it is a subset of the database. Because an empty database satisfies any set of FDs and INDs, it is a repair under the complete semantics. Therefore, in this case there is no nontrivial notion of consistent query answer. The exact semantics is uninteresting for a different reason: the set of repairs is empty if the database violates the constraints, and consists of the original database if the constraints are satisfied. The sound semantics is suitable if the constraints consist of INDs only; in the presence of FDs, the set of repairs may be empty (this is because the violations of FDs cannot be fixed by tuple insertions). However, solving a violation of an inclusion dependency by adding new tuples may lead to new violations, of other dependencies, and thus there is no clear upper bound on the size of a minimal repair, under the sound semantics. So one can expect the problem of consistent query answers to be undecidable here. And indeed, this undecidability is proved by Calì, Lembo, and Rosati [20].

To present the decidable cases identified by Calì, Lembo, and Rosati [20], we need to introduce some definitions.

Definition 9. *Let $IC = F \cup I$ be a set of constraints consisting of a set of key FDs F (with at most one key per relation) and a set of INDs I. Then an IND $P[X] \subseteq R[Y] \in I$ is* non-key-conflicting *w.r.t. F if either: (1) no nontrivial key FD is defined for R in F, or (2) Y is not a strict superset of the key of R.*

Theorem 13. *[20] Let $IC = F \cup I$ be a set of constraints consisting of a set of key FDs F (with at most one key per relation) and a set of non-key-conflicting INDs I. Let Q be a union of conjunctive queries. Then the problem of consistent query answers is in P (under sound semantics).*

Notice that Theorem 13 to some degree parallels Lemma 1. One has to bear in mind, however, that those results use different semantics of consistent query answers due to different notions of repair.

The notion of repair under the sound semantics is not powerful enough if some functional dependencies can be violated in the original database (the set of repairs may be empty). This observation leads to the notions of *loosely-complete*, *loosely-sound*, and *loosely-exact* semantics. Under those semantics, repairs are constructed by adding tuples, as well as by deleting them. The loosely-complete semantics does not impose the requirement that the set of deleted tuples be minimal in a repair; therefore, the empty database is a repair and, as under the complete semantics, the notion of consistent query answer is trivial. The notion of repair under the loosely-exact semantics is identical to that of Definition 4. Finally, loosely-sound semantics requires only that the set of deleted tuples is minimized.

Calì, Lembo, and Rosati [20] show that for general key FDs and INDs the problem of consistent query answers under loosely-sound and loosely-exact semantics is undecidable. The decidable cases identified in that paper involve again non-key-conflicting INDs.

Theorem 14. [20] *Let $IC = F \cup I$ be a set of constraints consisting of a set of key FDs F (with at most one key per relation) and a set of non-key-conflicting INDs I. Let Q be a union of conjunctive queries. Then the problem of consistent query answers is co-NP-complete (under loosely-sound semantics) and Π_2^p-complete (under loosely-exact semantics).*

Contrasting Theorem 14 with Theorem 13, we see that the loosely-sound semantics augments the sound semantics with the nondeterministic choice of the set of tuples to be deleted. The loosely-exact semantics adds another level of nondeterminism.

We conclude by noting that none of the six notions of repair coincides with the one proposed by Chomicki and Marcinkowski [28]. The latter notion, by forcing the repairs to be subsets of the original database, makes the problem of consistent query answers decidable (Theorem 12).

4.4   Repairing by Attribute Modification

In the framework of Arenas, Bertossi and Chomicki [5], which was adapted by the follow-up papers [6, 7, 8, 4, 9, 11, 12, 20, 21, 27, 28, 34, 41, 45, 46, 49, 62], the smallest unit to be deleted from (or added to) a database in the process of repairing is a tuple. A different choice is made by Wijsen [64] where tuples themselves are being repaired. The idea there is that even a tuple that violates the integrity constraints can possibly still yield some important information. Wijsen's motivating example is a relation of arity 5 containing information on dioxin levels in food samples. The attributes of this relation are: the sample number, the sample date, the analysis date, the lab and the dioxin level. The integrity constraint is "the sample date must be prior to the analysis date". This is a denial constraint, thus the only thing that can be done with a tuple violating this constraint is dropping it, possibly getting rid of the number and other data of the sample, which may indicate an alarming dioxin level.

Example 10. Consider the relation *Emp* with attributes *Name*, *Salary*, and *Manager*, where *Name* is the primary key. The constraint that *no employee can have a salary greater than that of her manager* is a denial constraint:

$$\forall n, s, m, s', m'. \left(\neg Emp(n, s, m) \vee \neg Emp(m, s', m') \vee s \leq s'\right).$$

Consider the following instance of *Emp* that violates the constraint:

Name	Salary	Manager
Jones	120K	Black
Black	100K	Black

Under Definition 4, this instance has two repairs: one obtained by deleting the first tuple and the other – by deleting the second tuple. It might be more natural to consider the repairs obtained by adjusting the individual salary values in such a way that the constraint is satisfied.

The basic idea of the approach proposed by Wijsen [64] is to define the notion of repair by means of the ordering defined by the *subsumption of tableaux*, instead of the ordering $\leq_r$ defined by set inclusion (Definition 3). A tableau is a generalization of a relation: tuples can have not only constants but also variables as components. Wijsen [64] considers only single-relation databases.

Definition 10. [64] *If S and T are two tableaux, then:*
- *S subsumes T ($S \succeq T$) if there is a substitution σ such that $\sigma(T) \subseteq S$;*
- *S one-one subsumes T ($S \sqsupseteq T$) if there is a substitution σ such that $\sigma(T) \subseteq S$ and $|\sigma(T)| = |T|$.*

Definition 11. [64] *A tableau T subsatisfies a set of integrity constraints IC if there is a relation R satisfying IC and such that $R \succeq T$. A fix, with respect to IC, of a relation D is any tableau T such that*
(i) $D \sqsupseteq T$ and T subsatisfies IC;
(ii) T is subsumption-maximal among tableaux satisfying (i).

A repair of D is now any minimal relation D_1 which satisfies IC and for which there exists a fix T of D such that $D_1 \succeq T$.

The notion of consistent query answer in Wijsen's framework is that of Definition 6 in which the notion of repair of Definition 4 is substituted by that of Definition 11.

Example 11. If the dioxin database contains just one tuple

$$\langle 120, 17Jan2002, 16Jan2002, ICI, 150 \rangle,$$

then there are two fixes of it:

$$\langle 120, x, 16Jan2002, ICI, 150 \rangle$$

and
$$\langle 120, 17Jan2002, y, ICI, 150 \rangle.$$

A repair is any database resulting from the first fix by substituting for x any date prior to 16 Jan 2002 or from the second fix by substituting for y any date later than 17 Jan 2002. In each repair there is a tuple with the dioxin level 150.

The class of integrity constraints considered by Wijsen consists of tuple- and equality-generating dependencies [55, 2]. The first are simply universal Horn constraints, the second – restricted denial constraints. The queries studied by Wijsen [64] are conjunctive queries.

Wijsen [64] considers cases where answers to conjunctive queries can be computed by means of *early repairs*, which means, that for a given relation D, another relation D' is computed, such that a query is consistently true in D if and only if the query is true in D'. There are questions left open by the paper regarding the size of D', and in consequence, regarding the efficiency of this algorithm. Recently [Jef Wijsen, unpublished], *NP*-hardness of repair checking has been established under Definition 11 of repair:

Theorem 15. *There exists a denial constraint ϕ_0 with one database literal, such that repair checking is NP-hard.*

Note that for denial constraints repair checking under Definition 4 is in P. Thus, unless $P = NP$, there is a considerable computational price for using Wijsen's framework.

We note that the notions of repair discussed so far do not exhaust all the possibilities. For example, in Example 11 the database could also be repaired by swapping the values of the second and third attributes.

5   Aggregation

So far we have considered only first-order queries but in databases aggregation queries are also important. In fact, aggregation is essential in scenarios, like data warehousing, where inconsistencies are likely to occur and keeping inconsistent data may be useful.

We consider here a restricted scenario: there is only one relation and integrity constraints are limited to functional dependencies. Thus, every repair in the sense of Definition 4 is a maximal consistent subset of the given instance. Aggregation queries consist of single applications of one of the standard SQL-2 aggregation operators (MIN, MAX, COUNT(*), COUNT(A), SUM, and AVG). Even in this case, it was shown by Arenas, Bertossi and Chomicki [7] that computing consistent query answers to aggregation queries is a challenging problem for both semantic and complexity-theoretic reasons.

Example 12. Consider the following instance r of the relation *Emp*:

Name	Salary	Manager
Brown	50K	Black
Brown	70K	Black
Green	40K	Brown

It is inconsistent w.r.t. the FD: *Name* $\rightarrow$ *Salary*. The repairs are:

Name	Salary	Manager
Brown	50K	Black
Green	40K	Brown

Name	Salary	Manager
Brown	70K	Black
Green	40K	Brown

If we pose the query

```
SELECT MIN(Salary) FROM Emp
```

we should get 40K as a consistent answer: `MIN(Salary)` returns 40K in each repair. Nevertheless, if we ask

```
SELECT MAX(Salary) FROM Emp
```

then the maximum, 70K, comes from a tuple that participates in the violation of the FD. Actually, `MAX(Salary)` returns a different value in each repair: 50K or 70K. Thus, there is no consistent answer in the sense of Definition 6.   □

We give a new, slightly weakened definition of consistent answer to an aggregation query that addresses the above difficulty.

Definition 12. [7] *Given a set of integrity constraints F, an aggregation query f and a database instance r, the* set of possible answers $Poss_F^f(r)$ *is defined as*

$$Poss_F^f(r) = \{f(r') \mid r' \in Repairs_F(r)\}.$$

The greatest-lower-bound (glb) answer $glb_F(f, r)$ *to f w.r.t. F in r is defined as*

$$glb_F(f, r) = glb\ Poss_F^f(r).$$

The least-upper-bound (lub) answer $lub_F(f, r)$ *to f w.r.t. F in r is defined as*

$$lub_F(f, r) = lub\ Poss_F^f(r).$$

□

According to this definition, in Example 12, 50K (resp. 70K) are the *glb-answer* (resp. *lub-answer*) to the query

```
SELECT MAX(Salary) FROM Emp.
```

Notice that the interval [*glb answer,lub answer*] represents in a *succinct* form a superset of the values that the aggregation query can take in all possible repairs of the database r w.r.t. a set of FDs. The representation of the interval is always polynomially sized, since the numeric values of the endpoints can be represented in binary.

Example 13. Along the lines of Example 3, consider the functional dependency $A \rightarrow B$ and the following family of relation instances S_n, $n > 0$:

r_n									
A	a_1	a_1	a_2	a_2	a_3	a_3	$\cdots$	a_n	a_n
B	0	1	0	2	0	4	$\cdots$	0	2^n

The aggregation query `SUM(B)` takes all the exponentially many values between 0 and $2^{n+1} - 1$ in the (exponentially many) repairs of the database [7]. An explicit representation of the possible values the aggregation function would then be exponentially large. Moreover, it would violate the 1NF assumption. On the other hand, the glb/lub representation has polynomial size.   □

Arenas et al. [4] provide a complete classification of the tractable and intractable cases of the problem of computing consistent query answers (in the sense of Definition 12) to aggregation queries. Its results can be summarized as follows:

Theorem 16. [4] *The problem of computing glb/lub answers is in P for all the aggregate operators except* `COUNT(A)`, *if the set of integrity constraints contains at most one non-trivial FD.*

Theorem 17. [4] *The problem of checking whether the glb-answer to a query is $\leq k$ and the problem of checking whether the lub-answer to a query is $\geq k$ are NP-complete for* `COUNT(A)` *already in the presence of one non-trivial FD, and for the remaining operators in the presence of more than one non-trivial FD.*

For the aggregate operators `MIN`, `MAX`, `COUNT(*)` and `SUM` and a single FD, the glb- and lub-answers are computed by SQL2 queries (so this is in a sense an analogue of the query rewriting approach for first-order queries discussed earlier). For `AVG`, however, the polynomial-time algorithm is iterative and cannot be formulated in SQL2.

Example 14. Continuing Example 12, the greatest lower bound answer to the query

`SELECT MAX(Salary) FROM Emp`

is computed by the following SQL2 query

```
SELECT MAX(C) FROM
  (SELECT MIN(Salary) AS C
   FROM Emp
   GROUP BY Name).
```

□

Arenas et al. [7, 4] identify some special properties of conflict graphs in restricted cases, paving the way to more tractable cases. For example, for two FDs and the relation schema in Boyce-Codd Normal Form, the conflict graphs are claw-free and perfect [15], and computing lub-answers to COUNT(*) queries can be done in P.

Given the intractability results, it seems appropriate to find approximations to consistent answers to aggregation queries. Unfortunately, "maximal independent set" seems to have bad approximation properties [51].

6   Related Work

We only briefly survey related work here. Arenas, Bertossi and Chomicki [5, 14] provide a more comprehensive discussion.

There are several similarities between our approach to consistency handling and those followed by the belief revision community [42]. Database repairs (Definition 4) coincide with revised models defined by Winslett [65]. Winslett's framework is mainly propositional. However, Chou and Winslett [29] study a preliminary extension to first order knowledge bases. Those papers concentrate on the computation of the models of the revised theory, i.e., the repairs in our case. Comparing our framework with that of belief revision, we have an empty domain theory, one model: the database instance, and a revision by a set of ICs. The revision of a database instance by the ICs produces new database instances, the repairs of the original database. We consider a specific notion of minimal change, namely one that minimizes the set of literals in the symmetric differences of two instances. Other possibilities have also been explored in the belief revision community, for example minimizing the cardinality of symmetric difference, as proposed by Dalal [30].

The complexity of belief revision (and the related problem of counterfactual inference which corresponds to our computation of consistent query answers) in the propositional case is exhaustively classified by Eiter and Gottlob [35]. They show, among others, that counterfactual inference under Winslett's semantics is Π_2^p-complete. Subsequently, they provide a number of restrictions on the knowledge base and the revision formula to reduce the complexity. We note that among the constraint classes considered in the current paper, only universal constraints can be represented propositionally by grounding. However, such grounding results in an unbounded revision formula, which prevents the transfer of any of the polynomial-time upper bounds obtained by Eiter and Gottlob [35] into our framework. Similarly, their lower bounds require different kinds of formulas from those that we use.

The need to accommodate violations of functional dependencies is one of the main motivations for considering disjunctive databases (studied, among others, by Imieliński, van der Meyden, Naqvi, and Vadaparty [53, 54, 61] and has led to various proposals in the context of data integration (Agarwal et al. [3], Baral et al. [10], Dung [32], and Lin and Mendelzon [58]). There seems to be an intriguing connection between relation repairs w.r.t. FDs and databases with disjunctive information [61]. For example, the set of repairs of the relation *Person* from Example 3 can be represented as a disjunctive database D consisting of the formulas

Person(Brown, Amherst, 115 Klein) $\vee$ *Person*(Brown, Amherst, 120 Maple)

and

Person(Green, Clarence, 4000 Transit).

Each repair corresponds to a minimal model of D and vice versa. We conjecture that the set of all repairs of an instance w.r.t. a set of FDs can be represented as a disjunctive table (with rows that are disjunctions of atoms with the same relation symbol). The relationship in the other direction does not hold, as shown by the folowing example [4].

Example 15. The set of minimal models of the formula

$$(p(a_1, b_1) \vee p(a_2, b_2)) \wedge p(a_3, b_3)$$

cannot be represented as a set of repairs of any set of FDs.   □

Known tractable classes of first-order queries over disjunctive databases typically involve conjunctive queries and databases with restricted OR-objects [53, 54]. In some cases, like in Example 3, the set of all repairs can be represented as a table with OR-objects. But in general a correspondence between sets of repairs and tables with OR-objects holds only in the very restricted case when the relation is binary, say $R(A, B)$, and there is one FD $A \rightarrow B$ [4]. Imieliński, van der Meyden, and Vadaparty [54] provide a complete classification of the complexity of conjunctive queries for tables with OR-objects. It is shown how the complexity depends on whether the tables satisfy various schema-level criteria, governing the allowed occurrences of OR-objects. Since there is no exact correspondence between tables with OR-objects and sets of repairs of a given database instance, the results of the paper [54] do not directly translate to our framework, and vice versa. A different interesting direction to explore in this context is to consider *conditional tables*, proposed by Imieliński and Lipski [52], as a representation for infinite sets of repairs, as in Example 8.

There are several proposals for language constructs specifying nondeterministic queries that are related to our approach: *witness*, proposed by Abiteboul, Hull and Vianu [2], and *choice*, proposed by Giannotti, Greco, Pedreschi, Saccà, and Zaniolo [43, 44, 47]. Essentially, the idea is to construct a maximal subset of a given relation that satisfies a given set of functional dependencies. Since there is usually more than one such subset, the approach yields nondeterministic queries in a natural way. Clearly, maximal consistent subsets (choice models [43]) correspond to repairs. Datalog with choice [43] is, in a sense, more general than our approach, since it combines enforcing functional dependencies with inference using Datalog rules. Answering queries in all choice models ($\forall G$-queries [47]) corresponds to our notion of computation of consistent query answers (Definition 6). However, the former problem is shown to be *co-NP-complete* and no tractable cases are identified. One of the sources of complexity in this case is the presence of Datalog rules, absent from our approach. Moreover, the procedure proposed by Greco, Saccà and Zaniolo [47] runs in exponential time if there are exponentially many repairs, as in Example 3. Also, only conjunctions of literals are considered as queries by Greco, Saccà and Zaniolo.

A purely proof-theoretic notion of consistent query answer comes from Bry [17]. This notion, described only in the propositional case, corresponds to evaluating queries after all the tuples involved in inconsistencies have been eliminated. No complexity results have been established for Bry's approach.

Representing repairs as answer sets of logic programs with disjunction and classical negation has been proposed in a number of papers [6, 8, 12, 34, 45, 46, 49, 62]. Those papers consider computing consistent answers to first-order queries. While the approach is very general, no tractable cases beyond those already implicit in the results of Arenas, Bertossi and Chomicki [5] are identified. This is because the classes of logic programs used are Π_2^p-complete [31]. Eiter et al. [34] propose several optimizations that are applicable to logic programming approaches. One is localization of conflict resolution, another - encoding tuple membership in individual repairs using bitvectors, which makes possible efficient computation of consistent query answers using bitwise operators. However, we have seen in Example 3 even in the presence of one functional dependency there may be *exponentially* many repairs [4]. With only 80 tuples involved in conflicts, the number of repairs may exceed 10^{12}! It is clearly impractical to efficiently manipulate bitvectors of that size.

7 Conclusions and Future Work

We envision several possible directions for future work.

First, one can consider various *preference orderings* on repairs. Such orderings are often natural and may lead to further tractable cases. Some preliminary work in this direction is reported by Greco et al. [45, 48].

Second, the connection between the semantics of repairs and the complexity of repair checking and consistent query answers should be investigated further, in particular the impact of adopting a *cardinality-based* minimality criterion for repairs.

Third, a natural scenario for applying the results developed in this paper is *query rewriting* in the presence of distributed data sources [33, 50, 57]. Abiteboul and Duschka [1] show, among others, that assuming that data sources are complete has a negative influence on the computational complexity of query answering. However, originally, this line of work didn't address problems due to database inconsistency. Only recently the research on data integration [13, 16, 19, 56] has started to deal with issues involved in data sources being inconsistent. These works largely remain within the answer-set-based paradigm discussed above. A new scenario for data integration, *data exchange*, has been recently proposed by Fagin et al. [37]. In this scenario, a target database is materialized on the basis of a source database using source-to-target dependencies. In the presence of target integrity constraints, a suitable consistent target database may not exist. This issue is not considered by Fagin et al. [37]. The work of Calì, Lembo and Rosati [20], discussed earlier, can be viewed as addressing the problem of consistent query answering in a restricted data exchange setting.

Finally, as XML is playing an increased role in data integration, it would be interesting and challenging to develop the appropriate notions of repair and consistent query answer in the context of XML databases. A first attempt in this direction is reported by Flesca et al. [40]. It is limited, however, since it does not consider DTDs. Recent integrity constraint proposals for XML have been made by Buneman et al. [18] and Fan, Kuper, and Siméon [38, 39].

Acknowledgments

The comments of Jef Wijsen, Ariel Fuxman, and the anonymous referees are gratefully acknowledged.

References

1. O. Abiteboul and O. Duschka. Complexity of Answering Queries Using Materialized Views. In *ACM Symposium on Principles of Database Systems (PODS)*, pages 254–263, 1998.
2. S. Abiteboul, R. Hull, and V. Vianu. *Foundations of Databases*. Addison-Wesley, 1995.
3. S. Agarwal, A. M. Keller, G. Wiederhold, and K. Saraswat. Flexible Relation: An Approach for Integrating Data from Multiple, Possibly Inconsistent Databases. In *IEEE International Conference on Data Engineering (ICDE)*, pages 495–504, 1995.
4. M. Arenas, L. Bertossi, J. Chomicki, X. He, V. Raghavan, and J. Spinrad. Scalar Aggregation in Inconsistent Databases. *Theoretical Computer Science*, 296(3):405–434, 2003.
5. M. Arenas, L. Bertossi, and J. Chomicki. Consistent Query Answers in Inconsistent Databases. In *ACM Symposium on Principles of Database Systems (PODS)*, pages 68–79, 1999.
6. M. Arenas, L. Bertossi, and J. Chomicki. Specifying and Querying Database Repairs Using Logic Programs with Exceptions. In *International Conference on Flexible Query Answering Systems (FQAS)*, pages 27–41. Springer-Verlag, 2000.
7. M. Arenas, L. Bertossi, and J. Chomicki. Scalar Aggregation in FD-Inconsistent Databases. In *International Conference on Database Theory (ICDT)*, pages 39–53. Springer-Verlag, LNCS 1973, 2001.
8. M. Arenas, L. Bertossi, and J. Chomicki. Answer Sets for Consistent Query Answering in Inconsistent Databases. *Theory and Practice of Logic Programming*, 3(4–5):393–424, 2003.
9. M. Arenas, L. Bertossi, and M. Kifer. Applications of Annotated Predicate Calculus to Querying Inconsistent Databases. In *International Conference on Computational Logic*, pages 926–941. Springer-Verlag, LNCS 1861, 2000.
10. C. Baral, S. Kraus, J. Minker, and V. S. Subrahmanian. Combining Knowledge Bases Consisting of First-Order Theories. *Computational Intelligence*, 8:45–71, 1992.
11. P. Barcelo and L. Bertossi. Repairing Databases with Annotated Predicate Logic. In S. Benferhat and E. Giunchiglia, editors, *Ninth International Workshop on Non-Monotonic Reasoning (NMR02), Special Session: Changing and Integrating Information: From Theory to Practice*, pages 160–170, 2002.

12. P. Barcelo and L. Bertossi. Logic Programs for Querying Inconsistent Databases. In *International Symposium on Practical Aspects of Declarative Languages (PADL)*, pages 208–222. Springer-Verlag, LNCS 2562, 2003.
13. L. Bertossi, J. Chomicki, A. Cortes, and C. Gutierrez. Consistent Answers from Integrated Data Sources. In *International Conference on Flexible Query Answering Systems (FQAS)*, pages 71–85, Copenhagen, Denmark, October 2002. Springer-Verlag.
14. L. Bertossi and J. Chomicki. Query Answering in Inconsistent Databases. In J. Chomicki, R. van der Meyden, and G. Saake, editors, *Logics for Emerging Applications of Databases*, pages 43–83. Springer-Verlag, 2003.
15. A. Brandstädt, V. B. Le, and J. P. Spinrad. *Graph Classes: A Survey*. SIAM, 1999.
16. L. Bravo and L. Bertossi. Logic Programs for Consistently Querying Data Integration Systems. In *International Joint Conference on Artificial Intelligence (IJCAI)*, pages 10–15, 2003.
17. F. Bry. Query Answering in Information Systems with Integrity Constraints. In *IFIP WG 11.5 Working Conference on Integrity and Control in Information Systems*, pages 113–130. Chapman &Hall, 1997.
18. P. Buneman, S. Davidson, W. Fan, C. Hara, and W. Tan. Keys for XML. *Computer Networks*, 39(5):473–487, 2002.
19. A. Cali, D. Lembo, and R. Rosati. On the Decidability and Complexity of Query Answering over Inconsistent and Incomplete Databases. In *ACM Symposium on Principles of Database Systems (PODS)*, pages 260–271, 2003.
20. A. Cali, D. Lembo, and R. Rosati. Query rewriting and answering under constraints in data intergation systems. In *International Joint Conference on Artificial Intelligence (IJCAI)*, pages 16–21, 2003.
21. A. Celle and L. Bertossi. Querying Inconsistent Databases: Algorithms and Implementation. In *International Conference on Computational Logic*, pages 942–956. Springer-Verlag, LNCS 1861, 2000.
22. U. S. Chakravarthy, J. Grant, and J. Minker. Logic-Based Approach to Semantic Query Optimization. *ACM Transactions on Database Systems*, 15(2):162–207, 1990.
23. A. K. Chandra and D. Harel. Computable Queries for Relational Databases. *Journal of Computer and System Sciences*, 21:156–178, 1980.
24. A. Chandra and P. Merlin. Optimal Implementation of Conjunctive Queries in Relational Databases. In *ACM SIGACT Symposium on the Theory of Computing (STOC)*, pages 77–90, 1977.
25. J. Chomicki, J. Marcinkowski, and S. Staworko. Computing Consistent Query Answers Using Conflict Hypergraphs. Submitted, 2004.
26. J. Chomicki, J. Marcinkowski, and S. Staworko. Hippo: A System for Computing Consistent Answers to a Class of SQL Queries. In *International Conference on Extending Database Technology (EDBT)*, pages 841–844. Springer-Verlag, LNCS 2992, 2004. System demo.
27. J. Chomicki and J. Marcinkowski. On the Computational Complexity of Consistent Query Answers. Technical Report arXiv:cs.DB/0204010, arXiv.org e-Print archive, April 2002.
28. J. Chomicki and J. Marcinkowski. Minimal-Change Integrity Maintenance Using Tuple Deletions. *Information and Computation*, 2004. To appear. Earlier version: Technical Report cs.DB/0212004, arXiv.org e-Print archive.
29. T. Chou and M. Winslett. A Model-Based Belief Revision System. *Journal of Automated Reasoning*, 12:157–208, 1994.

30. M. Dalal. Investigations into a Theory of Knowledge Base Revision. In *National Conference on Artificial Intelligence*, St.Paul, Minnesota, August 1988.

31. E. Dantsin, T. Eiter, G. Gottlob, and A. Voronkov. Complexity and Expressive Power of Logic Programming. *ACM Computing Surveys*, 33(3):374–425, 2001.

32. Phan Minh Dung. Integrating Data from Possibly Inconsistent Databases. In *International Conference on Cooperative Information Systems (COOPIS)*, pages 58–65, Brussels, Belgium, 1996. IEEE Press.

33. O.M. Duschka, M.R. Genesereth, and A.Y. Levy. Recursive Query Plans for Data Integration. *Journal of Logic Programming*, 43(1):49–73, 2000.

34. T. Eiter, M. Fink, G. Greco, and D. Lembo. Efficient Evaluation of Logic Programs for Querying Data Integration Systems. In *International Conference on Logic Programming (ICLP)*, pages 163–177, 2003.

35. T. Eiter and G. Gottlob. On the Complexity of Propositional Knowledge Base Revision, Updates, and Counterfactuals. *Artificial Intelligence*, 57(2-3):227–270, 1992.

36. S. M. Embury, S. M. Brandt, J. S. Robinson, I. Sutherland, F. A. Bisby, W. A. Gray, A. C. Jones, and R. J. White. Adapting integrity enforcement techniques for data reconciliation. *Information Systems*, 26(8):657–689, 2001.

37. R. Fagin, P. G. Kolaitis, R. J. Miller, and L. Popa. Data Exchange: Semantics and Query Answering. In *International Conference on Database Theory (ICDT)*, pages 207–224. Springer-Verlag, LNCS 2572, 2003.

38. W. Fan, G. Kuper, and J. Simeon. A Unified Constraint Model for XML. *Computer Networks*, 39(5):489–505, 2002.

39. W. Fan and J. Simeon. Integrity Constraints for XML. *Journal of Computer and System Sciences*, 66(1):254–201, 2003.

40. S. Flesca, F. Furfaro, S. Greco, and E. Zumpano. Repairs and Consistent Answers for XML Data with Functional Dependencies. In *International XML Database Symposium*, pages 238–253. Springer-Verlag, LNCS 2824, 2003.

41. A. Fuxman and R. Miller. Towards Inconsistency Management in Data Integration Systems. In *IJCAI-03 Workshop on Information Integration on the Web (IIWeb-03)*, 2003.

42. P. Gärdenfors and H. Rott. Belief Revision. In D. M. Gabbay, J. Hogger, C, and J. A. Robinson, editors, *Handbook of Logic in Artificial Intelligence and Logic Programming*, volume 4, pages 35–132. Oxford University Press, 1995.

43. F. Giannotti, S. Greco, D. Sacca, and C. Zaniolo. Programming with Non-determinism in Deductive Databases. *Annals of Mathematics and Artificial Intelligence*, 19(3-4), 1997.

44. F. Giannotti and D. Pedreschi. Datalog with Non-deterministic Choice Computes NDB-PTIME. *Journal of Logic Programming*, 35:75–101, 1998.

45. G. Greco, S. Greco, and E. Zumpano. A Logic Programming Approach to the Integration, Repairing and Querying of Inconsistent Databases. In *International Conference on Logic Programming (ICLP)*, pages 348–364. Springer-Verlag, LNCS 2237, 2001.

46. G. Greco, S. Greco, and E. Zumpano. A Logical Framework for Querying and Repairing Inconsistent Databases. *IEEE Transactions on Knowledge and Data Engineering*, 15(6):1389–1408, 2003.

47. S. Greco, D. Sacca, and C. Zaniolo. Datalog Queries with Stratified Negation and Choice: from P to D^P. In *International Conference on Database Theory (ICDT)*, pages 82–96. Springer-Verlag, 1995.

48. S. Greco, C. Sirangelo, I. Trubitsyna, and E. Zumpano. Preferred Repairs for Inconsistent Databases. In *International Database Engineering and Applications Symposium (IDEAS)*, pages 202–211. IEEE Computer Society Press, 2003.

49. S. Greco and E. Zumpano. Querying Inconsistent Databases. In *International Conference on Logic for Programming, Artificial Intelligence, and Reasoning (LPAR)*, pages 308–325. Springer-Verlag, LNCS 1955, 2000.

50. A. Y. Halevy. Answering Queries Using Views: A Survey. *VLDB Journal*, 10(4):270–294, 2001.

51. D. S. Hochbaum. Approximating Covering and Packing Problems: Set Cover, Vertex Cover, Independent Set, and Related Problems. In D. S. Hochbaum, editor, *Approximation Algorithms for NP-Hard Problems*. PWS Publishing Co., 1997.

52. T. Imieliński and W. Lipski. Incomplete Information in Relational Databases. *Journal of the ACM*, 31(4):761–791, 1984.

53. T. Imieliński, S. Naqvi, and K. Vadaparty. Incomplete Objects - A Data Model for Design and Planning Applications. In *ACM SIGMOD International Conference on Management of Data*, pages 288–297, Denver, Colorado, May 1991.

54. T. Imieliński, R. van der Meyden, and K. Vadaparty. Complexity Tailored Design: A New Design Methodology for Databases With Incomplete Information. *Journal of Computer and System Sciences*, 51(3):405–432, 1995.

55. P. C. Kanellakis. Elements of Relational Database Theory. In Jan van Leeuwen, editor, *Handbook of Theoretical Computer Science*, volume B, chapter 17, pages 1073–1158. Elsevier/MIT Press, 1990.

56. D. Lembo, M. Lenzerini, and R. Rosati. Source Inconsistency and Incompleteness in Data Integration. In *9th International Workshop on Knowledge Representation meets Databases (KRDB'02)*, Toulouse, France, 2002.

57. M. Lenzerini. Data Integration: A Theoretical Perspective. In *ACM Symposium on Principles of Database Systems (PODS)*, pages 233–246, 2002. Invited talk.

58. J. Lin and A. O. Mendelzon. Merging Databases under Constraints. *International Journal of Cooperative Information Systems*, 7(1):55–76, 1996.

59. B. Ludäscher, W. May, and G. Lausen. Referential Actions as Logical Rules. In *ACM Symposium on Principles of Database Systems (PODS)*, pages 217–227, 1997.

60. Jim Melton and Alan R. Simon. *SQL:1999 Understanding Relational Language Components*. Morgan Kaufmann, 2002.

61. R. van der Meyden. Logical Approaches to Incomplete Information: A Survey. In J. Chomicki and G. Saake, editors, *Logics for Databases and Information Systems*, chapter 10, pages 307–356. Kluwer Academic Publishers, Boston, 1998.

62. D. Van Nieuwenborgh and D. Vermeir. Preferred Answer Sets for Ordered Logic Programs. In *European Conference on Logics for Artificial Intelligence (JELIA)*, pages 432–443. Springer-Verlag, LNAI 2424, 2002.

63. M. Y. Vardi. The Complexity of Relational Query Languages. In *ACM Symposium on Theory of Computing (STOC)*, pages 137–146, 1982.

64. J. Wijsen. Condensed Representation of Database Repairs for Consistent Query Answering. In *International Conference on Database Theory (ICDT)*, pages 378–393. Springer-Verlag, LNCS 2572, 2003.

65. M. Winslett. Reasoning about Action using a Possible Models Approach. In *National Conference on Artificial Intelligence*, pages 79–83, 1988.

On the Complexity of
Paraconsistent Inference Relations

Sylvie Coste-Marquis and Pierre Marquis*

CRIL-CNRS/Université d'Artois,
rue de l'Université - S.P. 16,
F-62307 Lens Cedex - France
{coste, marquis}@cril.univ-artois.fr

Abstract. Reasoning in a non-trivial way from inconsistent pieces of information is a major challenge in artificial intelligence, and its importance is reflected by the number of techniques designed so far for dealing with inconsistency (especially the few ones reported in this handbook). Many of these techniques have been investigated in depth from a logical point of view, but far less to what concerns the computational complexity aspects. The purpose of this chapter is to present in a structured way the main complexity results identified so far for paraconsistent inference based on multi-valued propositional logics.

1 Introduction

Classical logic cannot be used as such to deal with inconsistent information since every formula can be derived from a contradiction. This well-known trivialization problem leads to consider that an inconsistent information base is totally meaningless: Since all contradictory formulas are equivalent and since a replacement (meta)theorem holds in classical logic, every contradictory base can be substituted by the boolean constant *false*, i.e., the unique irreducible contradiction. In order to escape from such a problem and offer a way to exploit inconsistent information bases in a cleverer way, *paraconsistent* inference relations must be considered. Using such inference relations, every formula is not a consequence anymore of every (classically) inconsistent formula.

The trivialization of classical entailment in presence of inconsistency appears as an important issue in AI for several reasons. A major reason is that it is actually a concrete problem: Like the beliefs of human beings in everyday life, the beliefs of artificial agents can easily be jointly inconsistent, especially when their databases are large or when they integrate information stemming from several sources (sensors, other agents, etc.). The problem is all the most salient when societies of agents are considered instead of individuals: Due to their different

---

* Many thanks to the anonymous reviewers of this chapter for many interesting comments. Many thanks as well to the Région Nord / Pas-de-Calais, the IUT de Lens and the IRCICA Consortium for their support.

L. Bertossi et al. (Eds.): Inconsistency Tolerance, LNCS 3300, pp. 151–190, 2004.

abilities and evolutions, agents have often conflicting beliefs about some topics, even if they share some consistent pieces of knowledge. Would it be rational to consider the common belief of such a society as meaningless? Clearly, intuition gives a negative answer: Since inconsistencies are typically local (i.e., they are due to proper subparts of the information base), it would be definitely unreasonable to accept that everything (or nothing) follows from the available information base whenever this information base is inconsistent.

Assume for instance that a given agent has the following beliefs, encoded as a propositional formula Σ (it will serve as a running example throughout the chapter):

Example 1. $\Sigma = a \wedge \neg a \wedge (a \vee b) \wedge c \wedge (\neg c \vee d)$

The agent has contradictory beliefs about the truth value of a (for instance, because she received conflicting evidence about it, she has been told by a reliable acquaintance that a holds, and by a second as reliable acquaintance that a does not hold). She also has fully consistent pieces of beliefs, $a \vee b$, c and $\neg c \vee d$. Because Σ is inconsistent, every formula is a logical consequence of Σ. Nevertheless, because the unique contradiction in Σ concerns only a and $\neg a$, it does not seem always relevant to conclude that the agent has trivial beliefs. In particular, since Σ does not tell anything about atom e, an expected conclusion could be that e is undetermined (i.e., contingent) given Σ in the sense that neither e nor $\neg e$ are consequences of Σ. In addition, since c and $\neg c \vee d$ do not participate to any contradiction, it is not absurd to desire viewing them as consequences of Σ as well.

A second factor explaining the prominence of the trivialization problem in AI is the close connection it has with the problem of *handling exceptions*, another main challenge in AI. Indeed, an exception to a rule is just a case which contradicts the rule. As a matter of fact, many interesting approaches to inconsistency tolerant reasoning can be used to address the exception handling issue as well (as we will see, most valuable paraconsistent inference relations are non-monotonic ones), and the connections between belief revision (in the AGM framework) and rational inference relations are known for a while [39, 38]. Nevertheless, it must be noted that paraconsistency and non-monotony are two logically independent notions: One can find inference relations that are paraconsistent and monotonic (e.g., inference in LP, see Section 3.2), one can find as well inference relations that are paraconsistent and non-monotonic (e.g., inference in LP_m, see Section 3.3) while a third (non-empty) family gathers inference relations that are not paraconsistent and monotonic (e.g., classical entailment) and a last family consists of inference relations that are neither paraconsistent nor monotonic (e.g., circumscription).

In the following, we assume that the information at hand are *beliefs*, and the main goal is the *inference* one: Making explicit some pieces of beliefs hidden in implicit ones. This issue contrasts with the problem of aggregating mutually inconsistent goals (or preferences or desires). The latter problem is not less concrete than the inference problem from inconsistent beliefs — on the contrary, it is at the core of both multicriteria decision making and group decision making

— and connections exist between the two issues (e.g., belief merging operators can also be used to goal fusing in some situations). However, the main objectives are different ones: On the one hand, it consists in characterizing consequences of a belief base; on the other hand, it consists in determining a global preference relation over goals.

The significance of handling inconsistent beliefs in AI is reflected by the many approaches developed so far to address the paraconsistency issue under its various forms. Let us just mention paraconsistent logics, belief revision, belief merging, reasoning from preferred consistent subsets, knowledge integration, argumentative logics, purification, etc. All these words actually name many different techniques described in an abundant literature (see [10, 44, 65] for a survey).

The large number of such techniques can be explained by the fact that paraconsistency can be achieved in various ways, depending on the exact nature of the problem at hand (hence, the available information at the start). Thus, when Σ represents the (conflicting) beliefs of several agents, a merged base giving the beliefs of the group of agents can be designed by logically weakening some local belief bases (associated to the agents) in order to restore global consistency [43, 54, 68, 49, 50]. Several weakening mechanisms can be used: Dilation [16] is at work when merging operators based on a selection of models are considered (a i-dilation of a belief base ϕ for a "distance" d is obtained by adding to the set of its models all these interpretations which are at a distance at most $i \in \mathbb{N}$ from a model of ϕ), formula inhibition is used within merging operators based on a selection of formulas. Thus, when Σ is an inconsistent set of formulas, focusing on the consistent subsets – eventually restricted to the most preferred ones, when some preferential information can be exploited – is sufficient to give rise to several families of paraconsistent inference relations (depending on the entailment principle under consideration, e.g., the skeptical one) [67, 36, 41, 5, 62, 7, 20]. Such techniques are closely related to so-called syntax-based approaches to belief revision [58, 59] and to the framework for supernormal default reasoning with priorities from [18]. Variable forgetting can be used as well as a weakening mechanism [52]. Another way to give rise to paraconsistent inference relations consists in associating to each inferred formula a justification under the form of a subset of Σ used to derive it, and by reasoning on such arguments whenever some mutually inconsistent formulas can be derived. This is the basic idea of argumentative logics, see e.g., [29, 33, 17]. It can be sophisticated through the use of preferential information in order to consider some arguments more acceptable than some other arguments [1].

Now, there are several definitions of what a paraconsistent logic is; in this chapter, the following (quite restricted) definition is considered: A propositional logic $\langle L, \vdash_L \rangle$ where L is a propositional language and $\vdash_L$ a binary relation over L is said to be paraconsistent whenever there exists a belief base $\Sigma \in L$ and a query $\gamma \in L$ s.t. Σ is classically inconsistent and $\Sigma \not\vdash_L \gamma$ nevertheless. Thus, within a paraconsistent logic, the trivialization issue of inference is addressed in some situations when the input consists of a *single inconsistent formula* (representing the belief base) and a query.

Compared with the other approaches listed above, paraconsistent logics (*stricto sensu*) give *more basic* ways to address the trivialization issue. Indeed, belief revision, belief merging, knowledge integration, reasoning from preferred inconsistent subsets and purification need some extra-logical information in order to be well-defined and avoid trivializing. Such extra-logical information can be rather poor (a splitting between the belief base and the revision formula in the belief revision setting, a set (or multi-set) organization of the elementary (or agents) beliefs in a belief merging scenario) or rather sophisticated (preference relations over the beliefs, knowledge gathering actions for purification) but they are required. Thus, none of the approaches listed above will be considered further in this chapter.[1]

Several (non mutually exclusive) techniques can be used to define an inference relation that avoid trivialization from an inconsistent formula (see [65] for a brilliant survey of them). One of them consists in *making the truth value of α (more or less) independent from the truth value of $\neg\alpha$* (e.g., this is what is done in C_ω logic [24] and the whole family of C_i logics). A second one consists in *restricting the proof theory* of classical logic so as to retain only a subset of the classical proofs as admissible (this is at work in quasi-classical logic [15, 45]). A third one consists in *preventing inconsistent belief bases from having no model*, through the consideration of more general notions of interpretations. Several *multi-valued logics* are related to this line of research (among others, see [27, 6, 37, 53, 63, 64, 13, 14, 2, 3, 48, 56]).

Just like belief revision or belief merging gather many operators from which many inference relations are induced, there is no universal consensus on what paraconsistent inference should be but several intuitions of what is expected. While paraconsistent inference relations designed so far share some common principles (for instance, any irrelevant piece of belief would not be considered as a consequence of some inconsistent belief bases – stepping back to the previous example, e would never be considered as a conclusion from Σ), they do not give the same closure (set of consequences) for all inconsistent belief bases Σ. On the previous example, some approaches lead to consider b as a conclusion of Σ (given that the conjunction Σ has both $\neg a$ and $a \vee b$ among its conjuncts) while others reject such a conclusion (given the logically strongest conjunct a of Σ, $a \vee b$ is considered irrelevant). Both approaches look reasonable in some specific contexts (thus, it can be the case that $a \vee b$ is an explicit belief whose origin differs from the one of a and that the agent wants to keep it but the opposite conclusion also makes sense in other situations). This tends to show that a purely descriptive approach to paraconsistency (i.e., modeling paraconsistent inference by considering how human beings reason in presence of inconsistency) is hard to be achieved when a so simple input (an inconsistent formula, nothing else) is considered.

---

[1] The definition of paraconsistency we used also sets aside several logics that are usually considered as paraconsistent logics, like Jaśkowski's discussive logic [46], one of the first logic defined so far to address the inconsistency handling issue.

This raises the issue of how to evaluate and compare paraconsistent inference relations. Several independent criteria can be used for such a purpose. A first criterion consists in investigating the logical properties of the relations. Many normative postulates which should be satisfied by common-sense inference relations have been proposed so far. For instance, it is interesting to determine whether the paraconsistent inference relation under consideration $\vdash_L$ satisfies reflexivity, transitivity, ... It is also valuable to determine whether $\vdash_L$ is subclassical (i.e., a subset of classical entailment) whenever the fragment of L from which both the belief bases and the queries are built up can be viewed as well as a fragment of classical propositional logic. It is interesting to determine whether usual metatheorems hold (substitution theorem, deduction theorem, compactness theorem, ...) and whether sound and complete axiomatisations (à la Hilbert or à la Gentzen) have been exhibited. All those logical features give a first dimension for a comparison. In the following, we will not focus on them but let the reader look at the bibliography for more about the logical aspects of the inference relations we consider (the logical dimension of paraconsistent relations is already presented with much details in several papers from the literature, in particular [65]).

Another criterion is the cautiousness one; it is important to consider this dimension together with the logical one since it is quite easy to design strongly rational inference relations which are useless just because they are too cautious (they do not lead to consider as consequences of a base many ones which are expected).

In this chapter, we mainly consider a third criterion, orthogonal to the previous ones but very relevant from an AI perspective: *The computational complexity one.* Indeed, in order to be able to simulate a paraconsistent inference relation on a computer, the computational resources (time and space) required must be taken into account. Complexity theory offers theoretical tools (especially, complexity classes and reductions) for a fine-grained classification of the computational difficulties. Particularly, it helps in identifying the complexity sources within a problem; polynomial reductions among problems are useful when they show the existence of a translation from the decision problem associated to a given paraconsistent relation to the decision problem associated to another one; this is particularly significant when sophisticated algorithms have been designed for the latter: It is then possible to take advantage of them for solving the former decision problems, avoiding thus an expensive software development (furthermore, if there is no guarantee that it is computationally valuable to do so from the practical side, it can actually be the case). Anyway, identifying complexity results for paraconsistent inference relations gives a third dimension allowing the comparison of these relations. From an AI point of view, it can make sense to prefer a more tractable inference relation over a less tractable one, even if the latter exhibits a more rational behavior than the former.

Quite surprisingly, the complexity of paraconsistent inference relations has been investigated only for the past few years. This contrasts with many other approaches to inconsistency tolerant reasoning for which many complexity results have been obtained; indeed, complexity results for belief revision can be found in [31, 60], complexity results for belief merging in [47], complexity of reasoning from preferred consistent subsets in [60, 20, 32], complexity of argumentative reasoning in [26, 25, 30].

It is also amazing to compare the (few) number of papers dedicated to the study of the complexity of paraconsistent inference relations to the (quite large) number of papers where such inference relations have been pointed out. Subsequently, we do not claim that this chapter covers exhaustively the complexity results for all the paraconsistent inference relations from the literature:[2] Much work remains to be done at that time to reach such a goal. The present chapter can be considered as a first step toward this objective. The focus is laid on paraconsistent inference relations based on propositional multi-valued logics. Especially, we do not consider first-order paraconsistent logics in the following (the extension to the first-order case does not raise any technical difficulty in general and, as expected, the corresponding inference relations are typically not recursive, see [65] for details). Furthermore, we refrain ourselves to presenting the various proof systems (typically, tableau-based) that have been designed so far for the inference relations considered in this chapter, unless the existence of such systems gives a reduction from which a membership result or a hardness one can be derived (again, we let the reader look at the bibliography to learn more about proof systems for paraconsistent inference relations).

The rest of this chapter is organized as follows. After some formal preliminaries (Section 2), we present in Section 3 many paraconsistent inference relations based on multi-valued logics; we focus on relations introduced in [27, 6, 37, 53, 63, 64, 69, 15, 13, 14, 44, 2, 48, 56] for which complexity results have been identified in [53, 19, 21, 55, 11, 48, 56]. Each relation is illustrated on the running example and its main logical properties are given. Then Section 4 presents complexity results for such relations in the general case and in some restricted cases. Finally, we conclude the chapter in Section 5.

2   Formal Preliminaries

In this section, we briefly present the basic notions about propositional logic and complexity theory necessary to understand the rest of the chapter. More details about such notions can be found e.g., in [34] and [40, 61].

2.1   Propositional Logic

Given a denumerable set PS of propositional symbols, $PROP^2_{PS}$ denotes the propositional language built up from PS, the boolean constants *true* and *false*, and the connectives $\neg$, $\vee$, $\wedge$ in the standard way. $\Rightarrow$ can also be introduced as a connective, where $\alpha \Rightarrow \beta$ is a short for $(\neg\alpha) \vee \beta$. The elements of $PROP^2_{PS}$ are

---

[2] For instance, we do not consider here inference relations based on multimodal logics for representing incoherent beliefs [57].

called formulas. $Var(\Sigma)$ denotes the set of propositional symbols occurring in the formula Σ. The size of a formula Σ noted $|\Sigma|$, is the number of occurrences of symbols and connectives used to write it.

For every subset V of PS, L_V is the set of literals built up from the propositional symbols of V. A negative literal is a literal of the form $\neg x$, where $x \in PS$. A symbol from PS is also called a positive literal. The complementary literal of a positive literal $l = x$ (resp. a negative literal $l = \neg x$) is $\bar{l} = \neg x$ (resp. $\bar{l} = x$). Every finite disjunction of literals is called a clause and every finite conjunction of literals is called a term. A positive clause contains only positive literals. A CNF formula is a (finite) conjunction of clauses, also viewed as a set of clauses when it is convenient. A k-CNF formula is a CNF formula in which every clause contains no more than k literals (where k is a non-negative integer). A Krom formula is a CNF formula in which every clause contains at most two literals. A Horn (resp. reverse Horn) CNF formula is a CNF formula in which each clause contains at most one positive (resp. negative) literal. A formula Σ is renamable Horn CNF if and only if there exists a substitution σ from L_{PS} to L_{PS} s.t. $\sigma(l) = l$ for every literal l of L_{PS} except those of a set L, and for every literal l of L, $\sigma(l) = \bar{l}$ and $\sigma(\bar{l}) = l$, and $\sigma(\Sigma)$ is a Horn CNF formula. A belief base is a finite, conjunctively-interpreted, set of formulas from $PROP^2_{PS}$. A DNF formula is a finite disjunction of terms. An NNF (Negation Normal Form) formula is a formula from $PROP^2_{PS}$ s.t. the scope of any occurrence of $\neg$ in the formula is a propositional symbol.

Formulas are interpreted in the classical way. An interpretation over $PROP^2_{PS}$ is a mapping I which associates every propositional symbol to one of the two truth values of $TWO = \{0,1\}$. The semantics of a formula Σ is a boolean function: A truth value can be associated to Σ as long as an interpretation I is considered. $I(\Sigma)$ denotes the truth value taken by Σ within I; it is defined in the usual compositional way. When I is s.t. $I(\Sigma) = 1$, I is said to be a model of Σ, noted $I \models^2 \Sigma$; otherwise, I is a counter-model of Σ. When a formula has no model (resp. no counter-model), it is said to be unsatisfiable or inconsistent (resp. valid). The binary relation $\models^2$ over $PROP^2_{PS}$ is defined by $\Sigma \models^2 \gamma$ if and only if every model of Σ is a model of γ. $\models$ is referred to as logical entailment: Whenever $\Sigma \models^2 \gamma$ holds, γ is said to be a logical consequence of Σ. Whenever $\Sigma \models^2 \Phi$ and $\Phi \models^2 \Sigma$ both hold, Σ and Φ are said to be logically equivalent, noted $\Sigma \equiv^2 \Phi$.

2.2 Computational Complexity

A decision problem (encoded as a language) belongs to P (resp. NP) if and only if there exists a deterministic (resp. non-deterministic) Turing machine which can classify every instance of it in a number of computational steps polynomially bounded in the input size. The decision problems of P are usually considered as efficiently solvable.

Because a deterministic Turing machine can be considered as a non-deterministic one, the inclusion P $\subseteq$ NP is established. However, the converse is the famous open problem: P $\stackrel{?}{=}$ NP (which is conjectured false). Among all the problems in NP, the hardest ones are those from which every problem in NP can be polynomially many-one reduced: Such problems are referred to as NP-complete. If any of them has a polynomial (deterministic) algorithm, then P = NP holds. Accordingly, it is believed that it is impossible to solve NP-complete problems in deterministic polynomial time. SAT, the problem of determining whether a propositional formula in CNF is satisfiable, is the prototypical NP-complete problem. Its complementary problem UNSAT (which consists in determining whether a propositional formula in CNF is unsatisfiable) is not necessarily in NP (in contrast to P, NP is not known to be closed under complementation). UNSAT is assigned to the class coNP which contains the complementary problems to problems in NP. It is conjectured that NP $\neq$ coNP.

Let X be a class of decision problems. P^X (resp. NP^X) is the class of all decision problems that can be solved in polynomial time using a deterministic (resp. non-deterministic) Turing machine which can use an oracle for deciding the membership to X for "free" (i.e., within a constant, unit time). The classes Δ_k^p, Σ_k^p and Π_k^p (with $k \in I\!N$) can be defined by:

- $\Delta_0^p = \Sigma_0^p = \Pi_0^p = P$,
- $\Delta_{k+1}^p = P^{\Sigma_k^p}$,
- $\Sigma_{k+1}^p = NP^{\Sigma_k^p}$,
- $\Pi_{k+1}^p = co\Sigma_{k+1}^p$.

Thus, $\Sigma_1^p = NP$ and $\Pi_1^p = coNP$. For any integer k, the complexity class D_k^p contains every decision problem that belongs to the intersection of a language from Σ_k^p and a language from Π_k^p. The *polynomial hierarchy* PH is the union of all Σ_k^p (for k integer). A decision problem is said to be at the kth level of the polynomial hierarchy if and only if it belongs to Δ_{k+1}^p, and is either Σ_k^p-hard or Π_k^p-hard. While it is easy to check that $\Delta_k^p \subseteq \Sigma_k^p$, $\Delta_k^p \subseteq \Pi_k^p$, $\Sigma_k^p \subseteq D_k^p$, $\Pi_k^p \subseteq D_k^p$, $D_k^p \subseteq \Delta_{k+1}^p$ hold for every k, it is unknown whether the inclusions are proper (but it is strongly conjectured that they are). Indeed, it is strongly believed that the polynomial hierarchy does not collapse (at any level), i.e., is a truly infinite hierarchy (for every integer k, PH $\neq \Sigma_k^p$).

3   Multi-valued Logics and Related Frameworks

In this section, we successively describe the syntax and the semantics of many paraconsistent multi-valued logics introduced so far, and some related propositional systems [15, 45, 27, 6, 37, 53, 63, 64, 13, 14, 2, 48, 56]. On this ground, we present a dozen of paraconsistent inference relations (both monotonic ones and non-monotonic ones). Their complexity will be given and discussed in the following section.

3.1   Syntax and Semantics

The logics considered in this chapter are typically based on the following propositional languages, or on proper fragments of them:

Definition 1 ($PROP_{PS}^4$ $PROP_{PS}^3$ $PROP_{PS}^2$).
Let PS be a finite set of propositional symbols.

- $PROP_{PS}^4$ *is the propositional language over PS inductively generated from the constant symbols true, false, both, and unknown and the connectives ¬, ∨, ∧, ⊃, ⊕, and ⊗.*
- $PROP_{PS}^3$ *is the propositional language over PS inductively generated from the constant symbols true, false and both and the connectives ¬, ∨, ∧, ⊃, and ⊕.*
- $PROP_{PS}^2$ *is the propositional language over PS inductively generated from the constant symbols true and false and the connectives ¬, ∨, ∧, and ⊃.*

As we will see, the constant symbols *both, unknown*, the consensus connective ⊗ and the gullability connective ⊕ are not interpreted in a classical way, using only the two standard "truth values" 0 (falsum) and 1 (verum). This explains why they are not used to generate formulas from $PROP_{PS}^2$, which coincides with a standard language for classical propositional logic. We can observe from the definition that $PROP_{PS}^2$ is a proper subset of $PROP_{PS}^3$ and that $PROP_{PS}^3$ is a proper subset of $PROP_{PS}^4$; none of the constants *both, unknown* (resp. *unknown*) and the connectives ⊕, ⊗ (resp. ⊗) can be used to generate formulas from $PROP_{PS}^2$ (resp. $PROP_{PS}^3$) because the set of "truth values" under consideration must be closed under the connectives.

Proper fragments of $PROP_{PS}^2$ consist of the set of formulas generated from *PS* and the three connectives ¬, ∨, ∧ (the so-called {¬, ∨, ∧} fragment also referred to as the monotonic fragment), and the subset of it containing all CNF formulas.

We must now explain how the formulas of $PROP_{PS}^4$ and its subsets can be interpreted. Obviously, a key feature of multi-valued logics from the semantics point of view is the presence of non-standard "truth values", i.e., different from the classical ones (0, denoting falsity and 1 denoting truth). The two additional "truth values" considered in such a setting are denoted ⊥ and ⊤. Intuitively, ⊥ denotes lack of information, while ⊤ indicates inconsistency. The latter "truth value" ⊤ is central when the goal is to achieve paraconsistency.

Definition 2 (Interpretations).
A 4-interpretation (resp. a 3-interpretation, a 2-interpretation) over PS is a total function I from PS to $FOUR = \{0, 1, \top, \bot\}$ (resp. $THREE = \{0, 1, \top\}$, $TWO = \{0, 1\}$).

Some alternative definitions of the set of "truth values" are sometimes given; for instance, *FOUR* can be defined as $TWO \times TWO$, or as the power set of *TWO*. All these definitions are equivalent to the one given here, the intuition is that ⊥ means "neither true nor false" while ⊤ means "both true and false".

Whatever the definition, it is useful to associate *FOUR* with two (partial) orderings, the usual *truth ordering* $\leq_t$ for which 0 is the least element, 1 is the greatest element and ⊤ and ⊥ are incomparable, and the *knowledge ordering* $\leq_k$ for which ⊥ is the least element, ⊤ is the greatest element and 0 and 1 are

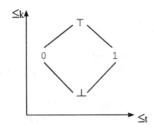

Fig. 1. FOUR

incomparable. *FOUR* with $\leq_t$ and $\leq_k$ is a bilattice, called Belnap's billatice. It is often represented by the double Hasse diagram given on Figure 1.

For every 4-interpretation I over PS, we define $I(true) = 1$, $I(false) = 0$, $I(both) = \top$, $I(unknown) = \bot$. Thus, the non-classical constants are mainly used to denote the corresponding non-classical "truth values" within the object language. Table 1 gives the truth table of the remaining connectives.

Table 1. Truth tables

α	β	$\neg\alpha$	$\alpha \wedge \beta$	$\alpha \vee \beta$	$\alpha \supset \beta$	$\alpha \otimes \beta$	$\alpha \oplus \beta$
0	0	1	0	0	1	0	0
0	1	1	0	1	1	$\bot$	$\top$
0	$\top$	1	0	$\top$	1	0	$\top$
0	$\bot$	1	0	$\bot$	1	$\bot$	0
1	0	0	0	1	0	$\bot$	$\top$
1	1	0	1	1	1	1	1
1	$\top$	0	$\top$	1	$\top$	1	$\top$
1	$\bot$	0	$\bot$	1	$\bot$	$\bot$	1
$\top$	0	$\top$	0	$\top$	0	0	$\top$
$\top$	1	$\top$	$\top$	1	1	1	$\top$
$\top$	$\top$	$\top$	$\top$	$\top$	$\top$	$\top$	$\top$
$\top$	$\bot$	$\top$	0	1	$\bot$	$\bot$	$\top$
$\bot$	0	$\bot$	0	$\bot$	1	$\bot$	0
$\bot$	1	$\bot$	$\bot$	$\bot$	1	$\bot$	1
$\bot$	$\top$	$\bot$	0	1	1	$\bot$	$\top$
$\bot$	$\bot$	$\bot$	$\bot$	$\bot$	1	$\bot$	$\bot$

It can be observed that the semantics of the gullability connective $\oplus$ (resp. the consensus connective $\otimes$) is the supremum (resp. infimum) w.r.t. $\leq_k$; thus, $\oplus$ (resp. $\otimes$) plays a role similar to the one of the classical connective $\vee$ (resp. $\wedge$) but w.r.t. the knowledge ordering (and not the truth one).

Now, the semantics $I(\phi)$ of a formula ϕ from $PROP^4_{PS}$ in I is defined compositionally in the usual way (every connective is truth functional).

The semantics of a formula from $PROP^3_{PS}$ (resp. $PROP^2_{PS}$) in a 3-interpretation (resp. a 2-interpretation) is obtained by considering the reductions of the previous truth tables to $THREE$ (resp. TWO).

A further step to obtain inference relations consists in defining the set of *designated values*. Unlike many other multi-valued logics, the set considered in $FOUR$ and its restriction $THREE$ is $\{1, \top\}$. Accordingly, a formula ϕ is satisfied in a world I when its semantics in I is at least 1 w.r.t. the knowledge ordering.

Once this is stated, the following notions of models can be defined:

Definition 3 (Models).
Let I be a 4-interpretation (resp. a 3-interpretation, a 2-interpretation) I over PS and ϕ be a formula from $PROP^4_{PS}$ (resp. $PROP^3_{PS}$, $PROP^2_{PS}$). I is a 4-model (resp. a 3-model, a 2-model) of ϕ if and only if $I(\phi) \in \{1, \top\}$. We note $4\text{-}mod(\Sigma)$ (resp. $3\text{-}mod(\Sigma)$) the set of all 4-models (resp. 3-models) of a formula Σ from $PROP^4_{PS}$ (resp. $PROP^3_{PS}$).

Now, equivalence can be defined: Two formulas ϕ and ψ from $PROP^4_{PS}$ (resp. $PROP^3_{PS}$) are said to be equivalent, noted $\phi \equiv^4 \psi$ (resp. $\phi \equiv^3 \psi$) if and only if they have the same set of 4-models (resp. 3-models). Note that a stronger notion of equivalence exists (two formulas are strongly equivalent when their semantics coincide in every interpretation) and that a replacement metatheorem holds for the strong notion but not for the weak one in the general case. For instance, while $a \vee \neg a \equiv^3 b \vee \neg b$ holds, it is not the case that $\neg(a \vee \neg a) \equiv^3 \neg(b \vee \neg b)$ ($a \vee \neg a$ and $b \vee \neg b$ are not strongly equivalent in $THREE$).

Because $\top$ is a designated value, it can be the case that a formula from $PROP^2_{PS}$ that is classically inconsistent has some 4-models (and this is what was expected in the purpose of avoiding trivialization). For instance:

Example 2. Let $\Sigma = a \wedge \neg a \wedge (a \vee b) \wedge c \vee (\neg c \wedge d)$. Σ has no 2-model. The 4-interpretation given by $I(a) = \top$, $I(b) = 1$, $I(c) = 1$ and $I(d) = 1$ is a 4-model of Σ. This interpretation can also be considered as a 3-model of Σ.

Contrariwise to what this example may suggest, it is not the case that inconsistency is always avoided in $FOUR$ or in $THREE$; some formulas in $PROP^4_{PS}$ (resp. $PROP^3_{PS}$) have no 4-models (the simplest one reduces to the constant *false*). Hence, only a weak form of paraconsistency is achieved in the general case (some inconsistent theories are not trivial ones, but not all of them). Nevertheless, it is easy to prove (by structural induction) that the interpretation mapping every symbol from PS to $\top$ is a 3-model (hence, a 4-model) of every formula from the $\{\neg, \vee, \wedge\}$ fragment.

Other connectives can be considered in the languages $PROP^4_{PS}$ and $PROP^3_{PS}$, as syntactic sugars. In particular:

- $\phi \Leftrightarrow \psi =_{def} (\phi \supset \psi) \wedge (\psi \supset \phi)$;
- $\phi \rightarrow \psi =_{def} (\phi \supset \psi) \wedge (\neg\psi \supset \neg\phi)$;
- $\phi \leftrightarrow \psi =_{def} (\phi \rightarrow \psi) \wedge (\psi \rightarrow \phi)$;
- $\phi! =_{def} \phi \wedge \neg\phi$;

- $\Box\phi =_{def} (\neg\phi \supset false) \wedge \neg(\phi \supset \neg\phi);$
- $\phi \leq \psi =_{def} (\Box\phi \wedge \Box\psi) \vee (\Box\neg\phi \wedge \Box\neg\psi) \vee (\neg\Box\psi \wedge \neg\Box\neg\psi);$
- $\Diamond\phi =_{def} \neg\Box\neg\phi;$
- $\sim \phi =_{def} \Box\neg\phi;$
- $\odot\phi =_{def} \Box\phi \vee \Box\neg\phi.$

The language considered in [6] is the restriction of $PROP^2_{PS}$ where $\supset$ is not nestable. The language used in [2] to define $FOUR$ is the extension of $PROP^4_{PS}$ where $\rightarrow$ and $\leftrightarrow$ are used as additional (binary) connectives. The language of the logic of 3-inference of [53] (resp. the language of LP [63] or equivalently the language of RP [37]) is the propositional language over PS generated from the constant $false$ and the connectives $\neg$, $\wedge$, $\vee$ (resp. from the connectives $\neg$, $\wedge$, $\vee$); $\supset$ and $\leftrightarrow$ are also introduced but as syntactic sugars ($\phi \supset \psi =_{def} \neg\phi \vee \psi$ and $\phi \leftrightarrow \psi =_{def} (\phi \supset \psi) \wedge (\psi \supset \phi)$). The language of LP_m [63, 64] is the propositional language over PS generated from the connectives $\neg$, $\wedge$, $\vee$ and $!$.[3] The language of J_3 is the propositional language over PS generated from the connectives $\neg$, $\wedge$, $\vee$, $\supset$, $\leftrightarrow$, $\Box$, $\Diamond$, $\sim$, $\odot$. The language considered in [13] is the propositional language over PS generated from the constants $true$, $false$ and the connectives $\neg$, $\wedge$, $\vee$, $\supset$, $\leftrightarrow$, $\Box$, $\leq$. The language considered in [14] is the propositional language over PS generated from the connectives $\neg$, $\wedge$, $\vee$, $\supset$ and $\leftrightarrow$.

The semantics of all such derived connectives can be easily defined by considering their truth tables. For instance, $\Box\phi$ means that ϕ is *necessarily* true, i.e., for every 4-interpretation I over PS, $I(\Box\phi) = 1$ if $I(\phi) = 1$ and $I(\Box\phi) = 0$ otherwise. All these additional connectives can be directly incorporated in $PROP^3_{PS}$ and $PROP^2_{PS}$ since both $THREE$ and TWO are closed w.r.t. any of them. When the truth values of TWO are considered, only, $\supset$ and $\rightarrow$ coincide and are equivalent to classical material implication (especially, we have $\phi \supset \psi \equiv^2 (\neg\phi) \vee \psi$ for every $\phi, \psi \in PROP^2_{PS}$); in the same vein, $\leftrightarrow$ and $\leftrightarrow$ coincide and are equivalent to classical equivalence, and we have $\phi \equiv^2 \Box\phi \equiv^2 \Diamond\phi$, $\neg\phi \equiv^2 \sim \phi$, $\phi! \equiv^2 false$, and $\odot\phi \equiv^2 true$ for every $\phi \in PROP^2_{PS}$. None of these equivalences holds as soon as $\top$ is considered as an additional "truth value".

The main observation here is that the incorporation of such additional connectives into $PROP^4_{PS}$ or $PROP^3_{PS}$ does not increase the expressiveness of the corresponding logic:[4] As $PROP^2_{PS}$ is functionally complete for TWO, $PROP^4_{PS}$ is functionally complete for $FOUR$ (Theorem 3.8 from [2]) and $PROP^3_{PS}$ is functionally complete for $THREE$ (Theorem 5.1 from [2]). This contrasts with the language of J_3 [27] (and its restrictions like LP [63], RP [37] and the logic of 3-inference of Levesque [53]) which includes neither $\oplus$ nor $both$, and despite the

---

[3] To be more precise, $!$ is introduced as a notation of the metalanguage in [63], and an element of the object language in [64].

[4] Nevertheless, like in classical logic, it may have an impact on the succinctness of the language; for instance, despite the fact that every classical propositional formula has an equivalent CNF form, it is well-known that a formula like $a_1 \leftrightarrow a_2 \leftrightarrow \ldots \leftrightarrow a_n$ where every $a_i \in PS$ cannot be represented by an equivalent CNF formula of size polynomial in n.

presence of other connectives, is not expressive enough to enable the representation of a formula equivalent to *both* (see [35]). The functional completeness of $PROP_{PS}^4$ (resp. $PROP_{PS}^3$) w.r.t. *FOUR* (resp. *THREE*) explains why the focus has been laid on them; in some sense, all the logics considered in this paper (including classical logic) are restrictions of *FOUR*.

3.2   Monotonic Inference Relations

Let us now define some paraconsistent inference relations. The simplest one are based on model containment.

Definition 4 ($\models^4$-inference and $\models^3$-inference).
Let Σ and γ be two formulas from $PROP_{PS}^4$ (resp. $PROP_{PS}^3$). We note $\Sigma \models^4 \gamma$ (resp. $\Sigma \models^3 \gamma$) if and only if every 4-model (resp. 3-model) of Σ is a 4-model (resp. 3-model) of γ.

Example 3. Let $\Sigma = a \wedge \neg a \wedge (a \vee b) \wedge c \vee (\neg c \wedge d)$. We have $\Sigma \models^4 a$, $\Sigma \models^4 \neg a$ and $\Sigma \models^4 c$, but we have neither $\Sigma \models^4 b$, nor $\Sigma \models^4 d$. Similar conclusions can be derived using $\models^3$ instead of $\models^4$. However, $\models^3$ and $\models^4$ do not coincide: *true* $\models^3 a \vee \neg a$ holds while *true* $\models^4 a \vee \neg a$ does not hold since interpreting a as $\perp$ leads to interpret $a \vee \neg a$ as $\perp$ as well.

Since J_3, *LP*, RP^5 and Levesque's logic of 3-inference can be viewed as restricted cases of *THREE* (what differs is the underlying language which is a subset of $PROP_{PS}^3$), the corresponding inference relations are just restrictions of $\models^3$:

Definition 5 ($\models_{J_3}$-inference, $\models_L$-inference and $\models_{LP}$-inference).
Let Σ and γ be two formulas from the language of J_3 (resp. Levesque's logic of 3-inference, LP). We note $\Sigma \models_{J_3} \gamma$ (resp. $\Sigma \models_L \gamma$, $\Sigma \models_{LP} \gamma$) if and only if every 3-model of Σ is a 3-model of γ.

$\vdash\!\!\!\sim\, = \models^4$, (resp. $\models^3$, $\models_{J_3}$, $\models_L$ and $\models_{LP}$) is obviously four-valued (resp. three-valued) *preferential*, i.e., it satisfies the following properties (provided that $\vdash$ in **(RW)** denotes $\models^4$ (resp. $\models^3$)):

(Ref) $\alpha\!\!\mid\!\!\sim\!\alpha$	Reflexivity
(LLE) If α and β are strongly equivalent	
and $\alpha\!\!\mid\!\!\sim\!\gamma$, then $\beta\!\!\mid\!\!\sim\!\gamma$	Left Logical Equivalence
(RW) If $\alpha\!\!\mid\!\!\sim\!\beta$ and $\beta \vdash \gamma$, then $\alpha\!\!\mid\!\!\sim\!\gamma$	Right Weakening
(Or) If $\alpha\!\!\mid\!\!\sim\!\gamma$ and $\beta\!\!\mid\!\!\sim\!\gamma$, then $\alpha \vee \beta\!\!\mid\!\!\sim\!\gamma$	Or
(Cut) If $\alpha \wedge \beta\!\!\mid\!\!\sim\!\gamma$ and $\alpha\!\!\mid\!\!\sim\!\beta$, then $\alpha\!\!\mid\!\!\sim\!\gamma$	Cautious Cut
(CM) If $\alpha\!\!\mid\!\!\sim\!\beta$ and $\alpha\!\!\mid\!\!\sim\!\gamma$, then $\alpha \wedge \beta\!\!\mid\!\!\sim\!\gamma$	Cautious Monotony

These properties have been stated in the framework of classical logic [51], but they can be extended to multi-valued settings in a straightforward way as above (such an extension has also been considered in [2]).

---

[5] Actually, we have $\models_{RP} = \models_{LP}$. In order to save some space, we will mainly focus on $\models_{LP}$ in the following.

$\models^4$, $\models^3$, $\models_{J_3}$, $\models_L$ and $\models_{LP}$ are even *monotonic* since the set of 4-models (resp. 3-models) of $\Sigma \wedge \phi$ is a subset of the set of 4-models (resp. 3-models) of Σ. As the previous example illustrates, the relations $\models^4$, $\models^3$, $\models_{J_3}$, $\models_L$ and $\models_{LP}$ are also *paraconsistent* [2]: There exist classically inconsistent formula $\Sigma \in PROP^2_{PS}$ whose closure w.r.t. any of the above mentioned relation is not the whole language $PROP^2_{PS}$. Furthermore, the restrictions of such relations over $PROP^2_{PS}$ are proper subsets of the classical entailment relation (noted $\models^2$ here instead of $\models$ for homogeneity). Stated otherwise, $\models^4$, $\models^3$, $\models_{J_3}$, $\models_L$ and $\models_{LP}$ are sub-classical over $PROP^2_{PS}$ (they can be viewed as approximations by default of classical entailment).

As usual when approximations are concerned, an important question is: What is the quality of the approximation? In this context, what are the classical consequences missed? And specifically, what happens when Σ is classically consistent?

Unfortunately, the news are not so good: $\models^4$, $\models^3$, $\models_{J_3}$, $\models_L$ and $\models_{LP}$ typically miss many expected consequences. A reason is that the disjunctive syllogism inference rule of classical logic fails for each of them. Thus, we do *not* have

$$c \wedge (\neg c \vee d) \not\models^4 d$$

because every 4-interpretation I s.t. $I(c) = \top$ and $I(d) = 0$ is a 4-model of $c \wedge (\neg c \vee d)$, but not a 4-model of d. Thus, on the running example, d is not found as a consequence of Σ despite the fact it comes logically from the sub-formulas c and $\neg c \vee d$ of Σ which are not involved in a contradiction. Since the disjunctive syllogism inference rule fails, none of the relations above coincides with $\models^2$ on $PROP^2_{PS}$ in the situation Σ is classically consistent - while we would expect it.

3.3   Non-monotonic Inference Relations

Inference Based on Preferred Models. In order to circumvent such difficulties, more refined inference relations have been pointed out. The principle is to focus on some preferred models of Σ in order to keep as much information as possible. Preferential information typically characterize a preordering $\leq$ over the set of interpretations, and the $\leq$-preferred models of a base Σ are defined as the models of Σ that are minimal w.r.t. $\leq$. This approach leads to the paraconsistent inference relations $\models^4_{I1}$, $\models^4_{I2}$, $\models_{LP_m}$, $\models_{BS}$ and other variants.

Let us first consider $\models^4_{I1}$ and $\models^4_{I2}$ [2]. Each of these relations is characterized by a specific preference criterion. The first one consists in giving more credit to the 4-models of Σ which minimize the amount of inconsistent beliefs in Σ. The second one consists in preferring the 4-models of Σ which are as close as possible to its classical models. In a formal way, two (partial) preorderings $\leq_1$ and $\leq_2$ over the set of 4-interpretations over PS are used:

- $I \leq_1 J$ if and only if $\{x \in PS \mid I(x) \in \{\top\}\} \subseteq \{x \in PS \mid J(x) \in \{\top\}\}$;
- $I \leq_2 J$ if and only if $\{x \in PS \mid I(x) \in \{\top, \bot\}\} \subseteq \{x \in PS \mid J(x) \in \{\top, \bot\}\}$.

The preferred 4-models of Σ w.r.t. the first (resp. second) preference criterion is the set of 4-models of Σ which are minimal w.r.t. $\leq_1$ (resp. $\leq_2$).

Definition 6 ($\models^4_{I1}$-inference and $\models^4_{I2}$-inference).
Let Σ and γ be two formulas from $PROP^4_{PS}$. We note $\Sigma \models^4_{I1} \gamma$ (resp. $\Sigma \models^4_{I2} \gamma$) if and only if every 4-model of Σ minimal in its set w.r.t. $\leq_1$ (resp. $\leq_2$) is a 4-model of γ.

Example 4. Let $\Sigma = a \wedge \neg a \wedge (a \vee b) \wedge c \wedge (\neg c \vee d)$. We have $\Sigma \models^4_{I1} d$ and $\Sigma \models^4_{I2} d$ (while we do *not* have $\Sigma \models^4 d$). On the contrary, we have neither $\Sigma \models^4_{I1} b$ nor $\Sigma \models^4_{I2} b$; the reason is that $a \wedge (a \vee b)$ is strongly equivalent to a in $FOUR$ (this shows that Σ is independent from b, so the impossibility to derive b is in some sense expected).

In [2], it is shown that both $\models^4_{I1}$ and $\models^4_{I2}$ are valuable inference relations since they are (four-valued) preferential, i.e., any of them satisfies reflexivity, left logical equivalence, right weakening, or, cautious monotony and cautious cut. They are also paraconsistent and sub-classical over $PROP^2_{PS}$. Contrariwise to $\models^4$, they are *non-monotonic*: While $\neg a \wedge (a \vee b) \models^4_{I1} b$ and $\neg a \wedge (a \vee b) \models^4_{I2} b$ hold, none of these two relations holds any longer when $\neg a \wedge (a \vee b)$ is logically strengthened by conjoining it with a. Hence, the scope of disjunctive syllogism remains limited whenever these inference relations are considered. Actually, this is mandatory under the paraconsistency requirement whenever the inference relation is s.t. $\alpha \vee \beta$ is a consequence of α since *ex contradictione quodlibet sequitur* comes from their unrestricted interaction (known as Lewis independent argument, cf. [65]):

$$\neg\alpha, \frac{\alpha}{\alpha \vee \beta} \texttt{ disj.intro}$$
$$\frac{}{\beta} \texttt{ disj. syllogism}$$

Similarly, none of $\models^4_{I1}$ and $\models^4_{I2}$ is a transitive relation (and obviously, this contrasts with $\models^4$). Thus, while $\neg a \wedge a \models^4_{I1} \neg a \wedge (a \vee b)$ and $\neg a \wedge (a \vee b) \models^4_{I1} b$, we do *not* have $\neg a \wedge a \models^4_{I1} b$ (the same example can be used to show that $\models^4_{I2}$ is not transitive, *mutatis mutandis*).

Nevertheless, every classical model of a formula Σ of $PROP^4_{PS}$ is minimal in the set of 4-models of Σ w.r.t. any of the two preorderings. Therefore, both $\models^4_{I1}$ and $\models^4_{I2}$ coincide with $\models^2$ on the $PROP^2_{PS}$ fragment whenever Σ is classically consistent.

Finally, each of $\models^4_{I1}$ and $\models^4_{I2}$ is a proper superset of $\models^4$ but those relations do not coincide (see counterexamples in [2]).

Similar preference criteria have been considered in a three-valued framework [63, 64] in order to design the logic LP_m, less cautious than LP. Formally, the partial preordering $\leq_{LP_m}$ over the set of 3-interpretations over PS defined by $I \leq_{LP_m} J$ if and only if $\{x \in PS \mid I(x) \in \{\top\}\} \subseteq \{x \in PS \mid J(x) \in \{\top\}\}$ is considered:[6]

---

[6] Obviously, the sole difference between $\leq_1$ - equal to $\leq_2$ when $\perp$ is not allowed - and $\leq_{LP_m}$ is the underlying set of non-classical interpretations.

Definition 7 ($\models_{LP_m}$-inference).
Let Σ and γ be two formulas from the language of LP_m. We note $\Sigma \models_{LP_m} \gamma$ if and only if every 3-model of Σ that is minimal in its set w.r.t. $\leq_{LP_m}$ is a 3-model of γ.

Example 5. Let $\Sigma = a \wedge \neg a \wedge (a \vee b) \wedge c \wedge (\neg c \vee d)$. We have $\Sigma \models_{LP_m} d$ (while we do *not* have $\Sigma \models^3 d$). But, we do *not* have $\Sigma \models_{LP_m} b$.

$\models_{LP_m}$ is (three-valued) preferential, non-monotonic, paraconsistent and subclassical over $PROP_{PS}^2$. Unlike $\models^3$, it is not transitive. Like $\models_{I1}^4$ and $\models_{I2}^4$, it coincides with $\models^2$ on the $PROP_{PS}^2$ fragment whenever Σ is classically consistent.

Other preference criteria result from giving more significance to the syntax of the database (especially, considering an additional comma connective). Indeed, when Σ is a finite set of formulas, it is possible to give more credit to the 3-models of Σ which maximize (w.r.t. $\subseteq$) the subset of formulas from Σ interpreted to 1. Formally, a partial preordering $\leq_{BS}$ over the set of 3-interpretations over PS can be defined as follows: $I \leq_{BS} J$ if and only if $\{\phi \in \Sigma \mid I(\phi) = 1\} \supseteq \{\phi \in \Sigma \mid J(\phi) = 1\}$. On this ground, another inference relation can be defined:

Definition 8 ($\models_{BS}$-inference).
Let Σ be a finite set of formulas and γ be a formula from the language considered in [13]. We note $\Sigma \models_{BS} \gamma$ if and only if every 3-model of every formula from Σ minimal in its set w.r.t. $\leq_{BS}$ is a 3-model of γ.

Example 6. Let $\Sigma = \{a, \neg a, (a \vee b), c, (\neg c \vee d)\}$. We have $\Sigma \models_{BS} d$. We also have $\Sigma \models_{BS} b$ (while we do *not* have $\Sigma \models_{LP_m} b$).

$\models_{BS}$ is three-valued preferential if left logical equivalence is stated as: If $E \cup \{\alpha\} \mathrel{|\!\!\sim} \gamma$ and $\vdash (\alpha \leftrightarrow \beta)$ then $E \cup \{\beta\} \mathrel{|\!\!\sim} \gamma$ (a set is required instead of a formula). It is also paraconsistent and coincides with $\models^2$ on the $PROP_{PS}^2$ fragment whenever Σ is a classically consistent set.

Other Inference Relations Other inference relations have been investigated in [21, 48]. A basic idea consists in characterizing inference in other ways than set containment, e.g., using *reductio ad absurdum*.[7]

Definition 9 ($\models^{4,inc}$-inference and $\models^{3,inc}$-inference).
Let Σ, γ be two formulas from $PROP_{PS}^4$. $\Sigma \models^{4,inc} \gamma$ (resp. $\Sigma \models^{3,inc} \gamma$) if and only if $\Sigma \wedge \neg\gamma$ has no 4-model (resp. no 3-model).

Such inference relations make sense when the language is not restricted to the monotonic fragment (or a subset of it); otherwise, they trivialize to the empty

---

[7] Another approach would consist in taking advantage of material implication and in defining $\models^{4,\supset}$ by $\Sigma \models^{4,\supset} \gamma$ if and only if $\models^4 \Sigma \supset \gamma$, and similarly for the three-valued setting. However, it is easy to prove that $\models^{4,\supset}$ coincides with $\models^4$, while $\models^{3,\supset}$ coincides with $\models^3$.

relation since every formula from the monotonic fragment has a 4-model and a 3-model.

Other relations can be defined by taking advantage of additional mechanisms. Among such mechanisms are the following ones:

- considering only argumentative consequences of the belief bases.
- selecting the consequences of the belief base that are necessarily true.
- selecting as consequences of the belief base formulas that are so to speak "at least as true" as the belief base.

Definition 10 ($\models_{\leq}^{4,arg}$-inference, $\models_{\leq}^{4,1}$-inference and $\models_{\leq}^{4,t}$-inference).
Let $\leq$ be a binary relation over the set of all 4-interpretations over PS. Let Σ, γ be two formulas from $PROP_{PS}^4$. We define $\Sigma \models_{\leq}^4 \gamma$ by $\forall I \in \min(4\text{-}mod(\Sigma), \leq)$, $I(\gamma) \in \{1, \top\}$. Then:

- $\Sigma \models_{\leq}^{4,arg} \gamma$ *if and only if* $\Sigma \models_{\leq}^4 \gamma$ *and* $\Sigma \not\models_{\leq}^4 \neg\gamma$.
- $\Sigma \models_{\leq}^{4,1} \gamma$ *if and only if* $\forall I \in \min(4\text{-}mod(\Sigma), \leq)$, $I(\gamma) = 1$.
- $\Sigma \models_{\leq}^{4,t} \gamma$ *if and only if* $\forall I \in \min(4\text{-}mod(\Sigma), \leq)$, $I(\Sigma) \leq_t I(\gamma)$.

Example 7. Let $\Sigma = a \wedge \neg a \wedge (a \vee b) \wedge c \wedge (\neg c \vee d)$. We have:

- $\Sigma \models_{\leq_1}^{4,arg} c$ and $\Sigma \models_{\leq_1}^{4,arg} d$
- $\Sigma \models_{\leq_1}^{4,1} c$ and $\Sigma \models_{\leq_1}^{4,1} d$
- $\Sigma \models_{\leq_1}^{4,t} c$ and $\Sigma \models_{\leq_1}^{4,t} d$ and $\Sigma \models_{\leq_1}^{4,t} a$
- $\Sigma \models_{\leq_2}^{4,arg} c$ and $\Sigma \models_{\leq_2}^{4,arg} d$
- $\Sigma \models_{\leq_2}^{4,1} c$ and $\Sigma \models_{\leq_2}^{4,1} d$
- $\Sigma \models_{\leq_2}^{4,t} c$ and $\Sigma \models_{\leq_2}^{4,t} d$ and $\Sigma \models_{\leq_2}^{4,t} a$

Let us now present some logical properties for these three inference relations. $\models_{\leq}^{4,arg}$, $\models_{\leq}^{4,1}$ and $\models_{\leq}^{4,t}$ satisfy or, cautious cut and cautious monotony but they satisfy neither monotony nor right weakening in the general case. Neither $\models_{\leq}^{4,arg}$ nor $\models_{\leq}^{4,1}$ satisfy reflexivity in general, but $\models_{\leq}^{4,t}$ does. $\models_{\leq}^{4,1}$ satisfies left logical equivalence but none of $\models_{\leq}^{4,arg}$ or $\models_{\leq}^{4,t}$ does.

Again, similar inference relations can be stated in a three-valued setting. [48] investigated the logical properties of such relations, as well as their relative cautiousness, in the general case (i.e., for any $\leq$). A similar analysis has also been conducted in the specific case preorderings $\leq$ are considered. In particular, we considered both the universal ordering (i.e., the minimal 3-models of Σ are all its 3-models), $\leq_{LP_m}$, $\leq_{BS}$ (assuming that Σ is a finite set of formulas), and the variant of the latter based on cardinality instead on set containment. All the relations under consideration are paraconsistent and non-monotonic (when the universal ordering is not chosen).

One of the purposes for designing these relations is to derive paraconsistent inference relations more discriminating toward their consequences. Indeed, the three-valued inference relations depicted before suffer from a relative myopia: They do not make sufficient distinctions between the conclusions they provide given a belief base Σ. For instance, let $\Sigma = \Box a \wedge b \wedge c \wedge \neg c$. Both a, b and c are consequences of Σ but they have different epistemic status w.r.t. Σ: a is necessary in Σ (it must be true, and only true, in every model of Σ), b is plausible since we have some evidence about its truth but no evidence about its falsity, and c is only possible since we have contradictory evidence about it.

Beyond S-3 Logic. As we will see in the next section, taking a preference relation into account in order to retain only the 3-models that are as close as possible to the classical ones (in a certain sense) has a computational cost. The complexity of the corresponding inference relations is at least one level higher in the polynomial hierarchy compared with $\models^3$. This just reflects that preference handling is a source of complexity (this is not a major surprise for any reader aware of the complexity of many preferential (and not paraconsistent) inference relations): Looking for preferred models requires searching an exponential space, and this source of complexity is typically orthogonal to the other source (exponentially many preferred models are possible).

In order to avoid such a complexity shift while refining $\models^3$ nevertheless, an approach is S-3 logic [69]. In a nutshell, instead of preferring only those models of the base Σ that are "as classical as possible" (or "as consistent as possible"), all the models of Σ that are classical over a prespecified set of symbols are kept. Thus, S-3-models are 3-models that are classical over the set S of propositional symbols. More formally, given a subset S of PS, an S-3-model I of $\Sigma \in PROP^3_{PS}$ is any 3-model of Σ s.t. $\forall x \in S$, $I(x) \neq \top$. Whenever S is fixed (and a part of the input), determining whether a given 3-model I of Σ is an S-3-model of it can be achieved in polynomial time (while the problem of determining whether a given 3-model I of Σ is a 3-model of it that is minimal w.r.t. $\leq_{LP_m}$ cannot be achieved in polynomial time – under the standard assumptions of complexity theory).

Given such a notion of S-3-model, another inference relation can be defined:

Definition 11 ($\models^3_S$-inference).
Let S be a subset of PS. Let Σ and γ be two formulas from $PROP^3_{PS}$. We note $\Sigma \models^3_S \gamma$ if and only if every S-3-model of Σ is an S-3-model of γ.

Now, the problem with S-3-logic is that a classically inconsistent belief base Σ may also be S-3-inconsistent, even if it is 3-consistent (especially when it is from the monotonic fragment). This happens when S contains all the propositional symbols that are brought into play in a conflict of Σ:

Example 8. Let $\Sigma = a \wedge \neg a \wedge (a \vee b) \wedge c \wedge (\neg c \vee d)$. Σ has no $\{a\}$-3-model.

In order to deal with the inconsistencies that may be revealed when using S-3 inference in $PROP^3_{PS}$, it was suggested in [56] to focus on some subsets S' of

S, the ones for which the corresponding inference relations are not trivial. The approach is similar to the standard coherence-based approach to inconsistency handling, except that the inference relation is weakened by removing symbols from S instead of removing explicit beliefs from Σ:

Definition 12 (Consistent subsets).
Let Σ be a belief base from $PROP^3_{PS}$. Let $S \subseteq PS$ and $S_0 \subseteq S$ s.t. $\Sigma \not\models^3_{S_0}$ false. A consistent subset S' of S w.r.t. Σ and S_0 is a subset of S containing S_0 and s.t. $\Sigma \not\models^3_{S'}$ false. $\mathcal{S}(\Sigma, S, S_0)$ denotes the set of all consistent subsets of S w.r.t. Σ and S_0.

In this definition, S_0 is a given set of symbols which must be interpreted classically. The condition $\Sigma \not\models^3_{S_0}$ *false* means that the set of consequences of Σ is not the whole language $PROP^3_{PS}$. Note that the existence of such a set S_0 (possibly empty) is ensured provided that Σ is 3-consistent.

Example 9. Let $\Sigma = a \wedge \neg a \wedge (a \vee b) \wedge c \wedge (\neg c \vee d)$. Every subset S of PS s.t. $a \notin S$ is a consistent subset of Σ.

Among the consistent subsets, we are interested in those from which the maximum amount of information is kept but trivialization is avoided. This calls for a selection policy $\mathcal{P}$ which aims at pointing out a preferred subset of $\mathcal{S}(\Sigma, S, S_0)$. In [56], the authors adhered to a skeptical approach: Any piece of belief is considered as a consequence of Σ given S and S_0 if and only if it is S'-3 entailed by Σ for every preferred consistent subset S' of S w.r.t. Σ and S_0.

Definition 13 ($\approx^{\mathcal{P},S_0}_S$-inference).
Let Σ be a belief base from $PROP^3_{PS}$ and S_0 be a subset of PS s.t. $\Sigma \not\models^3_{S_0}$ false. Let $\mathcal{P}$ be a selection policy s.t. $\mathcal{S}_{\mathcal{P}}(\Sigma, S, S_0)$ is a subset of $\mathcal{S}(\Sigma, S, S_0)$ and let γ be a formula from $PROP_{PS}$. γ is a consequence of Σ w.r.t. $\mathcal{P}$ and S_0, noted $\Sigma \approx^{\mathcal{P},S_0}_S \gamma$, if and only if $\forall S' \in \mathcal{S}_{\mathcal{P}}(\Sigma, S, S_0)$, $\Sigma \models^3_{S'} \gamma$.

Example 10. Let $\Sigma = a \wedge \neg a \wedge (a \vee b) \wedge c \wedge (\neg c \vee d)$. If $S = (\emptyset, \{b, c, d\})$ and $\mathcal{S}_{\mathcal{P}}(\Sigma, S, S_0) = \{\{b, c, d\}\}$, we have $\Sigma \approx^{\mathcal{P},S_0}_S d$. We also have $\Sigma \approx^{\mathcal{P},S_0}_S a$, $\Sigma \approx^{\mathcal{P},S_0}_S \neg a$ but $\Sigma \not\approx^{\mathcal{P},S_0}_S b$.

Many selection policies for consistent subsets that are similar to the ones defined for consistent subbases in the standard coherence-based approach to inconsistency handling [62, 7, 8] are given in [56]. Thus, the possibilistic policy $\mathcal{PO}$ (or best-out), the linear-order policy $\mathcal{LO}$, the inclusion-preference policy $\mathcal{IP}$ (or discrimin) and the lexicographic policy $\mathcal{LE}$ (or leximin) have been defined for stratified S (i.e., S is given by a totally ordered partition of its propositional symbols); such policies consist in selecting the minimal elements in $\mathcal{S}_{\mathcal{P}}(\Sigma, S, S_0)$ w.r.t. the corresponding preorderings.
Every $\approx^{\mathcal{P},S_0}_S$ inference relation is a proper subset of $\models^3_S$ and is equal to it when $\Sigma \not\models^3_S$ *false* for many reasonable $\mathcal{P}$ (including $\mathcal{PO}$, $\mathcal{LO}$, $\mathcal{IP}$, $\mathcal{LE}$). The family of $\approx^{\mathcal{P},S_0}_S$ inference relations also includes $\models^3$ (just set S to $\emptyset$). All these

relations are paraconsistent when Σ is assumed to be 3-consistent. However, in contrast to $\models_S^3$ that is monotonic, the $\approx_S^{\mathcal{P},S_0}$ inference relations are typically non-monotonic:

Example 11. Let $\Sigma = \neg a \wedge (a \vee b)$. If $S = (\emptyset, \{a, b\})$ and $\mathcal{S}_\mathcal{P}(\Sigma, S, S_0) = \{\{a, b\}\}$, we have $\Sigma \approx_S^{\mathcal{P},S_0} b$. Now, if $\Sigma = a \wedge \neg a \wedge (a \vee b)$, then $\{a, b\}$ may not belong any longer to $\mathcal{S}_\mathcal{P}(\Sigma, S, S_0)$. If this set becomes $\mathcal{S}_\mathcal{P}(\Sigma, S, S_0) = \{\{a\}\}$, then we have $\Sigma \not\approx_S^{\mathcal{P},S_0} b$.

3.4   Other Related Systems for Paraconsistent Inference

We finally describe two logical approaches to paraconsistency that are related to the propositional multi-valued logics framework: Quasi-classical logic [15, 44] and the signed systems for paraconsistent inference [14].

Quasi-classical Logic. As explained before, *ex contradictione quodlibet sequitur* is obtained whenever full disjunctive syllogism (or more generally resolution) and disjunction introduction are allowed inference rules. Removing any of those rules is a drastic way to escape from trivialization in presence of inconsistency. However, it clearly leads to too cautious inference relations.

Quasi-classical logic, as defined in [15] and in [45], relies on the idea that it is sufficient to limit the way resolution and disjunction introduction interact in order to avoid trivialization in presence of inconsistency. In this logic, an application of the resolution rule can never follow an application of the disjunction introduction rule; additionally, applications of the resolution rule that would produce an inconsistency (i.e., the empty clause) are forbidden.

The language of quasi-classical propositional logic is the restriction of $PROP_{PS}^2$ where no constant symbols occur.

Quasi-classical logic has a simple proof theory; when considering CNF formulas only, it is sufficient to consider the resolution rule and the disjunction introduction rule (disjunction and conjunction being implicitly taken as associative and commutative). Starting from a CNF formula Σ, a CNF γ is derivable if and only if each clause of it is derivable, and a clause is derivable if and only if it has a resolution proof from Σ in which the empty clause does not occur and no applications of the resolution rule follow an application of the disjunction introduction rule.

Example 12. Let $\Sigma = a \wedge \neg a \wedge (a \vee b) \wedge c \wedge (\neg c \vee d)$. Here is a proof of d from Σ:

$$\frac{c, \neg c \vee d}{d} \text{ resolution}$$

Here is a proof of b from Σ:

$$\frac{\neg a, a \vee b}{b} \text{ resolution}$$

Here is a proof of $d \vee e$ from Σ:

$$\frac{\dfrac{c, \neg c \vee d}{d} \text{ resolution}}{d \vee e} \text{ disj.intro.}$$

Contrastingly, neither the empty clause nor e are derivable from Σ in quasi-classical logic.

Quasi-classical logic also has a semantics w.r.t. which the proof theory is sound and complete. In order to define the quasi-classical logic entailment relation $\models_{QC}$, we first need to make precise the underlying notion of interpretation, as well as the notions of *strong satisfaction* and *weak satisfaction*. The first part is easy: An interpretation in quasi-classical logic (QC interpretation for short) is a 4-interpretation over PS. For the other notions, our presentation slightly departs from the one reported in [15, 44] so as to keep as much as possible the notations used in this chapter:

Definition 14 (Strong Satisfaction).
The notion of strong satisfaction of a formula Σ (from the language of quasi-classical logic) by a QC interpretation I, noted $I \models_s \Sigma$, is defined as follows:

- *If $\alpha \in PS$, then $I \models_s \alpha$ if and only if $I(\alpha) \in \{1, \top\}$;*
- *If $\alpha \in PS$, then $I \models_s \neg\alpha$ if and only if $I(\alpha) \in \{0, \top\}$;*
- *If $\alpha_1 \vee \ldots \vee \alpha_n$ is a clause, then $I \models_s \alpha_1 \vee \ldots \vee \alpha_n$ if and only if there exists $i \in 1 \ldots n$ s.t. $I \models_s \alpha_i$ and for every $i \in 1 \ldots n$, if $I \models_s \bar{\alpha}_i$ then $I \models_s \alpha_1 \vee \ldots \vee \alpha_{i-1} \vee \alpha_{i+1} \vee \ldots \vee \alpha_n$;*
- *$I \models_s \alpha \wedge \beta$ if and only if $I \models_s \alpha$ and $I \models_s \beta$;*
- *$I \models_s (\neg\neg\alpha) \vee \beta$ if and only if $I \models_s \alpha \vee \beta$;*
- *$I \models_s \neg(\alpha \wedge \beta) \vee \gamma$ if and only if $I \models_s \neg\alpha \vee \neg\beta \vee \gamma$;*
- *$I \models_s \neg(\alpha \vee \beta) \vee \gamma$ if and only if $I \models_s (\neg\alpha \wedge \neg\beta) \vee \gamma$;*
- *$I \models_s \alpha \vee (\beta \wedge \gamma)$ if and only if $I \models_s (\alpha \vee \beta) \wedge (\alpha \vee \gamma)$;*
- *$I \models_s \alpha \wedge (\beta \vee \gamma)$ if and only if $I \models_s (\alpha \wedge \beta) \vee (\alpha \wedge \gamma)$;*
- *$I \models_s (\alpha \supset \beta) \vee \gamma$ if and only if $I \models_s \neg\alpha \vee \beta \vee \gamma$;*
- *$I \models_s \neg(\alpha \supset \beta) \vee \gamma$ if and only if $I \models_s (\alpha \wedge \neg\beta) \vee \gamma$.*

Clearly enough, the definition for disjunction is more restricted than the classical definition. Actually, the notion of strong satisfaction implicitly translates the formula into CNF whenever disjunction applies to more sophisticated subformulas than literals. As to clauses $\alpha_1 \vee \ldots \vee \alpha_n$, it asks at least one disjunct to be satisfied, and in addition, when the interpretation strongly satisfies a complementary literal $\bar{\alpha}_i$ ($i \in 1 \ldots n$), it must satisfy the subclause obtained by removing α_i in the clause. This is necessary to restore the connection between a literal and its complementary literal which is decoupled when 4-interpretations are considered (remember that $\models^4$ does not satisfy the disjunctive syllogism).

The notion of strong satisfaction can be relaxed to the less demanding notion of weak satisfaction defined by:

Definition 15 (Weak satisfaction).
The notion of weak satisfaction *of a formula* Σ *(from the language of quasi-classical logic) by a QC interpretation* I, *noted* $I \models_w \Sigma$, *is defined as follows:*

- *If* $\alpha \in PS$, *then* $I \models_w \alpha$ *if and only if* $I(\alpha) \in \{1, \top\}$;
- *If* $\alpha \in PS$, *then* $I \models_w \neg\alpha$ *if and only if* $I(\alpha) \in \{0, \top\}$;
- $I \models_w \alpha \vee \beta$ *if and only if* $I \models_w \alpha$ *or* $I \models_w \beta$;
- $I \models_w \alpha \wedge \beta$ *if and only if* $I \models_w \alpha$ *and* $I \models_w \beta$;
- $I \models_w (\neg\neg\alpha) \vee \beta$ *if and only if* $I \models_w \alpha \vee \beta$;
- $I \models_w \neg(\alpha \wedge \beta) \vee \gamma$ *if and only if* $I \models_w \neg\alpha \vee \neg\beta \vee \gamma$;
- $I \models_w \neg(\alpha \vee \beta) \vee \gamma$ *if and only if* $I \models_w (\neg\alpha \wedge \neg\beta) \vee \gamma$;
- $I \models_w (\alpha \supset \beta) \vee \gamma$ *if and only if* $I \models_w \neg\alpha \vee \beta \vee \gamma$;
- $I \models_w \neg(\alpha \supset \beta) \vee \gamma$ *if and only if* $I \models_w (\alpha \wedge \neg\beta) \vee \gamma$.

When $I \models_s \Sigma$ holds, I is said to be a *strong model* of Σ. When $I \models_w \Sigma$ holds, I is said to be a *weak model* of Σ. Obviously, every strong model of Σ is a weak model of Σ but the converse does not hold in the general case.

It is not very difficult to show that every CNF formula Σ has a strong model (hence a weak one as well), even if it is classically inconsistent (the interpretation I s.t. $I(x) = \top$ for every $x \in PS$ does the job).

Definition 16 ($\models_{QC}$-inference).
Let Σ *and* Φ *be two formulas from the language of quasi-classical logic. We have* $\Sigma \models_{QC} \Phi$ *if and only if for every QC interpretation* I, *if* $I \models_s \Sigma$, *then* $I \models_w \Phi$.

A detailed study of the logical properties of quasi-classical inference is given in [45]; it is shown that quasi-classical entailment satisfies reflexivity, monotony, and-introduction, or-elimination and consistency preservation, but none of supra-classicality, right modus ponens, conditionalization, deduction, cut, transitivity, unit cumulativity, right weakening and left logical equivalence is satisfied.

An interesting feature of quasi-classical logic is that it coincides with classical entailment in the clausal case when the CNF belief base Σ is consistent and the CNF query γ does not contain any valid clauses.

Finally, let us note that quasi-classical logic has been extended recently to quasi-classical possibilistic logic [28]. This logic extends both possibilistic logic and quasi-classical logic, whilst preserving their merits. Thus, conflicts taking place at the same level of certainty are handled as in quasi-classical logic, while the remaining conflicts are handled as in possibilistic logic. $\models_{QIL}$ denotes the corresponding paraconsistent inference relation.

Signed Systems for Paraconsistent Inference. To conclude this section, let us consider the paraconsistent inference relations introduced in [14] in a default logic approach.

In Besnard and Schaub's work [14], the language used is the set of NNF formulas from $PROP^2_{PS}$, i.e., formulas built up from the connectives $\neg$, $\wedge$, $\vee$, only, and for which the scope of every occurrence of $\neg$ is a propositional symbol from PS.[8] Every formula Σ is associated to a default theory $\langle \Sigma^{\pm}, D_{\Sigma} \rangle$ where:

- $\Sigma^{\pm}$ is a formula in the language $PROP^2_{PS^{\pm}}$ where $PS^{\pm} = \{x^+ \mid x \in PS\} \cup \{x^- \mid x \in PS\}$; $\Sigma^{\pm}$ is obtained by replacing in Σ every occurrence of a positive literal x by the positive literal x^+ and every occurrence of a negative literal $\neg x$ by the positive literal x^-.
- $D_{\Sigma} = \{\delta_x \mid x \in PS\}$ is a set of default rules

$$\delta_x = \frac{: x^+ \Leftrightarrow \neg x^-}{(x \Leftrightarrow x^+) \wedge (\neg x \Leftrightarrow x^-)}$$

Negation is given a special treatment; first, every literal is rendered independent from its negation through renaming; then the corresponding dependence relations are re-introduced in a parsimonious way, so that no inconsistency occurs. Based on the extensions of the default theory $\langle \Sigma^{\pm}, D_{\Sigma} \rangle$, several paraconsistent consequence relations can be defined, especially the relations $\vdash_s$ and $\vdash^{\pm}_s$:

Definition 17 ($\vdash_s$-inference and $\vdash^{\pm}_s$-inference).
Let Σ and γ be two formulas from $PROP^2_{PS}$.

- γ is a skeptical unsigned consequence of Σ, noted $\Sigma \vdash_s \gamma$, if and only if γ belongs to every extension of $\langle \Sigma^{\pm}, D_{\Sigma} \rangle$.
- γ is a skeptical signed consequence of Σ, noted $\Sigma \vdash^{\pm}_s \gamma$, if and only if $\gamma^{\pm}$ belongs to every extension of $\langle \Sigma^{\pm}, D_{\Sigma} \rangle$.

Example 13. Let $\Sigma = a \wedge \neg a \wedge (a \vee b) \wedge c \wedge (\neg c \vee d)$. Σ is associated with:

- $\Sigma^{\pm} = a^+ \wedge a^- \wedge (a^+ \vee b^+) \wedge c^+ \wedge (c^- \vee d^+)$.
- $D_{\Sigma} = \{\dfrac{: x^+ \Leftrightarrow \neg x^-}{(x \Leftrightarrow x^+) \wedge (\neg x \Leftrightarrow x^-)} \mid x \in PS\}$.

This default theory has two extensions. We have:

- $\Sigma \vdash_s c \wedge d \wedge (a \vee b)$ but $\Sigma \nvdash_s a$, $\Sigma \nvdash_s \neg a$ and $\Sigma \nvdash_s b$.
- $\Sigma \vdash^{\pm}_s c \wedge d \wedge a \wedge \neg a \wedge (a \vee b)$ but $\Sigma \nvdash^{\pm}_s b$.

Reflexivity is satisfied by $\vdash^{\pm}_s$ while it is not ensured for $\vdash_s$. On the contrary, right weakening is ensured for $\vdash_s$ but not for $\vdash^{\pm}_s$. Both $\vdash^{\pm}_s$ and $\vdash_s$ coincide with classical entailment as soon as Σ is (classically) consistent.

Other inference relations can be obtained by considering other inference mechanisms (credulous inference, prudent inference), other ways to render each propositional symbol independent from its negation, other kinds of extensions when some preferential information (under the form of a total preordering over PS) are available. It must be noted that, unsurprisingly, taking advantage of such preferential information does not lead to a complexity shift (see [11] for details).

---

[8] The NNF assumption can be relaxed through the notion of polarity (see [14]) but every occurrence of a subformula $\phi \Leftrightarrow \psi$ must be replaced first by $(\phi \supset \psi) \wedge (\psi \supset \phi)$.

4   Complexity Results

4.1   Main Results

In this section, we report the complexity of inference problems for the different (paraconsistent) inference relations presented in the previous section. For each inference relation considered $\vdash_L$, the decision problem is defined as follows:

Definition 18 (Decision Problem for $\vdash_L$).
Input: *A pair $\langle \Sigma, \gamma \rangle$ (plus a possibly stratified subset S of PS for the relations for which this is relevant) of formulas from the language L of the logic $\langle L, \vdash_L \rangle$ considered.*
Question : *Does $\Sigma \vdash_L \gamma$ hold?*

Complexity results for most of the relations come from [53, 19] for the monotonic ones and from [21, 48] for the non-monotonic ones. [55] gives complexity results for quasi-classical logic and [28] for quasi-possibilistic logic. The complexity of the inference relations based on signed systems have been investigated in [21, 11]. Finally, [56] presents complexity results for the $\approx_S^{\mathcal{P}, S_0}$ relations.

Proposition 1. *The complexity of the decision problem for $\vdash_L$ has been identified as follows:*

- coNP-*complete when* $\vdash_L$ *is* $\models^4$, $\models^3$, $\models_{J_3}$, $\models_{LP}$, $\models_L$, $\models_S^3$, $\models^{4,inc}$, $\models^{3,inc}$.

- $\Delta_2^p[\mathcal{O}(\log n)]$-*complete when* $\vdash_L$ *is* $\approx_S^{\mathcal{PO}, S_0}$.

- Δ_2^p-*complete when* $\vdash_L$ *is* $\approx_S^{\mathcal{LO}, S_0}$ *or* $\approx_S^{\mathcal{LE}, S_0}$.

- Π_2^p-*complete when* $\vdash_L$ *is* $\models_{I1}^4$, $\models_{I2}^4$, $\models_{LP_m}$, $\models_{BS}$, $\vdash_s^{\pm}$, $\vdash_s$, $\approx_S^{\mathcal{IP}, S_0}$, $\models_{\leq_1}^{4,1}$, $\models_{\leq_2}^{4,1}$, $\models_{\leq_1}^{4,t}$, $\models_{\leq_2}^{4,t}$, $\models_{\leq_{LP_m}}^{3,1}$ *or* $\models_{\leq_{LP_m}}^{3,t}$.

- D_2^p-*complete when* $\vdash_L$ *is* $\models_{\leq_1}^{4,arg}$, $\models_{\leq_2}^{4,arg}$ *or* $\models_{\leq_{LP_m}}^{3,arg}$.

To conclude this section, let us sketch some of the proofs of the results given in the proposition above (the remaining ones can be found in [19, 55, 56]).

All the membership proofs are easy. For any relation $\vdash_L$ among $\models^4$, $\models^3$, $\models_{J_3}$, $\models_{LP}$, $\models_L$, $\models_S^3$, membership can be easily proven by showing that the corresponding complementary problems are in NP, thanks to the following non-deterministic algorithm:

```
1. Guess an interpretation I over Var(Σ) ∪ Var(γ);
2. Check that I is a model of Σ but not a model of γ
```

By interpretation (resp. model) here, it is meant a 4-interpretation (resp. a 4-model) when $\models^4$ is concerned, an S-3-interpretation (resp. an S-3-model) when $\models_S^3$ is concerned, and a 3-interpretation (resp. a 3-model) otherwise.

The membership results for $\models^{4,inc}$, $\models^{3,inc}$ comes from a similar non-deterministic algorithm (only step. 2 changes and consists in checking that I is a model of $\Sigma \wedge \neg \gamma$).

For any relation $\vdash_L$ among $\models_{I1}^4$, $\models_{I2}^4$, $\models_{LP_m}$, $\models_{BS}$, membership is proven by showing that the corresponding complementary problems are in Σ_2^p. This is achieved through the following non-deterministic algorithm:

1. Guess an interpretation I over $Var(\Sigma) \cup Var(\gamma)$;
2. Check that I is a model of Σ minimal w.r.t. $\leq$
   through a call to an NP oracle;
3. Check that I is not a model of γ

This time, by interpretation (resp. model), it is meant a 4-interpretation (resp. a 4-model) when $\models_{I1}^4$ or $\models_{I2}^4$ is concerned, a 3-interpretation (resp. a 3-model) otherwise.

Indeed, checking that I is not minimal w.r.t. any relation $\leq$ that can be decided in deterministic polynomial time can be easily done in non-deterministic polynomial time, just by guessing an interpretation J over $Var(\Sigma) \cup Var(\gamma)$, and by checking in deterministic polynomial time that J is a model of Σ, and that $J \leq I$ holds while $I \leq J$ does not hold. Obviously, $\leq=\leq_1$, $\leq_2$, $\leq_{LP_m}$ or $\leq_{BS}$ can be decided in deterministic polynomial time.

A similar non-deterministic algorithm can be used for $\models_{\leq_1}^{4,1}$, $\models_{\leq_2}^{4,1}$, $\models_{\leq_{LP_m}}^{3,1}$ (resp. $\models_{\leq_1}^{4,t}$, $\models_{\leq_2}^{4,t}$, $\models_{\leq_{LP_m}}^{3,t}$) (only step. 3 changes and consists in checking that $I(\gamma) \neq 1$ (resp. $I(\Sigma) \not\leq_t I(\gamma)$)).

As to $\vdash_s^\pm$, $\vdash_s$, the membership results are are direct consequences of Theorem 5.2 from [42] (see also [70]) showing that skeptical default reasoning is in Π_2^p in the general case.

As to the relations $\approx_S^{PO,S_0}$, $\approx_S^{CO,S_0}$, $\approx_S^{IP,S_0}$ and $\approx_S^{LE,S_0}$, the membership results come from modular and faithful polytime translations from the inference problem for such relations to the corresponding inference problems from stratified belief bases (Proposition 3.11 from [56]), and the membership results for the latter decision problems as reported in [60, 20].

As to the argumentative relations $\models_{\leq_1}^{4,arg}$, $\models_{\leq_2}^{4,arg}$ or $\models_{\leq_{LP_m}}^{3,arg}$, the membership results come directly from the definitions and the membership results for $\models_{\leq_1}^4$, $\models_{\leq_2}^4$ and $\models_{\leq_{LP_m}}^3$.

All the hardness proofs come from the corresponding restrictions to the CNF case, except to what concerns $\models^4$, $\models^3$, $\models_{J_3}$, $\models_{LP}$, $\models_L$, $\models^{4,inc}$, $\models^{3,inc}$.

As to $\models^4$, hardness comes from the following polytime reduction from the canonical NP-complete problem SAT; let Σ be a CNF formula s.t. $Var(\Sigma) = \{x_1, \dots, x_n\}$; we have that Σ is classically consistent if and only if $\Sigma \wedge \bigwedge_{i=1}^n (x_i \vee \neg x_i) \not\models^4 \bigvee_{i=1}^n (x_i \wedge \neg x_i)$ (see [19]).

As to $\models^3$, $\models_{J_3}$, $\models_{LP}$, $\models_L$, hardness comes from the following polytime reduction from SAT; let Σ be a CNF formula s.t. $Var(\Sigma) = \{x_1, \dots, x_n\}$; we have that Σ is classically consistent if and only if $\Sigma \not\models^3 \bigvee_{i=1}^n (x_i \wedge \neg x_i)$ (see [19]).

As to $\models^{4,inc}$ and $\models^{3,inc}$, we associate in polynomial time to any CNF Σ the formula $\Sigma_\square$ obtained by replacing in Σ every occurrence of any literal l by $\square l$. Now, Σ has a 2-model if and only if $\Sigma_\square$ has a 4-model if and only if $\Sigma_\square$ has a 3-model, due to the truth table of $\square$. Accordingly, Σ is classically consistent if and only if $\Sigma_\square \not\models^4 new$ if and only if $\Sigma_\square \not\models^3 new$, where $new \in PS \setminus Var(\Sigma)$.

4.2   Restrictions

Let us now give more specific results, obtained by imposing further restrictions to the decision problem.

The CNF Case. Significant decreases in complexity can be obtained for some inference relations when Σ and γ are restricted to CNF formulas (from $PROP_{PS}^2$).

Proposition 2. *The complexity of the decision problem for* $\vdash_L$ *has been identified as follows in the case* Σ *and* γ *are CNF formulas (from* $PROP_{PS}^2$*):*

- *trivial (i.e., in time $\mathcal{O}(1)$) when $\vdash_L$ is $\models^{4,inc}$ or $\models^{3,inc}$ because such relations are empty.*

- *in P when $\vdash_L$ is $\models^4$ or $\models^3$, $\models_{J_3}$, $\models_{LP}$ or $\models_L$.*

- *coNP-complete when $\vdash_L$ is $\models_S^3$.*

- *$\Delta_2^p[\mathcal{O}(log\ n)]$-complete when $\vdash_L$ is $\approx_S^{\mathcal{PO},S_0}$.*

- *Δ_2^p-complete when $\vdash_L$ is $\approx_S^{\mathcal{LO},S_0}$ or $\approx_S^{\mathcal{LE},S_0}$.*

- *Π_2^p-complete when $\vdash_L$ is $\models_{I1}^4$, $\models_{I2}^4$, $\models_{LP_m}$, $\models_{BS}$, $\models_s^{\pm}$, $\models_s$, $\approx_S^{\mathcal{IP},S_0}$, $\models_{\leq 1}^{4,1}$, $\models_{\leq 2}^{4,1}$, $\models_{\leq 1}^{4,t}$, $\models_{\leq 2}^{4,t}$, $\models_{\leq LP_m}^{3,1}$ or $\models_{\leq LP_m}^{3,t}$.*

- *D_2^p-complete when $\vdash_L$ is $\models_{\leq 1}^{4,arg}$, $\models_{\leq 2}^{4,arg}$ or $\models_{\leq LP_m}^{3,arg}$.*

Again, let us sketch some of the proofs of the results given in the proposition above. The Π_2^p-hardness proof for $\models_{LP_m}$ is fully detailed; it is a bit long, but on the one hand, it is central (in the sense that the other Π_2^p-hardness proofs are based on it) and on the other hand, it exhibits an interesting connection with the notion of conflict (a minimally inconsistent subset of formulas), which is at the core of many approaches to inconsistency tolerant reasoning based on formula inhibition.

Membership to P for $\models^4$ or $\models^3$, (and their restrictions $\models_{J_3}$, $\models_{LP}$ or $\models_L$) intuitively comes from the fact that the disjunctive syllogism rule fails for each of them. Thus, when Σ and γ are CNF formulas, $\Sigma \models^4 \gamma$ holds (resp. $\Sigma \models^3 \gamma$ holds) if and only if every clause of γ is subsumed by a clause from Σ (resp. every clause of γ is subsumed by a clause from Σ or it contains a pair of complementary literals) [53].

Hardness for $\models_S^3$ simply comes from the fact that classical entailment is coNP-hard and coincides with $\models_S^3$ when $S = PS$.

Hardness for $\approx_S^{\mathcal{PO},S_0}$ comes from the $\Delta_2^p[\mathcal{O}(log\ n)]$-hardness of inference from stratified belief bases interpreted under the possibilistic policy (Theorem 6.5 from [60]) and a (modular and faithful) polytime translation of this inference problem into the decision problem for $\approx_S^{\mathcal{PO},S_0}$-inference (Proposition 3.10 in [56]).

Similarly, hardness for $\approx_S^{\mathcal{LO},S_0}$ (resp. $\approx_S^{\mathcal{LE},S_0}$) comes from the Δ_2^p-hardness of inference from stratified belief bases interpreted under the linear-order policy

(Theorem 5.9 from [60]) (resp. the lexicographic policy (see [20])) and a (modular and faithful) polytime translation of such inference problems from stratified belieb bases into the corresponding decision problem for $\approx_S^{\mathcal{LO},S_0}$-inference (resp. $\approx_S^{\mathcal{LE},S_0}$) (again, see Proposition 3.10 in [56]).

Hardness for $\models_{I1}^4$ and $\models_{I2}^4$ comes from hardness for $\models_{LP_m}$, together with the fact that in the fragment $\{\neg, \wedge, \vee, true, false\}$, we have $\Sigma \models_{I2}^4 \gamma$ if and only if $\Sigma \models_{LP_m} \gamma$ and when in addition γ is a CNF formula that does not contain any valid clause, we have $\Sigma \models_{I1}^4 \gamma$ if and only if $\Sigma \models_{LP_m} \gamma$ (Proposition 5.4 from [2]).

Hardness for $\vdash_s^\pm$ and $\approx_S^{\mathcal{IP},S_0}$, comes from the fact that $\vdash_s^\pm$ and $\approx_{PS}^{\mathcal{IP},\emptyset}$ coincide with $\models_{LP_m}$ on the monotonic fragment (see Propositions 3.8 and 3.9 in [56] and Lemma 5).

The Π_2^p-hardness results for $\models_{LP_m}$, $\vdash_s$, $\models_{BS}$ remain to be proven. Let us do it in a gentle way, through a number of intermediate lemmata. We first need the following notions:

Definition 19. *Let $\Sigma = \{\phi_1, \ldots, \phi_n\}$ be a finite set of formulas from $PROP_{PS}^2$. Let α be a formula from $PROP_{PS}^2$.*

- *A subset S of Σ is an α-conflict of Σ if and only if $S \cup \{\alpha\}$ is classically inconsistent but every proper subset of it is consistent. We note $Conf(\Sigma, \alpha)$ the set of all formulas ϕ_i from Σ where ϕ_i belongs to at least one α-conflict of it. When $\alpha \equiv^2 true$ holds, an α-conflict of Σ is simply referred to as a conflict of Σ.*
- *A var-conflict of Σ is a subset V of $Var(\Sigma)$ s.t. there exists a conflict S of Σ satisfying $V = Var(S)$.*
- *A minimal var-conflict of Σ is a var-conflict of Σ that is minimal w.r.t. $\subsetneq$.*

Given a CNF formula $\Sigma = \{\phi_1, \ldots, \phi_n\}$ (we represent it as the set of its clauses instead of the conjunction of them for simplicity), we are going to prove successively that:

(1) Determining whether $\phi_i \in \Sigma$ does not belong to any conflict of Σ is Π_2^p-hard (this holds even in the case when ϕ_i is a propositional symbol).
(2) Determining whether $p \in Var(\Sigma)$ does not belong to any minimal var-conflict of Σ is Π_2^p-hard.
(3) Determining whether $p \in Var(\Sigma)$ satisfies $\Sigma \models_{LP_m} p$ (resp. $\Sigma \vdash_s p$) is Π_2^p-hard.

We prove (1) by considering a polynomial reduction from the inference problem related to WIDTIO belief revision operator [71]. Let $\Sigma = \{\phi_1, \ldots, \phi_n\}$ be a finite set of formulas from $PROP_{PS}^2$. Let α be a formula from $PROP_{PS}^2$. Let us recall that the revised database $\Sigma \circ_W \alpha$ can be defined up to classical equivalence by the formula $\alpha \wedge \bigwedge_{\phi_i \in \Sigma \setminus Conf(\Sigma, \alpha)} \phi_i$. Eiter and Gottlob proved in [31] that the corresponding inference problem is Π_2^p-hard. Looking carefully at the proofs of Lemma 6.2 and Theorem 8.2 from [31], it is easy to show that $\Sigma \circ_W p \overset{?}{\models} q$ remains Π_2^p-hard in the restricted case when Σ is a classically consistent CNF formula, p and q are propositional variables from PS, $q \in \Sigma$, and $p \notin \Sigma$ (especially, we can assume without loss of generality that the matrix of the $2 - QBF_\forall$ formula E used in the proof of Lemma 6.2 is a CNF formula). On this ground, we prove the following lemma:

Lemma 1. *Let $\Sigma = \{\phi_1, \ldots, \phi_n\}$ be a classically consistent CNF formula. Let p and q be two propositional symbols from PS, $q \in \Sigma$, and $p \notin \Sigma$. Determining whether q does not belong to any p-conflict of Σ is Π_2^p-hard.*

Proof of the lemma: It is sufficient to show that $\Sigma \circ_W p \models^2 q$ holds if and only if q does not belong to any p-conflict of Σ. In order to simplify a bit the writing, let us note $no - conflict(\Sigma, p) =_{def} \Sigma \setminus Conf(\Sigma, p)$ (this is the set of formulas from Σ not appearing in any p-conflict of it). The "only-if" way is obvious since $\Sigma \circ_W p \equiv^2 p \wedge \bigwedge_{\phi_i \in no - conflict(\Sigma, p)} \phi_i$ and $q \in no - conflict(\Sigma, p)$ by assumption. Conversely, let us assume that $\Sigma \circ_W p \models^2 q$ holds and there exists a p-conflict S of Σ s.t. $q \in S$. First of all, $\Sigma \circ_W p \models^2 q$ holds if and only if $no - conflict(\Sigma, p) \models^2 \neg p \vee q$. Now, let $S' = S \setminus \{q\}$. Since $S \models^2 \neg p$, we also have $S' \cup \{q\} \models^2 \neg p$, or equivalently $S' \models^2 \neg q \vee \neg p$. Moreover, by minimality of a conflict, we have $S' \not\models^2 \neg p$. Consider the subset $S' \cup no - conflict(\Sigma, p)$ of Σ. By monotony of $\models$, we have $S' \cup no - conflict(\Sigma, p) \models^2 (\neg q \vee \neg p) \wedge (\neg p \vee q)$. This is equivalent to state that $S' \cup no - conflict(\Sigma, p) \models^2 \neg p$. Accordingly, this implies that there exists a p-conflict $S'' \subseteq S' \cup no - conflict(\Sigma, p)$ of Σ. Since $S' \not\models^2 \neg p$, this implies that $S'' \cap no - conflict(\Sigma, p) \neq \emptyset$, contradiction. ∎

Let us now show that considering conflicts (instead of p-conflicts) is sufficient:

Lemma 2. *Let $\Sigma = \{\phi_1, \ldots, \phi_n\}$ be a classically consistent CNF formula. Let p be a propositional symbol from PS and ϕ_i a clause from Σ. ϕ_i belongs to a p-conflict of Σ if and only if ϕ_i belongs to a conflict of $\Sigma \cup \{p\}$ and $\phi_i \not\equiv^2 p$.*

Proof of the lemma: Let us first show that S is a p-conflict of Σ if and only if $S \cup \{p\}$ is a conflict of $\Sigma \cup \{p\}$. Obviously, we have $S \models^2 \neg p$ if and only if $S \cup \{p\}$ is inconsistent. It remains to show that $\forall \phi_i \in S, S \setminus \{\phi_i\} \not\models^2 \neg p$ if and only if $\forall \phi_i \in S \cup \{p\}, (S \cup \{p\}) \setminus \{\phi_i\} \not\models^2 false$.

- "if" way: Assume that there exists $\phi_i \in S \cup \{p\}$ s.t. $(S \cup \{p\}) \setminus \{\phi_i\} \models^2 false$. If $\phi_i \neq p$, then we have $(S \cup \{p\}) \setminus \{\phi_i\} = (S \setminus \{\phi_i\}) \cup \{p\}$. Accordingly, we have $(S \setminus \{\phi_i\}) \cup \{p\} \models^2 false$, which contradicts our assumption (minimality of a p-conflict).
  Otherwise, $\phi_i = p$ and $(S \cup \{p\}) \setminus \{\phi_i\}$ is a subset of S, hence a subset of Σ. The fact that $(S \cup \{p\}) \setminus \{\phi_i\} \models^2 false$ contradicts the assumption that Σ is consistent.
- "only-if" way: Assume that there exists $\phi_i \in S$ s.t. $S \setminus \{\phi_i\} \models^2 \neg p$. This is equivalent to state that $(S \setminus \{\phi_i\}) \cup \{p\} \models^2 false$. If $\phi_i \neq p$, then we have $(S \setminus \{\phi_i\}) \cup \{p\} = (S \cup \{p\}) \setminus \{\phi_i\}$. Accordingly, we have $(S \cup \{p\}) \setminus \{\phi_i\} \models^2 false$, with $\phi_i \in S$, which contradicts our assumption (minimality of a conflict).

Otherwise, $\phi_i = p$ and $(S \setminus \{\phi_i\}) \cup \{p\} = S$, hence a subset of Σ. The fact that $(S \setminus \{\phi_i\}) \cup \{p\} \models^2 false$ contradicts the assumption that Σ is consistent.

Once this is established, it is sufficient to show that p does not belong to any p-conflict of Σ in the case $p \in \Sigma$. Assume that this is not the case: Let S be a p-conflict of Σ s.t. $p \in S$. Let $S' = S \setminus \{p\}$. Since $S = S' \cup \{p\}$ and S is a p-conflict, we have $S' \cup \{p\} \models^2 \neg p$. This is equivalent to state that $S' \models^2 \neg p$ through the (meta)deduction theorem for propositional logic. Hence, S' is a p-conflict of Σ and a proper subset of S, which contradicts the existence of S. ∎

We are now ready to prove (1): To every triple $\langle \Sigma = \{\phi_1, \ldots, \phi_n\}, p, \phi_i \rangle$ where Σ is a classically consistent CNF formula, $p \notin \Sigma$ and $\phi_i \in \Sigma$, we associate in polynomial time the ordered pair $\langle \Sigma \cup \{p\}, \phi_i \rangle$. From Lemma 2, ϕ_i does not occur in any p-conflict of Σ if and only if ϕ_i does not occur in any conflict of $\Sigma \cup \{p\}$ or $\phi_i = p$. Now, the case $\phi_i = p$ can be excluded since $p \notin \Sigma$. The Π_2^p-hardness result given in Lemma 1 completes the proof.

In order to prove (2), we associate in polynomial time to every ordered pair $\langle \Sigma = \{\phi_1, \ldots, \phi_n\}, \phi_i \rangle$ (where Σ is a CNF formula and ϕ_i a clause from Σ) the following ordered pair: $\langle \bigcup_{\phi_i \in \Sigma} \{\phi_i \vee \neg new_i, new_i\}, new_i \rangle$, where $\{new_1, \ldots, new_n\}$ are new symbols from $PS \setminus Var(\Sigma)$. We have that ϕ_i belongs to a conflict of Σ if and only if new_i belongs to a minimal var-conflict of $\bigcup_{\phi_i \in \Sigma} \{\phi_i \vee \neg new_i, new_i\}$. Indeed, $S \subseteq \Sigma$ is a conflict of Σ if and only if $S_{new} = \{\phi_j \vee \neg new_j, new_j \mid \phi_j \in S\}$ is a conflict of $\bigcup_{\phi_i \in \Sigma} \{\phi_i \vee \neg new_i, new_i\}$ (intuitively, this is just a naming operation, hence every conflict is mainly preserved and no new conflict is added). The point is that every conflict S_{new} of $\bigcup_{\phi_i \in \Sigma} \{\phi_i \vee \neg new_i, new_i\}$ gives rise to a *minimal* var-conflict $Var(S_{new})$ of it by construction (this is not the case in general). The Π_2^p-hardness result stated in (1) completes the proof.

In order to prove (3), we first prove the two following lemmata:

Lemma 3. *Let $\Sigma = \{\phi_1, \ldots, \phi_n\}$ be a CNF formula and $p \in Var(\Sigma)$. p belongs to a minimal var-conflict of Σ if and only if there exists a 3-model I of Σ that is minimal w.r.t. $\leq_{LP_m}$ in its set and s.t. $I(p) = \top$.*

Proof of the lemma: We assume that no clause ϕ_i in Σ contains both a literal and its negation. This assumption can be done without loss of generality since removing such classical tautologies from Σ does not change the set of its conflicts, hence the set of its minimal var-conflicts and does not change the set of its 3-models (every tautological clause is interpreted as 1 or $\top$ in *THREE*).

- "if" way: Let I be a 3-model of Σ that is minimal w.r.t. $\leq_{LP_m}$ in its set and s.t. $I(p) = \top$. Let us show that p belongs to a minimal var-conflict of Σ. Let $\Sigma_p =_{def} \{\phi_i \in \Sigma \mid \forall x \in Var(\phi_i)$ if $x \neq p$, then $I(x) \neq \top\}$ be the set of clauses from Σ whose symbols are classically interpreted in I, expect possibly for p. Σ_p can be partitioned into three sets:
  - The subset Σ_p^+ of Σ_p containing all the clauses in which p appears as a literal.
  - The subset Σ_p^- of Σ_p containing all the clauses in which $\neg p$ appears as a literal.

- The subset Σ_p^* of Σ_p containing all the clauses in which p does not appear (as a symbol).

Since I is minimal w.r.t. $\leq_{LP_m}$ in the set of 3-models of Σ and $I(p) = \top$, it must be the case that Σ_p is classically inconsistent (otherwise there would exist a 2-model J of Σ_p^+ and the 3-interpretation J' defined by $J'(x) = J(x)$ for every $x \in Var(\Sigma_p^+)$ and $J'(x) = I(x)$ otherwise would be a 3-model of Σ s.t. $J' \leq_{LP_m} I$ and $I \nleq_{LP_m} J'$: The minimality of I would be questioned). Accordingly, there exists at least one conflict of Σ_p, hence at least one conflict of Σ.

Now, Σ_p^* is classically satisfiable since the restriction of I to $Var(\Sigma_p^*)$ is a (partial but classical) model of it. Since p (resp. $\neg p$) is a *pure* literal in Σ_p^+ (resp. Σ_p^-) (i.e., $\neg p$ (resp. p) does not appear as a literal in any clause of the set), every conflict of Σ_p contains at least one clause from Σ_p^- and one clause from Σ_p^+. In particular, every conflict of Σ_p is s.t. $p \in Var(S)$.

It remains to show that p belongs to every minimal var-conflict of Σ. If it were not the case, for every conflict S of Σ_p, there would exist a conflict S' of Σ s.t. $p \notin Var(S')$ and $Var(S') \subset Var(S)$. Let ϕ_i be any clause from $\Sigma \setminus \Sigma_p$. By construction, there exists at least one propositional symbol $x_i \neq p$ occurring in ϕ_i s.t. $I(x_i) = \top$ and $x_i \notin Var(\Sigma_p)$. Every conflict S' containing ϕ_i is s.t. $x_i \in Var(S')$, and this prevents $Var(S') \subset Var(S)$ from being true since $Var(S) \subseteq Var(\Sigma_p)$ whenever S is a conflict of Σ_p. Accordingly, every conflict S' of Σ s.t. $Var(S') \subset Var(S)$ does not contain any clause from $\Sigma \setminus \Sigma_p$; in other words, S' is a conflict of Σ_p, hence it must satisfy $p \in Var(S')$, contradiction.

- "only-if" way: Let $VConf(\Sigma)$ be the set of all minimal var-conflicts of Σ. Let us first recall the following notion of a *minimal hitting set* (cf. [66]):

Definition 20 (Minimal Hitting Set). *Let E be a finite set and C a set of subsets of E (i.e., $C \subseteq 2^E$). Let I be a subset of E.*
- *I is a hitting set of C if and only if $\forall S \in C, I \cap S \neq \emptyset$.*
- *I is a minimal hitting set of C if and only if I is a hitting set of C and no proper subset of I is a hitting set of C.*

If p is a propositional symbol belonging to a minimal var-conflict of Σ, then there exists a minimal hitting set H_p of $VConf(\Sigma)$ s.t. $p \in H_p$ (the minimality requirement is important here, the conclusion would not hold if any var-conflict were considered).

Once this is observed, it is sufficient to show that for every minimal hitting set H of $VConf(\Sigma)$, there exists a 3-model I_H of Σ that is minimal w.r.t. $\leq_{LP_m}$ and s.t. $\forall x \in Var(\Sigma), I(x) = \top$ if and only if $x \in H$.

Indeed, let $\Sigma_H^* = \{\phi_i \in \Sigma \mid Var(\phi_i) \cap H = \emptyset\}$. Let us show that Σ_H^* is classically satisfiable. If it were not the case, Σ_H^* would include a conflict S so there would exist a minimal var-conflict V of Σ_H^* s.t. $V \subseteq Var(S)$. This means that there would exist at least one conflict S_V of Σ_H^* s.t. $V = Var(S_V)$. Since $\Sigma_H^* \subset \Sigma$, S_V would be a conflict of Σ, there would also exist a minimal var-conflict V' of Σ s.t. $V' \subseteq V$. Since H is a minimal hitting set of $VConf(\Sigma)$ and $V' \in VConf(\Sigma)$, there exists a variable x s.t. $x \in V'$ and $x \in H$. Since $V' \subseteq V \subseteq Var(S)$, we must have $x \in Var(S)$ but since $S \subseteq \Sigma_H^*$ and $x \in H$, no clause of S can contain x as a symbol, contradiction. We conclude that a 2-model I of Σ_H exists.

Now, since every clause ϕ_i from Σ except those from Σ_H^* contains at least one symbol from H (by definition of Σ_H^*), every 3-interpretation J s.t. $J(x) = \top$ for every $x \in H$ also satisfies $J(\phi_i) = \top$. Since $H \cap Var(\Sigma_H^*) = \emptyset$, the 3-interpretation I_H defined by $I_H(x) = \top$ whenever $x \in H$ and $I_H(x) = I(x)$ otherwise is well-defined. By construction, I_H is a 3-model of Σ.

It remains to show that I_H is minimal w.r.t. $\leq_{LP_m}$. This comes directly from the fact that H is a *minimal* hitting set of $VConf(\Sigma)$. Indeed, let us assume that I_H is not a minimal 3-model of Σ w.r.t. $\leq_{LP_m}$. Then there exists $x \in H$ and a 3-model $I_{H'}$ of Σ minimal w.r.t. $\leq_{LP_m}$ s.t. for every $y \in Var(\Sigma)$, if $I_{H'}(y) = \top$, then $I_H(y) = \top$, and $I_{H'}(x) \neq \top$. This implies that the set H' of propositional symbols interpreted as $\top$ in $I_{H'}$ is a proper subset of H. Since H is a minimal hitting set of $VConf(\Sigma)$, this implies that there exists at least one minimal var-conflict $V \in VConf(\Sigma)$ s.t. $H' \cap V = \emptyset$. This means that no conflict S_V of Σ s.t. $Var(S_V) = V$ contains an element of H' as a symbol. Since $I_{H'}$ restricted to the symbols outside H' behaves classically and $I_{H'}$ is a 3-model of Σ, $I_{H'}$ is a classical model of S_V. This contradicts the fact that S_V is a conflict.   ∎

Lemma 4. *Let* $\Sigma = \{\phi_1, \ldots, \phi_n\}$ *be a CNF formula and* $p \in Var(\Sigma)$. *Let* $new \in PS \setminus Var(\Sigma)$. *There exists a 3-model* I *of* Σ *that is minimal w.r.t.* $\leq_{LP_m}$ *in its set and s.t.* $I(p) = \top$ *if and only if* $\Sigma \cup \{p \vee new, \neg p \vee new\} \not\models_{LP_m} new$ *if and only if* $\Sigma \cup \{p \vee new, \neg p \vee new\} \not\vdash_s new$.

Proof of the lemma:

– We first prove that there exists a 3-model I of Σ that is minimal w.r.t. $\leq_{LP_m}$ in its set and s.t. $I(p) = \top$ if and only if $\Sigma \cup \{p \vee new, \neg p \vee new\} \not\models_{LP_m} new$. It is obvious that the expansion of Σ with the two clauses $p \vee new$ and $\neg p \vee new$ does not create any new conflict, hence any new minimal var-conflict. Accordingly, the 3-models of Σ that are minimal w.r.t. $\leq_{LP_m}$ are exactly the 3-models of $\Sigma \cup \{p \vee new, \neg p \vee new\}$ that are minimal w.r.t. $\leq_{LP_m}$ (see the "only-if" side of the proof of Lemma 3). Let I be a 3-model of Σ that is minimal w.r.t. $\leq_{LP_m}$ in its set and s.t. $I(p) = \top$. Since $new \notin Var(\Sigma)$, the minimality requirement ensures that there exists a 3-model I_0 of Σ that is minimal w.r.t. $\leq_{LP_m}$ and s.t. $I_0(new) = 0$. Since I_0 also is a 3-model of $\Sigma \cup \{p \vee new, \neg p \vee new\}$ that is minimal w.r.t. $\leq_{LP_m}$, it cannot be the case that $\Sigma \cup \{p \vee new, \neg p \vee new\} \models^2 new$. Conversely, let I_0 be a 3-model of $\Sigma \cup \{p \vee new, \neg p \vee new\}$ that is minimal w.r.t. $\leq_{LP_m}$ and s.t. $I_0(new) = 0$. Since I_0 is a 3-model of both $p \vee new$ and $\neg p \vee new$, it must be the case that I_0 is a 3-model of both p and $\neg p$, which requires that $I_0(p) = \top$. Since I_0 also is a 3-model of Σ that is minimal w.r.t. $\leq_{LP_m}$, the conclusion follows.
– Let us now prove that $\Sigma' \not\models_{LP_m} new$ if and only if $\Sigma' \not\vdash_s new$, where $\Sigma' = \Sigma \cup \{p \vee new, \neg p \vee new\}$. Let us first prove the following lemma:

Lemma 5. *Let Σ and γ be two formulas from $PROP^2_{PS}$.[9] We have $\Sigma \vdash^\pm_s \gamma$ if and only if $\Sigma \models_{LP_m} \gamma$.*

Proof of the lemma: By definition, γ is a skeptical signed consequence of Σ if and only if $\gamma^\pm$ belongs to every extension of $\langle \Sigma^\pm, D_\Sigma \rangle$. From Theorems A.1 and A.2 of [14], this is equivalent to state that $\gamma^\pm$ belongs to every extension of supernormal default theory $\langle \Sigma^\pm, \{x^+ \Leftrightarrow \neg x^- \mid x \in PS\} \rangle$. Now, from the well-known preferred models characterization of skeptical inference, this is still equivalent to state that every preferred (2-)model of $\Sigma^\pm$ is a 2-model of $\gamma^\pm$, where the preferred models of $\Sigma^\pm$ are the minimal models of $\Sigma^\pm$ w.r.t. the partial ordering $\leq$ over $TWO^{PS^\pm}$ defined by $I \leq J$ if and only if $\{x \in PS \mid I(x^+) = I(x^-)\} \subseteq \{x \in PS \mid J(x^+) = J(x^-)\}$ (indeed, I satisfies $x^+ \Leftrightarrow \neg x^-$ if and only if $I(x^+) \neq I(x^-)$).

By construction, $\Sigma^\pm$ is a monotone (positive) formula from $PROP^2_{PS^\pm}$. As a consequence, if I is a 2-model of $\Sigma^\pm$ s.t. $I(x^+) = I(x^-) = 0$ for some $x \in PS$, then every interpretation J that coincides with I for every propositional symbol from $PS^\pm$ (except possibly on x^+ and x^-) is still a 2-model of $\Sigma^\pm$. This is specifically the case for any interpretation J s.t. $J(x^+) \neq J(x^-)$. Since $J < I$ holds (where $<$ is the strict ordering associated with $\leq$), every preferred model M of $\Sigma^\pm$ is s.t. for every symbol $x \in PS$, we do *not* have $M(x^+) = M(x^-) = 0$. Denoting $(TWO^{PS^\pm})^*$ the subset of all interpretations I from $TWO^{PS^\pm}$ s.t. for every $x \in PS$, we do not have $I(x^+) = I(x^-) = 0$, every preferred model M of $\Sigma^\pm$ belongs to $(TWO^{PS^\pm})^*$. Now, every interpretation I from $(TWO^{PS^\pm})^*$ can be associated to the 3-interpretation $3(I)$ over PS defined by $3(I)(x) = I(x^+)$ and $3(I)(\neg x) = I(x^-)$ for every variable $x \in PS$. It is obvious that $3(.)$ is a bijection from both sets of interpretations. It is also obvious to show (by structural induction on $\phi \in PROP^2_{PS}$) that I is a 2-model of the monotone (positive) formula $\phi^\pm$ from $PROP^2_{PS^\pm}$ if and only if $3(I)$ is a 3-model of ϕ.

Finally, we know that $\Sigma \models_{LP_m} \gamma$ holds if and only if every preferred 3-model of Σ is a 3-model of γ, where the preferred 3-models of Σ are the minimal 3-models of it w.r.t. $\leq_{LP_m}$. Since every preferred model of $\Sigma^\pm$ can be associated to a 3-model of Σ through the $3(.)$ bijection, and since for every pair of interpretations I and J from $(TWO^{PS^\pm})^*$, we have $I \leq J$ if and only if $3(I) \leq_{LP_m} 3(J)$, we obtain that M is a preferred model of $\Sigma^\pm$ w.r.t. $\leq$ if and only if $3(M)$ is a preferred 3-model of Σ w.r.t. $\leq_{LP_m}$, which concludes the proof.   ∎

Thanks to this lemma, we know that we have that $\Sigma' \not\models_{LP_m} new$ if and only if $\Sigma' \not\vdash_s new$, where $\Sigma' = \Sigma \cup \{p \vee new, \neg p \vee new\}$ if and only if we have that $\Sigma' \not\vdash^\pm_s new$ if and only if $\Sigma' \not\vdash_s new$. This equivalence is quite obvious since new and new^+ always appear in the same extensions of $\langle \Sigma^\pm, D_{\Sigma'} \rangle$; indeed, every extension of $\langle \Sigma'^\pm, D_{\Sigma'} \rangle$ contains the consequent

---

[9] Note that $\supset$ and $\Leftrightarrow$ are considered as syntactic sugars here ($\phi \supset \psi =_{def} (\neg\phi) \vee \psi$ and $\phi \Leftrightarrow \psi =_{def} (\phi \supset \psi) \wedge (\psi \supset \phi)$).

formula $(new \Leftrightarrow new^+) \wedge (\neg new \Leftrightarrow new^-)$ because the corresponding justification $(new^+ \Leftrightarrow \neg new^-)$ is (classically) consistent with Σ' (no occurrence
of $\neg new$ appears in Σ'). ■

(3) is a straightforward consequence of (2), Lemma 3 and Lemma 4.

The hardness of $\models_{BS}$ finally remains to be proven. Let us reduce the inference
problem of LP_m to the inference problem for the logic of [13]. Let Σ be a CNF
formula and γ a symbol. We associate to $\langle \Sigma, \gamma \rangle$ in polynomial time the following
ordered pair $\langle \{\Sigma \wedge new \wedge \neg new\} \cup \bigcup_{p \in Var(\Sigma) \cup Var(\gamma)} \{p \vee \neg p\}, \gamma \rangle$, where $new \in$
$PS \setminus (Var(\Sigma) \cup Var(\gamma))$. We have $\Sigma \models_{LP_m} \gamma$ if and only if $\{\Sigma \wedge new \wedge \neg new\} \cup$
$\bigcup_{p \in Var(\Sigma) \cup Var(\gamma)} \{p \vee \neg p\} \models_{BS} \gamma$. Indeed, since new does not occur elsewhere in
Σ or γ, we have $\Sigma \models_{LP_m} \gamma$ if and only if $\Sigma \wedge new \wedge \neg new \models_{LP_m} \gamma$. Accordingly, it
is sufficient to consider the 3-models I of Σ s.t. $I(new) = \top$. Once this is stated,
let us observe that the set S of 3-models I of Σ over $Var(\Sigma) \cup Var(\gamma) \cup \{new\}$
s.t. $I(new) = \top$ coincide with the set of 3-models of $\{\Sigma \wedge new \wedge \neg new\} \cup$
$\bigcup_{p \in Var(\Sigma) \cup Var(\gamma)} \{p \vee \neg p\}$ over $Var(\Sigma) \cup Var(\gamma) \cup \{new\}$. Indeed, for every
propositional symbol p and every 3-interpretation I, we always have $I(p \vee \neg p) \in$
$\{1, \top\}$. Now, it remains to show that $\leq_{LP_m}$ and $\leq_{BS}$ coincides over S. To do it,
it is sufficient to remark that for every $I \in S$, (1) we have $I(\Sigma \wedge new \wedge \neg new) = \top$
(this explains why new has been introduced), and (2) for every $p \in Var(\Sigma) \cup$
$Var(\gamma)$, we have $I(p) = \top$ if and only if $I(p \vee \neg p) = \top$. This completes the proof
of Π_2^p-hardness of $\models_{BS}$-inference in the case when the belief base is a finite set
of CNF formulas and the query a symbol.

Hardness for $\models_{\leq_1}^{4,arg}$ and $\models_{\leq_2}^{4,arg}$ comes from the hardness result for $\models_{\leq_{LP_m}}^{3,arg}$
and the fact that $\models_{\leq_1}^4$, $\models_{\leq_2}^4$ and $\models_{\leq_{LP_m}}^3$ coincide when Σ is CNF and γ a literal
(see Proposition 5.4 from [2]). Since $\models_{\leq_{LP_m}}^3$ is Π_2^p-hard in this situation, it is
sufficient to point out a polytime reduction that maps every tuple $\langle \Sigma_1, p_1, \Sigma_2, p_2 \rangle$
(where Σ_1 and Σ_2 are CNF formulas and p_1 and p_2 are propositional symbols)
to a pair $\langle \Sigma, \gamma \rangle$ (where Σ and γ are CNF formulas) s.t. $\Sigma \models_{\leq_{LP_m}}^{3,arg} \gamma$ if and only
if $\Sigma_1 \models_{\leq_{LP_m}}^3 p_1$ and $\Sigma_2 \not\models_{\leq_{LP_m}}^3 p_2$. Without loss of generality, we can assume
that Σ_1 and Σ_2 share no propositional symbols. Let us take $\Sigma = \Sigma_1 \wedge \Sigma_2 \wedge$
$new_2 \wedge \neg new_2$ and $\gamma = (p_1 \vee new_1) \wedge (\neg p_2 \vee new_2)$, where new_1 and new_2 are
new propositional symbols, not occurring in $Var(\Sigma_1) \cup Var(\Sigma_2) \cup \{p_1, p_2\}$.

Let us first assume that $\Sigma_1 \models_{\leq_{LP_m}}^3 p_1$ and $\Sigma_2 \not\models_{\leq_{LP_m}}^3 p_2$. If $\Sigma_1 \models_{\leq_{LP_m}}^3 p_1$,
then $\Sigma \models_{\leq_{LP_m}}^3 p_1 \vee new_1$ because $Var(\Sigma_1) \cap Var(\Sigma_2) = \emptyset$; furthermore, we necessarily have $\Sigma \models_{\leq_{LP_m}}^3 \neg p_2 \vee new_2$ because, by construction, every 3-model
I of Σ is s.t. $I(new_2) = \top$; hence, $\Sigma \models_{\leq_{LP_m}}^3 \gamma$. It remains to show that
$\Sigma \not\models_{\leq_{LP_m}}^3 \neg\gamma$. We have $\neg\gamma \equiv^3 (\neg p_1 \vee \neg new_2) \wedge (\neg new_1 \vee \neg new_2) \wedge (\neg p_1 \vee p_2) \wedge$
$(\neg new_1 \vee p_2)$. Since $\Sigma_2 \not\models_{\leq_{LP_m}}^3 p_2$, there exists a $\leq_{LP_m}$-preferred 3-model I_2 of
Σ_2 s.t. $I_2(p_2) = 0$; since $new_1 \notin Var(\Sigma_2)$, the 3-interpretation I_2' that coincides
with I_2 on every symbol, except possibly on new_1 and satisfies $I_2'(new_1) = 1$,
also is a $\leq_{LP_m}$-preferred 3-model of Σ_2. Accordingly, $I_2'(\neg new_1 \vee p_2) = 0$ and
$\Sigma_2 \not\models_{\leq_{LP_m}}^3 \neg new_1 \vee p_2$; now, since $Var(\Sigma_1) \cap Var(\Sigma_2) = \emptyset$ and new_1 and new_2

are new propositional symbols, we obtain that $\Sigma \not\models^3_{\leq LP_m} \neg new_1 \vee p_2$, hence $\Sigma \not\models^3_{\leq LP_m} \neg \gamma$.

Conversely, let us assume that $\Sigma \models^{3,arg}_{\leq LP_m} \gamma$ and prove that $\Sigma_1 \models^3_{\leq LP_m} p_1$ and $\Sigma_2 \not\models^3_{\leq LP_m} p_2$. If $\Sigma \models^3_{\leq LP_m} p_1 \vee new_1$, then it must be the case that $\Sigma_1 \models^3_{\leq LP_m} p_1$; otherwise, there would exist a $\leq LP_m$-preferred 3-model I_1 of Σ_1 s.t. $I_1(p_1) = 0$; since $new_1 \notin Var(\Sigma_1)$, the 3-interpretation I'_1 that coincides with I_1 on every symbol, except possibly on new_1 and satisfies $I'_1(new_1) = 0$, also is a $\leq LP_m$-preferred 3-model of Σ_1. Accordingly, $I'_1(p_1 \vee new_1) = 0$, and since $Var(\Sigma_1) \cap Var(\Sigma_2) = \emptyset$ and new_1 and new_2 are new propositional symbols, we would have $\Sigma \not\models^3_{\leq LP_m} p_1 \vee new_1$, contradiction. Finally, it is the case that $\Sigma_2 \not\models^3_{\leq LP_m} p_2$. Otherwise, we would have $\Sigma_2 \models^3_{\leq LP_m} (\neg p_1 \vee p_2) \wedge (\neg new_1 \vee p_2)$, hence $\Sigma \models^3_{\leq LP_m} (\neg p_1 \vee p_2) \wedge (\neg new_1 \vee p_2)$. Since by construction every 3-model I of Σ is s.t. $I(new_2) = \top$, we also have $\Sigma \models^3_{\leq LP_m} (\neg p_1 \vee \neg new_2) \wedge (\neg new_1 \vee \neg new_2)$. As a consequence, we obtain that $\Sigma \models^3_{\leq LP_m} \neg \gamma$, contradiction.

The complexity of $\models_{QC}$ and $\models_{Q\Pi L}$ has been identified in [55] and [28], respectively, when both Σ and γ are CNF formulas:

Proposition 3. *The complexity of the decision problem for $\models_{QC}$ and $\models_{Q\Pi L}$ is* coNP*-complete when both Σ and γ are CNF formulas.*

The membership proof is by a reduction to classical entailment (more specifically, by a modular and faithful polytime translation to classical logic, see Propositions 1 and 2 in [55]).

Tractability Results. As to $\models^4$ or $\models^3$, tractability is achieved as soon as the query is a CNF formula when the belief base belongs to the monotonic fragment [19]. Tractability is still the case for $\models^4$ when the base is a DNF formula, while $\models^3$ remains coNP-complete in this situation [19].

Other tractability results for $\models^3_S$ and the $\approx^{\mathcal{P},S_0}_S$ relations can be obtained by imposing in addition that $|S|$ is bounded (see Theorem A.3 in [69] and Proposition 3.15 in [56]).

Proposition 4. *The complexity of the decision problem for $\vdash_L$ is in* P *in the case when Σ and γ are CNF formulas (from $PROP^2_{PS}$) and the size of $S \subseteq PS$ is bounded, when $\vdash_L$ is $\models^3_S$, $\approx^{\mathcal{PO},S_0}_S$, $\approx^{\mathcal{LO},S_0}_S$, $\approx^{\mathcal{IP},S_0}_S$ or $\approx^{\mathcal{LE},S_0}_S$.*

Clearly enough, under the CNF assumption – a strict subset of the monotonic fragment –, the key for tractability is the fact that the size of S is bounded (hence only polynomially many S-3-interpretations are to be considered).

Finally, the translation from the decision problem for $\models_{QC}$ (in the CNF case) to the decision problem for classical entailment reported in [55] gives two tractable subcases as by-products: The decision problem for $\models_{QC}$ for CNF queries γ is in P given that the base Σ is a Krom formula or a renamable Horn k-CNF formula (see Propositions 4 and 5 in [55]).

5   Conclusion

The main purpose of this chapter was to put together in a coherent way complexity results for paraconsistent inference relations defined in multi-valued propositional settings (or related frameworks), and already identified in the literature. In a nutshell, the corresponding decision problems are located at the first or the second level of the polynomial hierachy; to be more precise, the relations under consideration are either as hard as classical entailment (coNP), or mildly harder ($\Delta_2^p[\mathcal{O}(log\ n)]$ or Δ_2^p), or finally strongly harder (Π_2^p-complete or D_2^p-complete) (under the usual assumptions of complexity theory); only few tractable cases have been exhibited.

The complexity results above can be related to similar complexity results for belief revision [31, 60] and reasoning from preferred consistent subsets in [60, 20, 32]. Actually, the Π_2^p-hardness of the problem of determining whether a given formula is a consequence of a belief base revised according to the WIDTIO policy – or equivalently, whether it is a so-called free consequence of a stratified belief base – has been exploited in some of the hardness proofs for non-monotonic relations. Conversely, some reductions to inference problems considered in belief revision or when reasoning from preferred consistent subsets can be used to prove membership results (even if we did not systematically adhere to such an approach when presenting membership results).

Roughly, the derived results show the complexity of paraconsistent inference to vary from P in some restricted cases to the first level of the polynomial hierarchy for many monotonic relations and even to the second level of the polynomial hierarchy for the non-monotonic ones. This reflects that there is typically a computational price to be paid for preserving more beliefs through the exploitation of preferential information (contrariwise to the model checking problem when no preferences are considered, determining whether a given interpretation is a preferred model of a belief base is intractable). It is interesting to observe that tractability is obtained in restricted situations when classical entailment is not tractable (under the standard assumptions of complexity theory). For instance, $\models^4$, $\models^3$ and its restrictions are tractable when the belief base is a CNF formula and clausal queries are considered, only. Indeed, restricting the language to its clausal fragment is sufficient to lower the complexity of many monotonic relations (this can be easily explained by the fact that each clause from the belief base can be considered independent to the other ones in the sense that the disjunctive syllogism fails). Contrastingly, focusing on the clausal fragment is not sufficient to decrease the complexity of the non-monotonic relations.

Among the inference relations considered before, $\approx_S^{\mathcal{LE},S_0}$ and $\models_{QC}$ (when CNF formulas are considered) appear as achieving an interesting compromise in the sense that many expected consequences are preserved while complexity remains at the first level of the polynomial hierarchy. Furthermore, $\approx_S^{\mathcal{P},S_0}$ relations allow for resource-bounded reasoning by limiting the size of S.

Much work remains to be done in this area. First, the complexity of many propositional paraconsistent inference relations is still unknown; this is particularly the case for many proof-theoretically defined relations.

Second, the tractability islands are not so numerous, especially for the most sophisticated relations that have been considered, so it is important to identify ways to deal with the complexity of paraconsistent inference relations. In such an objective, one can improve existing inference engines so as to increase the set of instances that are feasible from the practical side. Importantly, the complexity results we have reported show the existence of polynomial reductions from decision problems for paraconsistent inference to complete problems at the first or at the second level of the polynomial hierarchy; among the latter problems are, on the one hand, validity problems for quantified boolean formulas (QBFs) – including UNSAT as a specific case – and on the other hand, for the problems located at the second level of the polynomial hierarchy, inference problems for many non-monotonic logics considered in AI (e.g., skeptical reasoning from default theories, forms of closed-world reasoning) for which automated deduction tools have been developed). If such reductions are practically feasible, it is possible to take advantage of existing QBFs solvers and other programs for non-monotonic inference to implement forms of paraconsistent inference. Observing that QBFs solvers are more and more efficient in practice over years, this possibility is particularly interesting. In fact, reductions (and among them, modular and faithful translations) have already been exploited to encode several non-monotonic paraconsistent inference problems into validity problems for QBFs or circumscriptive inference problems (see [11, 4, 12]). Of course, it would be nice to compare from the empirical side the performances of such reduction-based approaches with the ones achieved by implementations of some proof systems (usually, tableau-based) for paraconsistent inference.

Another approach consists in circumventing complexity, and three main techniques prevail: Restriction, approximation and compilation. We have mainly focused on the first technique, showing for instance that quasi-classical inference is tractable under clausal queries when the belief base is a Krom formula or a renamable Horn k-CNF formula. Many other tractable fragments for classical satisfiability appear as interesting candidates to be investigated. The second technique is at work in [56]; approximation is used for reaching two goals: Considering $\models_S^3$ with a bounded S instead of its superset $\models^2$ allows for ensuring tractability, while considering $\approx_S^{\mathcal{LE}, S_0}$ instead of its superset $\models_S^3$ is sufficient for avoiding trivialization when it would occur. Similar ideas could be applied to other inference relations. Finally, it seems that the last technique mentioned above (compilation) has almost never been used in the purpose of enhancing paraconsistent inference; the principle would be to pre-process the belief base during an off-line compilation stage so as to obtain better performances when queries are considered at the on-line stage. In the case when a translation to inference problems from stratified belief bases exist (as for the $\approx_S^{\mathcal{P}, S_0}$ relations), it is possible to take advantage of some recent work about the compilation of stratified belief bases (see in particular [9, 22, 23]). Developing other compilation techniques for paraconsistent inference or fitting the compilation techniques for classical inference to paraconsistent inference is another perspective for further research.

References

1. L. Amgoud and C. Cayrol. On the acceptability of arguments in preference-based argumentation framework. In *Proceedings of the 14th Conference on Uncertainty in Artificial Intelligence*, pages 1–7, Madison (WI), 1998.

2. O. Arieli and A. Avron. The value of four values. *Artificial Intelligence*, 102:97–141, 1998.

3. O. Arieli and A. Avron. A model-theoretic approach for recovering consistent data from inconsistent knowledge bases. *Journal of Automated Reasoning*, 22(2):263–309, 1999.

4. O. Arieli and M. Denecker. Reducing preferential paraconsistent reasoning to classical entailment. *Journal of Logic and Computation*, 13(4):557–580, 2003.

5. C. Baral, S. Kraus, and J. Minker. Combining multiple knowledge bases. *IEEE Transactions on Knowledge and Data Engineering*, 3(2):208–220, 1991.

6. N. Belnap. *Modern Uses of Multiple-Valued Logic*, chapter A useful four-valued logic, pages 8–37. Reidel, 1977.

7. S. Benferhat, C. Cayrol, D. Dubois, J. Lang, and H. Prade. Inconsistency management and prioritized syntax-based entailment. In *Proceedings of the 13th International Joint Conference on Artificial Intelligence (IJCAI'93)*, pages 640–645, Chambéry (France), 1993.

8. S. Benferhat, D. Dubois, and H. Prade. How to infer from inconsistent beliefs without revising. In *Proceedings of the 14th International Joint Conference on Artificial Intelligence (IJCAI'95)*, pages 1449–1455, Montreal (Canada), 1995.

9. S. Benferhat, S. Kaci, D. Le Berre, and M.-A. Williams. Weakening conflicting information for iterated revision and knowledge integration. *Artificial Intelligence*, 153(1–2):339–371, 2004.

10. Ph. Besnard and A. Hunter. *Handbook of Defeasible Reasoning and Uncertainty Management Systems*, volume 2, chapter Introduction to actual and potential contradictions, pages 1–11. Kluwer Academic, 1998.

11. Ph. Besnard, T. Schaub, H. Tompits, and S. Woltran. Paraconsistent reasoning via Quantified Boolean Formulas I: Axiomatizing signed systems. In *Proceedings of the 8th European Conference on Logics in Artificial Intelligence (JELIA'02)*, pages 320–331, Cosenza (Italy), 2002.

12. Ph. Besnard, T. Schaub, H. Tompits, and S. Woltran. Paraconsistent reasoning via Quantified Boolean Formulas II: Circumscribing inconsistent theories. In *Proceedings of the 7th European Conference on Symbolic and Quantitative Approaches to Reasoning with Uncertainty*, pages 528–539, Aalborg (Denmark), 2003.

13. Ph. Besnard and T. Schaub. Circumscribing inconsistency. In *Proceedings of the 15th International Joint Conference on Artificial Intelligence (IJCAI'97)*, pages 150–155, Nagoya (Japan), 1997.

14. Ph. Besnard and T. Schaub. Signed systems for paraconsistent reasoning. *Journal of Automated Reasoning*, 20:191–213, 1998.

15. P. Besnard and A. Hunter. Quasi-classical logic: Non-trivializable classical reasoning from inconsistent information. In *Proceedings of the European Conference on Symbolic and Quantitative Approaches to Reasoning and Uncertainty*, volume 946 of *LNAI*, pages 44–51, Fribourg (Switzerland), 1995. Springer-Verlag.

16. I. Bloch and J. Lang. Towards mathematical morpho-logics. In *Proceedings of the 8th International Conference on Information Processing and Management of Uncertainty in Knowledge based Systems (IPMU'00)*, pages 1405–1412, Madrid (Spain), 2000.

17. A. Bondarenko, P. Dung, R.A. Kowalski, and F. Toni. An abstract, argumentation-theoretic framework for default reasoning. *Artificial Intelligence*, 93:63–101, 1997.
18. G. Brewka. Preferred subtheories: An extended logical framework for default reasoning. In *Proceedings of the 11th International Joint Conference on Artificial Intelligence (IJCAI'89)*, pages 1043–1048, Detroit (MI), 1989.
19. M. Cadoli and M. Schaerf. On the complexity of entailment in propositional multivalued logics. *Annals of Mathematics and Artificial Intelligence*, 18:29–50, 1996.
20. C. Cayrol, M.-C. Lagasquie-Schiex, and Th. Schiex. Nonmonotonic reasoning: From complexity to algorithms. *Annals of Mathematics and Artificial Intelligence*, 22(3–4):207–236, 1998.
21. S. Coste-Marquis and P. Marquis. Complexity results for paraconsistent inference relations. In *Proceedings of the 8th International Conference on Knowledge Representation and Reasoning (KR'02)*, pages 61–72, Toulouse (France), 2002.
22. S. Coste-Marquis and P. Marquis. On stratified belief base compilation. *Annals of Mathematics and Artificial Intelligence*, 42(4):399–442, 2004.
23. A. Darwiche and P. Marquis. Compiling propositional weighted bases. *Artificial Intelligence*, 157:81–113, 2004.
24. N. C. A. da Costa. On the theory of inconsistent formal systems. *Notre Dame Journal of Formal Logic*, 15:497–510, 1974.
25. Y. Dimopolos, B. Nebel, and F. Toni. Finding admissible and preferred arguments can be very hard. In *Proceedings of the 7th International Conference on Knowledge Representation and Reasoning (KR'00)*, pages 53–61, Breckenridge (CO), 2000.
26. Y. Dimopoulos, B. Nebel, and F. Toni. Preferred arguments are harder to compute than stable extensions. In *Proceedings of the 16th International Joint Conference on Artificial Intelligence (IJCAI'99)*, pages 36–41, Stockholm (Sweden), 1999.
27. I.M.L. D'Ottaviano and N.C.A. da Costa. Sur un problème de Jaśkowski. Technical report, Comptes Rendus de l'Académie des Sciences de Paris, 1970.
28. D. Dubois, S. Konieczny, and H. Prade. Quasi-possibilistic logic and its measures of information and conflict. *Fundamenta Informaticae*, 57(2–4):101–125, 2003.
29. P. Dung. On the acceptability of arguments and its fundamental role in nonmonotonic reasoning, logic programming and n-person games. *Artificial Intelligence*, 77:321–357, 1995.
30. P. Dunne and T.J.M. Bench-Capon. Coherence in finite argument systems. *Artificial Intelligence*, 141:187–203, 2002.
31. Th. Eiter and G. Gottlob. On the complexity of propositional knowledge base revision, updates, and counterfactuals. *Artificial Intelligence*, 57:227–270, 1992.
32. Th. Eiter and Th. Lukasiewicz. Default reasoning from conditional knowledge bases: Complexity and tractable cases. *Artificial Intelligence*, 124(2):169–241, 2000.
33. M. Elvang-Goransson and A. Hunter. Argumentative logics: Reasoning from classically inconsistent information. *Data and Knowledge Engineering*, 16:125–145, 1995.
34. H.B. Enderton. *A mathematical introduction to logic*. Academic Press, New York, 1972.
35. R.L. Epstein. *Propositional Logics*, volume 1, chapter The Semantic Foundations of Logic. Kluwer Academic, 1990.
36. R. Fagin, J.D. Ullman, and M.Y. Vardi. On the semantics of updates in databases. In *Proceedings of the 2nd ACM Symposium on Principles of Database Systems (PODS'83)*, pages 352–355, 1983.
37. A.M. Frisch. Inference without chaining. In *Proceedings of the 10th International Joint Conference on Artificial Intelligence (IJCAI'87)*, pages 515–519, Milan (Italy), 1987.

38. P. Gärdenfors and D. Makinson. Relations between the logic of theory change and nonmonotonic logic. In *The Logic of Theory Change*, pages 185–205, 1990.
39. P. Gärdenfors. Belief revision and nonmonotonic logic: Two sides of the same coin? In *Proceedings of the 9th European Conference on Artificial Intelligence*, pages 768–773, Stockholm (Sweden), 1990.
40. M.R. Garey and D.S. Johnson. *Computers and intractability: A guide to the theory of NP-completeness*. Freeman, 1979.
41. M.L. Ginsberg. Counterfactuals. *Artificial Intelligence*, 30:35–79, 1986.
42. G. Gottlob. Complexity results for nonmonotonic logics. *Journal of Logic and Computation*, 2:397–425, 1992.
43. J. Grant and V.S. Subrahmanian. Reasoning in inconsistent knowledge bases. *IEEE Transactions on Knowledge and Data Engineering*, 7(1):177–189, 1995.
44. A. Hunter. *Handbook of Defeasible Reasoning and Uncertainty Management Systems*, volume 2, chapter Paraconsistent logics, pages 11–36. Kluwer Academic, 1998.
45. A. Hunter. Reasoning with contradictory information using quasi-classical logic. *Journal of Logic and Computation*, 10(5):677–703, 2000.
46. S. Jaśkowski. Propositional calculus for contradictory deductive systems. *Studia Logica*, 24:143–167, 1969.
47. S. Konieczny, J. Lang, and P. Marquis. DA^2 merging operators. *Artificial Intelligence*, 157(1-2):49–79, 2004.
48. S. Konieczny and P. Marquis. Three-valued logics for inconsistency handling. In *Proceedings of the 8th European Conference on Logics in Artificial Intelligence (JELIA'02)*, volume 2424 of *Lecture Notes on Artificial Intelligence*, pages 332–344, Cosenza (Italy), 2002. Springer-Verlag.
49. S. Konieczny and R. Pino Pérez. On the logic of merging. In *Proceedings of the 6th International Conference on Knowledge Representation and Reasoning (KR'98)*, pages 488–498, Trento (Italy), 1998.
50. S. Konieczny. On the difference between merging knowledge bases and combining them. In *Proceedings of the 7th International Conference on Knowledge Representation and Reasoning (KR'00)*, pages 135–144, Breckenridge (CO), 2000.
51. S. Kraus, D. Lehmann, and M. Magidor. Nonmonotonic reasoning, preferential models and cumulative logics. *Artificial Intelligence*, 44(1-2):167–207, 1990.
52. J. Lang and P. Marquis. Resolving inconsistencies by variable forgetting. In *Proceedings of the 8th International Conference on Knowledge Representation and Reasoning (KR'02)*, pages 239–250, Toulouse (France), 2002.
53. H.J. Levesque. A knowledge-level account of abduction (preliminary version). In *Proceedings of the 11th International Joint Conference on Artificial Intelligence (IJCAI'89)*, pages 1061–1067, Detroit (MI), 1989.
54. J. Lin. Integration of weighted knowledge bases. *Artificial Intelligence*, 83(2):363–378, 1996.
55. P. Marquis and N. Porquet. Computational aspects of quasi-classical entailment. *Journal of Applied Non-Classical Logics*, 11(3–4):295–312, 2001.
56. P. Marquis and N. Porquet. Resource-bounded paraconsistent inference. *Annals of Mathematics and Artificial Intelligence*, 39(4):349–384, 2003.
57. J.-J. Ch. Meyer and W. Van der Hoek. *Handbook of Defeasible Reasoning and Uncertainty Management Systems*, volume 2, chapter Modal logics for representing incoherent knowledge, pages 37–75. Kluwer Academic, 1998.
58. B. Nebel. Belief revision. In P. Gärdenfors, editor, *Cambridge Tracts in Theoretical Computer Science*, volume 29, chapter Syntax-based approaches to belief revision, pages 52–88. Cambridge University Press, Cambridge, 1992.

59. B. Nebel. Base revision operations and schemes: Semantics, representation and complexity. In *Proceedings of the 11th European Conference on Artificial Intelligence*, pages 341–345, Amsterdam (Netherlands), 1994.
60. B. Nebel. Belief revision. In D. Dubois and H. Prade, editors, *Handbook of Defeasible Reasoning and Uncertainty Management Systems*, volume 3, chapter How hard is it to revise a belief base?, pages 77–145. Kluwer Academic, 1998.
61. Ch. H. Papadimitriou. *Computational complexity.* Addison–Wesley, 1994.
62. G. Pinkas and R.P. Loui. Reasoning from inconsistency: A taxonomy of principles for resolving conflict. In *Proceedings of the 3rd International Conference on Knowledge Representation and Reasoning (KR'92)*, pages 709–719, Cambridge (MA), 1992.
63. G. Priest. Reasoning about truth. *Artificial Intelligence*, 39:231–244, 1989.
64. G. Priest. Minimally inconsistent LP. *Studia Logica*, 50:321–331, 1991.
65. G. Priest. *Handbook of Philosophical Logic*, volume 6, chapter Paraconsistent Logic, pages 287–393. Kluwer Academic, 2002.
66. R. Reiter. A theory of diagnosis from first principles. *Artificial Intelligence*, 32:57–95, 1987.
67. N. Rescher and R. Manor. On inference from inconsistent premises. *Theory and Decision*, 1:179–219, 1970.
68. P.Z. Revesz. On the semantics of arbitration. *International Journal of Algebra and Computation*, 7(2):133–160, 1997.
69. M. Schaerf and M. Cadoli. Tractable reasoning via approximation. *Artificial Intelligence*, 74:249–310, 1995.
70. J. Stillman. The complexity of propositional default logics. In *Proceedings of the 10th National Conference on Artificial Intelligence*, pages 794–799, San Jose (CA), 1992.
71. M. Winslett. *Cambridge Tracts in Theoretical Computer Science*, chapter Updating logical databases. Cambridge University Press, 1990.

Approaches to Measuring Inconsistent Information

Anthony Hunter[1] and Sébastien Konieczny[2]

[1] Department of Computer Science,
University College London, Gower Street,
London WC1E 6BT, UK
a.hunter@cs.ucl.ac.uk
[2] CRIL-CNRS, Université d'Artois, 62300 Lens, France
konieczny@cril.univ-artois.fr

Abstract. Measures of quantity of information have been studied extensively for more than fifty years. The seminal work on information theory is by Shannon [67]. This work, based on probability theory, can be used in a logical setting when the worlds are the possible events. This work is also the basis of Lozinskii's work [48] for defining the quantity of information of a formula (or knowledgebase) in propositional logic. But this definition is not suitable when the knowledgebase is inconsistent. In this case, it has no classical model, so we have no "event" to count. This is a shortcoming since in practical applications (e.g. databases) it often happens that the knowledgebase is not consistent. And it is definitely not true that all inconsistent knowledgebases contain the same (null) amount of information, as given by the "classical information theory". As explored for several years in the paraconsistent logic community, two inconsistent knowledgebases can lead to very different conclusions, showing that they do not convey the same information. There has been some recent interest in this issue, with some interesting proposals. Though a general approach for information theory in (possibly inconsistent) logical knowledgebases is missing. Another related measure is the measure of contradiction. It is usual in classical logic to use a binary measure of contradiction: a knowledgebase is either consistent or inconsistent. This dichotomy is obvious when the only deductive tool is classical inference, since inconsistent knowledgebases are of no use. But there are now a number of logics developed to draw non-trivial conclusions from an inconsistent knowledgebase. So this dichotomy is not sufficient to describe the amount of contradiction of a knowledgebase, one needs more fine-grained measures. Some interesting proposals have been made for this. The main aim of this paper is to review the measures of information and contradiction, and to study some potential practical applications. This has significant potential in developing intelligent systems that can be tolerant to inconsistencies when reasoning with real-world knowledge.

L. Bertossi et al. (Eds.): Inconsistency Tolerance, LNCS 3300, pp. 191–236, 2004.
© Springer-Verlag Berlin Heidelberg 2004

1   Introduction

Traditionally the consensus of opinion in the computer science community is that inconsistency is undesirable. Many believe that databases, knowledgebases, and software specifications, should be completely free of inconsistency, and try to eradicate inconsistency from them by any means possible. Others address inconsistency by isolating it, and perhaps resolving it locally. All seem to agree, however, that data of the form q and $\neg q$, for any proposition q cannot exist together, and that the conflict must be resolved somehow.

This view is too simplistic for developing robust intelligent systems, and furthermore, it fails to use the benefits of inconsistency in intelligent activities. Inconsistency in information is the norm in the real-world, and so should be formalized and used, rather than always rejected [23].

There are cases where q and $\neg q$ can be perfectly acceptable together and hence need not be resolved. Consider for example an income tax database where contradictory information on a taxpayer can be useful evidence in a fraud investigation. Maybe the taxpayer has completed one form that states the taxpayer has 6 children (and hence get the tax benefits for that) and completed another that states the taxpayer has 0 children. In other cases, q and $\neg q$ serve as a useful trigger for various logical actions. Inconsistency is useful in directing reasoning, and instigating the natural processes of argumentation, information seeking, multi-agent interaction, knowledge acquisition and refinement, adaptation, and learning.

Of course, there are inconsistencies that do need to be resolved. But, the decision to resolve, and the approach to resolution, needs to be context-sensitive. There is also the question of when to resolve inconsistencies. Immediate resolution of inconsistencies can result in the loss of valuable information if an arbitrary choice is made on what to reject. Consider for example the requirements capture stage in software engineering. Here premature resolution can force an arbitary decision to be made without the choice being properly considered. This can therefore overly constrain the requirements capture process.

Similarly when working with distributed databases, it cannot be expected that there are no conflicts between the databases. Conflicts in this case can have different meanings. It can sometimes denote an error in some database, in which case we can simply use a database repair. But more often conflicts will denote deeper disagreement between sets of databases, with no easy repair. So, in this case, resolution of all conflicts is not the solution, since we need to keep track of the conflict. The straighforward reason is that "having no information about some fact" or "having contradictory information about some fact" cannot be regarded as having the same epistemic status. After a repair of a set of databases, either we forget all information about the facts in conflict, or we decide what is the correct answer (among the conflicting ones). But, for the user (human or software), it is not the same thing to receive an answer "the fact A is true" or "the fact A seems to be true, but there is a conflict about it". Such answers, needed in high-level reasoning systems, require us to not resolve the conflicts (see for example [12]).

The call for robust, and intelligent, systems, has led to an increased interest in inconsistency tolerance in computer science. The central position is that the collapse of classical logic in cases of inconsistency should be circumvented. In other words, we need to suspend the axiom of absurdity (*ex falso quodlibet*) for many kinds of reasoning. A number of useful proposals have been made in the field of paraconsistent logics (see for example [28, 13]).

In addition, we need strategies for analysing inconsistent information. This need has in part driven the approach of argumentation systems which compare pros and cons for potential conclusions from conflicting information (for reviews see [58, 14]). Also important are strategies for isolating inconsistency and for taking appropriate actions, including resolution actions. This calls for uncertainty reasoning and meta-level reasoning. Furthermore, the cognitive activities involved in reasoning with inconsistent information need to be directly related to the kind of inconsistency. So, in general, we see the need for inconsistency tolerance giving rise to a range of technologies for inconsistency management. These in turn call for richer ways of describing and comparing conflicts.

Comparing heterogeneous sources often involves comparing conflicts. Suppose we are dealing with a group of clinicians advising on some patient, a group of witnesses of some incident, or a set of newspaper reports covering some event. These are all situations where we expect some degree of inconsistency in the information. Suppose that the information by each source i is represented by the set Φ_i. Each source may provide information that conflicts with the domain knowledge Ψ. Let us represent $\Phi_i \cup \Psi$ by Δ_i for each source i. Now, we may want to know whether one source is more inconsistent than another — so whether Δ_i is more inconsistent that Δ_j — and in particular determine which is the least inconsistent of the sources and so identify a minimal Δ_i in this inconsistency ordering. We may then view this minimal knowledgebase as the least problematical or most reliable source of information. This point is close to the notion of verisimilitude, as initiated by Popper [57, 44, 63].

When an autonomous system works with a set of information, beliefs, knowledge, preferences, ... expressed in a logical form (we will talk about pieces of information in the following instead of always specifying information, belief, knowledge, preferences), the notion of informational content of a piece of information and the notion of amount of contradiction are of crucial interest. Effectively, in many high-level reasoning tasks one needs to know what is the amount of information conveyed by a piece of information and/or what is the amount of contradiction involved with this piece of information. This is particularly important in complex information about the real world where inconsistencies are hard to avoid.

While information measures enable us to say how "valuable" a piece of information is by showing how precise it is, contradiction measures enable us to say how "unvaluable" a piece of information is by showing how conflicting it is. As joint/conditional information measures are useful to define a notion of pertinence of a new piece of information with respect to an old one (or more generally for a set of information), joint/conditional contradiction measures can be useful to define a notion of conflict between pieces of information, that can be useful for many applications. These two measures are to a large extent independent of one another, but needed in numerous applications, for instance:

- In diagnosis, some initial assumptions stating that each component works normally are made; those assumptions may conflict with actual observations. Measuring the conflict of the resulting base may be a good indication about how hard it will be to identify the faulty components.
- In belief revision, when an agent receives a new piece of information which contradicts her previous beliefs, evaluating how much this information is conflicting with the previous beliefs can be useful to decide whether the agent accepts or rejects the new piece of information.
- In belief merging, degrees of information and contradiction can be the basis on which one can decide whether to take account or not of the information being conveyed by an agent. If the degree of contradiction of the information given by an agent is high, it may be relevant to reject the information, since there is some significant evidence that the source is not reliable; however, this must be balanced by the quantity of information furnished by the agent, especially when she also gives some important and uncontroversial pieces of information.

One of the applications discussed above concerns the problem of iterated belief revision. The problem of belief revision is to incorporate a new piece of information which is more reliable than (and conflicting with) the old beliefs of the agent. This problem has received a nice answer in the work of Alchourron, Gardenfors, Makinson [1] in the one-step case. But when one wants to iterate revision (i.e. to generalize it to the n-step case), there are numerous problems and no definitive answer has been reached in the purely qualitative case [16, 22]. Using a partially quantitative framework, some proposals have given interesting results (see e.g. [69, 68]). Here "partially quantitative" means that the incoming piece of information needs to be labelled by a degree of confidence denoting how strongly we believe it. The problem in this framework is to justify the use of such a degree, what does it mean exactly and where does it come from. So if one can define composite measures, from the information measure and the contradiction measure, then one can define several policies for the agent (we can figure out an agent who accepts a new piece of information only if it brings more information than contradiction, etc). We can then use the "partially quantitative" framework to derive revision operators with a nice behaviour. In this setting, since the degree attached to the incoming information is not a given data, but computed directly from the incoming information and the agent policy (behaviour with respect to information and contradiction, encoded by a composite measure) then the problem of the justification of the meaning of the degrees is avoided.

Another related application is the use of degrees of conflict and information to the problem of belief merging. Given a set of agents with conflicting beliefs, the problem of belief merging is to know how to define the beliefs of the group. A natural way to define the result of the merging is to see the group as a set of agents involved in a game (this can be intuitively explained as a modelisation of a human meeting), and look for winning coalitions of agents. An example of a definition of coalition can be a set of agent with consistent beliefs (or minimal conflicting ones) and a maximal joint degree of information. Then for determining the winning coalition we can look at the degree of conflict and define the winning coalition as the one which is minimally conflicting with the others. Other interesting strategies can be defined as well.

These two examples show that the conjoint use of degree of information and contradiction can open a huge scope of research. The two given examples are actually original approaches to revision and fusion. Similar examples can be found for other reasoning tasks. This highlights the fact that we need to develop and study degrees of contradiction and degrees of information in logical frameworks to be able to carry out correctly those reasoning tasks.

We cover in the next section some preliminary definitions for notation, and then in the following section we discuss some key dimensions for measuring inconsistent information. In the subsequent five sections, we consider five key approaches to measuring inconsistent information: Consistency-based analysis that focuses on the consistent and inconsistent subsets of a knowledgebase in Section 4; Information theoretic analysis that is an adaptation of Shannon's information measure in Section 5; Probabilistic semantic analysis that assumes a probability distribution over a set of formulae in Section 6; Epistemic actions analysis that measures the degree of information in a knowledgebase in terms of the number of actions required to identify the truth value of each atomic proposition and the degree of contradiction in a knowledgebase in terms of the number of actions needed to render the knowledgebase consistent in Section 7; and in Section 8 model-theoretic analyses that are based on evaluating a knowledgebase in terms of three or four valued models that permit an "inconsistent" truth value. We follow this range of approaches with a section covering two potential applications areas, namely multi-agent negotiation and analysis of heterogeneous sources of information. Finally, we discuss what has been achieved so far in this subject, and some possible research issues.

2   Preliminaries

For a set X, let $\wp(X)$ be the power set of X. Let $\mathcal{L}_{PSi}$ be a language composed from a set of atoms PS and a set of logical connectives and let $\vdash_i \subseteq \wp(\mathcal{L}_{PSi}) \times \mathcal{L}_{PSi}$ denote the consequence relation for that language. Let $\Delta \subseteq \mathcal{L}_{PSi}$ be a knowledgebase and let $\alpha \in \mathcal{L}_{PSi}$ be a formula. Let $\models_i$ be a satisfaction relation for $\mathcal{L}_{PSi}$, let $\mathsf{Models}_i(\Delta) = \{M \mid M \models_i \alpha \text{ for all } \alpha \in \Delta\}$ be the set of models for Δ in some logic i and let $\mathcal{W}_i$ be the set of models for the language $\mathcal{L}_{PSi}$. Let $\mathsf{Consequences}_i(\Delta) = \{\alpha \mid \Delta \vdash_i \alpha\}$.

For classical logic, we drop the subscript. So $\vdash$ is the classical consequence relation and $\mathcal{L}_{PS}$ is the usual set of classical formulae formed from a set of atoms and the usual logical connectives using the usual inductive definition. If $\mathcal{L}_{PS}$ is a set of first-order formulae, then each variable in each formula is in the scope of a universal or existential quantifier as usual. For $\Delta \subseteq \mathcal{L}_{PS}$, Consequences($\Delta$) = $\{\alpha \mid \Delta \vdash \alpha\}$.

When it is not ambiguous we will not write the subscript PS, so we will simply write $\mathcal{L}_i$ for $\mathcal{L}_{PS_i}$, and $\mathcal{L}$ for $\mathcal{L}_{PS}$.

If $\Gamma \in \wp(\mathcal{L})$, then Atoms($\Gamma$) returns the set of atom symbols used in Γ.

Definition 1. *Let Δ be a knowledgebase and let $\vdash$ be the classical consequence relation.*

$$\mathsf{CON}(\Delta) = \{\Pi \subseteq \Delta | \Pi \not\vdash \bot\}$$
$$\mathsf{INC}(\Delta) = \{\Pi \subseteq \Delta | \Pi \vdash \bot\}$$
$$\mathsf{MC}(\Delta) = \{\Pi \in \mathsf{CON}(\Delta) | \forall \Phi \in \mathsf{CON}(\Delta) \Pi \not\subset \Phi\}$$
$$\mathsf{MI}(\Delta) = \{\Pi \in \mathsf{INC}(\Delta) | \forall \Phi \in \mathsf{INC}(\Delta) \Phi \not\subset \Pi\}$$
$$\mathsf{FREE}(\Delta) = \bigcap \mathsf{MC}(\Delta)$$

Hence $\mathsf{MC}(\Delta)$ is the set of maximally consistent subsets of Δ; $\mathsf{MI}(\Delta)$ is the set of minimally inconsistent subsets of Δ; and $\mathsf{FREE}(\Delta)$ is the set of information that all maximally consistent subsets of Δ have in common. We also have the following relationship.

$$\mathsf{FREE}(\Delta) = \bigcap \mathsf{MC}(\Delta) = \Delta - \bigcup \mathsf{MI}(\Delta)$$

Example 1. Let $\Delta = \{\alpha, \neg\alpha, \alpha \rightarrow \beta, \neg\alpha \rightarrow \beta, \gamma\}$. So $\mathsf{MC}(\Delta) = \{\Phi_1, \Phi_2\}$, where $\Phi_1 = \{\alpha, \alpha \rightarrow \beta, \neg\alpha \rightarrow \beta, \gamma\}$, and $\Phi_2 = \{\neg\alpha, \alpha \rightarrow \beta, \neg\alpha \rightarrow \beta, \gamma\}$. From this, $\mathsf{FREE}(\Delta) = \bigcap \mathsf{MC}(\Delta) = \{\alpha \rightarrow \beta, \neg\alpha \rightarrow \beta, \gamma\}$, and $\mathsf{MI}(\Delta) = \{\Psi\}$, where $\Psi = \{\alpha, \neg\alpha\}$.

We can consider a maximally consistent subset of a database as capturing a "plausible" or "coherent" view on the database. For this reason, the set $\mathsf{MC}(\Delta)$ is important in many of the definitions presented in Section 4. Furthermore, we consider $\mathsf{FREE}(\Delta)$, which is equal to $\bigcap \mathsf{MC}(\Delta)$, as capturing all the "uncontroversial" information in Δ. In contrast, we consider the set $\bigcup \mathsf{MI}(\Delta)$ as capturing all the "problematical" data in Δ.

3   Dimensions of Measuring Inconsistency

To move beyond classifying a set of formulae using a binary classification (of consistent or inconsistent), we need to consider some of the dimensions we have available for measuring inconsistency.

First, there are many ways of defining inconsistency. It is a logical concept. But, there are different ways that we can view it in a language and the reasoning with that language. Inconsistency can also be viewed in the semantics. We start by considering five ways of describing inconsistency that all apply to classical logic. In classical logic, all these definitions of inconsistency coincide (i.e. when $\vdash_i$ is the classical consequence relation and $\mathsf{Models}_i(\Delta)$ is the set of classical models of Δ).

Inconsistency as Explosive Reasoning. Explosive reasoning is reasoning that allows the derivation of every formula of the language in case of inconsistency. In other words, if $\text{Consequences}_i(\Delta) = \mathcal{L}_i$, then Δ is inconsistent.

Inconsistency as Conflicting Inferences. The knowledgebase Δ is inconsistent when there is the inference of both $\Delta \vdash_i \alpha$ and $\Delta \vdash_i \neg\alpha$ for some $\alpha \in \mathcal{L}_i$.

Inconsistency as Inference of a Contradiction Formulae. If the contradiction formula, denoted $\bot$, is an atom in $\mathcal{L}_i$, it can be treated in the proof theory $\vdash_i$ as logically equivalent to any inconsistent formula. So if $\Delta \vdash_i \bot$, then Δ is inconsistent. In classical logic any inconsistent formula is equivalent to any other inconsistent formula. So in an infinite classical logic language, there is an infinite number of inconsistent formulae.

Inconsistency as Trivial Reasoning. A trivial inference is an inference α from a knowledgebase Δ such that α is not a tautology and $\text{Atoms}(\Delta) \cap \text{Atoms}(\{\alpha\}) = \emptyset$. So if $\Delta \vdash_i \alpha$ and α is a trivial inference then Δ is inconsistent by trivial reasoning from $\vdash_i$.

Inconsistency as a Lack of a Model. If $\text{Models}_i(\Delta) = \emptyset$, then Δ is inconsistent. The motivation for this is that a model is a possible coherent view of the world involving Δ. So if there is no such view, then Δ is regarded as inconsistent. This definition holds for numerous logics including classical logic.

The first description of inconsistency, i.e. "inconsistency as explosive reasoning", is a stronger definition than any of "inconsistency as inference of a contradiction formulae", "inconsistency as conflicting inferences", or "inconsistency as trivial reasoning", in the sense that an inconsistency by the first definition, is an inconsistency by the other three. Whilst the above five descriptions apply to classical logic, there are many other logics for which one or more of the above descriptions apply. Below we consider two further descriptions that apply to some logics, though neither apply to classical logic.

Inconsistency as an Inconsistent Truth Value. Let B be an inconsistent truth value. Let $\alpha \in \Delta$. If for all models of Δ, α is assigned B, then α is inconsistent, and hence Δ is inconsistent. Whilst this does not hold for classical logic, many-valued logics, and hence many-valued models, can be used to evaluate a set of classical formulae (see for example [6, 29]).

Inconsistency as Delineated Falsity. Instead of a single falsity symbol, we can adopt numerous falsity sumbols of the form $\bot_k$ and defined as $\alpha_k \rightarrow \bot_k$ for some α_k (for a brief review see [10]). This notion of inconsistency does not have the same status as the ones above. It introduces several levels of inconsistency, whereas all the other definitions above only give a dichotomy inconsistent/consistent. Note that those different levels of inconsistency can be related to the ones obtained in possibilistic logic, where the formulae deduced at a level above the inconsistency level are still safe consequences of the base, despite the presence of an inconsistency [19, 20, 8].

When we have more complex information as input, we can state several other candidate definitions for inconsistency. This extra information may be a set of plans, constraints, norms, properties, etc. Inconsistency can then be viewed operationally. Some kinds of operational definitions include:

Inconsistency as Unrealisability. If Δ is a plan or specification for something, and it is unrealisable, then Δ is inconsistent (perhaps in the context of the environment for the plan or specification);

Inconsistency as Rule Violation. If some rule is violated, then the agent, process, entity, etc. that caused the violation is inconsistent.

Inconsistency as Violation of Normality. If in a set, most of the elements have some property X, then the elements of the set that do not have this property, are inconsistent with respect to X.

It is interesting to note that these last three types of inconsistency, defined in terms of two distinct types of information — a knowledgebase plus constraints/plans/norms/properties — can be either more or less demanding than by the "classical" one. If the constraints/plans/norms/properties give some domain of interest, then the base will be considered inconsistent only if there is a conflict on the domain. In other words, we can have a conflict on variables/formulae outside of the domain without the conflict being considered inconsistent by these definitions. In this case it is less demanding than the classical definition. Conversely when the constraints/plans/norms/properties give what can be regarded as a situation of "unrealisability": For example, if the three atoms a, b and c cannot all be true at the same time, and so the base {a,b,c} is classically consistent but it is not consistent for "unrealisability".

All these ten different definitions for inconsistency offer different features of a logic that can be analysed. In this review, we can see that not all these possibilities have been considered yet.

Having selected a definition for inconsistency, together with a language and an underlying logic, there are a number of dimensions that we may wish to consider in a framework for analysing inconsistent knowledgebases in that logic. We consider some of these dimensions below.

Atomic Inconsistency. To be able to measure inconsistency, we need a formalisation of an atomic inconsistency: An indivisable and discrete representation of contradictory information. There are a number of choices depending on whether we want to take a semantic or syntactic approach, and on which underlying logic we use. The main options are to put the atomicity either on formulae or on the propositional letters. So the options we will consider here are (1) minimal inconsistent subset of formulae and (2) a propositional letter assigned with an inconsistent truth value. Another possibility which we do not consider further in this review is regarding each delineated falsity as an atomic inconsistency.

Number of Inconsistencies. Once we have a notion of atomic inconsistency, we can count them. Increasing the number of inconsistencies in a knowledgebase may or may not be a factor that increases the measure of inconsistency for that knowledgebase.

Size of Inconsistency. Once we have a notion of atomic inconsistency, we can consider the size of each atomic inconsistency, since they are not necessarily the same size. Suppose we use "minimal inconsistent subset" as the definition for an atomic inconsistency. Suppose also that Δ_1 and Δ_2 are minimal inconsistent subsets of some knowledgebase Δ, and $|\Delta_1| \leq |\Delta_2|$ holds, then Δ_2 is a bigger inconsistency than Δ_1. This is only one way we may choose to evaluate the size of an inconsistency. Increasing the size of inconsistency may or may not be a factor that increase the measure of inconsistency.

Degree of Information. Measuring the amount of information in a message or source is well established with proposals such as Shannon's information theory. In the usual applications of Shannon's information theory, inconsistent information contains no information. This coincides with a classical logic perspective of inconsistency (i.e. there are no models of inconsistent information, and as a result it represents no information). However, information about the real-world frequently, or normally, incorporates inconsistency, and yet it is still informative. So the intuition that inconsistent information contains useful information, leads to proposals for measuring the degree of information in the context of inconsistency.

Further dimensions that we may consider include the following two. The first of these could be described as a composite measure, using both degree of information and degree of contradiction, and the second of these requires further (meta-level) information.

Ratio of Information to Noise. When considering inconsistent information, if there is a relatively large amount of information when compared with the amount of inconsistency, then that source is likely to be more acceptable than a source that has a relatively low amount of information when compared with the amount of inconsistency.

Significance of Inconsistency. As an illustration of the need to evaluate significance, consider two news reports on a World Cup match, where the first report says that Brazil beat Germany 2-0, and the second report says that Germany beat Brazil 2-0. This is clearly a significant inconsistency. Now consider two news reports on the same football match, where the first report says that the referee was Pierluigi Collina and the second report says that the referee was Ubaldo Aquino. This inconsistency would normally be regarded as relatively insignificant.

Amongst the five approaches to measuring inconsistent information in this review, namely consistency-based analysis, information-theoretic analysis, analysis of probabilistic semantic, analysis of epistemic actions, and model-theoretic analysis, we see these dimensions drawn out.

4   Consistency-Based Analyses

One of the most obvious strategies for handling inconsistency in a knowledgebase is to reason with consistent subsets of the knowledgebase. This is closely related to the approach of removing information from the knowledgebase that is causing an inconsistency (see for example [52, 7, 21]).

To measure the information, and the degree of inconsistency, we can take cardinality of the Δ and $\mathsf{MI}(\Delta)$ sets as the basis of an analysis. We can use this for the following ratio that captures the relative incompatibility of the formulae in the knowledgebase.

Definition 2. *The* **incompatibility ratio** *for a knowledgebase* $\Delta \subseteq \mathcal{L}_{PS}$ *is defined as follows.*

$$\frac{|\mathsf{MI}(\Delta)|}{|\Delta|}$$

Example 2. Let $\Delta = \{\alpha, \neg\alpha, \beta, \neg\beta, \gamma, \delta, \gamma \wedge \delta\}$

$$\frac{|\mathsf{MI}(\Delta)|}{|\Delta|} = \frac{2}{7}$$

Whilst this ratio provides an abstraction of the conflicts in the information in Δ, it says nothing about the relative size of the minimal inconsistent subsets, or the overlaps between members of $\mathsf{MI}(\Delta)$. Also the syntax sensitivity can be problematical.

Example 3. Let $\Delta_1 = \{\alpha \wedge \beta, \neg\alpha \wedge \neg\beta\}$ and $\Delta_2 = \{\alpha \wedge \neg\alpha, \beta \wedge \neg\beta\}$.

$$\frac{|\mathsf{MI}(\Delta_1)|}{|\Delta_1|} = \frac{1}{2} \qquad\qquad \frac{|\mathsf{MI}(\Delta_2)|}{|\Delta_2|} = \frac{2}{2}$$

These shortcomings in part stem from this measure being insufficiently fine grained. To address this, we will now review an approach based on scoring functions that provides a deeper consistency-based analysis of the inconsistencies arising in a set of formulae.

For a knowledgebase Δ, a scoring function S is from $\wp(\Delta)$ into the natural numbers defined so that $S(\Gamma)$ gives the number of minimally inconsistent subsets of Δ that would be eliminated if the subset Γ was removed from Δ [34]. This characterization offers an alternative means for articulating, in general terms, the nature of inconsistency in a set of formulae. Knowledgebases can be compared using their scoring functions giving an ordering relation over databases that can be described as "more conflicting than".

Definition 3. *Let* $\Delta \subseteq \mathcal{L}_{PS}$. *Let* S *be the* **scoring function** *for* Δ *defined as follows, where* $S : \wp(\Delta) \mapsto \mathbb{N}$ *and* $\Gamma \in \wp(\Delta)$

$$S(\Gamma) = |\mathsf{MI}(\Delta)| - |\mathsf{MI}(\Delta - \Gamma)|$$

The scoring function for a database is an abstraction of the information we have about the database, and it says much about the inconsistencies arising in the database.

Example 4. Let $\Delta = \{\alpha, \neg\alpha, \beta \wedge \neg\beta\}$, where S is the scoring function for Δ, defined as follows:

$$S(\{\alpha\}) = 1 \qquad S(\{\neg\alpha\}) = 1 \qquad\qquad S(\{\beta \wedge \neg\beta\}) = 1$$
$$S(\{\alpha, \neg\alpha\}) = 1 \quad S(\{\alpha, \beta \wedge \neg\beta\}) = 2 \qquad S(\{\neg\alpha, \beta \wedge \neg\beta\}) = 2$$
$$S(\{\alpha, \neg\alpha, \beta \wedge \neg\beta\}) = 2$$

Example 5. Let $\Delta = \{\alpha \wedge \neg\alpha, \beta, \gamma\}$, where S is the scoring function for Δ, defined as follows:

$$S(\{\alpha \wedge \neg\alpha\}) = 1 \quad S(\{\beta\}) = 0 \qquad\qquad S(\{\gamma\}) = 0$$
$$S(\{\alpha \wedge \neg\alpha, \beta\}) = 1 \quad S(\{\alpha \wedge \neg\alpha, \gamma\}) = 1 \quad S(\{\beta, \gamma\}) = 0$$
$$S(\{\alpha \wedge \neg\alpha, \beta, \gamma\}) = 1$$

We can make a few simple observations regarding scoring functions. Where S is the scoring function for Δ, $S(\cup\mathsf{MI}(\Delta)) = S(\Delta) = |\mathsf{MI}(\Delta)|$ and $S(\mathsf{FREE}(\Delta)) = 0$. Also from the scoring function for a database Δ, it is straightforward to calculate the cardinality of $\mathsf{FREE}(\Delta)$ and $\cup\mathsf{MI}(\Delta)$. However, there is no simple way for determining the cardinality of the set of maximally consistent subsets of a database directly from the scoring function for the database.

Proposition 1. *Let $\leq$ be the usual ordering relation over $\mathbb{N}$. For $\Gamma_i, \Gamma_j \in \wp(\Delta)$, where S is the scoring function for Δ,*

$$S(\Gamma_i \cap \Gamma_j) \leq \min(\{S(\Gamma_i), S(\Gamma_j)\})$$

$$\max(\{S(\Gamma_i), S(\Gamma_j)\}) \leq S(\Gamma_i \cup \Gamma_j)$$

Note, $S(\Gamma_i) + S(\Gamma_j) \leq S(\Gamma_i \cup \Gamma_j)$ does not necessarily hold as illustrated below.

Example 6. Let S be the scoring function for Δ, and let $\Gamma_1 = \{\neg\alpha, \alpha \wedge \beta\}$, and let $\Gamma_2 = \{\beta, \alpha \wedge \neg\beta\}$, and let $\Delta = \Gamma_1 \cup \Gamma_2$. So $S(\Gamma_1) = S(\Gamma_2) = 3$, but $S(\Gamma_1 \cup \Gamma_2) = 4$.

We can compare databases using the scoring function for each database. For this we define score orderings.

Definition 4. *A **score ordering**, denoted $\leq$, is defined as follows[1]. Assume Δ_i and Δ_j are of the same cardinality and S_i is the scoring function for Δ_i,*

---

[1] Note, we are now using the $\leq$ symbol for the usual ordering over the natural numbers and as defined here for an ordering over score functions. Hopefully, this overloading of the symbol will not cause confusion.

and S_j is the scoring function for Δ_j. $S_i \leq S_j$ holds iff there is a bijection $f : \wp(\Delta_i) \mapsto \wp(\Delta_j)$ such that the following condition is satisfied:

$$\forall \Gamma \in \wp(\Delta_i), S_i(\Gamma) \leq S_j(f(\Gamma))$$

Note, $S_i < S_j$ iff $S_i \leq S_j$ and $S_j \not\leq S_i$. Also, $S_i \simeq S_j$ iff $S_i \leq S_j$ and $S_j \leq S_i$. We say Δ_j is **more inconsistent** than Δ_i iff $S_i \leq S_j$.

Example 7. Let $\Delta_1 = \{\alpha, \neg\alpha\}$ and $\Delta_2 = \{\alpha, \beta \wedge \neg\beta\}$. Let S_1 be the scoring function for Δ_1 and S_2 be the scoring function for Δ_2, and so $S_2 < S_1$.

$$\begin{array}{ll} S_1(\{\alpha\}) = 1 & S_2(\{\alpha\}) = 0 \\ S_1(\{\neg\alpha\}) = 1 & S_2(\{\beta \wedge \neg\beta\}) = 1 \\ S_1(\{\alpha, \neg\alpha\}) = 1 & S_2(\{\alpha, \beta \wedge \neg\beta\}) = 1 \end{array}$$

Example 8. Consider $\Delta_1 = \{\alpha \wedge \neg\alpha, \beta, \gamma\}$ and $\Delta_2 = \{\alpha \wedge \neg\alpha, \beta \wedge \neg\beta, \delta\}$. If S_1 is the scoring function for Δ_1, and S_2 is the scoring function for Δ_2, then $S_1 < S_2$.

We can consider scoring functions as giving information about the overlaps of the minimally inconsistent subsets. For example, for Δ_i and Δ_j, if $|\Delta_i| = |\Delta_j|$ and $|\mathsf{MI}(\Delta_i)| = |\mathsf{MI}(\Delta_j)|$ and $S_i \leq S_j$ then the inconsistencies are more overlapping in Δ_j. In other words, more of the formulae are in more minimally inconsistent subsets. In case we want to compare sets of different cardinality, we can add dummy propositions to the smaller set to make it the same size as the larger set. These dummy propositions are literals that do not appear elsewhere and so can be assumed to not be in any of the minimally inconsistent subsets of the database.

For each $n \in \mathbb{N}$, the score ordering $\leq$ over knowledgebases is reflexive and transitive, but not antisymmetric. The following result shows in part how a score ordering can be viewed as an aggregation of parameters including the relative number of minimally inconsistent formulae and the relative number of free formulae.

Proposition 2. *If $|\Delta_i| = |\Delta_j|$, and S_i is the scoring function for Δ_i, and S_j is the scoring function for Δ_j, then*

$$S_i \leq S_j \text{ implies } |\mathsf{MI}(\Delta_i)| \leq |\mathsf{MI}(\Delta_j)|$$
$$S_i \leq S_j \text{ implies } |\mathsf{FREE}(\Delta_i)| \geq |\mathsf{FREE}(\Delta_j)|$$

Note, the converse does not hold.

With the same assumptions as those for Proposition 2, we do not get that $S_i \leq S_j$ implies $|\mathsf{MC}(\Delta_i)| \leq |\mathsf{MC}(\Delta_j)|$ or that it implies $|\mathsf{MC}(\Delta_i)| \geq |\mathsf{MC}(\Delta_j)|$. This is captured in the following example.

Example 9. Consider $\Delta_1 = \{\alpha, \beta\}$ and $\Delta_2 = \{\alpha, \neg\alpha\}$. So $S_1 \leq S_2$ and $|\mathsf{MC}(\Delta_1)| \leq |\mathsf{MC}(\Delta_2)|$. Now consider $\Delta_3 = \{\alpha, \neg\alpha\}$ and $\Delta_4 = \{\beta \wedge \neg\beta, \gamma \wedge \neg\gamma\}$. So $S_3 \leq S_4$ and $|\mathsf{MC}(\Delta_3)| \geq |\mathsf{MC}(\Delta_4)|$.

Clearly, scoring functions are syntax sensitive in the sense that we may have two knowledgebase Δ_1 and Δ_2 where $\mathsf{Consequences}(\Delta_1) = \mathsf{Consequences}(\Delta_2)$ and S_1 is the scoring function for Δ_1 and S_2 is the scoring function for Δ_2, but $S_1(\Delta_1) \neq S_2(\Delta_2)$. Scoring functions may also be regarded as being prone to semantic insensitivity. To illustrate semantic insensitivity, consider the following two examples.

Example 10. Consider Δ_1 and Δ_2 below. Let S_1 be the scoring function for Δ_1 and S_2 be the scoring function for Δ_2.

$$\Delta_1 = \{\alpha, \neg\alpha\}$$
$$\Delta_2 = \{\alpha \wedge \beta, \neg\alpha \wedge \beta\}$$

Here, $S_1 \simeq S_2$ and so the scoring functions do not differentiate Δ_1 and Δ_2. Yet it could be argued that semantically Δ_2 implies more (such as if paraconsistent logic inference were used) than Δ_1.

Example 11. Consider Δ_1 and Δ_2 below. Let S_1 be the scoring function for Δ_1 and S_2 be the scoring function for Δ_2.

$$\Delta_1 = \{\alpha \wedge \beta \wedge \gamma, \alpha \wedge \neg\beta \wedge \gamma, \neg\alpha \wedge \beta \wedge \neg\gamma\}$$
$$\Delta_2 = \{\alpha \wedge \beta \wedge \gamma, \alpha \wedge \neg\beta \wedge \gamma, \neg\alpha \wedge \beta \wedge \gamma\}$$

Here, the formulae in Δ_1 and Δ_2 are pairwise inconsistent, and the resulting scoring functions are such that $S_1 \simeq S_2$. It may be argued that Δ_2 is less inconsistent than Δ_1 since all formulae in Δ_2 agree on γ.

In response to the arguments raised in Example 10 and 11, we believe that this kind of semantic insensitivity is useful in some applications. We believe that when a connective is used, it is used with some intent. So for example, whilst $\alpha \wedge \beta$ and α, β are semantically equivalent, we may need to differentiate them also. This intent depends on the applications area, but to illustrate in negotiation, consider a strategy for weakening the preferences (represented by a set of classical formulae) of an agent is take a subset of the preferences. So if an agent starts with $\{\alpha \wedge \beta\}$ as its preferences then the only possible weakening (using the $\subseteq$ relation) is $\{\}$. Whereas if the agent starts with $\{\alpha, \beta\}$ then weakenings also include $\{\alpha\}$ and $\{\beta\}$. In this application, the preference $\alpha \wedge \beta$ is intended to mean that $\alpha \wedge \beta$ must occur together, and so if the preference α is dropped then so is the preference β.

In fact, this question is related to the status of the "comma" connective. In classical logic (in the consistent case) $\{\alpha \wedge \beta\}$ and $\{\alpha, \beta\}$ are logically equivalent. That shows that the comma in the second knowledgebase has exactly the same meaning as a conjunction. But as soon as the knowledgebase is not consistent, a lot of approaches give a different meaning to the comma and to the conjunction. As explained above, this can be sensible if the $\wedge$ connective means that the conjuncts must absolutely occur together, whereas it is not the case with the comma. This difference can be very intuitive, but it is not mandatory. And this choice leads to different approaches.

The general conclusion we draw from this discussion is that the syntax sensitivity, and the semantic insensitivity, found in scoring functions is useful in some applications.

5   Information Theoretic Analyses

First we consider how information theory can be used to measure the information content of propositional formulae [70].

Table 1. A 3×3 grid denoting 9 possible locations for an object

	β_1	β_2	β_3
α_1	×		×
α_2			
α_3			

Example 12. Let ϕ be a formula in the classical language composed of the following propositional letters $\{\alpha_1, \alpha_2, \alpha_3, \beta_1, \beta_2, \beta_3\}$. Now consider that ϕ represents the location of an object where there are 9 possible positions in a 3×3 grid (cf. Table 1). Information can be collected on the position in the grid. Now if we receive two messages: The first states that the position is α_1 and the second states that the position is $\neg\beta_2$. From these two statements, we can conclude that the position is $\alpha_1 \wedge (\beta_1 \vee \beta_3)$. This is represented by the × symbol in Table 1.

The basic idea behind Shannon's measure of information is that information eliminates possibilities. The more unlikely a piece of information, the more information is conveyed when that piece of information is asserted.

Definition 5. *Let ϕ be a piece of information, and let $P(\phi)$ be the probability of ϕ occuring.* **Shannon's information measure I is**

$$I(\phi) = -log P(\phi)$$

We can illustrate the use of Shannon's Information measure by the following example.

Example 13. Returning to Example 12, we can use the 3×3 grid as a probability space and we can assume a uniform distribution over this space (i.e. each position in the grid is equally probable). Using Definition 5 for $\phi = \alpha_1$ and $\phi' = \alpha_1 \wedge \neg\beta_2$, we get

$$I(\phi) = -log\frac{3}{9} = 0.48 \qquad\qquad I(\phi') = -log\frac{2}{9} = 0.65$$

Information theory can be used to measure the information content of sets of consistent formulae. The information in a set Γ, composed from n different atom symbols, is the logarithm of the number of models (2^n) divided by the number of models of Γ [48]. This idea can be traced back to Kemeny [35] and Hintikka [27], so we will call this measure the Kemeny and Hintikka measure of information.

Definition 6. *Let Γ be a consistent set of formulae, let n be the number of atoms in the language $\mathcal{L}_{PSi}$, and let* Models(Γ) *denote the collection of models for Γ. The information value of Γ is defined by the following equation.*

$$I(\Gamma) = log_2 \frac{2^n}{|\text{Models}(\Gamma)|}$$

Rewriting this equation, we get the following.

$$I(\Gamma) = n - log_2|\text{Models}(\Gamma)|$$

Notice that with this definition, if the set of formulae Γ is inconsistent, then the measure of information does not work. To address this, Lozinskii extends this approach to measure the information content of sets of inconsistent formulae. The information in a set Γ, composed from n different atom symbols, is the logarithm of the number of models (2^n) divided by the number of models for the maximum consistent subsets of Γ.

Definition 7. *Let Γ be a consistent set of formulae, let n be the number of atoms in the language $\mathcal{L}_{PSi}$, and let* MC(Γ) *be the set of maximally consistent subsets of Γ (see Definition 1). For each $\Delta \in$ MC(Γ), if $M(\Delta)$ is the collection of models of Δ, then the collection of quasi-models is defined by*

$$U(\Gamma) = \bigcup\{\text{Models}(\Delta) \mid \Delta \in \text{MC}(\Gamma)\}$$

The information value of Γ is defined by the following equation

$$I_l(\Gamma) = n - log_2|U(\Gamma)|$$

This measure increases with additions of consistent information and decreases with additions of inconsistent information.

Example 14. For $\Delta = \{\alpha \vee \beta, \alpha \vee \neg\beta, \neg\alpha \wedge \gamma\}$, $\Gamma = \Delta \cup \{\neg\gamma\}$, and $\Gamma' = \Delta \cup \{\delta\}$

$$I_l(\Gamma) < I_l(\Delta) \qquad\qquad I_l(\Gamma') > I_l(\Delta)$$

However, the approach is syntax sensitive, in the sense discussed in Section 4, as illustrated by the following example.

Example 15. For $\Delta = \{\alpha \vee \beta, \alpha \vee \neg\beta, \neg\alpha \wedge \gamma\}$, and $\Delta' = \{\alpha \vee \beta, \alpha \vee \neg\beta, \neg\alpha, \gamma\}$, but $I_l(\Delta') < I_l(\Delta)$.

To address this syntax sensitivity, a normal form can be used for application of Lozinskii's measure. One proposal is to rewrite all formulae into conjunctive normal form, and then exhaustively apply conjunction elimination and resolution [70]. Returning to Example 15, if we use this normal form of the knowledgebases, then they have the same result using Lozinskii's measure.

It should be noted, whether or not we use a normal form, this information-theoretic approach does not provide a direct evaluation of inconsistency since for example, the value for $\{\alpha\}$ is the same as for $\{\alpha, \neg\alpha, \beta\}$. As a result, we stress this approach provides a measure of information that may be inconsistent rather than a measure of the inconsistencies in the information.

An interesting application of Lozinskii's measure is in a form of belief revision [50].

6 Analysis of Probabilistic Semantics

There is an inconsistency analysis framework, with a probabilistic semantics, that assigns a measure of consistency in the range $[0,1]$ for each set of propositional formulae [37, 39]. For a set of formulae that contains a formula that is contradictory (logically equivalent to falsity), the measure of consistency is 0. For a set of formulae that is consistent, the measure of consistency is 1.

For any set of formulae, the measure of consistency is directly proportional to the size of the minimal inconsistent subsets. This conceptualizes the intuition that the more formulae required to obtain an inconsistency, the more tolerable the set becomes. Since, any formula equivalent to falsity causes that set to have a measure of consistency of 0, the framework collapses a number of interesting, different kinds of knowledgebase, to the same value. In this sense, the framework is less-fined grained than the other measures presented in the next sections in the propositional case.

On the other hand this measure is the only one among those presented here that takes into account the number of formulae required to lead to the inconsistency.

It is also possible to define two information measures based on the measure of consistency [39].

6.1 Probabilistic Measure of Consistency

First one needs to define a probability function over formulae:

Definition 8. *A probability function on $\mathcal{L}$ is a function $P : \mathcal{L} \to [0,1]$ s.t. :*

- *if $\models \alpha$, then $P(\alpha) = 1$*
- *if $\models \neg(\alpha \wedge \beta)$, then $P(\alpha \vee \beta) = P(\alpha) + P(\beta)$*

See [55] for more details on this definition. In the finite case, this definition gives a probability distribution on interpertations, and the probablity of a formula is the sum of the probabilities of its models[2].

Then the measure of consistency is defined as [37] :

Definition 9. *Let Δ be a knowledgebase.*

- *Δ is $\eta-$consistent $(0 \leq \eta \leq 1)$ if there exists a probability function P such that $P(\alpha) \geq \eta$ for all $\alpha \in \Delta$.*
- *Δ is maximally $\eta-$consistent if η is maximal (i.e. if $\gamma > \eta$ then Δ is not $\gamma-$consistent).*

So the notion of maximally $\eta-$consistency can be used as a measure of contradiction. This is a direct formalisation of the fact that the more formulae are

---

[2] It can be also defined, like in[37, 39], in terms of the logical formulae corresponding to the models of the knowledgebase (maximally coherent conjunction of literals of $\mathcal{L}$).

required to produced the inconsistency, the less the inconsistency is important. As easily seen, in a finite setting, a knowledgebase Δ is 0−consistent if and only if there is a contradictory formula (i.e. a formula logically equivalent to falsity) in it. And Δ is 1−consistent if and only if the knowledgebase is consistent. Let us see some examples to illustrate the non-extremal cases:

Example 16. $\Delta = \{a, b, \neg a \lor \neg b\}$ is maximally $\frac{2}{3}$−consistent. $\Delta = \{a \land b, \neg a \land \neg b, a \land \neg b\}$ is maximally $\frac{1}{3}$−consistent, whereas each of its subsets of cardinality 2 is maximally $\frac{1}{2}$−consistent.

For minimal inconsistent sets of formulae, computing the probabilistic measure of consistency is easy.

Proposition 3. *If $\Gamma \in \mathsf{MI}(\Delta)$, then Γ is maximally $\frac{|\Gamma|-1}{|\Gamma|}$−consistent.*

For a general knowledgebase, there is no direct way to compute it. But a lower bound can be stated:

Proposition 4. *If Δ is finite and $\Gamma \subseteq \Delta$ is a smallest minimally inconsistent subset of Δ, then Δ is $\frac{|\Gamma|-1}{|\Delta|}$−consistent.*

In fact, as underlined in [37], it can be computed using the simplex method.

6.2   Probabilistic Measures of Information

From this probabilistic measure of consistency, one can define two probabilistic measures of information [39]. Let us first give some definitions:

Definition 10. *Let Δ be a knowledgebase.*

- *A probability function P is Pareto optimal for Δ if there is no probability function P^* such that $P^*(\alpha) \geq P(\alpha)$ for all $\alpha \in \Delta$ and $P^*(\beta) > P(\beta)$ for one $\beta \in \Delta$.*
- *A probability function P is Δ−consistent if Δ is maximally η−consistent and $P(\alpha) \geq \eta$ for all $\alpha \in \Delta$.*
- *A probability function P is Rawls optimal for Δ if it Δ−consistent and Pareto optimal for Δ.*

Definition 11. *Let us note respectively R_Δ and V_Δ, the set of Rawls optimal probability functions for Δ and the set of Δ−consistent probability functions.*

Proposition 5. *Let Δ be a knowledge base. A probability function is Pareto/Rawls optimal only if $P(\alpha) = 1$ for all $\alpha \in \mathsf{FREE}(\Delta)$.*

The entropy [67] of a probability function P is defined as

$$H(P) = -\sum_{\omega \in W} P(\omega) \log_2 P(\omega)$$

Let X be a set of probabiliy functions, then $ME(X)$ is a random maximum entropy function from X. Then the two probabilistic measures of information are:

Definition 12. *Let Δ be a knowledgebase.*

- $I_{k1}^{\mathcal{L}}(\Delta) = |\mathcal{L}| - H(ME(R_\Delta))$
- $I_{k2}^{\mathcal{L}}(\Delta) = |\mathcal{L}| - H(ME(V_\Delta))$

These two definitions are two direct generalization of Kemeny and Hintikka measure of information (see definition 6) that do not trivialize to 0 when the knowledgebase is not consistent.

In terms of this probabilistic semantics the information measure of Kemeny and Hintikka of a knowledgebase is the size of the language minus the entropy of the probabilistic function that has a maximum entropy while giving a probability 1 to all of the formulae of the knowledgebase.

This view trivializes when the knowledgebase is not consistent, since, in this case, it is not possible to give a probability 1 to all the formulae of the knowledgebase. The two definitions proposed in Definition 12 are the two more intuitive modifications of this intuition to fit the inconsistent case. The second one ($I_{k2}^{\mathcal{L}}$) takes the maximum entropy probabilistic function that maximizes the minimum probability of the formulae of the knowledgebase. The first one ($I_{k1}^{\mathcal{L}}$) takes the maximum entropy probabilistic function that gives a probability 1 to the maximum of formulae of the knowledgebase (the free formulae of the knowledgebase) and a maximum probability to each of the other formulae of the knowledgebase. So, in both cases, the requirement of giving probability 1 to all the formulae of the knowledgebase, is "minimally" changed.

Let us see what those measures give on some simple example.

Example 17. $\Delta = \{a, b, c, \neg a \wedge \neg b\}$. Δ is maximally $\frac{1}{2}$–consistent. As FREE(Δ) = $\{c\}$, for the first information measure, the probabilistic function must satisfy $P(c) = 1$. The only probability distribution on interpretations that is Rawls optimal is $P(\{\neg a, \neg b, c\}) = \frac{1}{2}$ and $P(\{a, b, c\}) = \frac{1}{2}$. So $I_{k1}^{\mathcal{L}}(\Delta) = 2$. For the second information measure, we only consider Δ–consistent probabilistic functions, and the one of maximum entropy is the one that gives a probability of $\frac{1}{4}$ to all of $\{\neg a, \neg b, c\}$, $\{\neg a, \neg b, \neg c\}$, $\{a, b, c\}$ and $\{a, b, \neg c\}$. So $I_{k2}^{\mathcal{L}}(\Delta) = 1$. Note that on this example Lozinskii's measure of information gives $I_l^{\mathcal{L}}(\Delta) = 2$.

Knight advocates the superiority of those two measures on the one proposed by Lozinskii, since they take into account the knowledgebase as a whole (i.e. all the formulae of the knowledgebase), whereas Lozinskii's, which is based on maximal consistent subsets, takes into account only some subsets of the knowledgebase.

Indeed, the two approaches (Lozinskii and Knight) give significant different results on some illustrating case. See the following example.

Example 18. Let α be a non-tautological consistent formula, and let $\Delta = \{\alpha, \neg \alpha\}$.

Then $I_l^{\mathcal{L}}(\Delta) = 0$ for all α. But, this is not the case for Knight's measures of information. Since they are based on a probability distribution on interpretations and on maximum entropy, the result depends on the number of interpretations in α and its negation.

For example if α is a conjunction of atoms $\alpha = a_1 \wedge \ldots \wedge a_k$. Then for $k = 1$, then $I_{k1}^{\mathcal{L}}(\Delta) = I_{k2}^{\mathcal{L}}(\Delta) = 0$, for $k = n$, then $I_{k1}^{\mathcal{L}}(\Delta) = I_{k2}^{\mathcal{L}}(\Delta) = |\mathcal{L}| - \frac{1}{2} - \frac{1}{2}\log_2 \frac{1}{n}$. So $I_{k1}^{\mathcal{L}}$ and $I_{k2}^{\mathcal{L}}$ increase with the number of conjuncts.

To know what behaviour is the more intuitive one is not an easy task. We think that both behaviours have pro and cons.

But both approaches are highly syntax sensitive, in particular, they make a distinction between $\{a \wedge b\}$ and $\{a, b\}$. This is not the case with some of the other approaches presented in the rest of this paper. Let us see this on the following example:

Example 19. Let $\Delta = \{a, b, \neg a \vee \neg b\}$ and $\Delta' = \{a \wedge b, \neg a \vee \neg b\}$. Then $I_{k1}^{\mathcal{L}}(\Delta) = I_{k2}^{\mathcal{L}}(\Delta) = 0.42$ and $I_l^{\mathcal{L}}(\Delta) = 1$. While $I_{k1}^{\mathcal{L}}(\Delta') = I_{k2}^{\mathcal{L}}(\Delta') = 0.21$ and $I_l^{\mathcal{L}}(\Delta') = 0$.

Note that Lozinskii's approach is immune to the presence of a contradictory formula (i.e. adding a contradictory formula to a knowledgebase does not change the measure of information). $I_{k1}^{\mathcal{L}}(\Delta)$ is dependent to the addition of contradictory formulae: adding a contradictory formulae decreases the measure of information. So it seems that this measure melds together information and contradiction. Whereas $I_{k2}^{\mathcal{L}}(\Delta)$ trivializes as soon as the knowledgebase contains a contradictory formula.

Note that the three measures by Lozinskii and Knight trivialize as soon as the knowledgebase contains only one formula that is contradictory. This is not the case with the measures presented in the following sections.

7   Analysis of Epistemic Actions

An alternative approach to quantifying degrees of information and contradiction in propositional logic is based on a framework of "epistemic actions" [40]. Each epistemic action (called also *test*) reduces inconsistency and/or gains information. The degree of information in a knowledgebase is based on the number (or the cost) of actions needed to identify the truth value of each atomic proposition: The lower the cost, the more information is contained in the base. The degree of contradiction in a knowledgebase is based on the number (or the cost) of actions needed to render the knowledgebase classically consistent. Both measurements are dependent on the language, logic, and tests used.

So this framework does not define a unique measure of contradiction (and information), but a wide family of such measures. Since instantiating the parameters of the framework allows to define different measures. The main parameter is the underlying logic. Each propositional logic that satisfies some basic requirements can be used here, leading to different definitions of measures of contradiction (and measures of information). Another important parameter is the available epistemic actions (called *tests* in the following). Specifying the set of available tests, allows us to make a distinction between atoms/formulae. It can for example be used to state that only some atoms are of interest (i.e. contradiction or lack of information on the remaining atoms is not important), or that some atoms/formulae are more important (or more difficult to test) than other ones. We will present here only the measures of contradiction, see [40] for more details and for the definition of the corresponding measures of information.

One of the aim of this approach is to be able to say something on a single contradictory formula. Another way to express this idea is to say that in this approach the connector $\wedge$ is the same as the comma connective (i.e. $\{\alpha, \beta\}$ must be considered exactly as $\{\alpha \wedge \beta\}$). So in this section we will consider that the knowledgebase is a single formula (since, with the above hypothesis, we can take equivalently the formula that is the conjunction of all formulae of the knowledgebase).

So this approach needs an underlying propositional logic $\mathcal{L}_{PSi}$ that is required to have the following components :

1. A *consequence relation* $\models_i$ on $\mathcal{L}_{PSi} \times \mathcal{L}_{PSi}$.
2. An *acceptance function* $A_i \subseteq \mathcal{L}_{PSi} \times \mathcal{L}_{PSi}$: $A_i(\Delta, \alpha)$ means that given the knowledgebase Δ, α is accepted as true information (we say that Δ *accepts* α). By default, acceptance is defined by: $A_i(\Delta, \alpha)$ iff ($\Delta \models_i \alpha$ and $\Delta \not\models_i \neg\alpha$). We say that Δ is *informative about* α iff exactly one of $A_i(\Delta, \alpha)$ or $A_i(\Delta, \neg\alpha)$ holds, and that Δ is *fully informative* iff for any $\alpha \in \mathcal{L}_{PSi}$, Δ is informative about α.
3. A *contradiction indicator* $C_i \subseteq \mathcal{L}_{PSi} \times \mathcal{L}_{PSi}$: if $C_i(\Delta, \alpha)$ holds, then we say that Δ *is contradictory about* α. By default, we define $C_i(\Delta, \alpha)$ iff ($\Delta \models_i \alpha$ and $\Delta \models_i \neg\alpha$). Δ is said to be *contradiction-free* iff for every $\alpha \in \mathcal{L}_{PSi}$, we do not have $C_i(\Delta, \alpha)$.
4. A *weak revision* operator $\star : \mathcal{L}_{PSi} \times \mathcal{L}_{PSi} \to \mathcal{L}_{PSi}$: $\Delta \star \alpha$ represents the new knowledgebase obtained once taking account of the observation α into the knowledgebase Δ. For the sake of generality, we are not very demanding about $\star$. The only requirement is that $\Delta \star \alpha \models_i \alpha$, which expresses that our tests are assumed reliable (each test outcome must be true in the actual world). In the following we will simply refer to these operators as *revision* operators (omitting the *weak*).

Let us now define the set of tests (a test is an action that allows to truthfully know the truth value of a formula) that will be allowed to be used for computing the measure of contradiction.

Definition 13. *A test context* $C_{\mathcal{L}_{PSi}}$ *(w.r.t.* $\mathcal{L}_{PSi}$*) is a pair* $\langle T, c \rangle$ *where* T *is a finite set of tests and* c *is a cost function from* T *to* $\mathbb{N}^*$ *(the set of strictly positive integers). The outcome to any test* $t_\alpha \in T$ *is one of* $\alpha, \neg\alpha$*, where* $\alpha \in \mathcal{L}_{PSi}$*. We say that* t_α *is the[3] test about* α *. A context is said to be :*

- *standard iff* $\forall t_\alpha \in T$*, we have* $c(t_\alpha) = 1$ *(every test has a unit cost).*
- *universal iff for every* $\alpha \in \mathcal{L}_{PSi}$*, there is a test* $t_\alpha \in T$*.*
- *atomic iff the testable formulae are exactly the atoms of the language (*$t_x \in T$ *iff* $x \in PS$*).*

---

[3] It is assumed, without loss of generality, that at most one test t_α of T is about α for each $\alpha \in \mathcal{L}_{PSi}$.

Definition 14. *Given a test context* $C_{\mathcal{L}_{PS_i}}$, *a test plan* π *is a finite binary tree; each of its non-terminal nodes is labelled with a test action* t_α; *the left and right arcs leaving every non-terminal node labelled with* t_α *are respectively labelled with the outcomes* α *and* $\neg\alpha$. *An (outcome) trajectory* $\langle o_1, \ldots, o_n \rangle$ *with respect to* π *is the sequence of test outcomes on a branch of* π. *The* cost *of a trajectory* $\langle o_1, \ldots, o_n \rangle$ *with respect to* π *is defined as* $\sum_{i=1}^n c(t_{\alpha_i})$, *where each* t_{α_i} *is the test labelling the node of* π *reached by following the path* $\langle o_1, \ldots, o_{i-1} \rangle$ *from the root of* π.

Test plans are the basic tool used to determinate the tests needed to remove the inconsistency. It is the number (or more generally the cost) of the tests needed that will give the measure of contradiction for a knowledgebase.

Definition 15. *Let* π *be a test plan and* Δ *the initial knowledgebase.*

- *The* application *of* π *on* Δ *is the tree* $apply(\pi, \Delta)$, *isomorphic to* π, *whose nodes are labelled with knowledgebases defined inductively as follows:*
  - *the root* ϵ *of* $apply(\pi, \Delta)$ *is labelled with* $\Delta(\epsilon) = \Delta$;
  - *let* n *be a node of* $apply(\pi, \Delta)$, *labelled with the knowledgebase* $\Delta(n)$, *whose corresponding node in* π *is non-terminal and labelled with* t_α; *then* n *has two children in* $apply(\pi, \Delta)$, *labelled respectively with* $\Delta(n) \star \alpha$ *and* $\Delta(n) \star \neg\alpha$.
- π purifies α *given* Δ *iff for every terminal node* n *of* $apply(\pi, \Delta)$, $\Delta(n)$ *is not contradictory about* α *(i.e., not* $C_L(\Delta(n), \alpha)$).
- π *(fully)* purifies Δ *iff it eliminates all contradictions in* Δ, *i.e., iff for any terminal node* n *of* $apply(\pi, \Delta)$, $\Delta(n)$ *is contradiction-free.*

The degree of contradiction of Δ measures the minimal effort necessary to purify Δ.

Note that, clearly enough, it can be the case that there is no plan to purify a formula (if the test context is not atomic and not universal).

Definition 16. *Let us define the* cost $c(\pi)$ *of a test plan* π *as the maximum of the costs of its trajectories. Then the* degree of contradiction *of* Δ *is defined by* $d_C(\Delta) = \min(\{c(\pi) \mid \pi \text{ purifies } \Delta\})$. *When no plan purifies* Δ, *we let* $d_C(\Delta) = +\infty$.

In the previous definition, we actually define *pessimistic degrees* of contradiction (because the cost of a plan is defined as the *maximum* cost among its trajectories); this principle, consisting in assuming the worst outcome, is known in decision theory as *Wald criterion*. Other criteria could be used instead, such as the optimistic criterion obtained by replacing *max* by *min*. Also interesting, the criterion obtained by first using *max* and then *min* for tie-breaking, or the *leximax* criterion, allow for a better discrimination than the pure pessimistic criterion.

The interest of this framework is that we can define different degrees of contradiction, depending of the chosen underlying logic. We will only give an example of such instanciation here for illustrating the definition (see [40] for other examples).

We focus here on the LP_m logic as defined in [59]. This choice is mainly motivated by the fact that this logic is simple enough and has an inference relation that coincides with classical entailment whenever the knowledgebase is classically consistent (this feature is not shared by many paraconsistent logics).

- The language of LP_m is built up from the connectives $\wedge$, $\vee$, $\neg$, $\rightarrow$ and the constants $\top$, $\bot$.
- An interpretation ω for LP_m maps each atom to one of the three "truth values" $false$, $both$, $true$, the third truth value $both$ meaning intuitively "both true and false". 3^{PS} is the set of all interpretations for LP_m. "Truth values" are ordered as follows: $false <_t both <_t true$.
  - $M(\top) = true$, $M(\bot) = false$
  - $M(\neg\alpha) = both$ iff $M(\alpha) = both$
    $M(\neg\alpha) = true$ iff $M(\alpha) = false$
  - $M(\alpha \wedge \beta) = \min_{\leq_t}(M(\alpha), M(\beta))$
  - $M(\alpha \vee \beta) = \max_{\leq_t}(M(\alpha), M(\beta))$
  - $M(\alpha \rightarrow \beta) = \begin{cases} true & \text{if } M(\alpha) = false \\ M(\beta) & \text{otherwise} \end{cases}$
- The set of models of a formula α is $\mathsf{Models}_{LP}(\alpha) = \{M \in 3^{PS} \mid M(\alpha) \in \{true, both\}\}$.
  Define $M! = \{x \in PS \mid M(x) = both\}$.
  Then $\min(\mathsf{Models}_{LP}(\alpha)) = \{M \in \mathsf{Models}_{LP}(\alpha) \mid \nexists M' \in \mathsf{Models}_{LP}(\alpha) \text{ s.t. } M'! \subset M!\}$.
  The consequence relation is defined by $\Delta \models_{LP_m} \alpha$ iff $min(\mathsf{Models}_{LP}(\Delta)) \subseteq \mathsf{Models}_{LP}(\alpha)$.
- The definitions of $A_{LP_m}(\Delta, \alpha)$ and $C_{LP_m}(\Delta, \alpha)$ are those by default; $C_{LP_m}(\Delta, \alpha)$ holds only if Δ has no classical model.

We have also to define the revision operator. Actually, the issue of revision in paraconsistent logic has never been considered so far. Expansion is not satisfactory as a revision operator for LP_m because it does not enable the purification task when Δ has no classical model ω (i.e., such that $\omega(x) \neq both$ for each $x \in PS$), whatever the test context. Among the many possible choices, we have considered the following revision operator, defined model-theoretically (for the sake of brevity, we characterize only its restriction to the case the revision formula α is a literal l).

Let $force(M, l)$ be the interpretation of 3^{PS} defined by (for every literal $l = x$ or $\neg x$):
$$\begin{cases} force(M, x)(x) = true \\ \forall y \in PS, y \neq x, force(M, x)(y) = M(y) \end{cases}$$
$$\begin{cases} force(M, \neg x)(x) = false \\ \forall y \in PS, y \neq x, force(M, x)(y) = M(y) \end{cases}$$
Then the revision operator is defined by:
$$\mathsf{Models}_{LP}(\Delta \star l) = \begin{cases} \{M \models \Delta \mid M(l) = true\} & \text{if this set is non-empty,} \\ \{force(M, l) \mid M \models \Delta \text{ and } M(l) = both\}, & \text{otherwise.} \end{cases}$$

Example 20. Given the standard atomic test context, we have:

- $d_C(\{\top\}) = 0$
- $d_C(\{a\}) = 0$
- $d_C(\{a \wedge b\}) = 0$
- $d_C(\{a \wedge b \wedge \neg a\}) = 1$
- $d_C(\{a \wedge b \wedge \neg a \wedge \neg b\}) = 2$

Let us see the result on a more complex example:

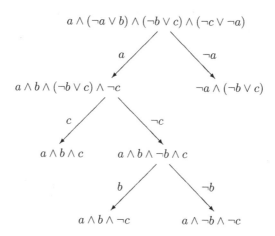

Fig. 1. Degree of contradiction in LP_m

Example 21. Let us consider the base $\Delta = \{a \wedge (\neg a \vee b) \wedge (\neg b \vee c) \wedge (\neg c \vee \neg a)\}$. Figure 1 reports a plan of minimal cost (given the standard atomic context) which purifies Δ. So the degree of contradiction of Δ is 3.

Note that what we define here is a measure of contradiction. To obtain a measure of coherence, as in the other sections, it is enough to define $I^{\mathcal{L}}_{klm_{(LP_m)}}(\Delta) = |\mathcal{L}| - d_C(\Delta)$ while considering the standard atomic test context.

Proposition 6. *Every knowledgebase that has a model $\in 3^{PS}$ has a finite degree of contradiction given any atomic or universal test context.*

Another example of instantiation with a paraconsistent logic can be obtained by taking the QC logic (see Section 8.2) as underlying logic. The revision operator in this case is the same one than for LP_m.

So this approach is highly configurable (underlying logic, test context), leading to several different particular measures of contradiction. It is less syntax-sensitive than the approaches in the previous sections, since a set of formulae is considered exactly as the conjunction of those formulae. This can be an advantage or a drawback, depending on the intended application. But the main advantage is that it does not trivialize when facing a single contradictory formula.

8   Model-Theoretic Analyses

Arguably, the most important logical language to analyse is that of classical logic. So far in this review we have considered a variety of approaches. Syntactic analysis is an obvious starting point for use with classical formulae. Useful alternatives for analysing classical formulae, which we have considered in previous sections, are based on information theory analysis, probability theory, and epistemic actions. Another alternative, which we consider in this section, is model-theoretic analysis. In this, inconsistent information is analysed in terms of the models of the information. Obviously this is not possible using classical models, because there is no model of a set of inconsistent formulae. To address this, we can use a three or four valued semantics, where one of the truth values denotes "inconsistency". In this section, we briefly consider an approach based on three-valued logic, and then review a framework based on quasi-classical logic which uses a four-valued semantics. Both of them can be used with a set of classical formulae.

8.1   Analysis of Three-Valued Models

In the proposal for three-valued models by [47], and a similar proposal by [26], a 3-interpretation is a truth assignment into {true,false} that does not map both a literal and its complement into false. This is extended to clauses so that a 3-interpretation satisfies a clause if and only if it satisfies some of the literals in the clause.

Example 22. For the set of formulae $\{\alpha, \neg\alpha \vee \neg\beta, \beta\}$, there are three 3-interpretations that satisfy: (X_1) $\alpha, \neg\alpha, \beta$ are true and $\neg\beta$ is false; (X_2) $\alpha, \beta, \neg\beta$ are true and $\neg\alpha$ is false; and (X_3) $\alpha, \neg\alpha, \beta, \neg\beta$ are true.

As shown by Grant [26], the 3-interpretations for a set of formulae can be analysed to obtained a degree of inconsistency. For this, the functions CCount and ICount are introduced. For a 3 interpretation X, CCount(X) gives the number of atoms in X for which either the atom or its complement is assigned false, and ICount(X) gives the number of atoms in X for which both the atom and its complement are assigned true. So CCount gives the number of atoms that are regarded as consistent, and ICount gives the number of atoms that are regarded as inconsistent, for X. In addition, LCount gives the total number of literals that are assigned by X. So LCount$(X) = $ CCount$(X) + (2 \times$ ICount$(X))$.

Definition 17. *The degree of inconsistency for a 3-interpretation X (in the finite case) is the ratio*

$$Inc_G(X) = \frac{\mathsf{CCount}(X)}{\mathsf{LCount}(X)}$$

Example 23. So, on the previous example, we have $Inc_G(X_1) = 1/3, Inc_G(X_2) = 1/3$ and $Inc_G(X_3) = 0$.

This definition has been generalized by Grant to deal with countable 3-interpretations, and to take into account the domain for the 3-interpretations. A problem with the proposal is that it takes into account "too many models". Consider the small knowledgebase in Example 22 for which there are three 3-interpretations. With quasi-classical (QC) logic reviewed in the next subsection, only the third 3-interpretation would be considered a model. The intuition behind this is that if we consider disjunctive syllogism, or equivalently, the resolution proof rule, as being applicable here, then neither the first 3-interpretation nor the second 3-interpretation would be valid models for this set of formulae.

As we shall see below, QC logic has a more constrained semantics and proof theory resulting in a "more appropriate" selection of models, and as a consequence, a measure of consistency can be defined with some useful properties. However, when we consider analysing first-order QC models, we will see how Grant's degree of inconsistency can also be harnessed.

8.2 Analysis of Quasi-classical Models

Quasi-classical (QC) logic, a form of paraconsistent logic can be used as the basis of a framework, to measure inconsistency [31, 32, 33]. In this, each inconsistent set of formulae is reflected in the quasi-classical models for the set, and then the inconsistency is measured in the models.

Review of Propositional QC Logic. We review the propositional version of quasi-classical logic (QC Logic) [9, 29]. The language of propositional QC logic is that of classical propositional logic.

Let α be an atom, and let $\sim$ be a complementation operation such that $\sim \alpha$ is $\neg\alpha$ and $\sim(\neg\alpha)$ is α. The $\sim$ operator is not part of the object language, but it makes some definitions clearer.

Definition 18. *Let* $\alpha_1 \vee .. \vee \alpha_n$ *be a clause that includes a disjunct* α_i *and* $n > 1$. *The* **focus** *of* $\alpha_1 \vee .. \vee \alpha_n$ *by* α_i, *denoted* $\otimes(\alpha_1 \vee .. \vee \alpha_n, \alpha_i)$, *is defined as the clause obtained by removing* α_i *from* $\alpha_1 \vee .. \vee \alpha_n$.

Example 24. Let $\alpha \vee \beta \vee \gamma$ be a clause where α, β, and γ are literals. Hence, $\otimes(\alpha \vee \beta \vee \gamma, \beta) = \alpha \vee \gamma$.

Focus is used to capture a form of resolution in the semantics of QC logic. A model in QC logic is a form of Herbrand model.

Definition 19. *Let* $\mathcal{A}$ *be a set of atoms. Let* $\mathcal{O} = \{+\alpha \mid \alpha \in \mathcal{A}\} \cup \{-\alpha \mid \alpha \in \mathcal{A}\}$ *be the set of objects defined as follows, where* $+\alpha$ *is a positive object, and* $-\alpha$ *is a negative object. We call any* $X \in \wp(\mathcal{O})$ *a* **QC model**. *So* X *can contain both* $+\alpha$ *and* $-\alpha$ *for some atom* α.

For each atom $\alpha \in \mathcal{L}$, and each $X \in \wp(\mathcal{O})$, $+\alpha \in X$ means that in X there is **a reason for** the belief α and $-\alpha \in X$ means that in X there is **a reason for** the belief $\neg\alpha$. This effectively gives us a four-valued semantics. Though for non-atomic formulae the semantics, defined next, is significantly different to [6].

Definition 20. *Let* $\models_s$ *be a satisfiability relation called* **strong satisfaction**. *For a model X, we define* $\models_s$ *as follows, where* $\alpha_1, ..., \alpha_n$ *are literals in $\mathcal{L}$, $n > 1$, and α is a literal in $\mathcal{L}$.*

$$X \models_s \alpha \text{ iff there is a reason for the belief } \alpha \text{ in } X$$

$$X \models_s \alpha_1 \vee ... \vee \alpha_n$$
$$\text{iff } [X \models_s \alpha_1 \text{ or } ... \text{ or } X \models_s \alpha_n]$$
$$\text{and } \forall i \text{ s.t. } 1 \leq i \leq n$$
$$[X \models_s \sim\alpha_i \text{ implies } X \models_s \otimes(\alpha_1 \vee ... \vee \alpha_n, \alpha_i)]$$

For $\alpha, \beta, \gamma \in \mathcal{L}$, we extend the definition as follows,

$$X \models_s \alpha \wedge \beta \text{ iff } X \models_s \alpha \text{ and } X \models_s \beta$$
$$X \models_s \neg\neg\alpha \vee \gamma \text{ iff } X \models_s \alpha \vee \gamma$$
$$X \models_s \neg(\alpha \wedge \beta) \vee \gamma \text{ iff } X \models_s \neg\alpha \vee \neg\beta \vee \gamma$$
$$X \models_s \neg(\alpha \vee \beta) \vee \gamma \text{ iff } X \models_s (\neg\alpha \wedge \neg\beta) \vee \gamma$$
$$X \models_s \alpha \vee (\beta \wedge \gamma) \text{ iff } X \models_s (\alpha \vee \beta) \wedge (\alpha \vee \gamma)$$
$$X \models_s \alpha \wedge (\beta \vee \gamma) \text{ iff } X \models_s (\alpha \wedge \beta) \vee (\alpha \wedge \gamma)$$

Definition 21. *For $X \in \wp(\mathcal{O})$ and $\Delta \in \wp(\mathcal{L})$, let $X \models_s \Delta$ denote that $X \models_s \alpha$ holds for every α in Δ. Let $\mathsf{QC}(\Delta) = \{X \in \wp(\mathcal{O}) \mid X \models_s \Delta\}$ be the set of QC models for Δ.*

A key feature of the QC semantics is that there is a model for any formula, and for any set of formulae.

Example 25. Let $\Delta = \{\neg\alpha \vee \neg\beta \vee \gamma, \neg\alpha \vee \gamma, \neg\gamma\}$, where $\alpha, \beta, \gamma \in \mathcal{A}$, and let $X = \{-\alpha, -\beta, -\gamma\}$. So $X \models_s \neg\alpha$, $X \models_s \neg\beta$ and $X \models_s \neg\gamma$. Also, $X \models_s \sim\gamma$. Hence, $X \models_s \neg\alpha \vee \gamma$, and $X \models_s \neg\alpha \vee \neg\beta$, and so, $X \models_s \neg\alpha \vee \neg\beta \vee \gamma$. Hence every formula in Δ is strongly satisfiable in X.

Strong satisfaction is used to define a notion of entailment for QC logic. There is also a natural deduction proof theory for propositional QC logic [29] and a semantic tableau version for first-order QC logic [30]. Entailment for QC logic for propositional CNF formulae is coNP-complete, and via a linear time transformation these formulae can be handled using classical logic theorem provers [53]. The definitions for QC models and for strong satisfaction provide us with the basic concepts for measuring inconsistency. QC logic exhibits the nice feature that no attention needs to be paid to a special form that the formulae in a set of premises should have. This is in contrast with other paraconsistent logics where two formulae identical by definition of a connective in classical logic may not yield the same set of conclusions. For example, in QC logic, β is entailed by both $\{(\neg\alpha \to \beta), \neg\alpha\}$ and $\{\alpha \vee \beta, \neg\alpha\}$ and γ is entailed by $\{\gamma \wedge \neg\gamma\}$ and $\{\gamma, \neg\gamma\}$. QC logic is much better behaved in this respect than other paraconsistent logics such as C_ω [17], and consistency-based logics such as [7]. Furthermore, the semantics of QC logic directly models inconsistent sets of formulae.

Definition 22. *Let* $\Delta \in \wp(\mathcal{L})$. *Let* $\mathsf{MQC}(\Delta) \subseteq \mathsf{QC}(\Delta)$ *be the set of minimal QC models for* Δ, *defined as follows:*

$$\mathsf{MQC}(\Delta) = \{X \in \mathsf{QC}(\Delta) \mid \text{if } Y \subset X, \text{ then } Y \notin \mathsf{QC}(\Delta)\}$$

Example 26. Consider the following sets of formulae.

$$\mathsf{MQC}(\{\alpha \wedge \neg\alpha, \alpha \vee \beta, \neg\alpha \vee \gamma\})$$
$$= \{\{+\alpha, -\alpha, +\beta, +\gamma\}\}$$
$$\mathsf{MQC}(\{\neg\alpha \wedge \alpha, \beta \vee \gamma\})$$
$$= \{\{+\alpha, -\alpha, +\beta\}, \{+\alpha, -\alpha, +\gamma\}\}$$
$$\mathsf{MQC}(\{\alpha \vee \beta, \neg\alpha \vee \gamma\})$$
$$= \{\{+\beta, +\gamma\}, \{+\alpha, +\gamma\}, \{-\alpha, +\beta\}\}$$

Whilst four-valued logic [6] also directly models inconsistent sets of formulae, there are too many Belnap models in many situations. Consider for example $\{\alpha \vee \beta, \neg\alpha\}$. There is one minimal QC model $\{-\alpha, +\beta\}$, but there are a number of Belnap models that satisfy this set. QC logic has a reduced number of models because of the constraint in the definition of strong satisfaction for disjunction that ensures that if the complement of a disjunct holds in the model, then the resolvent should also hold in the model. This strong constraint means that various other proposals for many-valued logic will tend to have more models for any given knowledgebase than QC logic. This increases the number of models that need to be analysed and it underspecifies the nature of the conflicts. These shortcomings of Belnap's four-valued logic also apply to three-valued logics such as 3-interpretations by [47], and a similar proposal by [26].

Measuring Coherence of QC Models. We now consider a measure of inconsistency called coherence [31]. The opinionbase of a QC model X is the set of atomic beliefs (atoms) for which there are reasons for or against in X, and the conflictbase of X is the set of atomic beliefs with reasons for and against in X.

Definition 23. *Let* $X \in \wp(\mathcal{O})$.

$$\mathsf{Conflictbase}(X) = \{\alpha \mid +\alpha \in X \text{ and } -\alpha \in X\}$$
$$\mathsf{Opinionbase}(X) = \{\alpha \mid +\alpha \in X \text{ or } -\alpha \in X\}$$

In finding the minimal QC models for a set of formulae, minimization of each model forces minimization of the conflictbase of each model. As a result of this minimization, if $\Delta \in \wp(\mathcal{L})$, and $X, Y \in \mathsf{MQC}(\Delta)$, then $\mathsf{Conflictbase}(X) = \mathsf{Conflictbase}(Y)$.

Increasing the size of the conflictbase, with respect to the size of the opinionbase, decreases the degree of coherence, as defined below.

Definition 24. *The* Coherence *function from* $\wp(\mathcal{O})$ *into* $[0,1]$, *is given below when* X *is non-empty, and* Coherence$(\emptyset) = 1$.

$$\text{Coherence}(X) = 1 - \frac{|\text{Conflictbase}(X)|}{|\text{Opinionbase}(X)|}$$

If Coherence$(X) = 1$, then X is a totally coherent, and if Coherence$(X) = 0$, then X is totally incoherent, otherwise, X is partially coherent/incoherent.

Example 27. Let $X \in$ MQC$(\{\neg\alpha \wedge \alpha, \beta \wedge \neg\beta, \gamma \wedge \neg\gamma\})$, $Y \in$ MQC$(\{\alpha, \neg\alpha \vee \neg\beta, \beta, \gamma\})$, and $Z \in$ MQC$(\{\neg\alpha, \beta, \neg\gamma\wedge\gamma\})$. So Coherence$(X) = 0$, Coherence$(Y) = 1/3$, and Coherence$(Z) = 2/3$.

Different minimal QC models for the same knowledgebase are not necessarily equally coherent, since different models for the same knowledgebase may have different opinionbases, though they will have the same conflictbase.

Example 28. Let $\Delta = \{\alpha, \neg\alpha, \beta \vee \gamma, \beta \vee \delta\}$, and let $X = \{+\alpha, -\alpha, +\beta\}$ and $Y = \{+\alpha, -\alpha, +\gamma, +\delta\}$. So MQC$(\Delta) = \{X, Y\}$, and Coherence$(X) = 1/2$ and Coherence$(Y) = 2/3$.

We extend coherence to knowledgebases as follows.

Definition 25. *Let* $\Delta \in \wp(\mathcal{L})$. *Assign* Coherence$(\Delta)$ *the maximum value in* $\{$Coherence$(X) \mid X \in$ MQC$(\Delta)\}$.

Example 29. Let $\Delta = \{\phi \wedge \neg\phi, \alpha \vee (\beta \wedge \gamma \wedge \delta)\}$ and $\Delta' = \{\phi \wedge \neg\phi, (\alpha \wedge \beta) \vee (\gamma \wedge \delta)\}$. Also let $X_1 = \{+\phi, -\phi, +\alpha\}$, $X_2 = \{+\phi, -\phi, +\beta, +\gamma, +\delta\}$, $Y_1 = \{+\phi, -\phi, +\alpha, +\beta\}$, and $Y_2 = \{+\phi, -\phi, +\gamma, +\delta\}$. So, MQC$(\Delta) = \{X_1, X_2\}$ and MQC$(\Delta') = \{Y_1, Y_2\}$. Also, Coherence$(X_1) = 1/2$, Coherence$(X_2) = 3/4$, Coherence$(Y_1) = 2/3$, and Coherence$(Y_2) = 2/3$. So Coherence$(\Delta) >$ Coherence(Δ').

Note that the definition of the coherence of a knowledgebase is an optimistic one, since it is based on the maximal coherence value of its models. But taking other aggregation functions could be interesting. For example taking a leximax function would allow for more discrimination. And taking the minimum or a mean can lead to other interesting measures. Such generalisations have not been considered yet, but can be a starting point for further work.

Significance Functions. The QC logic framework for measuring inconsistency has been extended to measuring the significance of inconsistencies arising in QC models, and thereby in sets of formulae [32]. The approach is based on specifying the relative significance of incoherent models using additional information, encoded as a mass assignment, which is defined below.

Definition 26. *A* **mass assignment** m *for* $\mathcal{O}$ *is a function from* $\wp(\mathcal{O})$ *into* $[0,1]$ *such that:*

(1) *If* $X \subseteq \mathcal{O}$ *and* Coherence$(X) = 1$, *then* $m(X) = 0$

(2) $\Sigma_{X \subseteq \mathcal{O}} \, m(X) = 1$

Condition 1 ensures mass is only assigned to models that contain conflicts and condition 2 ensures the total mass distributed sums to 1. A mass assignment can be localized on small subsets of $\mathcal{O}$, spread over many subsets of $\mathcal{O}$, or limited to large subsets of $\mathcal{O}$. A mass assignment can be regarded as a form of metaknowledge, and so it needs to be specified for an application area, where the application area is characterized by $\mathcal{O}$.

Example 30. Let $\mathcal{O} = \{+\alpha, -\alpha, +\beta, -\beta\}$. A mass assignment m is given by $m(\{+\alpha, -\alpha\}) = 0.2$ and $m(\{+\beta, -\beta\} = 0.8$. Another mass assignment m' is $m'(\{+\alpha, -\alpha\}) = 0.2$, $m'(\{+\alpha, -\alpha, -\beta\}) = 0.6$, and $m'(\{+\alpha, -\alpha, +\beta, -\beta\}) = 0.2$.

A significance function gives an evaluation of the significance of the conflicts in a QC model. This evaluation is in the range $[0,1]$ with 0 as least significant and 1 as most significant.

Definition 27. *Let m be a mass assignment for $\mathcal{O}$. A **significance function** for $\mathcal{O}$, denoted S, is a function ¿from $\wp(\mathcal{O})$ into $[0,1]$. A **mass-based significance function** for m, denoted S^m, is a significance function defined as follows for each $X \in \wp(\mathcal{O})$.*

$$S^m(X) = \Sigma_{Y \subseteq X} m(Y)$$

The definitions for mass assignment and mass-based significance correspond to mass assignment and belief functions (respectively) in Dempster-Shafer theory [66]. However, here they are used to formalise significance rather than uncertainty.

Proposition 7. *Let m be a mass assignment for $\mathcal{O}$. If S^m is a significance function, then the following property of simple cumulativity holds for all $X, Y \in \wp(\mathcal{O})$: $X \subseteq Y$ implies $S^m(X) \leq S^m(Y)$.*

Given that simple cumulativity holds, we see that specifying significance in terms of mass assignment is more efficient than directly specifying the significance.

Proposition 8. *Let m be a mass assignment for $\mathcal{O}$. Let S^m be a mass-based significance function. For all $X, Y \in \wp(\mathcal{O})$,*

$$(1)\ S^m(X \cup Y) \geq (S^m(X) + S^m(Y) - S^m(X \cap Y))$$
$$(2)\ S^m(X) + S^m(X^c) \leq 1$$

So mass-based significance is not additive. Also the remaining significance need not be for the complement of X (ie, X^c). Some may be assigned to models not disjoint from X. We now consider some constraints on mass assignments that give useful properties for mass-based significance.

Definition 28. *Let m be a mass assignment for $\mathcal{O}$. m is **focal** iff for all $X \in \wp(\mathcal{O})$ $m(X) \geq 0$ when $\mathsf{Coherence}(X) = 0$ and $m(X) = 0$ when $\mathsf{Coherence}(X) > 0$. m is **solo** iff for all $\{+\alpha, -\alpha\} \in \wp(\mathcal{O})$ $m(\{+\alpha, -\alpha\}) \geq 0$ and for all other $X \in \wp(\mathcal{O})$, $m(X) = 0$.*

A focal mass assignment puts the mass onto the totally incoherent models, and a solo mass assignment puts the mass on the smallest totally incoherent models. For all m, if m is a solo mass assignment for $\mathcal{O}$, then m is focal mass assignment for $\mathcal{O}$. Significance is additive for totally incoherent models when the mass assignment is solo.

Proposition 9. *Let m be a solo mass assignment for $\mathcal{O}$. Let S^m be a mass-based significance function and let $X \in \wp(\mathcal{O})$. If $\mathsf{Coherence}(X) = 0$, then $S^m(X) + S^m(X^c) = 1$.*

A useful feature of a focal mass-based significance function is that as the number of conflicts rises in a model, then the significance of the model rises. This is formalized by the following notion of conflict cumulativity.

Proposition 10. *Let m be a focal mass assignment for $\mathcal{O}$. If S^m is a significance function, then the following property of conflict cumulativity holds for all $X, Y \in \wp(\mathcal{O})$: $\mathsf{Conflictbase}(X) \subseteq \mathsf{Conflictbase}(Y)$ implies $S^m(X) \leq S^m(Y)$.*

We now extend the significance functions to knowledgebases. Since $\mathsf{MQC}(\Delta)$ is not necessarily a singleton, the significance for a set of formulae Δ is the lowest significance obtained for an $X \in \mathsf{MQC}(\Delta)$. This means we treat the information in Δ as a "disjunction" of QC models, and we regard each of those models as equally acceptable, or equivalently we regard each of those models as equally representative of the information in Δ. As with Definition 25, the following definition is an optimistic view, in the sense that taking the higher coherence value and lower significance value is better.

Definition 29. *Let $\Delta \in \wp(\mathcal{L})$. We extend the definition for a significance function S^m to knowledgebases as follows:*

$$S^m(\Delta) = \min(\{S^m(X) \mid X \in \mathsf{MQC}(\Delta)\})$$

Some knowledgebases have zero significance. Clearly, if $\Delta \nvdash \perp$, then $S^m(\Delta) = 0$.

Example 31. Let $\Omega = \{+\alpha, -\alpha, +\beta, -\beta, +\gamma, -\gamma\}$. Let $m(\{+\alpha, -\alpha, +\beta\}) = 0.3$, $m(\{+\alpha, -\alpha\}) = 0.6$, and $m(\{+\beta, -\beta, +\gamma\}) = 0.1$. So $S^m(\{\alpha \wedge \neg\alpha, \beta \vee \gamma\}) = 0.6$

In order to determine the set $\mathcal{O}$ for which a mass function is defined, we can use the delineation function as follows.

Definition 30. *For $\Delta \in \wp(\mathcal{L})$, $\mathsf{Delineation}(\Delta) = \{+\alpha, -\alpha \mid \alpha \in \mathsf{Atoms}(\Delta)\}$.*

Example 32. Let $\Delta_1 = \{\neg\alpha, \alpha \vee \beta, \neg\beta\}$, $\Delta_2 = \{\alpha \vee \beta, \neg\alpha \wedge \alpha\}$, and $\Delta_3 = \{\beta, \neg\alpha \vee \neg\beta\}$. Let $\mathcal{O} = \mathsf{Delineation}(\Delta_1 \cup \Delta_2 \cup \Delta_3) = \{+\alpha, -\alpha, +\beta, -\beta\}$. Also let $m(\{+\alpha, -\alpha, +\beta, -\beta\}) = 0.2$ and $m(\{+\alpha, -\alpha\}) = 0.8$. So $S^m(\Delta_1) = 1$, $S^m(\Delta_2) = 0.8$, and $S^m(\Delta_3) = 0$.

The next result captures a notion of monotonicity for mass-based significance.

Proposition 11. *Let $\Delta \in \wp(\mathcal{L})$ and $\alpha \in \mathcal{L}$. Let m be a mass assignment for* Delineation$(\Delta \cup \{\alpha\})$. *If S^m is a significance function, then $S^m(\Delta) \leq S^m(\Delta \cup \{\alpha\})$.*

Another approach to analysing the significance of inconsistency is possibility theory [19]. Let (ϕ, α) be a weighted formula where ϕ is a classical formula and $\alpha \in [0, 1]$. A possibilistic knowledgebase B is a set of weighted formulae. An α-cut of a possibilistic knowledgebase, denoted $B_{\geq \alpha}$, is $\{(\psi, \beta) \in B \mid \beta \geq \alpha\}$. The inconsistency degree of B, denoted $Inc(B)$, is the maximum value of α such that the α-cut is inconsistent. Possibility theory can also be used to extend classical logic, so that the proof rules propagate the possibility weights. This logic is called possibilistic logic and it offers complementary reasoning to that offered by QC logic.

Possibilistic logic and QC logic can be combined to give quasi-possibilistic logic [18]. This combined logic can handle plain conflicts taking place at the same level of certainty, as in QC logic, and take advantage of the stratification of the knowledgebase into certainty layers for introducing gradedness in conflict analysis, as in possibilistic logic. Moreover, quasi-possibilistic logic can be used to generalize the QC logic framework for measuring the degree and significance of inconsistencies.

Compromising on Inconsistency. In the following, we define the compromise relation to prefer knowledgebases with models with a greater opinionbase and a smaller conflictbase.

Definition 31. *Let $\Delta, \Delta' \in \wp(\mathcal{L})$. The **compromise relation**, denoted $\preceq$, is defined as follows:*

$$\Delta \preceq \Delta' \textit{ iff } \forall X \in \mathsf{MQC}(\Delta) \textit{ and } \exists Y \in \mathsf{MQC}(\Delta')$$
$$\textit{such that } \mathsf{Conflictbase}(X) \subseteq \mathsf{Conflictbase}(Y)$$
$$\textit{and } \mathsf{Opinionbase}(Y) \subseteq \mathsf{Opinionbase}(X)$$

We read $\Delta \preceq \Delta'$ as Δ is a preferred compromise to Δ'. Let $\Delta \prec \Delta'$ denote $\Delta \preceq \Delta'$ and $\Delta' \not\preceq \Delta$. Also let $\Delta \simeq \Delta'$ denote $\Delta \preceq \Delta'$ and $\Delta' \preceq \Delta$.

Example 33. If $\Delta = \{\alpha \wedge \beta \wedge \gamma\}$, and $\Delta' = \{\alpha \wedge \neg\alpha, \beta \vee \gamma\}$, then $\Delta \prec \Delta'$, since the following hold,

$$\mathsf{MQC}(\Delta) = \{\{+\alpha, +\beta, +\gamma\}\}$$
$$\mathsf{MQC}(\Delta') = \{\{+\alpha, -\alpha, +\beta\}, \{+\alpha, -\alpha, +\gamma\}\}$$

Example 34. If $\Delta = \{\alpha \wedge \neg\alpha \wedge \beta\}$ and $\Delta' = \{\beta\}$, then $\Delta \not\preceq \Delta'$, and $\Delta' \not\preceq \Delta$, since $\mathsf{MQC}(\Delta) = \{\{+\alpha, -\alpha, +\beta\}\}$ and $\mathsf{MQC}(\Delta') = \{\{+\beta\}\}$. Though $\mathsf{Coherence}(\Delta) < \mathsf{Coherence}(\Delta')$.

Example 35. If $\Delta = \{\alpha \vee \beta\}$ and $\Delta' = \{\alpha \vee \gamma\}$, then $\Delta \not\preceq \Delta'$, and $\Delta' \not\preceq \Delta$, since $\mathsf{MQC}(\Delta) = \{\{+\alpha\}, \{+\beta\}\}$ and $\mathsf{MQC}(\Delta') = \{\{+\alpha\}, \{+\gamma\}\}$. Though $\mathsf{Coherence}(\Delta) = \mathsf{Coherence}(\Delta')$.

We now motivate the compromise relation. For checking whether $\Delta \preceq \Delta'$ holds, we want to compare the minimal QC models of Δ with the minimal QC models of Δ'. First, we want each minimal QC model of Δ to have a conflictbase that is a subset of the conflictbase of each minimal QC model of Δ'. Second, we want for each minimal QC model X of Δ, for there to be a minimal QC model Y of Δ' such that the opinionbase of Y is a subset of the opinionbase of X. This is to ensure that Δ is not less conflicting than Δ' because Δ has less information in it. The reason we use the condition $\mathsf{Opinionbase}(Y) \subseteq \mathsf{Opinionbase}(X)$ rather than $Y \subseteq X$ is that if Y is more conflicting than X, then this will be reflected in the membership of Y but not in the membership of $\mathsf{Opinionbase}(Y)$. The reason we only seek one minimal QC model of Δ' for the comparison with all the minimal QC models of Δ is so that we can handle disjunction in Δ' as illustrated by Example 33. Useful properties of the compromise relation include it is a pre-order relation and it is syntax independent.

Let us note that, although the compromise relation and coherence function are logically independent notions, they are "philosophically" related, since in both case it is better when the conflicts decrease or when the information increase.

Measuring First-Order Inconsistency. Using the first-order version of quasiclassical logic [30], the QC logic framework for measuring inconsistency has been extended to first-order logic [33]. In first-order QC logic, the strong satisfaction relation is extended for universal and existential quantification.

- A QC model M, with a variable assignment A, satisfies a formula $\exists X \alpha$ if and only M satisfies α with some variable assignment A' that differs from A in at most the assignment for X.
- A QC model M, with a variable assignment A, satisfies a formula $\forall X \alpha$ if and only if M satisfies α with all variable assignments A' that differ from A in at most the assignment for X.

As with propositional QC logic, the models are a form of Herbrand model. The definitions for minimal QC model, for coherence, and for compromise relation can be used with first-order information.

In another development, the degree of inconsistency as presented by Grant [26], has been incorporated into the QC logic framework for measuring inconsistency in first-order information [25]. In this, both the language and the domain is taken into account. In the following, we restrict the presentation to a first-order language with constant symbols and no function symbols.

Definition 32. *For a language $\mathcal{L} = \langle \mathcal{P}, \mathcal{C} \rangle$, where $\mathcal{P}$ is a set of predicates represented in the form $P(n)$, with P being the predicate symbol and n being the arity of the predicate, $\mathcal{C}$ is a set of constants, and D is a domain,*

$$\mathsf{Groundatoms}(\mathcal{L}, D) = \{P(c_1, .., c_n) \mid P(n) \in \mathcal{P} \text{ and } c_1, .., c_n \in D\}$$

This is used for a measure as a ratio between 0 and 1 whose denominator is the total possible number of inconsistencies in the bistructure.

Definition 33. *The measure of inconsistency for a model M in the context of a language $\mathcal{L}$ and a domain D is given by the* Modellnc *function giving a value in $[0, 1]$ as follows.*

$$\mathsf{ModelInc}(M, \mathcal{L}, D) = \frac{|\mathsf{Conflictbase}(M)|}{|\mathsf{Groundatoms}(\mathcal{L}, D)|}$$

Example 36. Let $\mathcal{L} = \langle\{P(2), R(1)\}\{\}\rangle$. Hence, P is a binary predicate and R is a monadic predicate. Let $D = \{a, b, c\}$, and $M = \{+P(a, a), -P(a, a), +R(a), -R(b), +P(b, c)\}$, $|\mathsf{Groundatoms}(\mathcal{L}, D)| = 12$ (9 ground atoms for P and 3 for R). $\mathsf{Conflictbase}(M) = \{P(a, a)\}$. Hence, $\mathsf{ModelInc}(M, \mathcal{L}, D) = \frac{1}{12}$.

The Modellnc definition provides the basis of a richer framework for comparing first-order formulae. In the following example, we compare some inconsistent formulae. For this, we consider the preferred QC models: These are the minimal QC models with a minimal conflictbase. Given a language $\mathcal{L}$ and a domain D, the value of Modellnc is the same for all preferred QC models for a knowledgebase.

Example 37. Let $\mathcal{L} = \langle\{P(2)\}, \{\}\rangle$ and $D = \{a, b, c\}$.

1. $\Delta_1 = \{\forall x \forall y (P(x, y) \wedge \neg P(x, y))\}$ has one preferred QC model which is represented by $M_1 = \{+P(a, a), -P(a, a), \ldots, +P(c, c), -P(c, c)\}$, so $\mathsf{ModelInc}(M_1, \mathcal{L}, D) = \frac{9}{9} = 1$. M_1 is totally inconsistent.
2. $\Delta_2 = \{\exists x \exists y (P(x, y) \wedge \neg P(x, y))\}$ has 9 preferred QC models. One of them is $M_{21} = \{-P(a, b), + P(a, b)\}$, so $\mathsf{ModelInc}(M_{21}, \mathcal{L}, D) = \frac{1}{9}$.
3. $\Delta_3 = \{\forall x \exists y (P(x, y) \wedge \neg P(x, y))\}$ has 9 preferred QC models. One is $M_{31} = \{+P(a, a), - P(a, a), +P(b, c), -P(b, c), +P(c, a), -P(c, a)\}$, so $\mathsf{ModelInc}(M_{31}, \mathcal{L}, D) = \frac{3}{9} = \frac{1}{3}$.
4. $\Delta_4 = \{\exists x \forall y (P(x, y) \wedge \neg P(x, y))\}$ has 3 preferred QC models. One is $M_{41} = \{+P(b, a), - P(b, a), +P(b, b), -P(b, b), +P(b, c), -P(b, c)\}$, so $\mathsf{ModelInc}(M_{41}, \mathcal{L}, D) = \frac{3}{9} = \frac{1}{3}$.

Comparing quantified formulae is potentially important in diverse applications such as analysing systems specifications and analysing sources of information as a precursor to selecting sources for merging. These applications potentially include consideration of information that violates integrity constraints. This framework incorporates a notion of quasi-equality, which is weaker than classical equality, but can be formalized as an extension to QC logic for reasoning about integrity constraint violations.

9   Choosing a Good Measure

In the previous sections we have presented the existing measures of contradiction and of information for (possibly) inconsistent information. We have tried to highlight the advantages and the typical uses of each of its measures. In this section, we will try to compare them in order to highlight their differences and to guide the choice of a particular measure.

9.1   Logical Properties

A very convenient way to compare several approaches to the same problem is to propose a set of logical properties, aiming at capturing the typical wanted behaviours, and to compare the approaches with respect to the properties satisfied/dissatisfied.

Setting these properties have several advantages: first, it allows to "abstract" the discussion, i.e. to drop the discussion from the examples that are the particular approaches, for a discussion on the wanted behaviour for the given problem. Second, it gives a mean to compare the different approaches and to highlight the differences of behaviour and underlying rationale (in a much more explicit way that when building examples that are correctly handled by one approach and badly by an other). Thirdly, this allows us to define in one shot a whole family of methods (the ones that satisfy a set of properties), instead of only one particular one. And in the case where there is only one approach satisfying a set of properties, then it usually gives a nice comprehensive definition of the approach.

Setting a set of properties have usually accelerated the development of a corresponding field. We can cite for example the work of Arrow for social choice theory (voting theory) [3], Savage for decision theory [64]. In artificial intelligence, the same happened for non-monotonic inference relations [51, 43, 46], belief revision [1, 24], and belief merging [62, 41, 42].

So, it might be of great interest to find a set of logical properties for information measures (that allows non-trivial information content for inconsistent information), and for contradiction measures.

Information Measures. Lozinskii [49] gives a set of properties that a measure of quantity of information should satisfy.

He stated those properties in first order logic. Recasted in propositional logic, those conditions can be summarized as follows. I is a function from $\mathcal{L}_{PS}$ to a numeric scale with least element 0 such that:

1. If $\Delta = \emptyset$, then $I(\Delta) = 0$
2. If $\Delta = \{a \in \mathcal{L}_{PS}\} \cup \{\neg a \mid a \in \mathcal{L}_{PS}\}$, then $I(\Delta) = 0$
3. If Δ is consistent, and α is a consequence of Δ, then $I(\Delta \cup \{\alpha\}) = I(\Delta)$
4. If $\Delta \cup \{\alpha\}$ is consistent and α is not a consequence of Δ, then $I(\Delta \cup \{\alpha\}) > I(\Delta)$
5. If Δ is consistent and α is a consequence of Δ, then $I(\Delta \cup \{\neg\alpha\}) < I(\Delta)$
6. If $\forall a \in \mathcal{L}_{PS}$ $\Delta \vdash a$ or $\Delta \vdash \neg a$, then $\forall \Delta'$ $I(\Delta) \geq I(\Delta')$

The first condition states that an empty knowledgebase contains no information. The second condition states that if a knowledgebase contains all the atoms and their negation of the language, it gives also no information. In the first condition it was caused by a lack of information, in the second one it is because of an overload of (contradictory) information. The third condition states that adding a consequence of a knowledgebase does not change anything of the information content. That implies, in particular, an irrelevance of syntax, since there is no difference between an explicit formula of Δ and an implicit one[4]. It says also that several occurrences of the same formula (or several way to derive the same formula), do not improve the information content. The fourth condition says that adding a (consistent) formula that is not a consequence of a consistent knowledgebase increases the amount of information. The fifth condition says that adding a (consistent) formula that contradicts a consistent knowledgebase decreases the amount of information. This condition relates the contradiction of a base and its information content. Thus, as expected, the introduction of a contradiction decreases the amount of information. The sixth condition states that a complete knowledgebase, thus having exactly one classical model, has the highest possible information content. This condition is quite natural, and quite close to the idea of Shannon's information theory.

It is not surprising that the information measure $I_l(\Delta)$ of section 5 satisfies those conditions.

Knight in [39, 38] propose also a set of logical properties for measures of quantity of information. Most of them are equivalent to Lozinskii's ones. The different ones are:

7. $0 \leq I(\Delta) \leq |PS|$
8. $I(\{\alpha\}) = 0$ if and only if $\vdash \alpha$ or $\vdash \neg\alpha$
9. If Δ and Δ' are logically equivalent[5], then $I(\Delta) = I(\Delta')$

Condition 7 simply puts bounds on the value of the information measure. Putting 0 as minimum is quite natural (and is already asked in Lozinskii's conditions). So the addition of this property is to put a maximum on the value. It is clear that in a finite setting, the information value must have an upper bound, but we are not sure that giving a precise bound is useful (taking any strictly increasing function of $|PS|$ would basically give the same thing, as acknowledge by Knight [39]). Condition 8 states that the only singleton knowledgebase having null information value are tautologies and contradictions. Condition 9 is an irrelevance of syntax condition, basically saying that we can exchange any formula of a knowledgebase by a logically equivalent one without changing the amount of information in the knowledgebase.

Those two last conditions are not similar to the previous ones. They basically say that information measures can cope with inconsistency only because we work

---

[4] An explicit formula of a knowledge base is a formula $\alpha \in \Delta$. An implicit formula of a knowledge base is a formula $\alpha \notin \Delta$ and $\Delta \vdash \alpha$.

[5] We say that two knowledgebases are logically equivalent if for each formula of a base, there is a formula in the other base that is logically equivalent to the first one.

with sets of formulae. But if one is faced with a unique inconsistent formula, it continues to have a null information value. So it is a very strong assumption that forbids consideration of inconsistent formulae. Whereas the information measures proposed by Knight and Lozinskii satisfy those two properties, the one proposed by Konieczny et al. [40] do not satisfy them, since they differentiate the information content of inconsistent formulae.

In addition, there are also two conditions on the relation between the language and the information value. The first one is given by Lozinskii in [48], the second one by Knight [39, 38].

9. If $PS \subseteq PS'$, then $max_{\Delta \in \mathcal{L}_{PS}}(I(\Delta)) \leq max_{\Delta' \in \mathcal{L}_{PS'}}(I(\Delta'))$
10. If $PS \subseteq PS'$, then $I_{\Delta \in \mathcal{L}_{PS}}(\Delta) = I_{\Delta \in \mathcal{L}_{PS'}}(\Delta)$

Condition 10 says that extending the language does not change the information content of a given knowledgebase. But, as expected, condition 9 says that extending the language allows to express more things, and so the upper bound of the information measure in the extended language is higher than the one in the original language.

One can think of other meaningful conditions, but the ones given here seem to be a good place to begin.

Contradiction Measures. The story is not the same for contradiction measures. It is much more difficult to state properties for contradiction measures than for information ones. Since classical logic is not the right tool for talking about inconsistency, it is difficult to state interesting logical properties using only classical logic.

In order to state the wanted properties, one should need to use a paraconsistent logic. But there are a lot of different paraconsistent logics (see e.g. [28, 13, 60]), so choosing a particular logic is already a real, non-trivial commitment. So one has to be careful for avoiding stating *ad hoc* properties, according to a given paraconsistent logic.

This maybe explains why there is not yet any proposal of such set of properties for contradiction measures. But this is an interesting and important open question.

9.2   Comparison of the Measures

Let us first talk about the information measures presented in this paper. For comparing Lozinskii's measure (section 5) and Knight's ones (section 6.2), Let us quote Knight [39]:

> "For when we look at proper subsets of Γ we fail to account for the affect the remaining sentences of Γ have on the sentences of the subset. Thus the author asserts the superiority of $I_{k1}^{\mathcal{L}}$ - and, indeed, $I_{k2}^{\mathcal{L}}$ - over such information measures as Lozinskii's [48, 49] that analyze the information of a set by breaking it up into its maximal consistent subsets."

So, one drawback of Lozinskii' measure is that it is a "local" one, that takes into account subsets of the whole base, but not the base as a whole for the computation of the measure of information, whereas Knight's measures are "global" ones since they keep the knowledgebase in one piece. However, the maximal consistent subset semantics seem to be natural for a lot of people (it is for example the basis for several inference relations [52, 5, 4]), and if one looks at an inconsistent knowledgebase as a knowledgebase "polluted" by some false sentences, then trying to find the "plausible" information in the maximal consistent subsets can be sensible. Finally, as underlined in section 9.1, those two measures work with sets of formulae (with a single inconsistent formula still having a null information value). This behaviour can be discussed, and can be interesting for some applications. But, in some cases, one can wish to try to get some information from an inconsistent formula. In this case, the previous measures cannot be used. In this case, the information measure proposed by Konieczny et al. (section 7), based on epistemic tests, still succeeds in extracting some non-null information from a single inconsistent formula.

As for contradiction measures, the main measures presented in this paper are, first the scoring functions of section 4. The obtained score ordering allows to compare the contradiction level of different knowledgebases. Another contradiction measure is given by Knight's $\eta-$consistency (section 6.1). The idea here is also based on minimal inconsistent subsets, and, roughly, a knowledgebase is more contradictory than another one, if the contradictions (minimal inconsistent subsets) require more formulae. Intuitively, the more formulae are needed to produce a contradiction, the less the contradiction is strong. Knight illustrates this idea on the lottery paradox: saying that, if there is a sufficiently large number of tickets, a given lottery ticket is[6] not winning, but it is a fact that one of the tickets will win the lottery. That can be written: $\Gamma = \{\neg w_1, \ldots, \neg w_n, w_1 \vee \ldots \vee w_n\}$. This knowledgebase is clearly inconsistent, but it seems sensible to say that the bigger n, the more tolerable the inconsistency. As for information measures, the two previous approaches trivialize when they are applied to singleton knowledgebase, i.e. to only one formula. They both give the maximal contradiction value to an inconsistent formula. And, even more arguably than for information measures, it is important to be able to discriminate several inconsistent formulae. This can be achieved by the degree of contradiction proposed by Konieczny et al. (section 7), that do not take the formulae as atomic inconsistencies, but take propositional variables to this aim. In this framework, it is the (maximum) number of tests required for get rid of all inconsistencies that determine the degree of contradiction. In the same way, Grant's degree of inconsistency (section 8.1) and Hunter's degree of coherence take the propositional variable as atomic inconsistency, so they can cope with singleton inconsistent knowledgebase. Those two approaches can be used to measure the amount of contradiction in a knowledgebase. But in both cases, the amount of contradiction is related to the amount of information of the base. Basically, a knowledgebase is less contradictory than another one if it

---

[6] more exactly it is rational to believe that a given (random) ticket is not winning.

has a model that has a lowest noise[7] ratio than the models of the second one. The main difference between the two approaches lies in the underlying chosen logic. To be able to talk about models for classically inconsistent knowledgebase, one has to choose an underlying paraconsistent logic. Grant starts from Levesque 3-valued logic [47, 26], whereas Hunter starts from quasi-classical logic [9, 29]. Quasi-classical logic seems more adequate to handle inconsistent information (it has, for example, a more constrained semantics), so the degree of coherence of Hunter may seem more adequate that Grant's degree of inconsistency. Finally let us note the degree of significance of section 8.2, that allows us to compare the amount of contradiction in several knowledgebases when the potential contradictions are not as important. It often happens in real life that some parts of the agents beliefs are more important than others[8], so contradictions that concern the important beliefs are much more problematic than the ones concerning the less important ones. So if one can weight the importance of the (worries induced by potential) contradictions, the degree of significance allows us to measure the contradiction amount of a given knowledgebase.

10   Towards Applications

Formalisation of analyses of inconsistency information has been driven by more intelligent techniques for handling inconsistent information in applications. In this section, we briefly review two emerging applications, namely negotiation between agents and comparing heterogeneous sources of information, using two of the techniques we have presented in this review.

10.1   Negotiation Between Agents

For the following example of negotiation, we will keep the domain knowledge separate from the perspectives of the participants. In other words, we will consider the domain knowledge as being correct and not subject to negotiation. This will allow us to focus our attention on the perspectives of the participants. Note, we are not presenting a general framework for negotiation between agents. Rather we are trying to show how measurement of inconsistency can be used to evaluate each cycle in a negotiation to gauge how well the negotiation is proceeding. Formalisation of multi-agent negotiation is currently the subject of much research (see for example [2, 56]). Potentially, measures of inconsistency can be incorporated in an existing formalisation for multi-agent negotiation.

Example 38. Consider three members of a family who are discussing their wishes for their next family car. Let the domain knowledge Ψ be:

---

[7] amount of "contradiction" compared to the amount of "information".

[8] For example, an agent can posses some beliefs that have no importance for its goals, thus having very small importance.

```
red → fast
fast → ¬fuelEfficient
offRoad → expensive
sporty → (expensive ∧ (black ∨ red ∨ white))
¬expensive → under$20K
cabriolet → ¬bigCapacity
fuelEfficient → ¬offRoad
```

Let the initial preferences (requirements or demands) for each family member (participant 1, participant 2, and participant 3) be represented by Φ_1^1, Φ_1^2 and Φ_1^3 respectively.

$$\Phi_1^1 = \{\text{red}, \text{offRoad}\}$$
$$\Phi_1^2 = \{\neg\text{expensive}, \text{fuelEfficient}\}$$
$$\Phi_1^3 = \{\text{sporty}, \text{cabriolet}, \text{bigCapacity}\}$$

So the starting point of the discussions is captured by Δ_1.

$$\Delta_1 = \Psi \cup \Phi_1^1 \cup \Phi_1^2 \cup \Phi_1^3$$

Let S_1 be the scoring function for Δ_1. Now consider S_1 for some subsets of Δ_1.

$$S_1(\{\text{red}\}) = 1 \qquad S_1(\{\text{bigCapacity}\}) = 1$$
$$S_1(\{\text{sporty}\}) = 1 \qquad S_1(\{\text{offRoad}\}) = 2$$
$$S_1(\{\text{fuelEfficient}\}) = 2 \; S_1(\{\neg\text{expensive}\}) = 2$$
$$S_1(\{\text{cabriolet}\}) = 1 \qquad S_1(\{\text{red}, \text{bigCapacity}\}) = 2$$

$$S_1(\Phi_1^1) = S_1(\{\text{red}, \text{offRoad}\}) = 3$$
$$S_1(\Phi_1^2) = S_1(\{\neg\text{expensive}, \text{fuelEfficient}\}) = 4$$
$$S_1(\Phi_1^3) = S_1(\{\text{sporty}, \text{cabriolet}, \text{bigCapacity}\}) = 2$$
$$S_1(\Delta_1) = 5$$

We see from S_1 that each of the preferences is individually inconsistent with the domain knowledge. We also see that Φ_1^2 has the highest score (4) of the initial preferences and it would be a good starting point for discussion.

Suppose after some discussion, Φ_1^1 is changed to Φ_2^1 by participant 1, Φ_1^2 to Φ_2^2 by participant 2, and Φ_1^3 to Φ_2^3 by participant 3, as follows. How this multi-agent discussion is conducted is beyond the scope of this review. Potential formalisms for this include [2, 56]. However, we do assume that aim of the multi-agent discussion is that some of the agents have weakened their positions. The measurement of inconsistency is intended to monitor this.

$$\Phi_2^1 = \{\text{red} \vee \text{black}, \text{sporty} \vee \text{offRoad}\}$$
$$\Phi_2^2 = \{\neg\text{expensive}\}$$
$$\Phi_2^3 = \{\text{sporty}, \text{bigCapacity}\}$$

This intermediate point is captured by Δ_2.

$$\Delta_2 = \Psi \cup \Phi_2^1 \cup \Phi_2^2 \cup \Phi_2^3$$

Let S_2 be the scoring function for Δ_2. Now consider S_2 for some subsets of Δ_2.

$$S_2(\{\texttt{sporty}\}) = 1$$
$$S_2(\{\neg\texttt{expensive}\}) = 2$$
$$S_2(\{\texttt{sporty} \vee \texttt{offRoad}\}) = 1$$
$$S_2(\Delta_2) = 2$$

We see that $S_2 < S_1$. Furthermore, we see that the preference for $\neg\texttt{expensive}$ is the most problematical.

Now suppose after further discussion, Φ_2^2 is changed to Φ_3^2 by participant 2, and Φ_2^3 is changed to Φ_3^3 by participant 3.

$$\Phi_3^1 = \{\texttt{red} \vee \texttt{black}, \texttt{sporty} \vee \texttt{offRoad}\}$$
$$\Phi_3^2 = \{\texttt{interestFreeCredit}, \texttt{diesel}\}$$
$$\Phi_3^3 = \{\texttt{sporty} \vee \texttt{offRoad}, \texttt{bigCapacity}\}$$

This final situation is captured by Δ_3.

$$\Delta_3 = \Psi \cup \Phi_3^1 \cup \Phi_3^2 \cup \Phi_3^3$$

Let S_3 be the scoring function for Δ_3. We see that $S_3 < S_2$. Also for all $\Gamma \in \Delta_3$, we have $S_3(\Gamma) = 0$. So Δ_3 could be regarded as an acceptable end-point.

In the above example, we see that the scoring functions allow us to focus on the more problematical data, and use this to facilitate conflict resolution.

10.2   Comparing Heterogeneous Sources

We now return to the problem of comparing sources, discussed in the introduction. Here we consider how the compromise relation introduced in Section 4 can be used directly to reject sources of information that are too inconsistent. A threshold can be fixed and any source of information that is above this threshold is automatically rejected. For example, if we set the threshold at 0.5, then any report represented as a set of formulae Φ that together with background knowledge Ψ is such that coherence of $\Phi \cup \Psi < 0.5$, then "more than half of the information" in Φ is contradictory with respect to the background knowledge. Similarly, for infinite models, a selected profile can be used as a threshold for rejection of sources of information.

Definition 34. *Let $\Phi_i, \Phi_j, \Psi \in \wp(\mathcal{L})$. A **qualified compromise relation** $\preceq_\Psi$ is defined as follows, where Φ_i and Φ_j are sources and Ψ is background knowledge.*

$$\Phi_i \preceq_\Psi \Phi_j \ \textit{iff} \ \Phi_i \cup \Psi \preceq \Phi_j \cup \Psi$$

When using a qualified compromise relation, there may be an assumption that the background knowledge is correct, and we rank sources by their conflicts with the background knowledge.

Example 39. Let Δ incorporate a standard axiomatization for the equality predicate, denoted =, and the "less-than-or-equal-to" predicate, denoted $\leq$. Also suppose we know that the list price of a new Ferrari Maranello is $\$200K$. We represent this as $\text{Cost(Ferrari)} = \$200K$, and add this to the following background knowledge in Δ.

$$\forall X \; \text{Cost(X)} \leq \$1K \rightarrow \text{Cost(X)} \leq \$2K$$
$$\forall X \; \text{Cost(X)} \leq \$2K \rightarrow \text{Cost(X)} \leq \$3K$$
$$\vdots$$
$$\forall X \; \text{Cost(X)} \leq \$199K \rightarrow \text{Cost(X)} \leq \$200K$$

In general, the lower the purported value of a Ferrari in a report, the greater the number of formulae in the background knowledge that are contradicted. Now consider Report 1 with the information $\text{Cost(Ferrari)} = \$150K$ and Report 2 with the information $\text{Cost(Ferrari)} = \$15K$. With this, we see Report 1 is a preferred compromise to Report 2, and that Report 1 with Δ is more coherent than Report 2 with Δ.

$$\text{Cost(Ferrari)} = \$150K \preceq_\Delta \text{Cost(Ferrari)} = \$15K$$

We could extend the above example so that we have the following holding for any numbers V_1 and V_2 when $V_1 \leq V_2$.

$$\text{Cost(Ferrari)} = \$V_1 \preceq_\Delta \text{Cost(Ferrari)} = \$V_2$$

The situation above is reflected in many real-world situations where there is a range of possible values for the facts that are being reported, and the facts that take values "further away" from those delineated by the background knowledge are regarded as more inconsistent.

As an alternative approach to dealing with heterogeneous sources, we may assume that the sources are all individually consistent with the background knowledge, but combinations of sources are inconsistent. The $\preceq$ or $\preceq_\psi$ relations may then be used over all possible unions of sources. In either case, we may then choose to select the n least compromised sources of information. These n sources could then be used in some form of merging process such as arbitration [41, 42].

11   Discusssion

Current techniques for measuring the degree of inconsistency in a set of formulae are underdeveloped. There has been a marked increased interest in the past three years as reflected by new published articles on the subject. This has resulted in a range of interesting proposals based on syntactic coherence, information theory, probability theory, epistemic actions, and three/four-valued models. But it is a subject that is very much in flux. At this stage it is unclear what would constitute an ideal framework for measuring inconsistency: Though it seems that there is no unique measure of inconsistency. There are good arguments for a variety of factors to be taken into account.

Concerning the degree of inconsistency, there are two main ideas developed independently in the approaches presented in this paper. The first idea is to state that the importance of the conflict is reflected by the number of formulae of the knowledgebases implied in the contradiction. The more formulae needed, the less important the conflict. Another idea is to state that the importance of the conflict is described by the number of atoms on which we have contradictory information. An interesting question, in the quest for definition of "the" degree of consistency, is to know if it is possible to meld these two ideas, in order to take these two sensible intuitions into account.

Suggestions for desirable properties are at a tentative stage. More interrelationships between proposals need to be established. And perhaps most significantly, potential applications need to be developed. Since the more we know about how they can or should be used, the better we can develop the formalisms. In addition, there is a need to consider how some other formalisms in knowledge representation and reasoning are relevant to the subject.

Other formalisms in knowledge representation and reasoning that touch on the subject include: Diagnostic systems for which there are preferences for certain kinds of consistent subsets of inconsistent information [36, 61]; Belief revision for which epistemic entrenchment is an ordering over formulae which reflects the preference for which formulae to give up in case of inconsistency [24] and the Dalal distance which provides a model-theoretic characterisation of how inconsistent a formulae is with a consistent set of formulae [15]; Coherence-based reasoning (for drawing inferences from inconsistent information) for which there is a preference for inferences from some consistent subsets (e.g. [11, 7]); Paraconsistent logics for which there is an object operator denoting "acceptable" inconsistency that can be used to differentiate acceptable and unacceptable inconsistencies [13]; Approximate entailment for which two sequences of entailment relation are defined (the first is sound but not complete, and the second is complete but not sound) which converge to classical entailment [65]; and Partial consistency checking for which checking is terminated after the search space exceeds a threshold and so gives a measure of partial consistency of the data [54]. Whilst none of these proposals provide a direct definition for degree of inconsistency, there are clearly some important issues in common that could be explored.

As to the choice of a particular degree of inconsistency or degree of information, one important criterion, not mentionned until now, is its computational complexity. So a study of the complexity of the different proposals exposed in this paper should be a valuable work. And an open question is to know if there is a correlation between the discriminating power of the different approaches and their computational compelxity.

Finally, an interesting proposal for analysing the coherence of explanations could form an interesting development of the consistency-based analysis in Section 4. In the process of finding an explanation for some observations, there may be multiple theories that are mutually incompatible, but each constitutes an explanation for the observations. Consider a set of observation and a set of possible explanations Δ. A set $\Gamma \subseteq \Delta$ is a support for O in some context I iff $\Gamma \cup I$ implies O and no subset does so. Now we may have a number of these supports for O, and we may wish to evaluate the quality of the formulae that are used in them. In [45], a general framework for measuring support coherence is based on the average use of formulae in the supports. Highly coherent theories are those whose formulae that are tightly coupled to accounts for observations, while low coherence theories may contain disjointed and isolated statements.

Acknowledgements

The authors are grateful to Eliezer Lozinskii, Kevin M. Knight, and the anonymous referees for helpful feedback on this paper. The second author is supported by the IUT de Lens, the Université d'Artois, the Région Nord/Pas-de-Calais, and by the European Community FEDER Program. Both authors are grateful to the Royal Society and CNRS for funding travel while collaborating on this review.

References

1. C. Alchourrón, P. Gärdenfors, and D. Makinson. On the logic of theory change: partial meet contraction and revision functions. *Journal of Symbolic Logic*, 50:510–530, 1985.
2. L. Amgoud, S. Parsons, and N. Maudet. Arguments, dialogue, and negotiation. In *Proceedings of the 14th European Conference on Artificial Intelligence (ECAI'2000)*, 2000.
3. K. J. Arrow. *Social choice and individual values*. Wiley, New York, second edition, 1963.
4. C. Baral, S. Kraus, J. Minker, and V. S. Subrahmanian. Combining knowledge bases consisting of first-order theories. *Computational Intelligence*, 8(1):45–71, 1992.
5. C. Baral, S. Kraus, and J. Minker. Combining multiple knowledge bases. *IEEE Transactions on Knowledge and Data Engineering*, 3(2):208–220, 1991.
6. N. Belnap. A useful four-valued logic. In G Epstein, editor, *Modern Uses of Multiple-valued Logic*, pages 8–37. Reidel, 1977.
7. S. Benferhat, D. Dubois, and H. Prade. Argumentative inference in uncertain and inconsistent knowledge bases. In *Proceedings of Uncertainty in Artificial Intelligence*, pages 1449–1445. Morgan Kaufmann, 1993.
8. S. Benferhat, D. Dubois, and H. Prade. An overview of inconsistency-tolerant inferences in prioritized knowledge bases. In *Fuzzy Sets, Logic and Reasoning about Knowledge*, volume 15 of *Applied Logic Series*, pages 395–417. Kluwer, 1999.
9. Ph. Besnard and A. Hunter. Quasi-classical logic: Non-trivializable classical reasoning ¿from inconsistent information. In C Froidevaux and J Kohlas, editors, *Symbolic and Quantitative Approaches to Uncertainty*, volume 946 of *Lecture Notes in Computer Science*, pages 44–51, 1995.

10. Ph. Besnard and A. Hunter. Introduction to actual and potential contradictions. In Ph Besnard and A. Hunter, editors, *Handbook of Defeasible Resoning and Uncertainty Management Systems*, volume 2, pages 1–9. Kluwer, 1998. (Series editors: Dov Gabbay and Ph Smets).

11. G. Brewka. Preferred subtheories: An extended logical framework for default reasoning. In *Proceedings of the Eleventh International Conference on Artificial Intelligence*, pages 1043–1048, 1989.

12. L. Cholvy and C. Garion, Querying Several Conflicting Databases. *Journal Of Applied Non-Classical Logics*, 14(3):295–327, 2004.

13. W. Carnielli and J. Marcos. A taxonomy of C systems. In *Paraconsistency: The Logical Way to the Inconsistent*, pages 1–94. Marcel Dekker, 2002.

14. C. Chesnevar, A. Maguitman, and R. Loui. Logical models of argument. *ACM Computing Surveys*, 32:337–383, 2001.

15. M. Dalal. Investigations into a theory of knowledge base revision: Preliminary report. In *Proceedings of the 7th National Conference on Artificial Intelligence (AAAI'88)*, pages 3–7. MIT Press, 1988.

16. A. Darwiche and J. Pearl. On the logic of iterated belief revision. *Artificial Intelligence*, 89:1–29, 1997.

17. N. C. da Costa. On the theory of inconsistent formal systems. *Notre Dame Journal of Formal Logic*, 15:497–510, 1974.

18. D. Dubois, S. Konieczny, and H. Prade. Quasi-possibilistic logic and its measures of information and conflict. *Fundamenta Informaticae*, 57:101–125, 2003.

19. D. Dubois, J. Lang, and H. Prade. Possibilistic logic. In *Handbook of Logic in Artificial Intelligence and Logic Programming*, volume 3, pages 439–513. Oxford University Press, 1994.

20. D. Dubois and H. Prade. Properties of measures of information in evidence and possibility theories. *Fuzzy Sets and Systems*, 24:161–182, 1987. Reprinted in Fuzzy Sets and Systems, supplement to Vol. 100, 35-49, 1999.

21. M. Elvang-Goransson and A. Hunter. Argumentative logics: Reasoning from classically inconsistent information. *Data and Knowledge Engineering*, 16:125–145, 1995.

22. N. Friedman and J. Y. Halpern. Belief revision: a critique. In *Proceedings of the Fifth International Conference on Principles of Knowledge Representation and Reasoning (KR'96)*, pages 421–431, 1996.

23. D. Gabbay and A. Hunter. Making inconsistency respectable 1: A logical framework for inconsistency in reasoning. In *Fundamentals of Artificial Intelligence*, volume 535 of *Lecture Notes in Computer Science*, pages 19–32. Springer, 1991.

24. P. Gärdenfors. *Knowledge in Flux*. MIT Press, 1988.

25. J. Grant and A. Hunter. Measuring inconsistency in knowledgebases. Technical report, UCL Department of Computer Science, 2004.

26. J. Grant. Classifications for inconsistent theories. *Notre Dame Journal of Formal Logic*, 19:435–444, 1978.

27. J. Hintikka. On semantic information. *Information and Inference*, pages 3–27, 1970.

28. A. Hunter. Paraconsistent logics. In Dov Gabbay and Ph Smets, editors, *Handbook of Defeasible Resoning and Uncertainty Management Systems*, volume 2, pages 11–36. Kluwer, 1998.

29. A. Hunter. Reasoning with contradictory information using quasi-classical logic. *Journal of Logic and Computation*, 10:677–703, 2000.

30. A. Hunter. A semantic tableau version of first-order quasi-classical logic. In *Quantitative and Qualitative Approaches to Reasoning with Uncertainty*, LNCS. Springer, 2001. 544–556.

31. A. Hunter. Measuring inconsistency in knowledge via quasi-classical models. In *Proceedings of the 18th National Conference on Artificial Intelligence (AAAI'2002)*, pages 68–73. MIT Press, 2002. ISBN 0-262-51129-0.

32. A. Hunter. Evaluating the significance of inconsistency. In *Proceedings of the International Joint Conference on AI (IJCAI'03)*, pages 468–473, 2003.

33. A. Hunter. Measuring inconsistency in first-order knowledge. Technical report, UCL Department of Computer Science, 2003.

34. A. Hunter. Logical comparison of inconsistent perspectives using scoring functions. *Knowledge and Information Systems Journal*, 2004. (in press).

35. J. Kemeny. A logical measure function. *Journal of Symbolic Logic*, 18:289–308, 1953.

36. J. De Kleer and B. Williams. Diagnosing multiple faults. *Artificial Intelligence*, 32:97–130, 1987.

37. K. M. Knight. Measuring inconsistency. *Journal of Philosophical Logic*, 31:77–98, 2001.

38. K. M. Knight. *A theory of inconsistency*. PhD thesis, The university of Manchester, 2002.

39. K. M. Knight. Two information measures for inconsistent sets. *Journal of Logic, Language and Information*, 12:227–248, 2003.

40. S. Konieczny, J. Lang, and P. Marquis. Quantifying information and contradiction in propositional logic through epistemic tests. In *Proceedings of the 18th International Joint Conference on Artificial Intellignce (IJCAI'03)*, pages 106–111, 2003.

41. S. Konieczny and R. Pino-Pérez. On the logic of merging. In *Proceedings of the Sixth International Conference on Principles of Knowledge Representation and Reasoning (KR98)*, pages 488–498. Morgan Kaufmann, 1998.

42. S. Konieczny and R. Pino-Pérez. Merging information under constraints: a qualitative framework. *Journal of Logic and Computation*, 12(5):773–808, 2002.

43. S. Kraus, D. Lehmann, and M. Magidor. Nonmonotonic reasoning, preferential models and cumulative logics. *Artificial Intelligence*, 44:167–207, 1990.

44. T. Kuipers, editor. *What is closer-to-the-truth?* Rodopi, Amsterdam, 1987.

45. R. Kwok, N. Foo, and A. Nayak. Coherence of laws. In *Proceedings of the International Joint Conference on AI (IJCAI'03)*, 2003.

46. D. Lehmann and M. Magidor. What does a conditional knowledge base entail? *Artificial Intelligence*, 55:1–60, 1992.

47. H. Levesque. A logic of implicit and explicit belief. In *Proceedings of the National Conference on Artificial Intelligence (AAAI'84)*, pages 198–202, 1984.

48. E. Lozinskii. Information and evidence in logic systems. *Journal of Experimental and Theoretical Artificial Intelligence*, 6:163–193, 1994.

49. E. Lozinskii. Resolving contradictions: A plausible semantics for inconsistent systems. *Journal of Automated Reasoning*, 12:1–31, 1994.

50. E. Lozinskii. On knowledge evolution: Acquisition, revision, contraction. *Journal of Applied Non-Classical Logic*, 7:177–212, 1997.

51. D. Makinson. *Handbook of Logic in Artificial Intelligence and Logic Programming*, volume III, chapter General Pattern in nonmonotonic reasoning, pages 35–110. Clarendon Press, Oxford, 1994.

52. R. Manor and N. Rescher. On inferences from inconsistent information. *Theory and Decision*, 1:179–219, 1970.

53. P. Marquis and N. Porquet. Computational aspects of quasi-classical entailment. *Journal of Applied Non-classical Logics*, 11:295–312, 2001.
54. C. Papadimitriou. *Computational Complexity*. Addison-Wesley, 1994.
55. J. B. Paris. *The uncertain reasoner's companion: a mathematical perspective*. Number 39 in Cambridge Tracts in Theoretical Computer Science. Cambridge University Press, 1994.
56. S. Parsons, M. Wooldridge, and L. Amgoud. Properties and complexity of some formal inter-agent dialogues. *Journal of Logic and Computation*, 2003.
57. K. Popper. *Conjectures and Refutation*. Routlege and Kegan Paul, London, 1963.
58. H. Prakken and G. Vreeswijk. Logical systems for defeasible argumentation. In D Gabbay, editor, *Handbook of Philosophical Logic*. Kluwer, 2000.
59. G. Priest. Minimally inconsistent LP. *Studia Logica*, 50:321–331, 1991.
60. G. Priest. Paraconsistent logic. In *Handbook of Philosophical Logic*, volume 6. Kluwer, 2002.
61. R. Reiter. A theory of diagnosis from first principles. *Artificial Intelligence*, 32:57–95, 1987.
62. P. Revesz. On the semantics of arbitration. *International Journal of Algebra and Computation*, 7:133–160, 1997.
63. M. Ryan and P. Y. Schobbens. Belief revision and verisimilitude. *Notre Dame Journal of Formal Logic*, 36(1):15–29, 1995.
64. L. J. Savage. *The foundations of statistics*. Dover Publications, New York, 1971. Second revised edition.
65. M. Schaerf and M. Cadoli. Tractable reasoning via approximation. *Artificial Intelligence*, 74:249–310, 1995.
66. G. Shafer. *A Mathematical Theory of Evidence*. Princeton University Press, 1976.
67. C. Shannon. A mathematical theory of communication. *Bell System Technical Journal*, 27:379–423, 1948.
68. W. Spohn. Ordinal conditional functions: a dynamic theory of epistemic states. In W. L. Harper and B. Skyrms, editors, *Causation in Decision, Belief Change, and Statistics*, volume 2, pages 105–134. Princeton University Press, 1987.
69. M. Williams. Iterated theory base change: A computational model. In *Proceedings of the 14th International Joint Conference on Artificial Intelligence (IJCAI'95)*, pages 1541–1547, 1995.
70. P. Wong and Ph. Besnard. Paraconsistent reasoning as an analytic tool. *Journal of the Interest Group in Propositional Logic*, 9:233–246, 2001.

Inconsistency Issues in Spatial Databases

Andrea Rodríguez

Department of Computer Science
University of Concepción, Chile
andrea@udec.cl
http://inf.udec.cl/~andrea

Abstract. This chapter analyzes inconsistency issues in spatial databases. In particular, it reviews types of inconsistency, specification of integrity constraints, and treatment of inconsistency in multiple representations and data integration. The chapter focuses on inconsistency associated with the geometric representation of objects, spatial relations between objects, and composite objects by aggregation. The main contribution of this paper is a survey of existing approaches to dealing with inconsistency issues in spatial databases that emphasizes the current state of the art and that outlines research issues in the context of inconsistency tolerance.

1 Introduction

During the past several years traditional databases have been enhanced to include spatially referenced data. This type of data is an essential component of existing applications such as Geographic Information Systems (GIS), Computer-Aided Design (CAD), multimedia information systems, data warehousing, and NASA's Earth Observing System (EOS).

Spatial databases have been defined as database systems with a model and query language that support spatial data types and provide spatial indexing and efficient algorithms for spatial query processing [37]. Unlike classical database theory, where the content of databases is abstract, in spatial databases the content has some interpretation and laws of real geometry hold. This interpretation induces to much diverse classes of data structures and data manipulations. Spatial databases have no clear separation between what is handled by the database management system (DBMS) and what is handled by the software application [48]. For example, it is not always clear whether or not an operation that finds the shortest path in a network is part of the spatial DBMS. Consequently, there is no consensus of what properties and features should be part of spatial data manipulation languages.

In spatial databases, theory about spatial information is used to define *spatial data models or geomatic models*. Spatial data models represent information about the n-dimensional real space $\mathbb{R}^n$, a space that is infinite and cannot be represented with an extensional data model. Operations in spatial databases

L. Bertossi et al. (Eds.): Inconsistency Tolerance, LNCS 3300, pp. 237–269, 2004.

may or may not depend on the spatial data model underlying the data representation, an issue related to the concept of *genericity* that was introduced in classical databases [13] and then applied in the domain of spatial databases by Paredaens *et. al* [47] [48].

The integration of spatial data into traditional database systems requires addressing nontrivial issues at various levels. They range from ontological issues about the conceptualization of space to more technical issues about access mechanisms and file management [58]. As consequence, progress in SDBMS is the result of an interdisciplinary research effort. The treatment of inconsistency of spatial data also requires an interdisciplinary approach. Consistency of spatial information must deal with ontological issues concerning physical reality [18] [34] (e.g., an object can only have one physical location at a time). It needs to consider the appropriate conceptual frameworks for analyzing spatial consistency [24] [30] [43] [63], such as models for consistency at multiple representational levels or granularities. It also concerns the specification language of integrity constraints [9] [41] and the design of computational-geometry algorithms to implement consistency checkers.

This chapter analyzes inconsistency issues in spatial databases. Its main contribution is a survey of existing approaches to dealing with inconsistency issues that emphasizes the state of the art and outlines research issues in the context of inconsistency tolerance. The chapter focuses on the *geometric representation* of objects (i.e., location and shape), *spatial relations* between objects, and *composite objects by aggregations*. Positional information is often imprecise in spatial databases, which may result in conflicting geometric representations of objects (i.e., two different geometric representations for the same object). Spatial relations play an important role in spatial databases, since they are usually the basis for specifying integrity and query constraints [28]. *Spatial relations* are typically derived from positional information; however, they may not be affected by conflicting objects' geometric representations because objects may hold the same spatial relation in these representations [53]. *Nested aggregations* are fundamental abstraction mechanisms for modeling spatial phenomena. For example, countries contain states that contain counties. Aggregations impose requirements for data modeling and data consistency with respect to the relationships between parts and wholes.

The organization of this chapter is as follows. Section 2 gives a brief overview of spatial databases. Section 3 discusses the types and sources of inconsistency in spatial information. Section 4 discusses the specification of constraints, consistency at multiple representational levels, and consistency in the integration of spatial information. Section 5 addresses inconsistency tolerance of spatial information. Final conclusions are given in Section 6.

2   Spatial Database Overview

Spatial database systems consist of data about objects and properties in the world with respect to their locations [54]. These systems deal with diverse kinds of data, from natural to man-made features, which demands specific models that both capture the semantics of spatial data and also offer a high level of abstraction. At an abstract level, spatial objects can be *atomic* or *complex*. *Atomic spatial objects* are composed of a description and a spatial-component (e.g., a landparcel has a code number and a geometric component represented by a surface), and by aggregation, *complex spatial objects* are composed of a description and a set of spatial objects (e.g., a sport club may be composed of a sport field, tennis court, gymnasium, and so on).

Abstractions that need to be supported in a SDBMS are *partitions* and *networks* [37]. A partition represents either a spatial feature or space cell. Partitions are commonly used to represent thematic layers or maps (e.g., soil-type maps and administrative boundaries). A network is seen as a graph embedded in the plane with nodes (e.g., places) that are connected by edges (e.g., highways, rivers, channels, and so on). Other collections of spatial objects that are often relevant to spatial databases are *nested partitions* (e.g., a country is an aggregation of states and a state is an aggregation of counties) and *triangular irregular networks* (TIN) (e.g., terrain digital models).

Applications of spatial information, in particular geospatial applications, differ from traditional data applications for the following reasons [65]:

- Spatial information deals with spatial and non-spatial data, where the definition of spatial data types should be closed under the operations applicable to them.
- Data are highly structured by the notion of object aggregation.
- The existence of user-defined operations that require an extensible underlying model.
- Functions exist at both a low-level of abstraction (e.g., functions over points, lines and polygons) and a high-level of abstraction (e.g., functions over maps and configurations).

As an example of what is the kind of data that are modeled in a spatial database, consider the case of a land information system (LIS) composed of *landparcels* and information related to *land ownership* (Figure 1). A landparcel is a spatial object that has a spatial component (e.g., a landparcel may be represented by a surface) and attributes describing properties of the land (e.g., identification, owner, use, and so on). Aggregations of landparcels are *sections* in the LIS. Geometric operations may be defined at the level of an individual landparcel (e.g., the area of a landparcel) or at the level of thematic maps (e.g., the merge of landparels with topographic information). In addition to operations handled by the data manipulation language, a user may need to define a new operation over the landparcels' geometries. For example, a user may want to define a function that detects particular shapes of landparcels. This implies that the underlying data model must allow the definition of new types of operations.

2.1 Spatial Data Models or Geomatic Models

Spatial modelers often make the classical distinction between *field-based* and *entity-based* view of the space [22] [59]. In the field-based view of the space, each

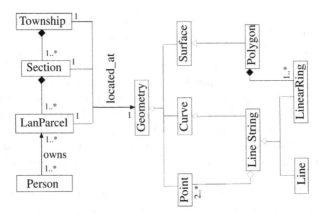

Fig. 1. A conceptual model of a portion of a land information system in UML

point in the space has one or more attribute values that are typically defined by continuous functions in coordinates x and y (e.g., temperature, altitude, and pollution). The view of the space is a continuous *field* that represents a phenomenon whose attribute values vary with the position in the space. In this view, the concept of entity or object is irrelevant. In the entity-based view of the space, by contrast, space is composed of spatial objects that are entities with explicit identity. Each of these views of space can be represented by using different spatial data models.

Spatial data models depend on the operations that have to be defined and the efficiency needs of the implementation. One of the simplest and common models is the *spaguetti model or vector model* [54]. Although the *vector model* is usually associated with an entity-based view of the space (e.g., Figure 1), it can also model a field-view of the space (e.g., a digital elevation model that is represented by a triangulated irregular network TIN). This model has efficient algorithms for detecting properties of spatial objects (e.g., overlapping, intersection, and spatial inclusion). In this model, the information in a n-dimensional space is represented by using m-dimensional geometric primitives, with $m < n$. The common types of primitives used in this model are, where $<>$ are lists, $[]$ are tuples and $\{\}$ are sets:

- *Points or zero-dimensional primitives* (e.g., the locations of utility poles can be represented by points): $[x : real, y : real]$.
- *Polylines or one-dimensional primitives*, whose data structure is a finite list of points (e.g., the access roads to landparcels can be represented by one-dimensional primitives) : $< point >$.
- *Polygons or two-dimensional primitives* are also represented by a list of points, but this list represents a non self-intersecting closed polylines (Figure 2) (e.g., the spatial component of a landparcel is described by a two-dimensional primitive): $< points >$. By aggregation, *complex polygons* or *regions* are sets of polygons: $\{polygon\}$.

Fig. 2. Polylines: (a) closed and non self-intersecting polyline and (b) closed and self-intersecting polyline

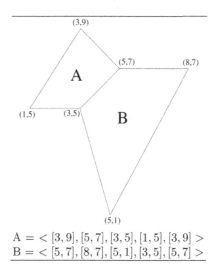

$$A = < [3,9],[5,7],[3,5],[1,5],[3,9] >$$
$$B = < [5,7],[8,7],[5,1],[3,5],[5,7] >$$

Fig. 3. An example of the Vector Model

Using the Vector Model, in a two-dimensional space, for example, any spatial object is presented by points or polylines, which are considered zero- and one-dimensional geometric primitives, respectively (Figure 3). In a tree-dimensional space, a polyhedra is represented by the boundaries of which contain planar facets (i.e., surfaces), polylines, and points.

Other types of models that concern with practical issues of efficiency are the *raster model* and the *piano model* [38] [39] [55], which are often, but not always, seen as the typical way to model a field view of the space. The *raster model* intentionally represents spatial information by a finite number of cells or raster points, where the infinite number of points associated with a cell share the same properties. The main problem of this model is the needed approximation of geometric elements to raster points of cells (Figure 4). The *piano model* combines techniques of space-filling curves and quadtrees [55]. This model encodes a linear order of cells that partition a space while maintaining locality (i.e., cells close to each other in the space are also close to each other in the linear order). This linear order is done recursively for a grid that is obtained by hierarchical subdivision of the space (Figure 4).

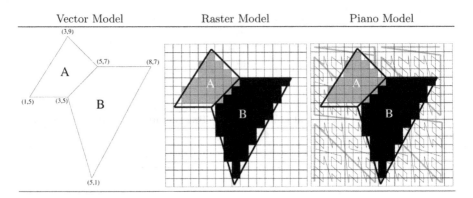

Fig. 4. The Vector Model, Raster Model, and Piano Model

Focusing on theoretical issues of an entity-based view of the space, other models are the *topological model* and the *constraint model*. The *topological model* addresses data manipulation that is topological in nature. This type of data manipulation involves concepts such as adjacency, connectivity and containment. For example, a query that can efficiently solve in this type of models is "find landparcels that are adjacent to the landparcel whose identifier is equal to X."

A topological model can be seen as a planar network, with the following primitives of interest:

- *Points* are pairs of real numbers: $[x : real, y : real]$.
- *Nodes* are tuples composed of a point and a list of arcs in which the node is one of the extremes: $[point, < arc >]$.
- *Arcs* are tuples composed of a starting node, ending node, left polygon, right polygon and list of internal points of the arcs :
  $[start\_node, end\_node, left\_polygon, right\_polygon, < point >]$.
- *Polygons* are lists of arcs $< arc >$.
- *Regions* are sets of polygons $\{polygon\}$.

To make clear the difference between the Vector model and Topological model, consider the same spatial objects represented with these two models in Figure 5. The difference between the two models is that the topological model handles explicitly common boundaries and adjacency between polygons.

The *constraint model* defines any geometrical figure by an elementary geometry expressed by first-order logic over the real numbers [42]. The constraint data model aims to handle infinite relations (i.e., infinite sets of points in a space), which are represented by quantifier-free formulas. For example, consider the same objects A and B in Figure 5, the corresponding representations in the constraint model are:

Object	Constraint-based Representation
A	$y \geq 5 \wedge y \leq 2x + 3 \wedge y \leq -x + 12 \wedge y \leq x + 2$
B	$y \leq 7 \wedge y \leq x + 2 \wedge y \leq 2x - 9 \wedge y \leq -2x + 11$

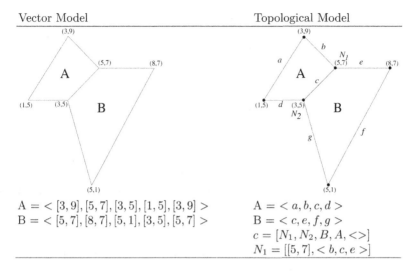

Fig. 5. Comparing representations of two landparcels in the Vector Model and Topological Model

In addition to the geometric representation of spatial objects (i.e., position and shape of objects), spatial relations between objects play an important role in spatial information systems, since such relations refer to the way people perceive, reason, and describe spatial information in a variety of languages [28]. Models of spatial information may be more or less efficient to determine spatial relations. Positional information is often used for determining the spatial relations between objects and, therefore, these relations can be determined when spatial data models, such as the vector or raster models, are used. Spatial relations such as adjacency and containment, however, do not require absolute positional data [11] and are efficiently handled with the topological model. For example, one could say that two objects meet because they share a common boundary, disregarding the exact location of the objects.

Common spatial relations are typically grouped into three kinds: *topological, orientation,* and *distance* [61] [66]. *Topological relations* deal principally with the concept of connectivity and are invariant under topological transformations, such as rotation, translation, scaling. *Orientation relations* presuppose the existence of a vector space and are subject to changes under rotation, while they are invariant under translation and scaling. *Distance relations* express spatial properties that reflect the concept of a metric and, therefore, they change under scaling, but are invariant under translation and rotation. Among these spatial relations, topological relations have spurred much recent research [17] [20] [25] [28] [46]. They are considered to capture the essence of a spatial configuration −topology matters, metric refines [11].

In summary, spatial databases deal with objects that have a position in a space as well as with spatial relations among these objects. Different models of spatial information exist that address the geometric representation of spatial objects, some of them concerning theoretical issues and others concerning issues of efficiency. It is still a research challenge to create models for spatial information that combine a solid theoretical foundation with efficiency considerations.

2.2   Data Model and Query Language

The previous Section has reviewed models for the geometric representation of spatial objects. Such models have been integrated into traditional database management systems to profit from well established data models and data structures of traditional database systems. This Section concentrates on the extended relation model, one of the possible data models that supports the representation and querying of spatial objects. The extended relational model is the widest used model in current spatial database management systems. Descriptions of other models, such as the object-oriented data model and the constraint data model can be found in [42][44][59][65].

In extended relational systems, end users manipulate values whose types are basic, such as integer or characters, but also abstract data types (ADT) that are accessible through the operations defined on them [35] [62]. In these systems, each type of spatial objects corresponds to a relation that contains a geometric-type attribute, such as *region* or *line*, among others. A link between relations is handled through the standard mechanism of relational schemas; i.e., by means of a foreign key.

Consider, for example, the cadastral application system presented in Figure 1. The corresponding data schema in the SQL data definition language (DDL) is:

create table Township(town_code: *integer*, name: *string*
geometry: *region*, **Primary Key** (town_code))
create table Section(town_code: *integer*, section_code: *integer*,
geometry: *region*, **Primary Key**(section_code),
Secondary Key(town_code))
create table LandParcel(section_code: *integer*, parcel_code: *integer*,
geometry: *region*, **Primary Key**(parcel_code),
Secondary Key(section_code))
create table Person(person_id: *integer*, name: *string*,
Primary Key(person_id))
create table Ownership(person_id: *integer*, parcel_code: *integer*,
Primary Key(person_id,parcel_code),
Foreign Key(person_id), **Foreign Key**(parcel_code))

A spatial selection query in SQL based on the previous schema could be "find the identifier of the town that contains the landparcel whose parcel_code is equal to X:

select   t.town_code **from** Township t, LandParcel l
where l.parcel_code= 'X' **and** inside(l.geometry,t.geometry)

The answer to this query will be inconsistent if two o more towns' identifiers (*town_code*) are retrieved, since a lanparcel must only be part of one town. A more complex query is, for example, "create a map and retrieve the area from the aggregation of landparcels grouped by sections." Such query could be expressed in SQL as:

select   area(o.geometry), sum(l.geometry) **from** LandParcel l, Section o
         where o.section_code = l.section_code **group** by l.section_code

The query answer is inconsistent if the area of the aggregation is different to the area of the spatial component of section (i.e., if $area(sum(l.geometry)) \neq area(o.geometry))$, since the aggregation of the geometric parts should be equal to the geometric whole.

3   Types and Sources of Inconsistency of Spatial Information

Spatial information systems often must deal with different kinds of data imperfections, which can be classified into *uncertainty, imprecision/vagueness, incompleteness,* and *inconsistency* [7] [10] [49]. Uncertainty is a kind of data imperfection that arises from the lack of information about the state of the world (e.g., "if the distance between Santiago and Concepción is unknown, the time that takes to travel from Santiago to Concepción is uncertain"); imprecision is a kind of data imperfection that arises from the granularity of the language used to make an imprecise statement (e.g., "Santiago is located in America"); vagueness is a kind of imprecision that arises from the use of terms when there are cases for which it is difficult to decide if they are covered or not by a particular concept (e.g., "Santiago is *close* to Concepción"); incompleteness is a kind of imperfection that arises from the absence of some data values (e.g., a missing road in a transportation network); and inconsistency is a kind of data imperfection that arises from the coexistence of two contradictory facts (e.g., "Concepción is located at 500 km from Santiago" and "Concepción is located at 600 km from Santiago").

From an ontological perspective, Frank [34] distinguishes consistency rules that capture the meaning of space and time. At a bottom level, the physical reality, which is independent of human-perception, satisfies "natural laws," rules that are thought to be universal; for example, the speed of an object is related to the acceleration. At the physical-observation level; that is, the physical reality observed through instruments, data should follow the distribution of measurement values according to the expected error. For example, the distance that is measured by an instrument must not be too different from the calculated distance between two stored points. At the object-property level, objects should satisfy necessary conditions. For example, a stadium must be composed of a sport field. At the social-definition level, context constrains the consistency of data in the form of X counts as Y in context Z. For example, a historical building is a building older than 150 years, but this is true in the context of Chile. Finally, at the cognitive-agent level (i.e., agents are people or organizations), there should be no contradiction with respect to the common understanding of reality by an agent.

For example, an organization (i.e., an agent) is composed of sub-agents that are departments of the organization. Consistency rules at this level enforce that each of the sub-agents behaves consistently with the organization's view of the world.

Considering ideas from [18] [69], spatial inconsistencies can be related to, but they are not the same than, forms of error. From the perspective of the type of characteristics the inconsistency refers to, inconsistency is related to what are called *primary* or *secondary* forms of error. The primary form of error corresponds to a wrong description of location or characteristics/qualities of spatial objects. A typical case is the conflicting geometric representation of a spatial object; for example, having an integrity constraint that states that objects have only one location, there is an inconsistency derived from a primary type of error if there exist more than one location for a spatial object. This type of inconsistency occurs because there exist differences in data accuracy or precision, but also because many observations of spatial phenomena are essentially vague. For example, the boundaries of cities, mountains, and oceans cannot be determined with precision, which may make two observers record two different locations for the same object.

In general, an inconsistency associated with a primary error violates a basic principle of *location or attribute uniqueness*. In spite of the desirable condition of positional uniqueness, spatial information often deal with inaccurate coordinates and imprecise data. Topological facts; however, may not require data about positions of objects [53] to be consistent. There may exist different geometric representations of objects (i.e., inconsistency); however, the spatial relations between objects may be the same in these representations (Figure 6).

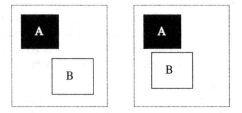

Fig. 6. A configuration of two objects with two different geometric representations, but with the same topological relation *disjoint* between objects

A spatial inconsistency related to a secondary error refers to a contradiction between stored data and constraints associated with *structural* definitions of geometric primitives. For example, a surface must be bounded by closed and non self-intersecting polylines. Inconsistency may also be related to *semantic* contradictions, such as when a road overlaps a body of water. These types of inconsistency, structural or semantic, depend on the spatial domain, and they are captured by rules that should be expressed within the data model.

Some relevant characteristics of spatial applications that should be considered in the treatment of consistency are [8] [53]:

- Spatial information deals with spatial and non-spatial data. In addition to inconsistency of non-spatial data, inconsistency may occur between spatial and non-spatial or within spatial data.
- Many spatial data are inherently vague, which may lead to conflicting data. Vagueness may make observations of a same spatial phenomenon be different and, therefore, have conflicting representations.
- Topological and other spatial relations are very important and are usually implicitly represented. Spatial relations are typically derived through data manipulation such that checking topological inconsistency involves not only to check stored facts in a database; but also to check for results of data manipulation.
- A modification in a spatial database may cause simultaneous updates in a large number of records. Depending on a spatial representation, a modification of an object's boundary may affect the representation of its neighboring objects' boundaries as well. For example, two partitions of the space that share a common boundary may need an update at the same time when one of them changes its boundaries; otherwise, partitions could overlap, which contradicts the definition of partitions of a space.
- Spatial databases may need to treat different levels of detail in the spatial representation. These representations may be handled as duplicate information or may be generated dynamically through a generalization process. For example, you may need to keep the representation of a city as a region and a point, depending on the visualization needs of an application. Since duplication of information may occur, it is necessary to keep consistency of multiple representational levels (e.g., a region cannot be a line at a coarse representation).
- Many queries are defined in terms of combinations of functions that exist at both a low-level of abstraction (e.g., geometry types) and a high-level of abstraction (e.g., maps, configurations). For example, a query may be to select the location of a lanparcel or may be to obtain a map by the merge of lanparcels with transportation networks.

As a conclusion, differences between traditional databases and spatial databases are based on the interpretation of data. The spatial domain brings up different types of inconsistency that may require ad-hoc treatments. A contradiction of facts in a traditional database is commonly determined by the property of equality of attribute values. In spatial databases, however, a spatial attribute (e.g., a region that represents a spatial object) is not only a single value, it underlies a model of the space composed of a number of geometric primitives. In this context, data consistency does not only concern with the comparison of spatial attribute values, but also, the analysis of contradictions between the stored data and the model of spatial information (e.g., a polygon that is represented by a self-intersecting polyline contradicts the classical model where a polygon is defined by a closed and non self-intersecting polyline).

4   Work on Consistency in Spatial Databases

Research in the area of consistency in spatial databases has tried to clarify concepts about types of consistency, incorporate integrity constraints at different levels of the database design, and conceptualize consistency problems in generalization and information-integration processes. In all cases, the research effort has focused on how to detect or prevent inconsistencies. Although issues about inconsistency tolerance have been addressed for traditional relational databases, spatial databases have not handled explicitly inconsistency tolerance in query answering.

4.1   Integrity Constraints in Spatial Databases

Inconsistency arises when integrity constraints are violated. Thus, constraints must be taken into account when updating a database so that the semantics and quality of data are preserved. In the spatial domain, integrity constraints have been mainly used for preventing structural inconsistency (i.e., inconsistency between stored data and rules of geometric primitives), whereas conflicting information about positional information has been treated as a problem of data accuracy.

In addition to traditional integrity constraints concerning static, transition, and transactional aspects of databases systems [31], rules about spatial data must ensure consistent updating of spatial information (i.e., consistency of the geometric representation of objects with respect to a model of spatial information). A typical classification of these spatial constraints is [18] :

- *Topological constraints.* Topological constraints are those constraints that address geometrical properties and spatial relations. They may be associated with structural considerations, such as that partitions only meet or are disjoint, or topological conditions, such as centerlines must meet at intersections. Considering a subset of topological constraints, Servigne *et al.* [57] defined *topo-semantic* constraints as those that relate geometry with semantic conditions, as in the constraint that a city's administrative region must be contained within its corresponding city limits.
- *Semantic integrity constraints.* These constraints are concerned with the meaning of geographic features; for example, landparcels are not contained in building_blocks.
- *user-defined integrity constraints.* These types of constraints are equivalent to business rules in non-spatial DBMS; for example, legal rules that constraints the installation of a gas station in a given region.

Like in traditional database systems, constraints at a conceptual and logical level in spatial databases are inherited by the implementation or physical level. These constraints are translated into a proprietary scripting language or into explicit constraints coded in the application programs [31]. At a logical level, Hadzilacos and Tryfona [41] describe a logical model with definitions of constraints based on topological relations. They state that it is possible but cumbersome to define topological constraints based on absolute positions. Therefore, they use a

Table 1. Definition of topological relations between regions

	$\delta\delta$	oo	δo	$o\delta$	Relation
disjoint	$\emptyset$	$\emptyset$	$\emptyset$	$\emptyset$	
meet	$\neg\emptyset$	$\emptyset$	$\emptyset$	$\emptyset$	
overlap	$\neg\emptyset$	$\neg\emptyset$	$\neg\emptyset$	$\neg\emptyset$	
cover	$\neg\emptyset$	$\neg\emptyset$	$\neg\emptyset$	$\emptyset$	
covered_by	$\neg\emptyset$	$\neg\emptyset$	$\emptyset$	$\neg\emptyset$	
contain	$\emptyset$	$\neg\emptyset$	$\neg\emptyset$	$\emptyset$	
inside	$\emptyset$	$\neg\emptyset$	$\emptyset$	$\neg\emptyset$	
equal	$\neg\emptyset$	$\neg\emptyset$	$\emptyset$	$\emptyset$	

formal framework for defining topological relations [25] [27] upon which integrity constraints are specified. This framework defines topological relations between subsets of a classical topological space by the emptiness or non-emptiness of the two-by-two intersections of the subsets' interiors (o) and boundaries (δ). Table 1 summarizes the resulting eight possible topological relations between two polygons. This table indicates, for example, that a *disjoint* relation exists when the intersections between boundaries, between interiors, between boundary and interior, and between interior and boundary are the empty set.

Within Hadzilacos and Tryfona's framework [41], spatial relations and integrity constraints are expressed by using first-order logic. Atomic topological formulae in combination create topological sentences. Atomic topological formulae include geometric operators over objects, elementary topological relations between objects, and comparison between objects' attributes. For example, consider the following statement in natural language of a semantic integrity constraint in a cadastral application: *land-parcels are not contained in build-*

ing_blocks. The formal specification of this constraint for land_parcels lp and building_blocks bl based on the topological relations defined in Table 1 is:

$$\forall(lp, bl)[\neg inside(lp, bl) \wedge \neg covered\_by(lp, bl)] \tag{1}$$

Some topological constraints define geometric primitives or some spatial dependences of composite objects. Consider, for example, partitions of a space. To define a partition rule in first-order logic, one needs to consider predicates of the type $P_i(x)$, with x being an interior point of an object P_i. The spatial aggregation of partitions $P_0() \ldots P_n()$ into $W()$, assuming that partitions can only *meet* or be *disjoint*, where *meet* and *disjoint* were defined in Table 1:

$$\forall(P_i, P_j) \; [meet(P_i, P_j) \vee disjoint(P_i, P_j)] \tag{2}$$

is then defined by the statement that a point x in the aggregation must belong to one partition $P_i()$:

$$\forall(x)[W(x) \equiv (P_0(x) \vee P_1(x) \vee \ldots \vee P_n(x))] \tag{3}$$

A graph-based model of maps has also been used to establish topological integrity constraints of objects and their aggregations as a map [53]. This model makes it possible to guarantee the consistency of a map through database updates with respect to a set of topological constraints over *vertices*, *edges* and *faces* on the map graph. Theses integrity constraints are equivalent to the mathematical axioms of maps that are defined by a graph that is plane, connected, nonseparable and formed by edges that are straight lines bounding internal faces.

Some attempts have been made to provide end users with easy mechanisms that hide the logic in specifying constraints [19] [52] [57]. An early work by Pizarro *et al.* [52] presents a visual language that depicts unacceptable database states. This visual language can then generate first-order predicates of spatial constraints. Another study allows users to define constraints in an English-like fashion. Basic components of the language are entity classes, relations, and qualifiers (e.g., forbidden, at least n times, at least most n times, or exactly n times) [57]. Following the same idea, Crockcroft's work [19] extends the previous specification to include attribute values in the topological constraints. For example, a butterfly valve must not intersect a pipe if the diameter of the pipe is greater than 40 inches. This interface for end-users is a standalone software tool that is integrated with a Geographic Information System (GIS).

4.2   Consistency at Multiple Representational Levels

The problem of multiple representations consists of data changing their geometric and topological structure due to changes in scale. Conceptually, multiple representations may be considered as different data sets that cover the same area with different levels of detail. Within the context of assessing consistency at multiple representations, topological relations are considered to be first-class information, which must prevail in case of conflicts [24] [29] [30] [43]. This means

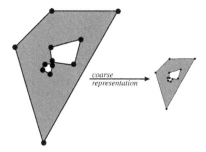

Fig. 7. Two representations of the same object

that, at different scales, there is no inconsistency in having different geometric representations of a same object if some topological constraints are satisfied.

Initially, topological consistency was treated at the low level of data structures, counting nodes and arcs to assure that an object's topology is complete [45]. This strategy accounts for changes in the geometry of objects, but it does not assure consistency of the relations between objects. For example, it does not handle consistency of the topological changes that may occur when, at a coarse representation, several parts become a single object or when holes of objects disappear. Figure 7 shows an object at two different representational levels. In a detailed representation, the object is composed of two holes and, in a more coarse representation, the two holes become only one. In both representations, however, the number of nodes and edges are the same.

Considering objects' relations, Egenhofer *et al.* [24] present a framework that treats consistency at multiple representational levels based on the comparison of topological invariants [26]. They defined two types of equivalence: object equivalence and relation equivalence between different representations. This framework assumes that changes of topology through consecutive representational levels can be ordered by a similarity relation "topologically less general than or topologically as general as" ($\leq$), a relation that is reflexive, antisymmetric, and transitive. In this context, a representation is characterized by a set of topological invariants $(T(O_x^i))$ of an object (O_x) at a given representation (i), and a set of topological invariants between objects $(T(O_x^i, O_y^i))$ at a given representation (i).

The set of topological invariants of an object A $(T(A))$ is described by the relation matrix between the generalized object A^* (i.e., the object A without holes) and the object A's holes H_i^A, and by the component invariant tables for the boundary-boundary intersections between holes and between the generalized object and the holes. The topological invariants of the boundary-boundary intersections include the sequence of intersections and the dimension of these intersections (i.e., zero-dimensional or point, one-dimensional or line). For example, Figure 8 shows a region A with three holes $H_1^A \ldots H_3^A$, the relation matrix of the generalized region A^* and the holes H_i^A, and the component invariant tables for the boundary-boundary intersections. In this case, there is one boundary intersection between A^* and H_1^A and two boundary intersections between H_2^A and H_3^A.

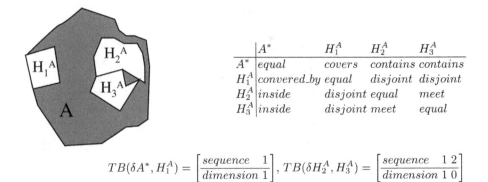

$$TB(\delta A^*, H_1^A) = \begin{bmatrix} sequence & 1 \\ \hline dimension & 1 \end{bmatrix}, \; TB(\delta H_2^A, H_3^A) = \begin{bmatrix} sequence & 1\;2 \\ \hline dimension & 1\;0 \end{bmatrix}$$

Fig. 8. A region A with three holes $H_1^A \ldots H_3^A$, the relation matrix between the generalized region A^* and the component invariant tables for the boundary-boundary intersections

The topological invariants between objects is characterized by the relation matrix between objects and by the topological invariants of the boundary-boundary intersections between objects. These invariants are the sequence of intersections, dimension of the intersections, type of intersections (i.e., an intersection crosses into or out of an object), and boundedness of boundary-boundary intersections (i.e., whether or not the components of boundary intersection are inside of the union of objects). As an example, consider the configuration in Figure 9 with two objects at a given representational level and their corresponding relation table and component invariant table of their boundaries.

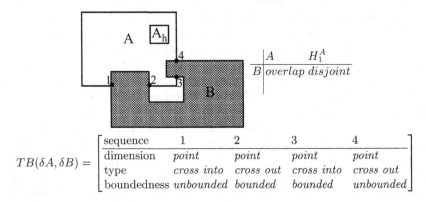

Fig. 9. A configuration with two objects and its corresponding relation table and component invariant tables

Egenhofer *et al.* classify the set of topological equivalences between representations into three types of similarity and three types of homeomorphism (Table 2). Within this framework, two representational levels are topologically

Table 2. Types of equivalence between representations S_i and S_j

Type	Rule
object-similar	$\forall(O_x^i \in S_i, O_x^j \in S_j)$ $[S_i \leq S_j \supset T(O_x^i) \leq T(O_x^j)]$
relation-similar	$\forall(O_x^i, O_y^i \in S_i, O_x^j, O_y^j \in S_j)$ $[S_i \leq S_j \supset T(O_x^i, O_y^i) \leq T(O_x^j, O_y^j)]$
similar	$\forall(O_x^i, O_y^i \in S_i, O_x^j, O_y^j \in S_j)$ $[S_i \leq S_j \supset (T(O_x^i, O_y^i) \leq T(O_x^j, O_y^j)) \wedge$ $(T(O_x^i) \leq T(O_x^j)) \wedge (T(O_y^i) \leq T(O_y^j))]$
object-homeomorphic	$\forall(O_x^i \in S_i, O_x^j \in S_j)$ $[S_i \leq S_j \supset T(O_x^i) = T(O_x^j)]$
relation-homeomorphic	$\forall(O_x^i, O_y^i \in S_i, O_x^j, O_y^j \in S_j)$ $[S_i \leq S_j \supset T(O_x^i, O_y^i) = T(O_x^j, O_y^j)]$
homeomorphic	$\forall(O_x^i, O_y^i \in S_i, O_x^j, O_y^j \in S_j)$ $[S_i \leq S_j \supset (T(O_x^i, O_y^i) = T(O_x^j, O_y^j)) \wedge$ $(T(O_x^i) = T(O_x^j)) \wedge (T(O_y^i) = T(O_y^j))]$

consistent if they satisfied the conditions of topological homeomorphism; that is, if they have the same topological invariants and relation matrices. Two different representational levels may also be consistent if they satisfy some basic conditions of topological similarity ($\leq$) from a coarse to a detailed representation. The basic assumption when defining these consistency rules is that the goal of a coarse representation is to reduce the complexity of objects. For objects with holes, this means that the number of holes should be reduced in a coarse representation. Likewise, the number of boundary-boundary intersections between holes and between a generalized region and a hole should get smaller. If the topological relation between holes change, it changes from *disjoint* to *meet*. Thus, the dimension may increase from one to another representation. For example, if two holes are moved closer to each other, a component intersection that meets in a node may change to a meet in an edge. Like these basic rules, many other rules exist for objects with holes and for relations between objects with holes in different representations, which can be found in [24].

Figure 10 shows a case of *relation* homomorphism, because both representations have the same relation matrices, except for the fact that in the representation j a disjoint relation between objects B^i and H^A is dropped; and the representations have identical component invariant tables for the relations between non-empty boundaries intersections (i.e., $T(A^i, B^i) = T(A^j, B^j)$). In this case, the representation j may be considered a coarse or less detailed representation than the representation i.

While the work by Egenhofer *et al.* [24] addresses consistency at multiple representational levels of objects with holes, a work by Tryfona and Egenhofer [63] focuses on the computational assessment of topological consistency across multiple representational levels of objects with disconnected parts. They define that the *generalized* region A^* of an object A with disconnected parts A_i is the union of all its parts and all relevant connectors ΔA_{ij} between parts A_i and

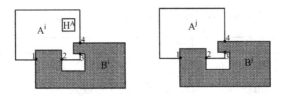

Fig. 10. Two relation-homeomorphic representations

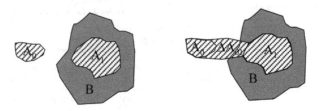

Fig. 11. Derivable relation between an aggregate object A and object B

A_j. A connector ΔA_{ij} between parts A_i and A_j is the region that links A_i and A_j, filling the exterior between the two parts such that A_i, ΔA_{ij}, and A_j are connected. The basic rules of the *generalized* object A^* and the parts A_i are:

$$\forall (i)[A^* covers A_i] \tag{4}$$

$$\forall (i \neq j)[A_i\ disjoint\ A_j] \tag{5}$$

$$\forall (i \neq j)[A_i\ meet \Delta A_{ij} \wedge A_j\ meet\ \Delta A_{ij}] \tag{6}$$

The goal of Tryfona and Egenhofer's work was to determine the relation between the generalized object A^* and another object B from the relations between B and A's parts. This derivation is based on the analysis of the topological invariants defined by the set intersections of interior, boundary and exterior of objects [26], and on the consistency-checking of scenes [30]. For example, consider the case of two disjoint parts A_0 and A_1 and a third object B that contains A_1 (Figure 11). Then, a unique possible relation of the generalized object A^* with respect to B is *overlap*. A constraint of a relation between an object B and A^* is terms of an A's part A_i can be expressed by:

$$\forall (A^*, B)[overlap(A^*, B) \equiv \exists (A_i)[overlap(A_i, B)]] \tag{7}$$

In summary, multiple representations in spatial databases may not imply inconsistent information, but rather, merely different levels of detail or scale. In such cases, topological consistency at the level of objects and objects' relations must be analyzed. Analyses of consistency at multiple representational levels are not included in current commercial DBMS, they are running as ad-hoc applications. From the perspective of consistency in spatial databases, models of consistency at multiple representational levels lack the specification in a formal language for their treatments as integrity constraints.

4.3   Consistency in Spatial Information Integration

This Section discusses consistency in spatial information integration that considers cases where spatial data sets to be integrated contain the same features or objects, which can be extracted from several sources at different times. The treatment of consistency when integrating data sets with different features (e.g., combining cadastral with water resource data) depends on the semantics of the features involved.

The integration of the same features from different sources may vary in reliability, accuracy and scale of representation. Thus, integrating spatial information may create conflicts due to the different representations for the same features concerning, for example, shape, dimension, and positional accuracy. As example, Figure 12 shows two objects, A and B, with different representations at the same representational level, each coming from a different source. The example in Figure 12 is inconsistent with respect to a constraint that specifies that objects must have only one geometric representation.

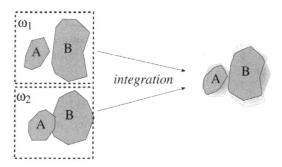

Fig. 12. Different representations of two objects

In the context of data integration, different types of consistency at the same representational level are distinguished [1]:

- *Total consistency* occurs when two configurations or data sets (i.e., when elements or objects that compose configurations) are identical.
- *Partial consistency* occurs when partial configurations are identical (i.e., when subsets of elements that compose configurations are identical).

As mentioned in Section 4.2 of consistency at multiple representational levels, two aspects of consistency when comparing data sets are object-based equivalence and relation-based equivalence. Object-based equivalence analyzes objects individually, so that it is possible to classify types of consistency in terms of the existence, shape, dimension, size, and degree of detail of objects. Relation-based equivalence focuses on objects' relationships, which are classified into topological, directional, or relative size equivalence.

The common approach to integrating different representations has assumed that when no further information exists about the origin of data, both representations are considered to equally contribute to the integration of information. In cases of multiple representational levels, a preliminary step is to check whether or not different representational levels are consistent. When representational levels are consistent, a more detailed level can be mapped onto and integrated into a less detailed level; that is, into a representation generated by a generalization process. If, at a common representational level, two different representations exist, partial consistency may still be possible (i.e., parts of the different representations of an object or configuration are identical). The idea is to merge both representations in such a way that the resulting representation is modeled as a vague or unclear one. In modeling these unclear boundaries, three alternatives are found [24]:

- *Fuzzy models* [2][56][64][71], which are based on fuzzy set theory and have been applied to spatial uncertainty. Fuzzy set theory is an extension of classical boolean set theory that deals with different degrees of possibility that an individual is a member of a set or that a given statement is true [70]. Examples of fuzzy spatial objects are mountains, cities, and oceans.
- *Probabilistic models* [12][33], which are based on probability theory to model positional and measurement uncertainty. Probabilistic approaches model uncertainty by determining a degree of membership of an entity in a set in terms of statistically defined functions. An example of an unclear boundary that can be modeled by a probabilistic model is the water level of a lake that is not certainly known.
- *Exact models* [15][16][21][32], which map data models for spatial objects with sharp boundaries onto spatial objects with broad boundaries.

Consider an example of a fuzzy representation of indeterminate regions (Figure 13). A membership function for area A can be specified in 8, where B stands for the region that is definitely outside of A, A/B is a region that can be part of A or B, and d_a and d_b are the distances from a point (x, y) in the region A/B to the core area of the region A (i.e. region where $\mu_A(x, u) = 1$) and the core area of the region B (i.e., region where $\mu_A(x, u) = 0$):

$$\mu_A(x, y) = \begin{cases} 1 & \text{if}(x, y) \in A \wedge (x, y) \notin B \\ 1 - d_a/(d_a + d_b) & \text{if}(x, y) \in A \wedge (x, y) \in B \\ 0 & \text{if}(x, y) \notin A \wedge (x, y) \in B \end{cases} \quad (8)$$

In the context of data integration, fuzzy theory can be used in the integration of two representations that overlap (i.e., a partial consistency). In such case,

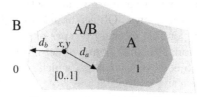

Fig. 13. A fuzzy region

one could consider that the overlapping areas or intersections between objects from different representations are the core areas of the integrated objects (i.e., dark grey of Figure 13 with membership function equal to 1) and the differences between the union and the intersection of representations are the unclear boundary of objects (i.e., light grey region with membership function in the range $[0 \ldots 1]$). The regions outside of objects in both representations are considered outside of the integrated objects. Following an exact approach to handle indeterminate boundaries, a broad boundary is associated with objects whose boundaries are unclear after integration. In the example of Figure 14, regions of broad boundaries are the regions that result from the difference between the union and intersection of objects in both representations, that is, the regions that do not clearly belong to the geometric representations of objects.

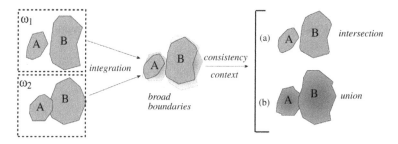

Fig. 14. Example of integration of spatial data based on previous knowledge of datasets

There are various possible strategies that can formalize the integration of more than one observation about location in a region with broad boundaries. These strategies make distinctions depending on the contextual information that characterizes the quality of representations [69]. For example, consider configurations in Figure 14, and assume that we know that both configurations (i.e., ω_1 and ω_2) are not accurate (i.e, there exist errors in positional information) then, only the intersection of both representations can be considered consistent (i.e., option (a) in Figure 14). If we consider that configuration ω_2 does not include regions that it should (i.e., incomplete representation), the union of both representations is considered consistent (i.e., option (b) in Figure 14).

Focusing on the integration of topological relations, the relation between objects with broad boundaries are described by an intersection matrix between interiors ($\circ$) (i.e., between the core of objects), broad boundaries (Δ) (i.e., between the unclear regions of objects), and exteriors ($^-$) [15] [60][67][68] (Figure 15). For topological relationships between regions with broad boundaries, 44 realizable matrices are possible.

Each intersection matrix of objects with broad boundaries has a set of topological relations that are realizable when considering changes from the core to the broad boundary of an object. In the case of Figure 15, three possible relations are realizables: *disjoint, meet* and *overlap*. Figure 16 shows these three alternatives when one considers that the geometry of objects change from the core to

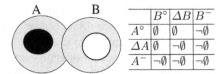

	B°	ΔB	B^-
A°	$\emptyset$	$\emptyset$	$\neg\emptyset$
ΔA	$\emptyset$	$\neg\emptyset$	$\neg\emptyset$
A^-	$\neg\emptyset$	$\neg\emptyset$	$\neg\emptyset$

Fig. 15. Intersection matrix of objects with broad boundaries

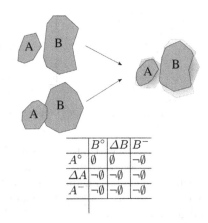

Fig. 16. Possible relations between objects with broad broundaries

	B°	ΔB	B^-
A°	$\emptyset$	$\emptyset$	$\neg\emptyset$
ΔA	$\neg\emptyset$	$\neg\emptyset$	$\neg\emptyset$
A^-	$\neg\emptyset$	$\neg\emptyset$	$\neg\emptyset$

Fig. 17. Integration of two representations

the broad boundaries. In this figure, gray lines represent the core boundary and broad boundary of objects.

To discuss the integration of different representations, consider the example in Figure 17, where two representations of two objects are integrated, resulting in objects with broad boundaries. The intersection of both representations define the core of objects and the difference between the union and the intersection defines the broad boundaries for each object. The idea here is not to analyze what the boundaries of individual objects are, but the relationship between objects; that is, what relationships are possible between the objects given that the integration of two representations results in objects with broad boundaries. From the point of view of consistency, if the analysis of broad boundaries determines that there exists only one possible relation between objects based on two representations, there is no conflicting information about the spatial relation between objects even in presence of different representations of objects. In presence of multiple possible relations and a constraint that enforces a unique relation between objects, multiple representations are inconsistent. In the example of Figure 17, the broad boundaries (Δ) make possible that objects are *disjoint, meet* or *overlap*, that is, consistency cannot be guarantee based on both representations.

In the same way than models for handling multiple representational levels of spatial objects, applications that integrate spatial information run as ad-hoc implementations, that is, they are user-defined applications rather than tools incorporated into current DBMS. These models also lack the specification in a formal language for their treatments as integrity constraints.

5   Consistency Tolerance in Spatial Databases

Although there has been active research on creating efficient spatial databases, the treatment of inconsistency in spatial databases is still a problem for current spatial information systems [8] [23]. The models described in the previous Sections about consistency at multiple representational levels and for data integration can be used in defining strategies for treating inconsistency in spatial databases; however, these models have not been integrated into a query process that explicitly addresses the answer and process of data despite the fact that the data are inconsistent (i.e., inconsistency tolerance). Inconsistency tolerance can be used to one's advantage when accessing or integrating data from different sources, or when it is inconvenient or impractical to enforce integrity constraints during data updates.

In traditional databases, studies have addressed inconsistency tolerance in query answers [3] [6] of a relational database schema with a set of integrity constraints over this schema. From these studies, possible alternatives for dealing with inconsistency in query answering are: *ignoring inconsistency* (i.e., using conflicting data in the answer), *eliminating inconsistency* data (i.e., considering none of the conflicting data for answer; data cleaning), and considering the *consistent answer that belongs to all consistent states* of the database based on *minimum repairs*. Conceptually, these alternatives could be applied in the spatial domain when issuing queries that rely on spatial operations from the relational algebra with spatial criteria.

For example, consider a spatial database that has conflicting representations of spatial objects (conflicting representation of object A in Figure 18).

Using an extended relational database, the data set in Figure 18 is represented by a relation *Spatial Object* with the following instances, where $region_i$ represents a value of the geometric primitive *region*:

Spatial Object	Name	Region
	A	$region_1$
	A	$region_2$
	B	$region_3$
	C	$region_4$
	D	$region_5$

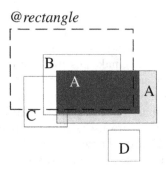

Fig. 18. An inconsistent database with different representations of an object A and a query defined by a window @*rectangle*

Having the functional dependency $Name \rightarrow Region$, meaning that the $Name$ functionally determines $Region$, the relation $Spatial\ Object$ violates the functional dependency, since there are two tuples with value A in attribute $Name$. In this example, two selection queries based on a space window (i.e., a rectangular area of the space @*rectangle*) that was defined by a user are:

1   **select** $clipping(r.geometry, @rectangle)$
     from $Regions\ r$
     where $Overlaps(r.geometry, @rectangle)$

2   **select** $r.geometry$
     from $Regions\ r$
     where $Overlaps(r.geometry, @rectangle)$

The first query returns the geometric parts of objects that overlap the window (@*rectangle*). The second query, on the other hand, returns the complete geometry of objects that totally or partially overlap the window. In answering these queries, the three alternatives of ignoring, eliminating, and considering minimum repairs of traditional databases can be applied (Figure 19). For the first query, ignoring inconsistency will return the geometric parts of both consistent and inconsistent data that overlap the query window. In this case, the conflicting representations of object A lay outside the overlapping region with the query window such that the answer does not have conflicting information. The situation is different, however, in the option of ignoring inconsistency for the second query, since the answer in that case will contain conflicting information, that is, two representations of object A that partially overlap the query window. In both queries, eliminating inconsistency data will not consider the conflicting data, that is, the geometry of object A is not considered as part of the answer.

The option of minimum repairs returns all the answers that belong to the result of query evaluation in every repair [6]. In this database, there are two possible repairs, each of them considering only one tuple of object A. In answering the first query in Figure 19, both repairs contain the same geometric area of objects A, B, and C that overlap the query window (Figure 20); therefore, these areas

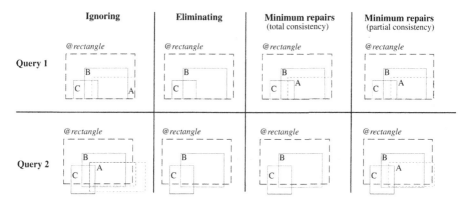

Fig. 19. Alternatives to consistent query answers from the inconsistent database

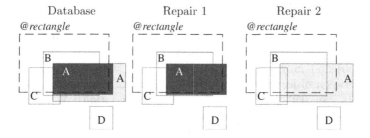

Fig. 20. Minimum repairs of the database

are part of the consistent answer. For answering the second query, since it is the complete geometry of objects that overlap the query window what is retrieved, only objects B and C can be considered consistent answers to this query.

The previous example of the second query illustrates that in the case of minimum repairs, one could consider two further alternatives that depend on the granularity of the determination of inconsistency in the geometric representation of spatial objects. One option is to take the geometry of an object as a whole, which is the basic case described before when making the repairs based on the complete geometries of objects (Figure 20). The second alternative of minimum repairs is to consider that the geometry of an object can be partially inconsistent, in which case, the repair of the database takes the consistent parts of objects' representations. Partial consistency may be defined by the part of the geometric representation of objects that is equivalent in conflicting information, that is, the intersection of geometric representations. For example, in the previous database, one of the representations of object A is inside of the other one such that the former corresponds to the intersection of both representations. This intersection region, by definition, is present in all representations of object A and, therefore, it is part of the database repair (Figure 21). In the example of the query 2 in Figure 19, the intersection of the geometric attribute of both tuples with value A in attribute *Name* will be considered in the answer.

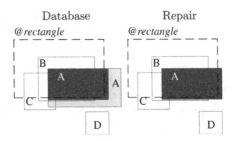

Fig. 21. The minimum repair of the database that considers partial consistency

Other interesting queries are those that uses criteria defined by spatial relations between objects. Spatial relations are usually derived during the query process, and they may not require accurate data about positional information. This type of query involves spatial joins between relations, which construct the pairs of tuples from the relations whose spatial components satisfy spatial predicates. When querying by spatial relations between objects, inconsistency with respect to the representation of objects (i.e., location and shape of objects) may not affect the consistency with respect to the spatial relation between objects (e.g., even with conflicting positional information exists, objects can still hold the same topological relation). What is more, by considering some metric refinements of topological relations (i.e., relative size and distance of objects) [36], one could also determine that objects keep the same topological relations despite the fact that they have conflicting geometric representations.

Consider the same database of spatial objects in Figure 18 and the following two selection queries based on a criteria of spatial relations between objects, where the difference is in the selection component (i.e., regions' ids or regions' geometries):

1 **select** $r_1.id$
   from $Regions\ r_1,\ Regions\ r_2$
   where $r_2.id =' B'$ and $Overlaps(r_1.geometry, r_2.geometry)$

2 **select** $r_1.geometry$
   from $Regions\ r_1,\ Regions\ r_2$
   where $r_2.id =' B'$ and $Overlaps(r_1.geometry, r_2.geometry)$

In answering these queries, the geometric representation is needed for applying the spatial criteria. The answer to the first query, however, does not concern the selection of the geometric representation of objects, but the selection of objects' ids. Thus, since the spatial criteria is satisfied in both representations of A, the answer to the query is the same in all repairs of the database. For the second query, in contrast, the answer is the geometric representation of objects so that, even if the spatial criteria is satisfied in all repairs of the database, the answer cannot include conflicting information (Figure 22).

	Ignoring	Elimining	Minimum repairs (total consistency)	Minimum repairs (partial consistency)
Query 1	A,C	C	A,C	A,C
Query 2				

Fig. 22. Alternatives to consistent query answers from the inconsistent database

Fig. 23. Aggregation of inconsistency representations by modeling objects with broad boundary

A different perspective for handling conflicting representations in answering a query is the use of broad boundaries in a query concerning the geometric aggregation of objects. This idea of objects with broad boundaries could be related to the way aggregate functions have been treated in consistent query answering from inconsistent traditional databases [4] [5] [14]. A consistent answer to an aggregation query is defined as a *minimum interval* such that the value of the aggregation function in every repair of the database belongs to this *minimum interval*. The end-points of the *minimum interval* corresponds to the greatest lower bound and the least upper bound answers to the query in the database.

In a query by aggregation of objects' geometry, two different geometric representations may lead to different aggregate objects. Answering a query may then involve treating the aggregate object as an object with broad boundaries, that is, an object with a crisp boundary defined by the intersection of all possible aggregations, and with a broad boundary defined by t the union of all aggregations (Figure 23). In this case, the *minimum interval* of possible answer are limited by the greatest lower bound that corresponds to the crisp region and the least upper bound that corresponds to the region defined by the broad boundary.

The previous examples have described conceptually the use of different alternatives for dealing with inconsistency tolerance with respect to geometric representations, without taking in consideration the computational mechanisms for obtaining consistent answers. Other examples with different types of inconsistencies, such as semantic inconsistency and topological inconsistency, and more complex queries are also possible. In all cases, much work need to be done with respect to what repairs and consistent answers are in spatial databases.

The treatment of inconsistency tolerance raises new issues respect to topological constraints. In such cases, the inconsistency is not the result of conflicting information about the position of objects, but rather of a lack of consistency with the rules that define the primitives of representation. For example, a typical structural constraint of a polygon is to be bounded by a non self-intersecting and closed polyline. The satisfaction of topological constraints ensures that some computational-geometry algorithms can be successfully executed; however, not all of these algorithms require the same structural constraints. For example, the boundary of a region must be defined by a closed polyline in order to calculate the area of a region. On the other hand, a closed and non self-intersecting polyline is the requirement of an algorithm for determining whether or not a point is inside of a region. So, if one only wants to compute the area of a polygon, polylines only need to be closed. This analysis may imply that topological constraints may be associated with the particular use of spatial operators rather than with a general definition of geometric primitives.

6   Conclusions

This chapter presents a review of the work on inconsistency in spatial databases. It discusses the kinds and origins of inconsistency, the specification of integrity constraints, and the treatment of inconsistency for representations at different levels and for data integration. Further, it discusses how inconsistency tolerance can be introduced in querying inconsistent spatial databases. This review highlightes issues about composite objects and spatial relations in the treatment of inconsistency.

Summarizing, important issues for the treatment of inconsistency that were discussed are:

- Inconsistency may relate to conflicting information with respect to positional or qualitative attributes of objects or to contradictions with respect to structural and semantic rules. Structural conditions of geometric primitives have been typically expressed as integrity constraints.
- Integrity constraints may refer to the geometric representation of objects by making reference to conditions on the geometric types of objects (i.e., point, polylines, regions), or they may refer to the semantic of spatial objects (e.g., a road cannot run into a body of water). Thus, constraints can be expressed, for example, by points or aggregations of points (i.e, by geometric primitives), or by objects or aggregations of objects (i.e., by objects that have a semantic meaning, such as rivers, building and roads).
- Queries concerning spatial relations may not need a unique geometric representation of objects and, therefore, such queries are less sensitive to conflicting positional information.
- Definitions of composite objects deal with sets of objects and impose constraints between wholes and parts to enforce consistency.
- Geometric information about spatial objects can be considered as a whole unit (i.e., a geometric representation is consistent or inconsistent as a whole)

or can be considered as an aggregation of spatial parts (i.e., a geometric representation is consistent, partially consistent, or totally inconsistent).
- Multiple representation levels with respect to different scales may be necessary in information systems. In such cases, multiple representations are considered consistent if they satisfy basic topological constraints.
- Different definitions of consistent answers and database repairs can be applied to spatial databases based on the interpretation and use of the geometric representations.

Since this chapter has outlined issues concerning the treatment of inconsistency of spatial databases, it leaves the door open for exploring aspects of formalization and implementation of mechanisms for consistent query answering from inconsistent spatial databases. Although it was not discussed in the chapter, there is an increasing interest in the research community of spatial databases toward the management of spatial-temporal applications. These types of applications raise issues of temporal, spatial, and spatial-temporal consistency [40] [50] [51].

Acknowledgment. Andrea Rodríguez's research work is partially funded by CONICYT under grant FONDECYT 1030301.

References

1. A. Abdelmoty and C. Jones. Towards maintening consistency in spatial databases. In *Proceedings of the Sixth International Conference on Information and Knowledge Management*, pages 293–300, Las Vergas, USA, 1997. ACM Press.
2. D. Altman. Fuzzy set theory approaches for hadling imprecision in spatial analysis. *International Journal of Geographic Information Science*, 8(3):271–289, 1994.
3. M. Arenas, L. Bertossi, and J. Chomicki. Consistent query answers in inconsistent databases. In *ACM Symposium on Principles of Database Systems (PODS)*, pages 68–79, 1999.
4. M. Arenas, L. Bertossi, and J. Chomicki. Specifying and querying database repairs using logic programs with exceptions. In *International Conference on Flexible Query Answering Systems (FGAS)*, pages 27–41. Springer-Verlag, 2000.
5. M. Arenas, L. Bertossi, and J. Chomicki. Answer sets for consistent query answering in inconsistent databases. *Theory and Practice of Logic Programming*, 3(4 & 5):393–424, 2003.
6. L. Bertossi and J. Chomicki. Query answering in inconsistent databases. In J. Chimicki, G. Saake, and R. van der Meyden, editors, *Logics for Emerging Applications of Databases*. Springer-Verlag, 2003.
7. P. Bonnissone and R. Tong. Reasoning with uncertainty in expert systems. *International Journal of Man and Machine Studies*, 22:241–250, 1985.
8. K. Borges, C. Davis, and A. Laender. Integrity constraints in spatial databases. In *Database Integrity: Challenges and Solutions*. Ideas Group, 2002.
9. K. Borges, A. Laender, and C. Davis. Spatial integrity constraints in object oriented geographic data modeling. In C. Bauzer-Medeiros, editor, *ACM International Symposium on Advances in GIS*, pages 1–6. ACM Press, 1999.

10. P. Bosc and H. Prade. An introduction to fuzzy set and possibility theory based approaches to the treatment of uncertainty and imprecision in datatabase management systems. In A. Motro and P. Smets, editors, *Uncertainty Management in Information Systems: From Needs to Solutions*, pages 285–324. Kluwer Academic Publishers, 1997.

11. T. Bruns and M. Egenhoger. Similarity of spatial scenes. In *International Symposium on Spatial Data Handling SDH'96*, pages 31–42, Delf, The Netherlands, 1996. Taylor and Francis.

12. P. Burrough. Natural objects with undeterminate boundaries. In A. Frank, editor, *Geographic Objects with Indeterminate Boundaries GISDATA*, pages 3–28. Taylor & Francis, 1996.

13. A. Chandra and D. Harel. Computable queries for relational database systems. *Journal of Computer and System Sciences*, 21(2):156–178, 1980.

14. J. Chomicki. Consistent query answering: Recent developments and future directions. In S. Jajodia and L. Strous, editors, *Working Conference on Integrity and Internal Control in Information Systems*, Lousanne, Switzerland, 2003. Kluwer Publishers.

15. E. Clementini and P. Di Felice. An algebraic model for spatial objects with undeterminate boundaries. In A. Frank, editor, *Geographic Objects with Indeterminate Boundaries*, pages 155–169, London, 1996. Taylor & Francis.

16. E. Clementini and P. Di Felice. Approximate topological relations. *International Journal of Approximate Reasoning*, 16:73–204, 1997.

17. E. Clementini, J. Sharma, and M. Egenhofer. Modeling topological relations: Strategies for query preprocessing. *Computers and Graphics*, 18(6):815–822, 1994.

18. S. Cockcroft. A taxonomy of spatial integrity constraints. *GeoInformatica*, 1(4):327–343, 1997.

19. S. Cockcroft. Modelling spatial data integrity constraints at the metadata level. In D. Pullar, editor, *GeoComputation*, Brisbane, Australia, 2001.

20. A. Cohn, B. Bennett, J. Gooday, and N. Gotts. Representing and reasoning with qualitative spatial relations about regions. In O. Stock, editor, *Spatial and Temporal Reasoning*, pages 97–134. Kluwer Academic Publishers, 1997.

21. G. Cohn and N. Gotts. The 'egg-yolk' representation of regions with indeterminate boundaries. In A. Frank, editor, *Geographic Objects with Indeterminate Boundaries*, pages 171–187, London, 1996. Taylor & Francis.

22. H. Couclelis. People manipulate objects (but cultivate fields): Beyond the raster-vecter debate in gis. In A. Frank, I. Campari, and U. Formentini, editors, *Theories and Methods of Spatio-Temporal Reasoning in Geographic Space. LNCS vol. 639*, pages 65–77. Springer-Verlag, 1992.

23. M. Egenhofer. Consistency revisited. *GeoInformatica*, 1(4):323–325, 1997.

24. M. Egenhofer, E. Clementini, and P. Di Felice. Evaluating inconsistency among multiple representations. In *Spatial Data Handling*, pages 901–920, Edinburg, Scotland, 1994.

25. M. Egenhofer and R. Franzosa. Point-set topological spatial relations. *International Journal of Geographical Information Systems*, 5(2):161–174, 1991.

26. M. Egenhofer and R. Franzosa. On the equivalence of topological relations. *International Journal of Geographical Information Systems*, 8(6):133–152, 1994.

27. M. Egenhofer and J. Herring. Categorizing topological spatial relations between point, line, and area objects. Technical Report Report 94-1, National Center for Geographic Information Analysis, 1994.

28. M. Egenhofer and D. Mark. Naive geography. In A. Frank and W. Kuhn, editors, *Theoretical Basis for Geographic Information Systems COSIT'95*, pages 1–14, Semmering, Austria, 1995. Springer-Verlag.

29. M. Egenhofer and J. Sharma. Topological consistency. In P. Bresnahan, E. Corwin, and D. Cowen, editors, *Proceedings of the 5th International Symposium on Spatial Data Handling*, pages 335–343, Charleston, USA, 1992. IGU Commission of GIS.

30. M. Egenhofer and J. Sharma. Assessing the consistency of complete and incomplete topological information. *Geographical Systems*, 1(1):47–68, 1993.

31. R. Elsmari and S. Navathe. *Fundamentals of Database Systems*. Addison Wesley, 3er edition edition, 2000.

32. M. Erwing and M. Schneider. Vague regions. In *5th Int. Symposium on Advances in Spatial Databases SSD97. LNCS 1262*, pages 298–320. Springer-Verlag, 1997.

33. J. Finn. Use of the average mutual information index in evaluating error and consistency. *International Journal of Geographic Information Science*, 7(4):349–366, 1993.

34. A. Frank. Tiers of ontology and consistency constraints in geographical information systems. *International Journal of Geographic Information Science*, 15(7):667–678, 2001.

35. G. Gardarin, J.P. Cheiney, G. Kiernan, D. Pastre, and H. Stora. Managening complex objects in an extensible relational DBMS. In *Proceedings of Very Large Data Bases*, 1989.

36. F. Gody and A. Rodríguez. A quantitative description of spatial configurations. In D. Richardson and P. van Oosterom, editors, *Proceedings of the 10th Symposium on Spatial Data Handling*, pages 299–311. Springer, 2002.

37. R. Güting. An introduction to spatial database systems. *VLDB Journal*, 3:357–399, 1994.

38. R. Güting and M. Schneider. *International Symposium on Spatial Databases, Lecture Notes in Computer Science Vol. 692*, chapter Realms: A Foundation for Spatial Data Types in Database Systems, pages 14–35. Springer-Verlag, 1993.

39. R. Güting and M. Schneider. Realm-based spatial data types: The rose algebra. Technical Report 141-3-93, Fern Universität, Hagen, 1993.

40. R. Guüting, M. Böhlen, M. Erwing, C. Jensen, N. Lorentzos, M. Schneider, and M. Vazirgiannis. Foundation for representing and querying moving objects. *ACM Transactions on Database Systems*, 25(1):1–42, 2000.

41. T. Hadzilacos and N. Tryfona. A model for expressing topological constraints in geographic databases. In A. Frank, I. Campari, and U. Formentini, editors, *Theories and Methods of Spatio-Temporal Reasoning in Geographic Space COSIT92*, pages 252–268, Pisa, Italy, 1992. Springer-Verlag.

42. P. Kanellakis, G. Kuper, and P. Revesz. Constraint query languages. *Journal of Computer and System Sciences*, 51(1):26–52, 1995.

43. B. Kuipers, J. Paredaens, and J. den Busshe. On topological equivalence of spatial databases. In F. Afrati and Ph. Kolaitis, editors, *6th International Conference on Database Theory ICDT97, LNCS 1186*, pages 432–446. Springer Verlag, 1997.

44. G. Kuper, L. Libkin, and J. Paredaens. *Constraint Databases*. Springer-Verlag, 2000.

45. R. Laurini and D. Thompson. *Fundamentals ofr Spatial Information Systems*. Academic Press, 1992.

46. D. Papadias and Y. Theodoridis. Spatial relations, minimum bounding rectangles and spatial data structures. *International Journal of Geographical Information Science*, 11(2):111–138, 1997.

47. J. Paredaens, J. Van den Bussche, and D. Van Gucht. Towards a theory of spatial databases queries. In *Proceedings of the 13th ACM SIGACT-SIGMOD-SIGART Symposium on Principles of Database Systems*, pages 128–288. ACM Press, 1994.

48. J. Paredaens and B. Kuipers. Data models and query languages for spatial databases. *Data Knowledge Engineering*, 25(1-2):29–53, 1998.

49. S. Parson. Current approaches to handling imperfect information in data and knowledge bases. *IEEE Transactions on Knowledge and Data Engineering*, 8(3):353–371, 1996.

50. D. Pfoser and C. Jensen. Capturing the uncertainty of moving-object representations. In R. Güting, D. Papdias, and F. Lochovsky, editors, *Proceedings of the 6th International Symposium on the Advances in Spatial Databases*, pages 111–132. Springer Verlag, 1999.

51. D. Pfoser and N. Tryfona. Capturing fuzziness and uncertainty of spatiotemporal objects. In A. Caplinskas and J. Eder, editors, *5th East-European Conference on Advances in Databases and Information Systems ADBIS01. LNCS 2151*, pages 112–126, Lithuania, 2001. Springer Verlag.

52. A. Pizzaro, A. Klinger, and A. Cardenas. Specification of spatial integrity constraints in pictorical databases. *Computer*, 22(12):59–71, 1989.

53. L. Plümer and G. Gröger. Achieving integrity constraints in geographic information systemsd. *GeoInformatica*, 1(4):345–367, 1997.

54. P. Ragaux, M. Scholl, and A. Voisard. *Spatial Databases: with Application in GIS*. Academic Press, 2002.

55. H. Samet. *The Design and Analysis of Spatial Data Structures*. Addison-Wesley, 1990.

56. M. Schneider. Metric operations on fuzzy spatial objects in databases. In *Proceedings of the 8th ACm Symposium on Geographic Information Systems*, pages 21–26, Washington DC, 2000. ACM Press.

57. S. Servige, T. Ubeda, A. Puricelli, and R. Laurini. A methodology for spatial consistency improvement of geographic databases. *GeoInformatica*, 4:7–24, 2000.

58. S. Shekhar and S. Chawla. *Spatial Databases: A Tour*. Prentice Hall, 2003.

59. S. Shekhar, M. Coyle, B. Goyal, D.-R. Liu, and S. Sarkar. Data models in geographic information systems. *Comm. ACM*, 40(4):103–111, 1997.

60. J. Stell and M. Worboys. Stratified map spaces. In T. Poiker and N. Chrisman, editors, *Spatial Data Handling*, pages 180–189, British Columbia, Canada, 1998. Taylor & Francis.

61. O. Stock. *Spatial and Temporal Reasoning*. Kluwer Acaddemic Publishers, 1997.

62. M. Stonebraker and L.A. Rowe. The design of POSTGRES. In *Proceedings of ACM SIGARCT-SIGMOD*, pages 340–355, 1986.

63. N. Tryfona and M. Egenhofer. Consistency among parts and aggregates: A computational model. *Transactions on GIS*, 1(3):189–206, 1997.

64. E. Usery. A conceptual framwork and fuzzy set implementation for geographic features. In A. Frank, editor, *Geographic Objects with Undeterminate Boundaries GISDATA*, pages 71–85. Taylor & Francis, 1996.

65. A. Voisard and B. David. A database pespective on geospatial data modeling. *IEEE Transactions on Knowledge and Data Engineering*, 14(2):226–246, 2002.

66. M. Worboys. A geometric model for planar geographical objects. *International Journal of Geographical Information Systems*, 6(5):353–372, 1992.

67. M. Worboys. Computation with imprecise geographic data. *Journal of Computers, Environment and Urvan Systems*, 22:85–106, 1998.

68. M. Worboys. Imprecision in finite resolution spatial data. *GeoInformatica*, 2:257–280, 1998.

69. M. Worboys and E. Clementini. Integration of imperfect spatial information. *Journal of Visual Languages and Computing*, 12:61–80, 2001.
70. L. Zadeh. Fuzzy sets. *Information and Control*, 8:338–358, 1965.
71. F. Zhan. Approximate analysis of binary topological relations between geographic regions with indeterminate boundaries. *Soft Computing*, 2:28–34, 1988.

Relevant Logic and Paraconsistency

John Slaney*

The Australian National University
and National ICT Australia,
Canberra, Australia
John.Slaney@anu.au.edu

Abstract. This is an account of the approach to paraconsistency associated with relevant logic. The logic **fde** of first degree entailments is shown to arise naturally out of the deeper concerns of relevant logic. The relationship between relevant logic and resolution, and especially the disjunctive syllogism, is then examined. The relevant refusal to validate these inferences is defended, and finally it is suggested that more needs to be done towards a satisfactory theory of when they may nonetheless safely be used.

1 Why Paraconsistency?

The core business of logic is to underpin reasoning. The distinction is important: a logic is a *theory*; reasoning is a *process*. The activities of a reasoner are not dictated by logic, but are described by it in the sense that logic issues permissions—assurances that certain forms of inference will never lead into error—and restrictions. The restrictions are not on inferences, for the reasoner may of course reason invalidly if it so wishes, but on the formation of theories not closed under the principles enunciated in the logic. Thus logic is a guide to reasoning as well as a description of it: a "normative science", as Ramsey succinctly put it.[1] That sets up the central paradox of the philosophy of logic: norms are necessarily prior to the behaviour they circumscribe or guide, but phenomena are prior to the science that describes them, so how is such a normative science possible? The nature of logic will not be settled in this paper, but we may at least investigate an important issue that bears directly upon it.

The problem arises in matching logic to the activity of reasoning with inconsistent information. Such reasoning is desirable in practice, and apparently rational, yet accommodating it challenges the most basic principles on which standard formal logic is built. The standard view of contradictions is that they are (necessarily) false, so no inference with contradictory premises can lead into error: if you start from a contradiction, you are already in error, so it simply

---

* National ICT Australia is funded through the Australian Government's *Backing Australia's Ability* initiative, in part through the Australian Research Council.
[1] This conversational remark of Ramsey's, reported by Wittgenstein in the *Philosophical Investigations*, applies equally to other formal sciences such as grammar.

L. Bertossi et al. (Eds.): Inconsistency Tolerance, LNCS 3300, pp. 270–293, 2004.

does not matter what inference you make. That is, logic validates the argument form:

$$\frac{A \qquad\qquad \neg A}{B}$$

On the other side of the coin, the classical account prohibits theories which are inconsistent in the sense of containing a contradiction but for which it is a non-trivial question what else they contain. This prohibition is not consonant with reasoning practice, in which it is fairly common to encounter bodies of information which are inconsistent in ways which should not inhibit reasoning.

Three examples of such reasoning situations in which giving up in the face of inconsistency is not an appropriate response will serve as illustrations:

1. Database management: data integration. It is common for databases to make available data from many sources, and important for them to be able to do this while imposing strong integrity constraints. Since the sources may have overlapping domains, in which they may conflict, and since they are not always expected to satisfy the integrity constraints, especially when taken in combination with each other, there arises a need for the deductive part of the database to cope with inconsistency. Many techniques for this have been suggested, sometimes based on nonmonotonic reasoning because it is expected that consistency should be restored through repeated revision of the data over time. However, the static logical description of inconsistent data also demands to be taken seriously, especially as there may be cases in which the inconsistency of the global database is undetected at the time of query answering and in which data may become obsolete and be replaced faster than the corpus can be checked for consistency and corrected.

2. Software engineering: merging specifications. Software specifications must frequently be put together from many sources, fragments being in different languages and contributed by different experts. There may be indeterminacy as to whether an apparent conflict (one expert says that a transition from state a to state b is possible, while another says that a transition from state α to state β is impossible) is to be resolved by distinguishing between a and α, b and β or whether it should remain in the proto-specification as a genuine disagreement, perhaps to be cleaned up later in some way. A standard move is to represent the amalgamated specification in a logical framework where the "truth values" are tuples of values (true, false, unknown) standing for the opinions of the various experts from whom the fragments are taken. An alternative is to use a four-valued scheme to allow the cases in which we have been told that something is true, told that it is false, both or neither. The logical manipulation of this "useful 4-valued logic" [4] requires paraconsistency in order to cope with the truth value gaps and gluts without collapse.

3. Epistemic logic: first order beliefs. It is usual in doxastic and epistemic logic to consider belief sets closed under logical entailment rather than sets of propositions immediately and explicitly available to an agent. This concentration on implicit beliefs is essential to any treatment based on normal [multi-]modal logics, since it is an outcome of the K principles that the belief sets in question are deductively closed—the *theories* of agents rather than their explicit contents. The question of whether an agent believes p is then one of whether p follows logically from the agent's explicit beliefs, not one of whether p is actually present to the agent. Thus it does not lie open to introspection. In a language as rich as first order logic, indeed, it does not lie open to effective determination at all. It is thus quite possible for an agent to arrive at a belief that p, unaware (explicitly) that $\neg p$ follows from its beliefs, and thus (implicitly) to embrace a contradiction. This situation is not particularly abnormal, and calls for paraconsistent logical treatment, not for dismissal as a case that "cannot happen".

There are three styles of approach to such inconsistency, very likely each with its appropriate range of applications. Firstly, the inconsistent theory may be regarded as a temporary departure from a previously consistent one and the problem as one of restoring consistency by revision or some other type of non-monotonic reasoning. Secondly, the formulae whose consequences are (globally) inconsistent may be treated like soft constraints in an overconstrained CSP, and "large" consistent subtheories sought without necessarily changing the inconsistent theory. Of course, these two responses may be combined in various ways. The third approach is to regard the inconsistent theory as logically respectable just as it stands, and therefore to adopt a genuinely paraconsistent logic as the underlying theory of valid inference. It is this third option which is the subject of the present paper.

Paraconsistency requires inconsistent theories to be entertained without collapse into triviality, and hence affects most directly the logic of negation. However, the logic of negation is obtained by fitting an account of denial into the framework provided by positive logic. Accordingly, it is with the negation-free part of logic that we begin the next section.

2   The Relevant Approach

There are many paraconsistent systems on the menu, but one of the oldest and most systematically developed is relevant logic [2, 3, 21, 23] in which paraconsistency is not itself the main motivation but arises naturally out of other concerns. Those other concerns historically included securing relevance—most simply that in the propositional part of the logic, no implication should be accounted valid unless antecedent and consequent share a variable. The classical inference from $p \wedge \neg p$ to q of course violates even this simple relevance requirement. However, the deeper motivation of the relevant family of logics is to formalise a notion of proof in which part of what constitutes a derivation of a conclusion *from* assumptions is that the assumptions be *used* in deriving the conclusion, and to marry this structural condition on derivations with systematic logical properties such as a decent deduction theorem and, importantly, with a very "ordinary" account of the familiar truth-functional connectives.

2.1   Relevant Positive Logic

Their truth-functional character gives the operations of conjunction and disjunction all of their logical properties from the relevant point of view. This puts relevant logic in the same family as intuitionist logic and the usual modal logics, rather than that of linear logic and the other substructural systems, as regards its treatment of the extensional connectives. Semantically, these connectives are evaluated at each world using only information local to that world—specifically, the values of the conjuncts or disjuncts at that world—in the standard way. This results in the set of "positive first-degree entailments" which may be characterised using $\wedge$ and $\vee$ as multiary connectives thus:

1. Where $p_1, \ldots, p_m$ and $q_1, \ldots, q_n$ are all atomic,
   $p_1 \wedge \ldots \wedge p_m \vdash q_1 \vee \ldots \vee q_n$ iff for some $i \leq m$ and $j \leq m$, $p_i = q_j$.
2. $A_1 \wedge \ldots \wedge A_{i-1} \wedge (B \vee C) \wedge A_{i+1} \wedge \ldots \wedge A_m \vdash D$ iff
   $A_1 \wedge \ldots \wedge A_{i-1} \wedge B \wedge A_{i+1} \wedge \ldots \wedge A_m \vdash D$ and
   $A_1 \wedge \ldots \wedge A_{i-1} \wedge C \wedge A_{i+1} \wedge \ldots \wedge A_m \vdash D$
3. $A \vdash B_1 \vee \ldots \vee B_{j-1} \vee (C \wedge D) \vee B_{j+1} \vee \ldots \vee B_n$ iff
   $A \vdash B_1 \vee \ldots \vee B_{j-1} \vee C \vee B_{j+1} \vee \ldots \vee B_n$ and
   $A \vdash B_1 \vee \ldots \vee B_{j-1} \vee D \vee B_{j+1} \vee \ldots \vee B_n$

Algebraically, the structures modelling this fragment of logic are simply distributive lattices. That is, a "propositional structure" for this logic is a set on which are defined binary operations $\wedge$ (meet) and $\vee$ (join) each of which is idempotent, commutative and associative, such that:[2]

$$a \wedge (a \vee b) = a$$
$$a \vee (a \wedge b) = a$$
$$a \wedge (b \vee c) = (a \wedge b) \vee (a \wedge c)$$
$$a \vee (b \wedge c) = (a \vee b) \wedge (a \vee c)$$

A model in such a propositional structure is just a homomorphism from the formula algebra into the lattice in the obvious sense, lattice meet corresponding to conjunction and lattice join to disjunction. There is nothing specific to relevant logic about this: the story for classical logic is exactly the same, as it is for intuitionist logic and many others. This is worth emphasising, since it is a feature of the relevant approach that it does not depend on any strange definition of entailment or the like, but agrees totally with the standard logics as regards the basic truth-functional connectives.

Classically, negation and implication are basic truth-functional connectives as well. Relevantly, although we shall urge below that negation can reasonably be regarded as truth-functional, implication is something else. The relevant theory of implication belongs firmly to the tradition of substructural logic. There

---

[2] As a trivial fact of lattice theory, only one of the first two and one of the last two of these postulates are needed, but all four are given here to emphasise the complete duality of the two operations.

is a semantic account, to be sure, but the fundamental intuitions concerning implication are deduction-theoretic in nature.

The essence of the implication operation, $\rightarrow$, is encapsulated in the deduction equivalence:

$$\Gamma \vdash A \rightarrow B \text{ iff } \Gamma, A \vdash B$$

That is, some information Γ suffices for an implication $A \rightarrow B$ iff the assumption of A in the context of Γ suffices for B. The implication records the availability of an inference from A to B. This much, too, is common to classical logic, intuitionist logic, the whole range of substructural logics, several many-valued logics and others. Those logics tend, however, to disagree about the details of which entailments hold among formulae involving the implication operator. Does $(p \rightarrow q) \rightarrow p$ entail p? Does $(p \rightarrow q) \rightarrow (q \rightarrow p)$ entail $q \rightarrow p$? Does p entail $q \rightarrow q$? Does $p \rightarrow (p \rightarrow q)$ entail $p \rightarrow q$? These questions are not answered by the deduction equivalence alone, but by the underlying theory of how inference is structured, which differs from logic to logic. Differences at that level affect the account of what it is to "assume A in the context of Γ", and hence the possible readings of the compound object Γ, A.

The fundamental idea of relevant implication is simple: a derivation of B is not "from" a structure Γ, A as required for the deduction equivalence unless A is in the appropriate sense *used* in reaching B. The paradigm cases of "use" are clear: both premises are used in an application of the rule of detachment in which D is derived from C and $C \rightarrow D$, but the first premise is *not* used in the derivation of D from C and D by the rule of iteration. Use is transitive, so whatever is used in deriving lemmas from axioms is used in the derivation of a theorem from those axioms by means of the lemmas.

The implicational fragment of the standard relevant logic **R** results by making this guiding idea rigorous in a very natural way. Let X, Y, etc be the sets of assumptions used in derivations. Note that the *sets* of assumptions correspond in general to *multisets* of formulae, since nothing prevents two or more distinct assumptions of the same formula. We write $X : A$ to mean that A is derived relevantly from assumptions X. Now the introduction and elimination rules for the implication connective $\rightarrow$ are simple and obvious. For introduction, we have

$$\frac{X : B}{X \setminus \{x\} : A \rightarrow B}$$

where x is an assumption of the formula A and (for relevance) it is required that $x \in X$. The elimination rule is detachment, as is familiar:

$$\frac{X : A \rightarrow B \qquad Y : A}{X \cup Y : B}$$

To get the calculus started, it is of course relevantly fine to derive a formula from an assumption of itself, though not in general from a set of assumptions of which it happens to be a member, since there may be no way to *use* all the side assumptions in the derivation. It will be apparent that this logic is the pure implication fragment of the substructural logic BCIW: that which allows collections of formulae to have the associative and commutative character of multisets, and allows the structural rule of contraction, but disallows weakening. Thus, despite its appearance and reputation as something exotic, the relevant logic of implication is actually a logic very much in the mainstream tradition: it is in fact exactly like intuitionist pure implicational logic except for the extra feature that due attention is paid to which assumptions are used and which are idle. In particular, it does not involve violent departures from logical tradition such as non-transitive entailment relations, restrictions on the nesting of connectives or special treatment for formulae of some distinguished kind such as inconsistent ones.

R is natural, given the motivation, but it is not the only possibility. There is not one relevant logic, just as there is not one modal logic, but a family, since the interpretation of the guiding notion of "relevance" is an equivocal matter. The paradigm cases of "use" may indeed be clear, but more delicate questions soon arise. Does the order of assumptions matter? – that is, is the effect of assuming B in the context of A different from that of assuming A in the context of B? For the standard relevant logic **R** there is no difference, but the systems **T** and **E** originally preferred by Anderson and Belnap [2] do make a distinction. Again, how are uses to be *counted*? Have we used *all* of the assumptions in deriving A from A, A? Not according to **R**: if you want to discharge A twice you have to use it twice; in the semi-relevant system **RM** [7] however, repetitions don't count. Conversely, according to **R**, once an assumption is in play it may be used as often as it takes to reach a conclusion, and then discharged in just one step, whereas in the weaker system **C**, whose pure implication fragment is that of linear logic, once an assumption is used it is consumed so to use it twice you must assume it twice. Different decisions as to the structural rules lead to different logics, although in a straightforward sense the *meaning* of the implication connective is the same in all of them.

It is not part of the present purpose to examine the differences between the many logics in the relevant family. Still less is it to declare one of them the One True Logic. Rather let it be noted that they are all constructed by fitting together the stable and relatively uncontroversial classical theory of conjunction and disjunction with a weakening-free substructural logic of implication. Because the fundamental motivation for the former is semantic, based on the "truth tables" for the dual pair of lattice connectives, while the latter arises from considerations concerning the structure of deduction and is thus essentially proof-theoretic, combining the two is not trivial. Specifically, the principle of distributivity of $\wedge$ over $\vee$ and *vice versa* is proof-theoretically unnatural except in the context of intuitionist logic and the like in which the fine distinctions required for substructurality are obliterated. The relevant logics, however, derive their distinctive character from the way in which they manage to maintain both the "intensional" and the "extensional" subtheories as motivated above, while combining them without restriction in the richer logic.

To specify the relevant positive logic R_+ deductively, we use two ways of combining assumptions: the formulae A_1 through A_n may be collected into a set $\{A_1, \ldots, A_n\}$ or a multiset $[A_1, \ldots, A_n]$.[3] The set represents "pooling" information, with no particular consideration for which subset is used in making a deduction, while the multiset represents pieces of information which have been all been used in combination. Bunching of formulae under these two operations may be nested arbitrarily: any formula A is both an S-bunch ("set bunch") and an M-bunch ("multiset bunch"); any non-singleton set of M-bunches is an S-bunch and any non-singleton multiset of S-bunches is an M-bunch. Our notation follows standard practice (e.g. [25]) whereby the comma-separated list $X_1, \ldots, X_n$ stands for $\{X_1, \ldots, X_n\}$ while the semicolon-separated list $X_1; \ldots; X_n$ stands for $[X_1, \ldots, X_n]$. We also write $\Gamma(\Delta)$ in the normal way to indicate a bunch in which Δ occurs in some place as a sub-bunch, so $\Gamma(\Delta')$ differs from it exactly in that Δ' occurs instead of Δ in that particular place. The logic may be presented in natural deduction style as a calculus of sequents with bunches of formulae on the left and single formulae on the right. The axioms are the sequents of the form $A \vdash A$ and the logical (introduction and elimination) rules are:

$$\frac{\Gamma \vdash A \qquad \Delta \vdash B}{\Gamma, \Delta \vdash A \wedge B} \ (\wedge I) \qquad\qquad \frac{\Gamma \vdash A \wedge B}{\Gamma \vdash A} \ (\wedge E)$$

$$\frac{\Gamma \vdash A \wedge B}{\Gamma \vdash B} \ (\wedge E)$$

$$\frac{\Gamma \vdash A \vee B \quad \Delta(A) \vdash C \quad \Delta(B) \vdash C}{\Delta(\Gamma) \vdash C} \ (\vee E) \qquad \frac{\Gamma \vdash A}{\Gamma \vdash A \vee B} \ (\vee I)$$

$$\frac{\Gamma \vdash B}{\Gamma \vdash A \vee B} \ (\vee I)$$

$$\frac{\Gamma \vdash A \rightarrow B \qquad \Delta \vdash A}{\Gamma; \Delta \vdash B} \ (\rightarrow E) \qquad\qquad \frac{\Gamma; A \vdash B}{\Gamma \vdash A \rightarrow B} \ (\rightarrow I)$$

Note that the arrow goes with intensional (multiset) combination of assumptions, while conjunction goes with extensional (set) combination.

There are also structural rules marking the difference between sets and multisets. Both operations, symbolised by the comma and semicolon respectively, are associative and commutative, and both satisfy contraction in the form:

---

[3] The idea of formulating these logics with two operations for combining assumptions goes back at least to Dunn [8] and has since become fairly standard and been elaborated by many authors [5, 6, 12, 20, 21, 25, 26].

$$\frac{\Gamma(\Delta, \Delta) \vdash A}{\Gamma(\Delta) \vdash A} \text{ (W-set)} \qquad \frac{\Gamma(\Delta; \Delta) \vdash A}{\Gamma(\Delta) \vdash A} \text{ (W-multiset)}$$

Set combination, though not multiset combination, also satisfies the standard rule of weakening:

$$\frac{\Gamma(\Delta) \vdash A}{\Gamma(\Delta, \Delta') \vdash A} \text{ (K-set)}$$

A small but important detail is that the empty set $\emptyset$ and the empty multiset $\mathbf{I}$ are different objects satisfying the conditions $\emptyset, \Gamma = \Gamma$ and $\mathbf{I}; \Gamma = \Gamma$ respectively. Formula A is a logical theorem iff $\mathbf{I} \vdash A$ is provable.

All of this looks very much as normal, except for the well-motivated distinction between assumptions which have been combined and those which just co-occur. The very ordinariness of the system is what needs to be stressed: this is a logic in the mainstream tradition of logical theory—static, monotonic and with a familiar look. But for a few wrinkles, it could have been proposed by Frege or Tarski.

Semantically, too, it is much what should be expected of a marriage between a substructural treatment of implication and a truth functional account of the lattice connectives. On the substructural side, the fundamental semantic idea is that of combining two bodies of information, and in particular taking one such body to supply the available inferences and applying it to another which supplies the facts available to serve as inputs to those inferences. Thus if the first body contains the information that all tigers are carnivores (an inference ticket) and the second gives us the information that Timmy is a tiger (a fact), then by applying the first to the second we may deduce that Timmy is a carnivore.

Formally [22] a frame for a logic in the relevant family is a set of evaluation points, which may be thought of as bodies of information, or information states. The set is partially ordered by increasing strength—intuitively, by inclusion of the information. We write $x \leq y$ to mean y is stronger than x. More generally, there is a *ternary* relation defined on the set: $Rxyz$ means that z contains everything that can be derived from y by applying an inference warranted by x.[4] What properties does this relation have? In the basic case, nothing beyond monotonicity. That is, if x or y is weakened, or if z is strengthened, the relation $Rxyz$ still holds. In the case of particular logics such as $\mathbf{R}$ there are more postulates on the relation, just as there are in the semantic stories corresponding to modal logics stronger than $\mathbf{K}$, but these are best considered as additions to the basic theory, again as in the modal case. There is one more component to a frame: a distinguished point 0 representing the truth, or the real world, or that which is logically correct. Its characteristic property is that if it says that x is included in y then x is really included in y. That is, $R0xy$ iff $x \leq y$.

---

[4] We have sometimes [26] written $Rxyz$ as $y \leq_x z$ which is suggestive of the meaning: y is contained in z from the perspective of x. However, the neutral 'R' notation is standard in the literature and is followed here for that reason.

A model in such a frame is a function assigning to each atomic formula p a set of points, intended to be those points at which p is evaluated to "true". Naturally, this satisfies a heredity condition that the set assigned to p is closed under $\leq$. The modelling condition for implications is the obvious one: $A \to B$ holds at a point x iff x warrants the inference from A to B; that is, for all points y and z such that $Rxyz$, if A holds at y then B holds at z. The true formulae in a model are those which hold at 0, and the valid formulae on a frame (or set of frames) are those which are true in all models on that frame (or on all frames in that set).

Accounting for the lattice connectives $\wedge$ and $\vee$ is simple: require the evaluation points to be world-like in that they treat truth-functional operators truth-functionally. That is, $A \wedge B$ holds at x iff A holds at x and B holds at x, and $A \vee B$ holds at x iff A holds at x or B holds at x.

To secure the usual relevant logic **R**, it is necessary to impose conditions saying that the "application" of points to each other is associative, commutative and square-increasing:

1. $Rabc \& Rcde \Longrightarrow \exists x(Rbdx \& Raxe)$
2. $Rabc \Longrightarrow Rbac$
3. $Raaa$

Of course, these postulates are not inescapable: other logics in the family result by modifying them in various ways, just as they result proof-theoretically by modifying the structural rules governing premise combination. For a wide range of such modifications, the first degree logic (with no nested arrows) is invariant, and conversely the positive logic is a conservative extension of the pure implication fragment.[5]

2.2   Negation

Just as there are many choices along the route to relevant positive logic, the motivating considerations being insufficiently precise to determine how those choices are to be made, so there are several more or less natural ways to add negative particles to the logic. One possible addition is an "absurd" constant $\bot$ with its characteristic property that it (relevantly) entails everything, or equivalently that it holds in no world. This constant is in some sense out of the spirit of the relevant view, though its addition is easily seen to be conservative over the positive logic and since it is a connective, not containing variables, it does not break the relevance conditions such as variable-sharing. It allows a sort of negation to be defined as in intuitionist logic:

$$\widehat{\neg} A =_{\mathrm{df}} A \to \bot$$

However, this kind of negation will hardly do for relevant knowledge representation purposes, since what we typically do with negation is to deny things

---

[5] Completeness theorems and similar results for logics in the relevant family may be found in many places: in [22] for instance, or more accessibly in [9] or [23].

on the grounds that we think they are false, and few of these things, we may suppose, are so false that they *relevantly* imply absolutely everything. Absurd negation, then, is too strong. On the other hand, relevant *minimal* negation is rather weak. This is obtained by introducing the constant f without any distinguishing properties, and defining another kind of negation:

$$\widehat{\sim} A =_{\mathrm{df}} A \rightarrow \mathsf{f}$$

This is better, but suffers from the usual drawback of minimal negation, that it does not yield much of a theory because there is nothing to mark the constant f as a *negative* expression.

A more interesting possibility, yielding a much less trivial account of negation, is to add to the language a connective corresponding to the operation of boolean complement [18]. This is easy enough both syntactically and semantically. Deductively, add to the system of positive logic outlined above the new connective, here symbolised by overscoring, with the rules:

$$\frac{\Gamma, A \vdash B \qquad \Gamma, \overline{A} \vdash B}{\Gamma \vdash B} \text{ SLEM}$$

$$\frac{\Gamma \vdash A \qquad \Gamma \vdash \overline{A}}{\Gamma \vdash B} \text{ ECQ}$$

Note that in the rule SLEM (strong law of the excluded midddle) the boolean negation goes essentially with the comma of set combination, establishing it as a connective in the truth functional group, like $\wedge$. Note also that both this rule and ECQ (*ex contradictione quodlibet*) are quite out of keeping with the concern for relevance. The addition to relevant positive logic is conservative, however, so there is a sense in which it does not upset relevant insights.

On the semantic side, boolean negation is naturally introduced by giving it the expected classical truth table at each world. To secure the necessary model-theoretic properties, however, the worlds need to be unordered. What that amounts to is that a new "base" world $0'$ be added with the property that $R0'xy$ iff $x = y$. It must then be shown that such an addition does not change the set of valid inferences in the old vocabulary, so that every counter-model to a nontheorem of the positive logic remains so after the addition of $0'$. In the case of a well-behaved propositional logic like **R**, this is routine, though in some cases, especially in richer vocabularies, it may be nontrivial.

The question of whether to add a boolean negation to relevant logic has traditionally divided the community of relevant logicians. There are those who, like the founders of the field Anderson and Belnap, wish to have none of it, and others such as Martin and Meyer [17] who wish to embrace it—at least as a kind of recommended optional extra. Certainly the relevant use criterion for valid implication does not sit well with inference principles such as SLEM: the latter allows the conclusion that there is a *relevant* deduction of B from Γ even in the case where all the work was done by the A and $\overline{A}$ and in which Γ may have been introduced by the explicitly irrelevant weakening rule K-set. Certainly also boolean negation does not readily mix with the relevant implication connective. Even the apparently innocent addition of relevant contraposition in the form

$$(A \rightarrow B) \rightarrow (\overline{B} \rightarrow \overline{A})$$

has unfortunate side effects such as the loss of conservative extension results.[6]

The standard approach to negation in relevant logics, also to be found in linear logic [13] and Łukasiewicz many-valued logics [15] among others, is to weaken the boolean theory sufficiently to bring it into line with the positive logic while keeping its most important systematic property of being an involution in the lattice sense—a dual automorphism of period 2. That is, it has the effect of reversing the order of implication, dualising the other connectives and maintaining left-right symmetry in the logical system. Its characteristic properties are equivalences:

$$\neg\neg A \dashv\vdash A$$
$$\neg A \rightarrow \neg B \dashv\vdash B \rightarrow A$$
$$A \rightarrow \neg B \dashv\vdash B \rightarrow \neg A$$
$$\neg A \rightarrow B \dashv\vdash \neg B \rightarrow A$$
$$\neg(A \wedge B) \dashv\vdash \neg A \vee \neg B$$
$$\neg(A \vee B) \dashv\vdash \neg A \wedge \neg B$$

Of course, there are one-way inference principles involving negation as well. In **R**, for instance, as a result of the structural rule of exchange (commutativity of the semicolon in the deductive system given above) we have

1. $A \dashv\vdash (A \rightarrow A) \rightarrow A$

from which, on substituting $\neg A$ for A, rewriting $\neg A \rightarrow \neg A$ as $A \rightarrow A$ and contraposing,

2. $\neg A \dashv\vdash A \rightarrow \neg(A \rightarrow A)$

hence

3. $A \rightarrow \neg A \dashv\vdash A \rightarrow (A \rightarrow \neg(A \rightarrow A))$

so by contraction (W-multiset) and rewriting $A \rightarrow \neg(A \rightarrow A)$ as $\neg A$:

4. $A \rightarrow \neg A \vdash \neg A$

This strong *reductio* principle does not hold in all logics in the relevant family; Anderson and Belnap [2] postulated it by fiat for their systems **T** and **E**, but in general it fails in systems without exchange and contraction. One of its outcomes

---

[6] See for example [23], p.379. With strong contraposition as above, we have $A \rightarrow (A \rightarrow C), (A \rightarrow B) \rightarrow C \vdash C$ which is not valid in **R**.

is the provability of the truth table tautologies in the vocabulary of $\wedge$, $\vee$ and $\neg$, in virtue of the theorem $A \vee \neg A$. To prove this, note that $A \wedge B$ entails $A \vee C$, as a special instance of which $A \wedge \neg A$ entails $A \vee \neg A$. But $A \vee \neg A$ is equivalent to $\neg(A \wedge \neg A)$, so by the strong *reductio* principle we have both $\neg(A \wedge \neg A)$ and $A \vee \neg A$ as theorems of **R**.

As logical rules sufficing to govern negation in the deductive calculus, we may take this pair:

$$\frac{\Gamma; A \vdash \neg B \qquad \Delta \vdash B}{\Gamma; \Delta \vdash \neg A} \; (\neg \mathrm{I})$$

$$\frac{\Gamma; \neg A \vdash B \qquad \Delta \vdash \neg B}{\Gamma; \Delta \vdash A} \; (\neg \mathrm{E})$$

Note that relevant negation is defined using multiset (use-sensitive) combination of assumptions and that it thus fits well into the substructural theory of implication underlying the intensional side of relevant logic.

It also fits the truth-functional account of the extensional connectives, with the twist that paraconsistency and its converse are allowed. Suppose that truth and falsehood are neither collectively exhaustive nor mutually exclusive, but rather are treated in the formal semantics of logic as two independent properties that propositions may have. That is, at each point in a frame, there are those formulae which are asserted, or accepted, or true according to that point, and there are those which are denied, rejected, false according to that point. A particular formula may be simply accepted, simply rejected, both accepted and rejected (if the evaluation is confused) or neither (if the evaluation is incomplete). Another view of the matter is that each evaluation point presents two theories: one consists of the formulae asserted and the other of the formulae not denied. Both of these theories are required to be closed under logic. The distinctive feature of the relevant semantics for negation is that to each evaluation point a there corresponds another a^* which asserts just what the first fails to deny, denies just what the first fails to assert. The conditions governing evaluation points in frames apply to both equally. Clearly $a^{**} = a$. Equally clearly, if a is contained in b then b^* is contained in a^*. In fact, to secure the full force of relevant reasoning with negation, this last condition holds also under assumptions, meaning that if $Rabc$ then Rac^*b^*. Naturallly, $\neg A$ holds at a point a iff A does not hold at a^*. The classical, boolean account of negation results by imposing the condition $a^* = a$ but relevant logic, leaving open the paraconsistent possibilities, does not require such a strong condition.[7]

---

[7] There is a large literature on this kind of negation and the semantic postulates governing it. The 'star' operation on worlds is due to Routley and was featured in [22], since when it has been attacked and defended many times. See [3] for an entry point to the literature.

As in the case of the { ∧ , ∨ } fragment, the logic of ∧ , ∨ and ¬ arises directly from the truth functional semantics. Atomic formulae may or may not be true, and orthogonally to that may or may not be false. Compound formulae have truth conditions and falsehood conditions exactly as in the boolean case except that the two are independent. Thus $A \wedge B$ is true iff its two conjuncts are both true (whether or not they are false as well) and false iff at least one of them is false (whether or not it is also true). Dually, $A \vee B$ is true iff at least one disjunct is true and false iff they are both false. $\neg A$ is true iff A is false and false iff A is true. A entails B iff B is true on every valuation on which A is true *and* A is false on every valuation falsifying B. This scheme gives rise to the logic **fde** of "first degree entailments" [2]. To check whether A entails B in **fde** it suffices to reduce A to disjunctive normal form and B to conjunctive normal form; the logic validates all of the DeMorgan laws, distribution principles and other moves necessary for this reduction. Then A entails B iff each disjunct of DNF(A) separately entails each conjunct of CNF(B). A disjunct of DNF(A) is a conjunction of literals and a conjunct of CNF(B) is a disjunction of literals; the former entails the latter in **fde** iff they have a literal in common.

fde is a well known paraconsistent logic. The reason for taking so long to come to this point is to emphasise that in the context of relevant logic **fde** is not an arbitrary choice but arises naturally from the background motivations and is of a piece with the larger logical system. In particular, it represents a theory of negation in harmony with the positive logic to which it is added. In the next section **fde** will be defended against some common objections, after which it will be noted that the first degree entailments themselves do not form an adequate logical system but stand in need of extension to something like a logic in the relevant tradition.

3   Disjunctive Syllogism: Baby or Bathwater?

It is easy enough to set up a logic to omit some unwanted principle of inference—here the inference from a contradiction to an arbitrary conclusion—but less easy to do this in such a way as not to lose with it too many other principles which are not so unwanted. A common view is that the weakened logic should remain as close as possible to classical logic while avoiding the "bad" principle, where "as close as possible" is taken to mean that as many inference forms as possible should be retained, and perhaps that outside the disputed area (say, in consistent domains) the logic should be exactly classical. The logic **fde** draws criticism on this point, usually for failing to validate the classical principle of the *disjunctive syllogism* in the form

$$\frac{A \vee B \qquad\qquad \neg A}{B}\ (DS)$$

Undeniably, we sometimes reason in this way: 'Somebody has eaten the last cookie, and it's not me, so it must be you!' Simply denying that the disjunctive syllogism is valid reasoning will not do, for such ordinary episodes of inference should be accounted for rather than legislated away.

On the other hand, from a paraconsistent point of view the case against DS is strong. Most famously, it is clearly implicated in the derivation of ECQ through the ancient argument re-discovered some eighty years ago by C. I. Lewis:

$$\frac{\dfrac{A}{A \vee B}\,(\vee \mathrm{I}) \qquad \neg A}{B}\,(DS)$$

In the light of this argument, every paraconsistent logic must either disallow $\vee$I, disallow DS or somehow allow that a two-step argument whereby a conclusion is derived from a lemma which is derived from an assumption is not really a derivation of the conclusion from the assumption. Of the possible suspects here, DS looks by far the most guilty. Consider the premises of DS. What does $(A \vee B) \wedge \neg A$ amount to? By the distributivity of $\wedge$ and $\vee$, it amounts to $(A \wedge \neg A) \vee (B \wedge \neg A)$. And we have no reason to think *that* entails B if we are not already wedded to the doctrine that its first disjunct does. The classical reasoning to obtain B from $(A \wedge \neg A) \vee (B \wedge \neg A)$ is that the first disjunct $A \wedge \neg A$ just cannot be the case and so can be ignored, leaving the second, from which B obviously follows. But if we are in a reasoning situation in which inconsistency is a serious possibility and in which we do not take $A \wedge \neg A$ to entail B, it simply is not true that the first disjunct can be ignored. In particular, in the Lewis argument, the classical thought is that because of the $\neg A$, the $A \vee B$ can't come from A, so it must come from B—but this is just plain wrong, because the $A \vee B$ did come from A, whatever the other premise says.

What, then, of the desideratum of staying as close as possible to classical logic? Is **fde** not throwing away the baby with the bathwater, retreating from well-motivated and useful logical principles just to be able to entertain theories of a kind nobody really wants to regard as first-class inhabitants of logical space?

There appear to be three reasons for wanting a paraconsistent logic to retain DS in spite of the *prima facie* case against it. The first is that it is essential to keeping the logic "almost classical". The second is that it is needed: that reasoning would be hamstrung without it. The third, which is perhaps the most persuasive in practice but also the least defensible is that it is *just obviously good reasoning*. This last reason is also puzzling. It rests, presumably, on examples like the one above ('Someone has eaten the last cookie. . . '). Yet we have seen that in the paraconsistent context, DS is equally obviously *not* good reasoning, so how is this conflict of "obvious" intuitions to be resolved? A first step is to note that too hasty generalisation from a meagre set of examples is the enemy of logical good sense. It may be true that we regard the reasoning in the above example as rational, but it by no means follows that whatever plausible formalisation we make of it may be applied with equal rationality to quite different types of reasoning. We shall return below to this question of what it is to apply locally inferential principles which are globally invalid, and in what sense it may be rational to do so.

The argument that DS is part of keeping as much as possible of classical logic is unconvincing. There is a particular reason why the classical paradigm is not a suitable goal for paraconsistent logic: classically, negation is *the* central connective, whereas in paraconsistent logic it occcupies a less important place. The mainspring of classical inference is the absolute intolerance of inconsistency, whereas a guiding principle of (monotonic) paraconsistent logic is that it is possible to come to rest on a contradiction without the collapse of all rationality. In a sense, the paradigm classical inference form is resolution: inference is driven by the existence of a clash (a contradiction) and only by that, and what inference does is to remove the clash leaving whatever parametric literals happen to be around. In paraconsistent logic, where even if there is nothing else around p and $\neg p$ together do not necessarily call for any action, resolution as classically construed[8] is an unmotivated style of reasoning. If paraconsistent logic is worth anything, it is a decent theory of reasoning in inconsistent theories whereas classical logic furnishes no such thing. And it is not a virtue of a good theory that it stays as close as possible to a bad one.

The remaining plea for DS, and for resolution more generally, is the pragmatic one that reason cannot get by without it. This may be an important consideration, though opponents of the classical paradigm should not concede the point until it has been established. Naturally, whether resolution is needed depends on the alternatives to it, and the best view of that at present is that not enough is known to enable it to be settled.

4   First Degree Entailment and Beyond

The relevant abandonment of DS, and of the classical tenet that inference is driven by the need to avoid contradictions, is not an arbitrary choice of response to the Lewis argument and the like, but is an outcome of a systematic account of logic. This account indeed stays within the orthodox logical tradition, but at a deeper level than just maintaining certain individual theorems. It is like classical logic and the other mainstream systems in that it allows unlimited nesting of connectives, validates cut, is monotonic everywhere and admits semantic treatment in terms of truth-preservation at worlds. However, the fragmentary logic **fde** which emerges from relevant logic is capable of being examined on its own terms as a medium for paraconsistent reasoning, and then of being re-extended to a full system which may eventually fit that application better than the parent relevant logic.

The best explanation of the potential value of **fde** in computer science applications comes by comparing it with a reasonable alternative in the form of a "vector of values" system. The domain is software specification, and in particu-

---

[8] There are other construals of resolution, as a form of cut rule, which is of course fine from a relevant perspective as from many others. The complaint is only about the view of it as resolving a clash, which makes sense only in a theory where clashes need to be resolved.

lar the fusion of partial specifications gleaned from several experts or users. On a specific question such as whether a transition is possible from state s_1 to state s_2, each expert may either assert 'yes', assert 'no' or be agnostic. This makes it natural to represent the expert's opinions in a three-valued fashion, where the values stand for 'true', 'false' and 'unknown'. It is quite standard to adopt the usual three-valued matrices, associated with Kleene, to extend the trivalent valuation to compound formulae. If there are several experts, then instead of obtaining just one of the three values, we obtain a vector, one value per expert. The logical operations such as conjunction, disjunction and negation extend in a pointwise fashion to operations on such vectors of values, permitting a semantic representation of the situation in which partial and possibly conflicting pieces of information are combined.

It may be suspected that since epistemic values are in question here, a multi-agent epistemic logic along modal lines could be a better option, but in fact in the attempt to build a theory as to the truth of the matter, rather than one as to the beliefs of the experts, many-valued approaches seem to perform not too badly. Let us therefore consider some advantages and shortcomings of **fde** as opposed to the vector approach. A first striking difference is that **fde** remains four-valued irrespective of the number of experts, whereas the vector-valued logic (henceforth **VVL**) has 3^k values where there are k experts. This extra complexity of **VVL** is more apparent than real, however, because the theories in the vector do not interact: the value (true, false or unknown) in each vector position can be calculated independently of the values in other positions, so the calculation of the value of a compound is no worse than linear in the number of experts (and in the length of the formula, of course). Still, for **fde** it is linear in just the formula length.

In a sense, the four values of **fde** are an abstraction from those of **VVL**. In passing from **VVL** to **fde**, information is lost: the information as to who said what. All that remains is whether at least one expert said 'true', and whether at least one said 'false'. The notion of the relationship between the logics as one of abstraction must, however, be treated with care, because the function taking a vector to the corresponding "abstracted" value is not a homomorphism between the two algebras (Figure 1). That is, they go on to treat compounds in very different ways.

Consider a simple case in which two experts a and b disagree about proposition p. a says p and b says $\neg p$. Suppose neither of the experts has any opinion about q. What should we conclude about the compounds $p \wedge q$ and $p \vee q$? On the **VVL** approach, $p \wedge q$ is false for expert b because p is, and it is unknown for expert a because for a it stands or falls with the unknown q. So it has value $\langle ?, \perp \rangle$. Similarly, $p \vee q$ gets value $\langle \top, ? \rangle$. In **fde** however, the conjunction and disjunction come out simply false and simply true respectively. I have seen incredulity at this: if we are confused about p, how can disjoining it with something about which we have no information at all remove the confusion and leave pure truth? We shall return to this response below, but for now note that there is a reasonable story to tell in reply: consider $p \vee q$; we have been told that it is

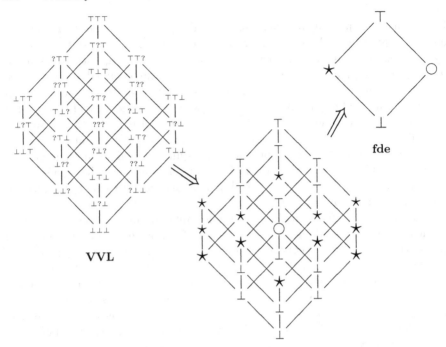

Fig. 1. The four values of **fde** as an abstraction of the twenty-seven vector values of three experts. The star represents 'confused' and the circle represents 'no value'. Note that with the trivial exception of 'no value', the preimages of the **fde** values are not sublattices of the **VVL** values

true, since we have been told that p by someone who is an expert on p (we have also been told $\neg p$, but never mind). Nobody, however, has told us that the disjunction is false, because nobody has any evidence against q. Therefore, the only truth value we have for $p \vee q$ is 'true'.[9]

Consider another case, in which **fde** appears closer to the intuitively correct view than **VVL**. Again the experts disagree about p, a saying p and b saying $\neg p$. This time, however, they also disagree about q: a says $\neg q$ and b says q. What now of $p \wedge q$ and $p \vee q$? On the **VVL** approach, the disjunction is true and the conjunction false, because the two experts agree on that much although their reasons for the compound assertions are completely opposite. On the **fde** approach, however, we mark $p \wedge q$ as false, because an expert has said that p is false (and for good measure another expert has said that q is false), but we also mark it as true for the very good reason that we have expert testimony that p is true and also that q is true. Therefore we take the experts in combination to

---

[9] We also have 'unknown', but this is better seen as the lack of a truth value than a third value in the same sense as the other two. On the **fde** story, at any rate, each proposition has a set of truth values, the values in the sets being just the classical 'true' and 'false'.

be confused, or in disagreement, about $p \wedge q$, and similarly about $p \vee q$. This is surely right: it is quite possible that a is the dominant expert about p and b about q, in which case it is quite correct to mark $p \wedge q$ as true despite their opinions to the contrary. Each of *them* has a reason to regard the conjunction as simply false and the disjunction as simply true, and of course we have these reasons as well, but we also have, as they do not, sufficient expert testimony to regard the conjunction as true and the disjunction false.

At the level of representation of simple propositions, therefore, **fde** compares reasonably well with certain other natural approaches to paraconsistent theory-building. It is worth pausing to note some more features of the logic. Importantly, there is a sense in which classical resolution-based reasoning can be reconstructed in **fde**, despite the invalidity of resolution as such. For this purpose it is convenient to enrich the logic slightly by adding the sentential constants t (true) and f (false). Intuitively, t is the infinite conjunction of all tautologies: we may think of it as $\bigwedge_i (A_i \vee \neg A_i)$. Dually, we may think of f, the minimally contradictory proposition, as $\bigvee_i (A_i \wedge \neg A_i)$. Now any resolution inference of the form

$$\frac{A \vee B \qquad\qquad \neg B \vee C}{A \vee C}$$

may be reproduced in **fde** with the addition of the false constant:

$$\frac{A \vee B \qquad\qquad \neg B \vee C}{A \vee C \vee \mathsf{f}}$$

Hence where there is classically a derivation of the empty clause from a set of clauses, in **fde** there is an analogous resolution derivation of f from the same set of clauses. More generally, any classical resolution derivation of any formula A has a corresponding **fde** derivation of $A \vee \mathsf{f}$. Of course, in **fde**, $A \vee \mathsf{f}$ does not imply A, because we cannot generally overlook the possibility that the situation in which we are reasoning is itself inconsistent and contains f. However, for showing the inconsistency of a set of clauses by resolution, **fde** lacks nothing in comparison with classical logic, and for deriving an arbitrary conclusion, it is as good provided we are prepared to tack the precautionary "...or I contradict myself" onto the conclusion.

fde is, however, inadequate for all but the most basic knowledge representation purposes. The reason is that it cannot express generality. It lacks quantifiers. Without the means to say that all men are mortal, all tigers are carnivores, all footballers are bipeds and so forth, there is *no hope* of serving the essential purpose of representing lawlike conditions or knowledge about relationships between sorts. Of course, it can easily be equipped with the familiar '$\forall x$' and '$\exists x$' with the obvious semantics, but this hardly helps. The problem is that it is not sufficient that the language contains some particles that *look* like quantifiers: to function as quantifiers, they have to validate the right inference forms. Just as an arrow is not an implication connective unless it satisfies a rule of detachment, so a variable-binding operator is not a universal quantifier unless it features appropriately in the passages of inference:

(a) Let ABC be a triangle;
   then ... ⟨*some reasoning*⟩ ... ABC has an acute angle;
   therefore every triangle has an acute angle.
(b) All footballers are bipeds;
   Socrates is a footballer;
   therefore Socrates is a biped.

These principles for the introduction and elimination of universal quantifiers are central to the logic of generality, and have nothing to do with the presence or absence of given structural rules or with attitudes towards inconsistency. In order to formalise such reasoning, a logic must contain, or have a way of securing, quantifiers as binary operators on formulae. It is not enough to be able to express 'Everything is a biped': there must be a way to say that every *footballer* is a biped. Classically, of course, 'Everything is either a biped or else not a footballer' will suffice, but in a weaker logic such as **fde** it will not because it does not validate argument (b) above.

The effect of introducing a binary universal quantifier is to add an implication operator to the logic. If there is an implication $\to$ in the language, the unary quantifier produces a binary one by the usual move of parsing 'All A are B' as $\forall x(A \to B)$. Conversely, if there is a suitable binary universal quantifier $(\forall x : A)B$ expressing 'All A are B', it can be used to define $A \to B$ neatly, if a little artificially, as $(\forall y : A)B$ where y is a variable not occurring free in either A or B. In previous work on this subject [27] it was suggested that if **fde** is to be equipped with universal and existential quantifiers in the most basic way, without stepping outside the truth functional part of the logic, the semantic conditions for these should be as follows. The notion of satisfaction (truth under an assignment to variables) has to be accompanied by a dual notion of dissatisfaction (falsehood under assignment to variables) in the obvious way. Then:

1. $(\forall x : A)B$ is satisfied by a valuation v iff B is satisfied by all x-variants of v that satisfy A and A is dissatisfied by all x-variants of v that dissatisfy B.
2. $(\forall x : A)B$ is dissatisfied by a valuation v iff for some x-variant v' of v, A is satisfied by v' and B is dissatisfied by v'.
3. $(\exists x : A)B$ is satisfied by a valuation v iff some x-variant of v satisfies both A and B.
4. $(\exists x : A)B$ is dissatisfied by a valuation v iff every x-variant of v either dissatisfies A or dissatisfies B.

This gives the implication connective the matrix:

$\to$	T	O	★	⊥
T	T	O	⊥	⊥
O	T	T	O	O
★	T	O	★	⊥
⊥	T	T	T	T

The valid formulae are those which always take values $\top$ or $\bigstar$ (if they were required to take only $\top$ then even $A \to A$ would not be valid). Now an interesting thing has happened, for the logic **BN4** with this implication matrix does not contain the relevant logic **R**. It rejects the structural rule of contraction (W-multiset) since $\bigcirc \to (\bigcirc \to \bot)$ evaluates to $\top$ and so does not imply $\bigcirc \to \bot$ which evaluates to $\bigcirc$. In fact, the four-valued structure contains the three-valued logic of Lukasiewicz as the subalgebra on $\{\top, \bigcirc, \bot\}$ and also the (unique) three-valued matrix for **R**, as the subalgebra on $\{\top, \bigstar, \bot\}$. We may note that *no* connective definable on the four values of **fde** is an implication in the sense of **R**.

R accommodates paraconsistency without strain, and has **fde** as its truth functional fragment, but it does not fit the interpretation of $\bigcirc$ as the lack of a truth value. As already noted, **R** has the theorem scheme $A \vee \neg A$ which requires that in any **R** model either A or $\neg A$ is true at the base world 0. Hence although there can be worlds in which A has no truth value, the real world cannot be one of them. This is not necessarily fatal to the advertised use of **fde** and its implicative extensions, to account for fusion of theory fragments, since after all even if the experts' knowledge leaves gaps, we may reasonably suppose that reality does not have gaps. However, it does suggest that we might do well to examine alternatives to the **R** theory of implication in the hope of finding a plausible logic with **fde** as its extensional fragment that can have as a model the partial and inconsistent theory resulting from amalgamating expert opinions.

While there are many options for enhancing **fde** with an implication in the relevant family, one particularly attractive suggestion [25] is the paraconsistent version of Nelson's logic [19] of constructible falsity, called **NP** in [14]. A frame for this system is a set of information states, partially ordered by inclusion. As in the models of **fde**, truth and falsehood are independently assigned at states in the frame, subject to the heredity condition that *both* truth and falsehood are preserved under the inclusion order. This gives rise to two modelling relations $\models^+$ (makes true) and $\models^-$ (does not make false). The semantics of conjunction, disjunction and negation at each state are as in **fde** while implication is evaluated:

$$w \models^+ A \to B \quad \text{iff} \quad \text{for every } x \text{ such that } w \subseteq x,$$
$$\text{(i) if } x \models^+ A \text{ then } x \models^+ B;$$
$$\text{(ii) if } x \models^- A \text{ then } x \models^- B.$$
$$w \models^- A \to B \quad \text{iff} \quad w \not\models^+ A \text{ or } w \models^- B.$$

Evidently, the four-valued matrix of **BN4** is the special case in which there is only one information state in the frame, so this logic is a refinement of the "truth functional" implication most naturally associated with **fde**.

NP is a strong logic, an extension of linear logic with a distinctly intuitionist flavour. It does not validate contraction, but comes as close to it as possible, validating the structural rule

$$\frac{\Gamma; \Gamma; \Delta \vdash A \qquad \Gamma; \Delta; \Delta \vdash A}{\Gamma; \Delta \vdash A}$$

This is not the place to go into a detailed account of constructible falsity. The interested reader would do well to start with [14] for a readable account and entry to the literature. **NP** has been noted not only half a century ago by Nelson and others, but more recently by a number of writers [1, 10, 11, 30] who see it as useful especially in the context of logic programming. What is worth noting is that it represents, at least arguably, an advance on **R** for the purposes of paraconsistent reasoning such as occurs in merging databases or system specifications. In the first place, it has the four-valued characteristic matrix of **BN4** as a model, and in the second place it is decidable in polynomial space, unlike **R** which is undecidable [28] and whose decidable fragments such as the pure implication fragment tend to have EXPSPACE-hard decision problems [29].

5   Finally: The Disjunctive Syllogism Again

Here we are thinking of the logics of constructible falsity as substructural systems related to the relevant logics, rather than in the more usual way as intuitionist logic with a "strong" negation. They wear both aspects, of course. Like **R** and the other relevant logics, they have **fde** as their fragment of entailments between extensional formulae, and therefore do not validate DS or resolution. the remaining task for the present paper is to revisit DS and consider the status of reasoning in that way in the framework of paraconsistent logics such as **R** or **NP**.

As noted in the opening section, logics which do not validate DS nonetheless do not prohibit its use in reasoning. They offer no guarantee that such reasoning will never go awry, and indeed those of their models which show the disputed principle to be invalid also show *how* it is unreliable. They provide examples of the circumstances in which it fails. In the case of DS, these examples are the obvious ones of inconsistent theories which should be regarded as non-trivial.

This also points to a set of circumstances in which resolution and DS are rational principles to use: those circumstances in which there is no threat of inconsistency (even in counter-factual suppositions) or at least in which no inconsistent state of information can possibly be of any interest. We must note carefully that taking ourselves to be in such circumstances is not a mater of making an assumption of consistency: an extra assumption cannot make an inconsistent theory consistent, even if the extra assumption is "...and this is consistent". Rather it is a methodological decision to regard any contradiction as rendering the reasoning state absolutely useless. As already observed,[10] resolution derivations can be copied inside paraconsistent logics which contain **fde** provided '...∨ f' is tacked onto every conclusion. We can choose to disregard the caveat, inferring A from $A \vee f$, if we wish, provided we do not care about the lack of a first-class logical guarantee for the move.

There is a class of reasoning situations in which an invalid rule such as DS may be applied with more logical backing, namely in making deductions in theories

---

[10] This observation has been made frequently enough before, by R. Meyer and D. Batens among others, so no claims of originality are made for it here.

in which the rule, though not derivable, is provably admissible. This is general: admissibility is all that is required, though of course derivability is the most direct argument for admissibility no matter what the logic. It is worth rehearsing the commonest technique for showing the admissibility of DS in theories based on relevant logics such as **R** since this is independently interesting and widely applicable (though hardly new, having been around for 35 years or so [2]).

Consider some logic **L** in the relevant family. By a *theory* we mean a set θ of formulae closed under **L** entailment in the sense that where $A_1, \ldots, A_n \vdash B$ in **L** if $\{A_1, \ldots, A_n\} \subseteq \theta$ then $B \in \theta$. We say that θ is *prime* if wherever it contains a disjunction $A \lor B$ it contains either A or B, that it is *normal* if it is prime and consistent, and that it is *regular* if it contains all the theorems of **L**. The key to showing that θ is closed under resolution is to show that θ is the intersection of its normal supertheories. For classical logic, this amounts to Lindenbaum's lemma (θ is the intersection of its maximal consistent supertheories) but for **L** it must be remembered that maximal theories are not in general normal, and that the lemma is not true of arbitrary θ—it is a rather special feature that must be proved again for each individual case. Clearly, if $A \lor B$ and $\neg A \lor C$ are both in θ, then every normal supertheory of θ contains $B \lor C$, because it either contains A or contains B and either contains $\neg A$ or contains C, and it does not contain both A and $\neg A$, so if θ is the intersection of such theories, it too contains $B \lor C$. Adding unification to resolution for the purposes of this observation is merely a technical detail.

The standard procedure is to construct normal extensions of θ by metavaluation, a technique dating back at least to the 1950s and Harrop's work on intuitionist logic. Where N is a nontheorem of θ, there is by Zorn's lemma a maximal θ' extending θ while excluding N (with appropriate machinery to deal with existentials as always in completeness proofs). Now set T to agree with θ' on atomic formulae, define it to contain $A \land B$ iff it contains both A and B, $A \lor B$ if it contains A or contains B, and $\exists x A$ iff it contains A_x^t for some term t free for x in A. $\neg A \in T$ iff both $A \notin T$ and $\neg A \in \theta'$. Similarly, $A \to B \in T$ iff both $A \to B \in \theta'$ and if $A \in T$ then $B \in T$. Finally, $\forall x A \in T$ iff $A_x^t \in T$ for every t free for x in A and $\forall x A \in \theta'$. It remains to show that T is normal (which is trivial) and that $\theta \subseteq T \subseteq \theta'$ (which is not trivial). The hard part of the proof is usually to show that all the axioms of θ are in T.

Many piecemeal results by metavaluation have been established, including crucially the cases in which θ is the set of theorems of a logic such as **R** or **E**. Some special theories have also been shown to admit DS, including the infinitary arithmetic $\mathbf{R}^{\#\#}$, and some others have been shown *not* to admit DS, including the relevant Peano arithmetic $\mathbf{R}^{\#}$ [16]. The technique has also been elaborated to deal with contraction-free logics in the family such as **C** and **NP** [24] but there remain serious limits to what has been done. Most annoyingly, the technique has been restricted to regular theories—this is natural, since in regular theories the closure conditions are just detachment and adjunction, the logical theorems supplying the rest—but many irregular theories are closed under resolution too, and it would be satisfying to have a routine way of applying metavaluations to them.

6   Conclusion

Relevant logic, considered as a family of systems rather than one specific theory, presents a coherent approach to paraconsistent reasoning while remaining within the mainstream logical tradition in many ways. This is not to deny a place to nonmonotonic reasoning as a way of restoring consistency in flawed theories, nor to soft constraint solving as an approach to overconstrained problems. It is merely to offer a logical point of view from which inconsistent theories may be admitted as first class logical citizens without putting an end to critical rationality.

An examination of one common source of resistance to the relevant approach, the supposed plausibility of resolution and its special case the disjunctive syllogism, suggests that these are in fact poorly motivated in inconsistent contexts, and that there is no particular virtue in trying to maximise preservation of them. It does, however, open the issue of when these inference forms can be used responsibly. To that question there is as yet no completely satisfactory answer.

What is clear, however, is that a thoroughgoing paraconsistency, seen as logical reasoning of the plain deductive variety rather than as a process of reconciling conflicting but individually consistent theories, is an option and is in tune with an account of logic that stands on its own terms, rather than as paraconsistent superstructure on a classical foundation.

References

1. S. Akama. Tableaux for Logic Programming with Strong Negation. *Proceedings of the Conference on Automated Reasoning with Analytic Tableaux and Related Methods (TABLEAUX'97)*, 1997, 31–42.
2. A. R. Anderson and N. D. Belnap. *Entailment: The Logic of Relevance and Necessity, Vol 1.* Princeton University Press, Princeton, 1975.
3. A. R. Anderson, N. D. Belnap and J. M. Dunn. *Entailment: The Logic of Relevance and Necessity, Vol 2.* Princeton University Press, Princeton, 1992.
4. N. D. Belnap. A Useful Four-Valued Logic. Dunn and Epstein (eds), *Modern Uses of Multiple-Valued Logics*, Reidel, Dordrecht, 1977: 8–37.
5. N. D. Belnap. Display Logic. *Journal of Philosophical Logic* 11 (1982): 375–417.
6. R. Brady. *Universal Logic.* Cambridge University Press, Cambridge, 2001.
7. J. M. Dunn. Algebraic Completeness Results for R-mingle and its Extensions. *Journal of Symbolic Logic* 35 (1970): 1–13. Reprinted in [2].
8. J. M. Dunn. A 'Gentzen' System for Positive Relevant Implication. *Journal of Symbolic Logic* 38 (1974): 356–357 (abstract). Reprinted in [2].
9. J. M. Dunn. Relevance Logic and Entailment. in D. Gabbay and F. Günthner (eds) *Handbook of Philosophical Logic* Vol. 3, Reidel, Dordrecht, 1986: 117–229.
10. T. Eiter, N. Leone and D. Pearce. Assumption Sets for Extended Logic Programs. *JFAK. Essays dedicated to Johan van Benthem on the occasion of his 50th birthday.* Amsterdam University Press, 1999. http://www.illc.uva.nl/j50/contribs/pearce/.

11. M. Gelfond. Representing Knowledge in A-Prolog. *Computational Logic* 2408: 'Logic Programming and Beyond: Essays in honour of Robert A. Kowalski' (2002): 413–451.

12. S. Giambrone and A. Urquhart. Proof theories for Semilattice Relevant Logics. *Zeitschrift für Mathematische Logik und Grundlagen der Mathematik* 33 (1987: 301–304.

13. J.-Y. Girard. Linear Logic. *Theoretical Computer Science* 50, 1987: 1–101.

14. I. Hasuo and R. Kashima. A Proof-Theoretical Study on Logics with Constructible Falsity. Report C-165, research Reports on Mathematical and Computing Sciences, Tokyo Institute of Technology, 2003, http://www.is.titech.ac.jp/research/research-report/C/

15. J. Łukasiewicz. *Selected Works* (ed. L. Borkowski), North-Holland, Amsterdam, 1970.

16. R. K. Meyer and H. Friedman. Whither Relevant Arithmetic? *Journal of Symbolic Logic* 57 (1992): 824–831.

17. R. K. Meyer and E. P. Martin. Logic on the Australian Plan. *Journal of Philosophical Logic* 15 (1986): 305–332.

18. R. K. Meyer and R. Routley, Classical Relevant Logics, I and II. *Studia Logica* 32 (1973): 51–66 and 33 (1973): 183–194.

19. D. Nelson. Constructible Falsity. *Journal of Symbolic Logic* 14 (1949): 16–26.

20. D. Pym. *The Semantics and Proof Theory of the Logic of Bunched Implications.* Kluwer, Dordrecht, 2002.

21. Relevant and Substructural Logics. in D. Gabbay and J. Woods (eds) *Handbook of the History and Philosophy of Logic* forthcoming.

22. R. Routley and R. Meyer. Semantics of Entailment. in H. Leblanc (ed) *Truth, Syntax, Modality*, North Holland, 1973: 194–243.

23. R. Routley, V. Plumwood, R. Meyer and R. Brady. *Relevant Logics and their Rivals.* Ridgeview, Atascadero CA, 1982.

24. J. Slaney. Reduced Models for Relevant Logics Without WI. *Notre Dame Journal of Formal Logic* 28 (1987): 395–407.

25. J. Slaney. A General Logic. *Australasian Journal of Philosophy* 68 (1990): 74–88.

26. J. Slaney and R. Meyer. Logic for Two: The Semantics of Distributive Substructural Logics. *Proceedings of the Conference on Qualitative and Quantitative Practical Reasoning (ECSQARU-FAPR)* (1997): 554–567.

27. J. Slaney. The Implications of Paraconsistency. *Proceedings of the 12th International Joint Conference on Artificial Intelligence* (1991): 1052–1057.

28. A. Urquhart. The Undecidability of Entailment and Relevant Implication. *Journal of Symbolic Logic* 49 (1984): 1059–1073.

29. The Complexity of Decision Procedures in Relevance Logic. J. M. Dunn and A. Gupta (ed), *Truth or Consequences: Essays in Honour of Nuel Belnap*, Kluwer, Dordrecht, 1990: 77–95.

30. H. Wansing. *The Logic of Information Structures (LNAI 681)*. Springer-Verlag, Berlin, 1993.

Author Index